Y0-BCD-787

# War, Diplomacy, and Development

# War, Diplomacy, and Development

# THE UNITED STATES AND MEXICO 1938–1954

## Stephen R. Niblo

A Scholarly Resources Inc. Imprint
Wilmington, Delaware

Scholarly Resources Inc.
104 Greenhill Avenue
Wilmington, DE 19805-1897

**Library of Congress Cataloging-in-Publication Data**

Niblo, Stephen R., 1941–
    War, diplomacy, and development : the United States and Mexico,
1938–1954 / Stephen R. Niblo.
        p.    cm. — (Latin American silhouettes)
    Includes bibliographical references (p.    ) and index.
    ISBN 0-8420-2550-2 (cloth : alk. paper)
    1. United States—Relations—Mexico. 2. Mexico—Relations—
United States. 3. Industrialization—Mexico—History—20th century.
4. Mexico—Economic conditions—1918–    I. Title. II. Series.
E183.8.M6N53    1995
303.48'273072—dc20                                                            94-37100
                                                                                                CIP

⊛ The paper used in this publication meets the minimum requirements of
the American National Standard for permanence of paper for printed
library materials, Z39.48, 1984.

# About the Author

After studying economics at the University of Colorado and working for the cooperative movement of Colombia, Stephen R. Niblo earned his Ph.D. in Latin American history from Northern Illinois University in 1972. He taught at two universities in Mexico from 1970 to 1976 and currently is a senior lecturer at La Trobe University in Melbourne. In addition to writing over twenty journal articles and book chapters, he is the author of *A Short History of the Cold War* (1994), coeditor of *Cuba: Thirty Years of Revolution* (1990), and coauthor of *Precursores de la revolución agraria en México: Las obras de Wistano Luis Orozco y Andrés Molina Enríquez* (1975). Dr. Niblo is a frequent media commentator in Australia on issues and developments relating to Latin America.

# Contents

Acknowledgments, **ix**
Introduction, **xi**
Abbreviations and Acronyms, **xvii**

**Part I  The Eve of World War II**
Chapter 1    Progress and Industrialization, **3**
Chapter 2    The "Good Neighbor" Copes with Cárdenas, **35**

**Part II  Wartime Cooperation**
Chapter 3    Mexico's Entry into World War II, **63**
Chapter 4    Politics and Wartime Cooperation, **89**
Chapter 5    The Impact of War, **123**

**Part III  Postwar Strategies**
Chapter 6    Strategies of Industrialization, **165**
Chapter 7    Battles over Foreign Investment, **191**
Chapter 8    The Political Nature of Industrialization, **221**
Chapter 9    Mexico and the Postwar Settlement, **249**

Conclusion:  The Great Evasion, **283**
Bibliography, **293**
Index, **305**

# Acknowledgments

I have had the good fortune of being associated with departments of history where there was a serious commitment to quality research and good teaching. As a postgraduate student, I was especially fortunate to study with Benjamin Keen and others in a dynamic department at Northern Illinois University. In my first academic job, Jim Hamon, Laurens Perry, and William Bischoff helped me a great deal. Moving to Australia enabled me not only to develop a different perspective on my field but also discover traditions from other parts of the English-speaking world that people from the United States frequently ignore.

Many friends and colleagues helped me in various ways: Peter Cook, Arnaldo Cordova, David La France, Peter Love, Moises González Navarro, James Levy, John Salmond, Enríque Semo, and Paul Vanderwood. Their insights and support have been invaluable. Particular thanks go to Alan Knight for his extremely valuable comments and, above all, to Barry Carr, an extraordinarily gifted and energetic colleague who provided support and stimulation from the earliest stages of the project. These generous people should rest assured that I acknowledge that the shortcomings of this book are entirely my own.

Without exception, the archivists at the Archivo General de la Nación, the National Archives of the United States, the Roosevelt Library, and the Truman Library, as well as the staff at Borchardt Library and the Department of History of La Trobe University, were extremely helpful. Without the university's overseas study program it would not have been possible to work from such a distance. I am especially grateful to William Beezley, Judy Ewell, and the anonymous reviewers at Scholarly Resources for their suggestions and support. Mary Aitken helped me get the manuscript into its final form.

I dedicate the book to the memory of my parents, Edith and Eugene, who provided an environment that made great issues part of daily life. Special thanks also go to my in-laws, Nathan and Lillian Cholodenko, for their generous help. My greatest debt is to my wife, Diane, for her endless support.

Finally, the candid autobiographical accounts of the period by Narciso Bassols, Valentín Campa, Laurence Duggan, John K. Galbraith, Jesse Jones, and, above all, Bruce Catton are especially valuable. My imagination was

especially fired by Catton's *War Lords of Washington*. After having learned about the cost of war by writing the great narrative account of the Civil War in the United States, he headed off to Washington, DC, during World War II to observe the politics of war firsthand. Reviewers frequently called his a "bitter" book. Perhaps this study will suggest an alternative perspective.

# Introduction

This study deals with an attempt by the people of Mexico in the midtwentieth century to reverse a birthright of colonial subjugation by, and dependence upon, a succession of great powers. The technique that the modern Mexicans chose to catch up with their more recently arrived neighbors to the north was no longer direct military conquest or even the reconquest of lost lands. The long and painful experience with its neighbor led most Mexicans to conclude that it was their lack of technical and industrial development that locked the country into continuing cycles of poverty, dependency, and disappointment.

A strong national commitment to industrialization emerged. Set in the context of the complex events that are known collectively as the Mexican Revolution, this passion for industrial modernization came close to being a common denominator shared by those who identified with one or another current of that great movement. Even Mexico's superb mural artists of the period, from Diego Rivera to David Siqueiros, painted visions of progress cast in industrial and scientific terms. And the breadth of that commitment generated great political legitimacy for the governing party.

We now know that the price the community paid for this program was far more than anyone had anticipated. The Mexican commitment to rapid industrialization has gone astray. Today the country suffers not only from age-old problems of poverty and underdevelopment but also from a new crisis of advanced environmental decay. Poverty and pollution have combined with the world's second largest burden of foreign debt, to such a degree that even occasional high rates of economic growth fail to ameliorate the conditions of life for the vast majority of the people. This book is an exploration of how the country's development program went astray.

My analysis begins in 1938 at the height of radical nationalism under President Lázaro Cárdenas and traces the dismantlement of Cardenismo from wartime cooperation with the United States to the postwar industrial project. Part I examines attitudes toward industrial modernization and the state of relations between Mexico and the United States on the eve of World War II. Starting from an awkward moment when President Cárdenas nationalized the foreign-owned petroleum, the Roosevelt administration pursued an unprecedented policy of accommodation with Mexico. After old disputes were settled, a period of intimate wartime cooperation followed. Part II focuses

on Mexico's decision to offer unconditional support to the Allies in World War II, as well as on the nature of that support and the politics of wartime cooperation. Finally, this section evaluates the impact of wartime cooperation on Mexican society.

Part III shows the postwar strategies that the governments of the day pursued as they sought industrial modernization in a rapidly changing environment. There is a discussion of their strategy of industrialization and the dispute over foreign investment, along with an analysis of the highly political nature of industrialization in Mexico and the country's place in the postwar settlement. This study is especially concerned with the mechanisms by which new forms of wartime cooperation evolved into unprecedented levels of foreign investment after the war.

Since the period has received little detailed attention by historians, few Mexicans have a clear understanding of the ways in which their revolution shifted course, and too many in the United States do not realize the dominant influence their country has exercised over the affairs of other nations. President Ronald Reagan's simplification of issues, in the wake of the U.S. invasion of Grenada—"America seeks no new territory, nor do we wish to dominate others"—does not tell the entire story.[1]

From time to time there are historical periods of great innovation, times when new institutions are established, resources are allotted, and patterns of development are set for surprisingly long periods. This was such an era. In the final years of the Cárdenas administration a number of factors, both foreign and domestic, began to shift the Mexican Revolution in a more conservative direction; and the next two presidents, Manuel Avila Camacho and Miguel Alemán, accelerated that process. It was not just that they wanted to move to the right, which they did; their desire scarcely accounts for their ability to chart Mexico's new course. Rather, two great historical phenomena—war and industrialization—interacted with domestic conservatism and U.S. pressure to shift the revolution to the right.

Unfortunately, war is the most common issue that creates a broad unity of purpose, at least in the absence of defeat. Sacrifice in the name of the nation gives leaders the power to discipline those who disagree with their positions, and it becomes possible to accomplish difficult goals. Sensing this, President Avila Camacho leaped at the chance to commit his country to the Allied side in World War II. Even though Mexico was scarcely involved in the military events of the war, the government's call for sacrifice and patriotism created a fabric into which a new political direction was sewn. The Mexican president used calls for wartime collaboration to escape from the enormous shadow of his predecessor and dominate the various factions in his party.

War also created a day-to-day intimacy of contact that enabled the United States to make up for the loss of influence suffered during the early Cardenista period. By looking at the history of the period from the perspec-

tive of the development program of the Mexican nation, one finds an unexpected centrality of World War II in that the shift to a more orthodox program of development took place under the exigencies of wartime cooperation with the Allies.

During the 1940s the convergence of the war effort with a drive for industrialization created an irresistible pressure for political change that grew unexpectedly out of a problem in the United States. Wartime price and production controls meant that Mexico could not buy much from the United States in return for its sales of raw materials in the early years of the war. Innovative forms of payment, including a return to barter at the level of advanced industrialization, had the effect of integrating Mexico into the U.S. economy. For example, any request to purchase imports—for which Mexico had the funds—had to be sent to the U.S. embassy in Mexico City and then forwarded to the Office of Price Administration, the War Production Board, or one of the other relevant wartime agencies in Washington that allocated production, transportation, and finance. Embassy assistance was indispensable in helping the Mexicans (in both the public and private sectors) find their way through the maze of wartime regulations and deal with foreign paperwork. Anything but close cooperation on the Mexicans' part would have placed their country's development program in desperate straits. Out of that day-to-day contact, the closest forms of collaboration emerged between U.S. and Mexican business. After the war the stage was set for a massive return of foreign capital to Mexico.

The United States had a fairly clear notion of the strategic resources it wanted from Mexico as its contribution to the war effort. It sent two ambassadors to Mexico who were extremely competent and had the ear of President Franklin D. Roosevelt. After the death of FDR, there is little doubt that Harry Truman's diplomats paid less attention to Latin America in general, but it was an inattentiveness based upon a domination of the situation. Latin America's importance was great, but little effort was required to keep the hemisphere in line with major U.S. priorities. Latin Americans' frustrations with their place in the postwar settlement were ignored by U.S. policymakers. The region's exclusion from the Marshall Plan was especially galling. (Only a generation later did the Latin American governments gain the credits they so desperately wanted, and then the debt crisis became the bitter result of that desire.) Their moment of leverage had passed as the Cold War replaced World War II.

The model of rapid industrial development that Mexico adopted under the administrations of Avila Camacho and Alemán inverted the populism of the 1930s and dropped the nationalist model of industrial development, although that battle was in some ways a central domestic political issue in the 1940s. The power of the state was placed at the disposition of both foreign and domestic developers, as long as they accommodated themselves to the fundamental rules of the Mexican political system. Goals of alleviating the

poverty of the Mexican people were dropped in favor of simply increasing production. Private capital accumulation was supported by the state, and an age of private opulence for a few Mexicans became a characteristic of the day. A conscious policy, culminating under President Alemán, of freezing wages in a period of rapid inflation made the weakest people contribute the most to the process of capital accumulation.

The interaction between daily politics and the overall strategy of development requires detailed attention. It helps us to understand how indirect pressure enabled the United States to set the broad rules of development for its allies. New techniques of influence and control emerged that were far more subtle and indirect than the old techniques of direct imperialism. As such, they were all the more effective. The informal empire was very real, and when Mexico occasionally violated the rules of the new international order, remedy was not long in coming, as the Pan American Trust episode or Mexico's intervention at Bretton Woods demonstrates. The new techniques of indirect influence offered unclear targets for nationalists in Mexico. The most fervent supporters of the country's radical nationalism—in certain business circles and in government, as well as in segments of the labor movement—all fundamentally misunderstood the nature and goals of U.S. policy after World War II. They thought in terms of the territorial expansion of the past, or they believed that the United States did not want them to know the secrets of industrial production. That was a great historical misunderstanding. The new order was effective because it incorporated elements of the Mexican elite into the system in innovative ways.

The period after the era of Cárdenas is only beginning to receive attention from historians.[2] Some distinguished colleagues have asked me why one would choose to study such an unsavory cast of characters. Such images as that of the death of Maximino Avila Camacho during a vigorous celebration on his estate in Puebla in honor of Fulgencio Batista of Cuba do tend to stand out.[3] Certainly, the epic events after 1910 have attracted far more inquiry and interest, but it is important to examine the groups, policies, and individuals that prevailed and not merely those that one might prefer.

Ultimately, limitations of space convinced me to divide the broad project into two parts. To keep the evolution of Mexico's development program on center stage, this volume stresses the interface between the two countries at a number of levels: diplomatic, political, military, and business. Comments on domestic politics are held to a minimum here; a separate manuscript under the working title "Mexico in the 1940s" is in preparation in order to explore further the domestic aspects of the topic. My aim is for each work to stand alone, but, taken in conjunction, they should juxtapose the domestic and the international factors that brought the economic nationalism of the Mexican Revolution under President Cárdenas to an end.

Fortunately, there are few periods richer in primary sources. We now have the possibility of using a quality of documentation that would have been unimaginable a few years ago, and for which many historians of more distant eras would give a great deal. In Mexico, the Archivo General de la Nación has an enormous amount of material that is now open to researchers. The problem is something of an embarrassment of riches, as they find themselves among many thousands of boxes of documents and aided only by an idiosyncratic card index used by the various presidential secretaries. Nevertheless, rewards await those patient enough to make the effort. The reader will note that material as confidential as President Avila Camacho's bank statement has been used in this study.

In the United States the Freedom of Information Act has led to a much greater, although not absolute, access to government documents. From 1938 to 1954 there is no open record of the covert action that was pursued, and the United States is still withholding a considerable amount of material relating to the man it viewed as the demon of the day, Vicente Lombardo Toledano. Ironically, Mexico's best-known labor leader played a dubious role during this time. In their concern to discredit Lombardo Toledano and simultaneously disguise the full nature of their involvement in Mexican affairs, U.S. functionaries may well have damaged their own cause.

The unique value of the U.S. archives during this period is to be found in the records of conversations between our embassy personnel and high Mexican officials and political activists. American Ambassador George Messersmith had sources of information so good that he boasted of knowing of the formation of the Partido Popular within two hours of the event. It is not often that investigators have the opportunity to hear top officials describing their views in confidence to the representatives of the hegemonic power. Of course, the historian must be aware of the U.S. filter through which these confidential discussions were reported and the purpose that people had when talking to foreign diplomats. Nevertheless, the newly opened Mexican and U.S. material allows the researcher to explore various historical episodes on the basis of remarkably candid documentary evidence. Thus, we can investigate more deeply the interests and decisions that set the basic rules for both growth and development in modern Mexico.

## Notes

1. *Washington Post*, November 5, 1983.

2. The most direct work on the period is by Medina and Torres, *Del cardenismo al avilacamachismo* and their *Civilismo y modernización del autoritarismo*. It is unfortunate that these volumes are based almost exclusively upon press reports. Well-researched, interpretative works for the period—such as Contreras, *México 1940: Industrialización y crisis política*—are few and far between. Research on the

labor movement and on the political left is the most advanced for the period, especially since the advent of the CEMOS research group.

3. The account of Maximino's party for Batista is found in USNA/RG 59, 812.00/2-647.

# Abbreviations and Acronyms

| | |
|---|---|
| A.C.&Co. | Anderson, Clayton, and Company |
| AFL-CIO | American Federation of Labor-Congress of Industrial Organizations |
| AMC | Asociación Mexicana de Caminos (Mexican Association of Roads) |
| ARMCO | American Rolling Mills Company |
| ASARCO | American Smelting and Refining Company |
| BANAMEX | Banco Nacional de México (National Bank of Mexico) |
| BEW | Board of Economic Warfare |
| CCC | Confederación de Cámaras de Comercio (Confederation of Chambers of Commerce) |
| CCI | Confederación de Cámaras Industriales (Confederation of Industrial Chambers) |
| CCRM | Cámaras de Comercio de la República Mexicana (Chambers of Commerce of the Mexican Republic) |
| CEIMSA | Compañía de Exportaciones e Importaciones Mexicana S.A. (Mexican Export and Import Corporation) |
| CEMOS | Centro de Estudios del Movimiento Obrero y Socialista (Center for Studies of the Labor Movement and Socialism) |
| CFB | Combined Foods Board |
| CFE | Comisión Federal de Electricidad (Federal Electricity Commission) |
| CFR | Council on Foreign Relations |
| CGOCM | Confederación General de Obreros y Campesinos de México (General Mexican Confederation of Workers and Peasants) |
| CGT | Confederación General de Trabajadores (General Confederation of Workers) |
| CIA | Central Intelligence Agency |
| CIO | Congress of Industrial Organizations |
| CNC | Confederación Nacional Campesina (National Confederation of Peasants) |
| CNIT | Cámara Nacional de Industrias de Transformación (National Chamber of Industries of Transformation) |

| | |
|---|---|
| COCM | Confederación de Obreros y Campesinos de México (Mexican Confederation of Workers and Peasants) |
| CONCAMIN | Confederación Nacional de Cámeras Industriales (National Confederation of Chambers of Manufacturing) |
| CONCANACO | Confederación Nacional de Cámeras de Comercio (National Confederation of Chambers of Commerce) |
| COPARMEX | Confederación Patronal de la República Mexicana (Employers' Confederation of the Mexican Republic) |
| CPN | Confederación Proletaria Nacional (National Proletariat Confederation) |
| CROM | Confederación Regional Obrera Mexicana (Regional Confederation of the Mexican Worker) |
| CTAL | Confederación de Trabajadores de América Latina (Latin American Confederation of Workers) |
| CTM | Confederación de Trabajadores de México (Confederation of Mexican Workers) |
| CUT | Confederación Unica de Trabajadores de México (The Only Confederation of Mexican Workers) |
| DDF | Departamento del Distrito Federal (Department of the Federal District) |
| EXIMBANK | Export-Import Bank |
| FBI | Federal Bureau of Investigation |
| FSTSE | Federación de Sindicatos de Trabajadores al Servico del Estado (Federation of Union of Workers at the Service of the State) |
| GDP | Gross Domestic Product |
| GNP | Gross National Product |
| HDI | Human Development Index |
| IBRD | International Bank for Reconstruction and Development (World Bank) |
| IEM | Industrias Electrónicas Mexicanas (Mexican Electronics Industries) |
| IMF | International Monetary Fund |
| IMSS | Instituto Mexicano de Seguro Social |
| INS | Immigration and Naturalization Service |
| ITII | Instituto Technológico de Investigaciones Industriales (Technological Institute of Industrial Research) |
| ITT | International Telephone and Telegraph Company |
| MEXLIGHT | Mexican Light and Power Company |
| MEXTELCO | Mexican Telephone Company |
| MIT | Massachusetts Institute of Technology |
| NAFISA | Nacional Financiera (National Finance Bank) |
| NAM | National Association of Manufacturers |

| | |
|---|---|
| NBER | National Bureau of Economic Research |
| ND&R | Nacional Distribuidora y Reguladora S.A. (National Distributor and Regulator) |
| NPA | National Planning Association |
| NRA | National Recovery Administration |
| OPA | Office of Price Administration |
| PAN | Partido de Acción Nacional (National Party of Action) |
| PAW | Petroleum Administration for the War |
| PCM | Partido Comunista Mexicano (Mexican Communist Party) |
| PEMEX | Petróleos Mexicanos (Mexican Petroleum Company) |
| PIPSA | Productores e Importadores de Papel S.A. (Producers and Importers of Paper) |
| PNR | Partido Nacional Revolucionario |
| PRI | Partido Revolucionario Institucional (Institutional Revolutionary Party) |
| PRM | Partido Revolucionario Mexicano (Revolutionary Mexican Party) |
| RFC | Reconstruction Finance Corporation |
| SITMMSRM | Sindicato Industrial de Trabajadores Mineros, Metalúrgicos, y Similares de la República Mexicana (Industrial Union of Mining, Metallurgical, and Similar Workers of the Mexican Republic) |
| SITTFDS | Sindicato Industrial de Trabajadores Textiles de Fibras Duras y Similares (Industrial Union of Textile Workers of Hard Fibers and Similar Occupations) |
| SNTE | Sindicato Nacional de Trabajadores de la Educación (National Union of Education Workers) |
| SOFINA | (Belgian holding company that owned MEXLIGHT) |
| SRE | Secretaría de Relaciones Exteriores (Foreign Relations Secretariat) |
| STERM | Sindicato de Trabajadores Electricos de la República Mexicana (Union of Electrical Workers of the Mexican Republic) |
| STFRM | Sindicato de Trabajadores Ferrocarrileros de la República Mexicana (Union of Railroad Workers of the Mexican Republic) |
| STIC | Sindicato de Trabajadores de la Industria Cinematográfica (Union of Workers in the Film Industry) |
| STPRM | Sindicato de Trabajadores Petroleros de la República Mexicana (Union of Petroleum Workers of the Mexican Republic) |

| | |
|---|---|
| UGOCM | Unión General de Obreros y Campesinos de México (General Union of Workers and Peasants of Mexico) |
| UNAM | Universidad Nacional Autónoma de México (National Autonomous University of Mexico) |
| UNS | Unión Nacional Sinarquista (National Union of the Enemies of Anarchy) |
| USDA | United States Department of Agriculture |
| USSR | Union of Soviet Socialist Republics |
| WASP | White Anglo-Saxon Protestant |
| WPB | War Production Board |

# I THE EVE OF WORLD WAR II

# 1 Progress and Industrialization

"Progress," an old term that originally signified travel toward one's goal, has come to mean—at least over the last 150 years—a general direction in which society is moving. In the wake of the expansion of Western industrial capitalism, several generations largely accepted a belief that material innovations were synonymous with social progress. The union of steam and steel seemed miraculous. Nations with industrial might seemed to prosper while those without the arms provided by the new industrial techniques found their shores visited by gunboats and other peoples' armies. Soon the development of electricity, chemicals, automobiles, and a myriad of other innovations changed the world beyond recognition. It is little wonder that theories of progress abounded—right, left, and center—in the wake of the second industrial revolution.

In the industrialized world, acutely exploited workers, the unemployed, dispossessed rural poor, and native peoples who were partially living in precapitalist subcultures paid the price for all of this progress. Yet to those who commanded capital and made political decisions, the deprived seemed to represent an anachronism, groups for whom modern prosperity had not arrived. Clearly, the orthodox vision of development anticipated the withering away of these groups and their replacement by members of the modern sector. Theories of dualism dominated the Western social sciences in these years, positing a belief that modern sectors were displacing traditional communities, and policymakers often confused the life-styles of the rich and powerful, or the structure of their beliefs, with the causes of their prosperity.

In recent decades, as the problems of mature capitalism compound at ever more rapid rates, doubts about earlier beliefs in industrial progress have proliferated. Today, some question defining progress in terms of the growth of industry. As many of the original regions of industrialization in Europe and North America turn into rust belts, contempt for the facile equation of industrialization with human progress has grown. Even Mexico already finds its early steel mills, such as Altos Hornos, being closed. Moreover, the contamination of the planet, congestion, and the tensions of urban life have undercut the optimism of earlier times. People are asking more serious and probing questions about the ways in which progress is defined. However, it is not at all clear that such doubts can prevail over the

*3*

profit motive. Yet, whatever emerges from our age of uncertainty, it is important not to project contemporary misgivings about orthodox development strategies onto Mexico's push for industrialization after 1940. Our doubts did not have currency when Mexico committed itself to a program of rapid industrial development. Today's romantic escapists, or the environmentalists, or the proponents of zero growth, or even the basic needs advocates will look long and hard before they find their spiritual ancestors in the Mexico of the 1940s.

Mexican governments worked hard to promulgate a view that placed the struggle for modernity at the heart of the nation's historical experience.[1] And modernity meant suppressing production of items of use value and petty commodity production—the peasant and artisan economies—and placing public policy at the service of the market. Keeping up with the latest consumer product or production technique from the United States was difficult, but Mexican industrialists addressed the problem by developing close relationships with their U.S. counterparts.

Mexicans of nearly all persuasions had concluded that the solution of the country's problems lay in a rapid industrial program of development. Only on the far right, within a tradition called hispanidad, did individuals such as the philosopher Agustín Aragón reject the value of industrial production as the essential aspect of human progress. Their call for retaining the spiritual values of conservative Spain had limited attraction. Still, there were bastions of the old Hispanic right within political circles in Mexico even into the 1940s. The Presidential Committee for Postwar Planning, which had been established along with a number of other U.S.-Mexican committees of wartime cooperation, was one such group. The committee opposed the reentry of U.S. capitalists into Mexico, from a perspective of hispanidad. When the committee was finally abolished on December 16, 1944, great relief was expressed by U.S. diplomats: "So far as our relationships with Mexico are concerned, it is perhaps significant that Véjar Vázquez [chairman of the committee] is strongly pro-Hispanidad and anti-American, and the abolition of the Post-war Planning Committee under his leadership can only be viewed with relief."[2] That tradition quickly atrophied under increased opportunity, although some lamented what they called the materialism that emanated from the English-speaking world.

It was far more common for Mexicans to call loudly for rapid programs of industrialization. The reorganization of the state and the emergence of mass organizations in the period of Lázaro Cárdenas's presidency seemed to make the tradition of hispanidad far less pertinent. As Joaquín de la Peña, president of the National Chamber of Manufacturing Industries, put it in 1947, "Today no one discusses the necessity and convenience for Mexico to industrialize, but . . . there are an infinity of criteria as to . . . the procedures for achieving industrialization."[3] The daily support for industrializa-

tion was implicit in the Mexican presidents' schedules. One day, in March 1948, President Miguel Alemán visited the industrial zone in the State of Mexico, from Tlalnepantla to Lechería, which had 116 factories representing 450 million pesos in investment. He managed to fit in enthusiastic visits to La Nacional S.A., Acero Estructural S.A., Herramientas de México S.A., Laminadora de Acero S.A., which was a subsidiary of the U.S.-owned steel mill La Consolidada, the Goodyear Oxo rubber factory, the aluminum plant of Reynolds Internacional de México S.A., and Westinghouse's Industria Eléctrica de México S.A. After lunch the president visited the Nash automobile factory and a series of smaller plants. His effort on the day was not unique; it reflected a deep belief in the importance of industrial projects.

## Business and Industrialization

There were a number of traditional obstacles to business and industry. Many were legacies of the country's colonial heritage, and others flowed from the endemic political instability. Time and again, agricultural producers and merchants saw itinerant armies or bandits destroy crops and merchandise.[4] The colonial tax system, which largely survived the establishment of independence, penalized production, exports, and trade quite severely.[5] On top of this, the alienation of community lands, in the name of liberal reform, further opened the gap between the rich and the poor, and made the country more vulnerable to predatory foreign investors and their Mexican allies.[6] Above all, there was a class system that had its origins in the Spanish conquest of middle America. Only a few of the poor escaped from the villages and the veritable sea of poverty that was rural Mexico, and they frequently improved their lot by turning on their neighbors. It is not by chance that the story of the *malinche* (the woman who betrayed her people to the Spanish conquerors for her personal gain) plays such an important role in Mexican thought. This class system denied mass markets to producers.

Into this world of weak states, poor capital accumulation, and a lethargic business class came a group of revolutionary entrepreneurs. Stephen Haber summarized the historical problem that faced new industrialists: "From its very beginning, Mexican manufacturing was characterized by its inability to export, the need for protection from foreign competition, and an extraordinarily high degree of market concentration."[7] These revolutionary capitalists joined earlier pockets of industry—most notably in Monterrey—and generated a new momentum toward industrial development. Men such as Abelardo Rodríguez, Aarón Sáenz, Plutarco Elías Calles, and many others found that their political connections enabled them to tap the growing resources of the state in order to start many new industries.

It was within the business community that the most intense debate about the terms of industrialization took place. Some tendencies were predictable. The Instituto de Estudios Económicos y Sociales, which published the magazine *El Economista*, was founded by MIT graduate Manuel A. Hernández, who succeeded in bringing together key figures in the public and private sectors. Founded in 1938, the institute was formed to oppose what it called the "Cárdenas labor squeeze method" of pushing land and businesses into the public sector. Claiming that Cárdenas had confiscated more than twenty-five thousand hectares without compensation, the institute brought together members of the Confederation of Chambers of Commerce, the Confederation of Industrial Chambers, the Bankers' Association of Mexico, the Union of Property Owners of the City of Mexico, and the Bar Association. Political members of the institute included Manuel Avila Camacho, as honorary president, Foreign Minister Ezequiel Padilla, Minister of the Interior Miguel Alemán, Minister of Health and Welfare Gustavo Baz, and General and former President Abelardo Rodríguez, as well as top bankers, industrialists, and property holders.[8]

Looking for ways to combat Cardenismo, the group initiated a number of private studies relating to the goal of industrialization. Some sixty-two of those studies were published in *Hoy* between May 1938 and January 1939. In a similar vein, *El Economista* opposed the labor legislation of the 1930s as well as the petroleum nationalization. The institute reiterated that capital was the crucial factor that determined a nation's progress. As Hernández expressed it in a radio broadcast on WEAF in New York City, America's advances in developing machinery and electricity in effect gave its citizens the equivalent of "three million slaves" to do their work. Capital was responsible for U.S. prosperity; therefore, above all, Mexico must pursue policies that would create capital. Members of the institute did try (as Hernández argued to diplomat Spruille Braden while asking the U.S. government to purchase one hundred thousand subscriptions to *El Economista*, an offer that was declined) to downplay the degree to which they viewed organized labor as an obstacle to development. Instead, the Instituto de Estudios Económicos y Sociales stressed the need to reward capital, to reduce costs, and to create a more favorable political attitude toward capital and private enterprise in general.[9] This kind of organization was similar to the American Manufacturing Association in the United States in essentially stressing the employers' perspective that to reduce wages is to reduce costs and therefore increase productivity. That accounting perspective among employers is depressingly predictable.

There was yet another tendency among some Mexican industrialists to support an economic nationalist position. Although they did not want to give up protectionism, they did view the Mexican population as their prospective customers. People in this school were the main figures in the Cámara Nacional de Industrias de Transformación (CNIT): José Domingo Lavín,

Jesús Cruz y Célis, Jorge Heyser, Antonio Ruiz Galindo, Evaristo Araiza, and José R. Colín, at least at some stage in their careers. This group wanted Mexican entrepreneurs, aided by the state, to lead the push for rapid industrialization. In their view, a wide variety of rules should be slanted to their advantage so that the benefits of industrial growth would accrue to the nation's entrepreneurs and workers. Tax breaks, favorable import and export regulations, labor law, rules governing banking and finance, and many other practical measures should favor national over foreign investors. Since these producers invariably came from light industry, they focused quite clearly upon the problem of sales. Given the extreme poverty of so many Mexicans, they understood that only by raising the purchasing power of the poor could they find markets for their products. In an anticipation of Keynesianism, they therefore saw a community of interests with organized labor in general, and with Vicente Lombardo Toledano in particular. It was extraordinary to find business leaders arguing for something other than ever-lower wages for their workers.[10]

It was this group of economic nationalists that Sanford Mosk focused upon when he wrote *Industrial Revolution in Mexico* in 1954.[11] He was unduly optimistic, as it turned out, in viewing them as the dominant group in the business community. The economic nationalists may have been numerous and even eloquent at times; however, they were not to predominate in the long run.[12] Both the United States and the Mexican governments of the 1940s opposed them. Tremendous pressure was generated against any policies that would tend to exclude U.S. entrepreneurs from Mexican markets, finance, or resources. A strong case can be made that, even at the height of the Cold War, anticommunism was of much less importance to U.S. diplomats than blocking the economic nationalists. Merwin L. Bohan, chief economic counselor to the U.S. embassy from 1946 through the early 1950s, left a vigorous record of his opposition to the economic nationalists.

Even the Mexican Communist Party (the PCM) joined in the rush to industrialize by calling for a policy of patriotic unity—a popular-front policy that aimed at giving all possible aid to the USSR after the German invasion. Eschewing strikes, under most circumstances—even in the face of falling real wages—that policy continued after the war in order to support a plan for industrial development under the leadership of the government and Mexican capitalists. To that end, the PCM favored the entry of foreign capital into Mexico, with only the Lombardista qualification that foreign capital should be productive rather than rapacious; there was to be no threat to the government's goal of rapid industrialization from this frequently purged party.[13]

It should be noted that even as U.S. officials vigorously opposed any Mexican defensive measures that might limit the "free" flow of capital or U.S. products into Mexico, those New Deal officials adopted some of the underconsumptionist analysis. At the time the level of scarcity was such

that industrial production was snapped up; saturation of internal markets had not yet emerged as the Achilles' heal of the development program. Even as the war began, Mexican borrowing for the large hydroelectric and irrigation projects was justified in terms of creating an internal market. And after the war, as enormous loans were being negotiated, U.S. Ambassador Walter Thurston argued that "it is now apparent that, if Mexico is to have an adequate market for the products of its new industries, it must stimulate the productivity of the land and put earning power into the hands of its cultivators and their families who make up an estimated three-quarters of the population, in addition to rounding out the industrialization and public utilities picture."[14]

In the long run the underconsumptionists' policies were ignored; Mexico based its industrialization upon a forced extraction of surplus from the poor to the rich and from the country to the cities, thus stimulating the rural exodus. The state was harnessed to the development project in order to provide both capital and markets. Yet, at the time, the presumed convergence of interests between those who would benefit from the borrowing and those who believed that massive irrigation projects would bring prosperity to the campo provided a powerful political alliance. That belief was not realized, as very quickly Mexican power relationships determined that there would be no continuation of the Cardenista redistribution toward the countryside. The political stock of the economic nationalists declined throughout the 1940s and fell so low by 1946 that José R. Colín, president of the CNIT in the last months of President Avila Camacho's administration, could not even gain an interview with the president, and Alemán was totally unsympathetic.[15]

Between the clear differences of the unreconstructed businessmen of the private sector, as represented by the *centros patronales* (employers' organizations), and the economic nationalists was a middle group that achieved practical dominance. Finance Minister Eduardo Suárez played a central role in shifting the government's economic program from the nationalist policies of Cardenismo in a direction more acceptable to presidents Avila Camacho and Alemán. An influential group emerged including Ramón Beteta, Eduardo Bustamente, Antonio Carrillo Flores, Josué Sáenz, and most of the senior staff at the Banco de México; the majority of this dominant group—excluding Sáenz, who cut himself off from the dominant party by insisting upon a laissez-faire position—was influenced by Alvin Hansen of Harvard University and the discovery of some aspects of Keynesianism. Although they ignored the redistribution analysis in that tradition, they accepted the need for an active economic state to stimulate investment; indeed, there was no other historical tradition in Mexico.[16]

These men pioneered new techniques to establish joint ventures, and their projects became the hallmark of the day. Sometimes figures in the private sector were the Mexican partners of U.S. firms that entered the country; more frequently, revolutionary leaders were silent partners. American

diplomats quickly got the picture. A fundamental rule of the day for most U.S. firms was not to go it alone in the Mexican business environment. Politics was too close to the day-to-day operation of business. To cite one of many such examples, James E. Henderson, American consul in Guadalajara in 1945, wrote to the State Department urging the United States to adopt a cooperative attitude toward Mexico's desire for industrialization and to provide engineers, scientists, and technicians for joint ventures. Henderson was reiterating a safe line.[17]

Under the Avila Camacho administration, Mexican industrialists who were willing to collaborate with foreign investors fared far better than the economic nationalists. Aarón Sáenz, Manuel Suárez, Agustín Legorreta, and others in the private sector dealt with political allies such as Maximino Avila Camacho and Abelardo Rodríguez in organizing the major business deals of the period.[18] The dominant political-industrialists were less sympathetic toward labor. During the 1940s, employers were certain that the CTM was a radical enemy, and many expressed the view that the Tri-Partite Pact of the war years was not a safe harbor. There was no hint that bosses viewed the CTM as a tamed institution, useful as a mechanism to control workers.[19] Whereas the economic nationalists accepted a coalition with labor, for reasons relating to the underconsumptionist analysis that saw higher wage rates as necessary to create demand for their products, the dominant industrialists with close links to foreign investors were less sympathetic. Nevertheless, even the nationalistic employers still opposed other forms of the social wage. There was, for example, a concerted campaign waged by captains of industry in 1944–45 against a levy of 1.3 percent of the wage bill to support the Instituto Mexicano de Seguro Social. Economic nationalists such as José Cruz y Célis of the Confederación de Cámaras Industriales, Jesús Grovas of the Confederación Nacional Cinematográfica, and José Rivera R. of the CNIT all vigorously opposed the social security system.[20] They saw no contradiction.

## Labor and Industrialization

Demands for industrialization abounded from the labor movement. Frequent and elaborate petitions from labor organizations bombarded the government calling for the commitment to industrialization projects. The most common pattern was for the petitioner to enumerate simply the kinds of industries that were desired. Archives are replete with such petitions; however, it is extremely rare to find any such petition that either expresses doubts about the self-evident value of industrialization or provides any concrete plan of industrial development. These petitions resembled shopping lists, cataloging the kinds of industries that petitioners thought it would be good to have.

It was at this point that the orthodox Marxist tradition was broadly influential. By adopting a historical analysis that posited stages through which all societies passed on their way to a progressive future, Mexico looked like a semicolony with strong feudal residues. Progress therefore consisted of helping the capitalists overcome the feudal remnants, a position accepted by Lombardo Toledano and the CTM. After the German attack on the USSR, labor and the Left were unable to oppose the new industrialists, whatever their action. Workers wanted jobs, and national pride required catching up with the industrial powers.

The commitment to industrialization created an ambiguity on matters of economic nationalism within the labor movement. Even the left-wing leaders of the labor movement continuously met with U.S. diplomats, assuring them that they supported U.S. participation in industrialization projects in Mexico. Alejandro Carrillo, for example, in meeting with the second secretary of the embassy, William K. Ailshie, in September 1944, "expressed his keen interest in the participation of American capital in the industrialization of Mexico under certain conditions." Labor leaders demanded that capital should be channeled into productive industries rather than tied up in real estate, as was the case all too frequently. As editor of *El Popular*, and close collaborator of Lombardo Toledano, Carrillo went to great lengths to convince the diplomats that his faction was eager to have U.S. participation in Mexico's industrialization program. Going beyond the mere requirements of the wartime alliance, he stressed that it was the political Right (here, he singled out the newspaper *La Nación* of the Acción Nacional and, within the cabinet, Octavio Véjar Vásquez, head of the postwar planning committee) that was anti-American in that it supported European investors over U.S. businessmen. He also assured the United States that Mexico could never become a rival in the industrial sphere. Ailshie agreed that the labor-left was not against U.S. investment in Mexico.[21]

*El Popular* had a running campaign to convince its readers that Lombardo Toledano headed a coalition of labor and capital that provided the best chance to industrialize the country. A sense of megalomania could be read into his speech on the seventh anniversary of the petroleum expropriation. A few days later *El Popular* reported the speech under the banner headline "THE BANKERS OF MEXICO ACCEPT THE CALL OF LOMBARDO TO BRING ABOUT AN INDUSTRIAL REVOLUTION."[22] At that time, Lombardo's capitalist allies included firm economic nationalists such as José Colín and Domingo Lavín, owners of small chemical and pharmaceutical companies, and others less committed, such as Evaristo Araiza of the Fundadora of Monterrey, the Spaniard Angel Urraza of Goodyear-Euzkadi, and Aarón Sáenz of financial and sugar interests.[23] The U.S. diplomats were eager to try to use their increasingly warm relationship with Sidney Hillman, vice president of the CIO and for a time a member of the War Production Board (WPB), to

block links that Lombardo Toledano was trying to forge with U.S. labor leaders. Only John L. Lewis had expressed sympathy for Lombardo Toledano's position; U.S. officials worked hard to keep the main Mexican labor leader isolated from the AFL-CIO.

The ambiguity of labor's position reflected a problem. The tradition of anti-imperialism made labor leaders oppose foreign investment as exploitative. However, the desire to bring industry to the country meant that foreign investment would come with the techniques of industrialization. Leaders such as Lombardo Toledano wanted to play it both ways. For years he had vociferously denounced foreign investment in terms of Lenin's theory of imperialism. Yet, in confidential discussions with the U.S. embassy, he took a different position. Ambitious, but with declining influence in government and labor circles, Lombardo Toledano privately argued that foreign investment was welcome in Mexico. The ploy was too transparent to work. Unbeknownst to him, his statements to the U.S. embassy in favor of foreign investment after the war were contradicted by reports from Foreign Minister Padilla, who told the diplomats that Lombardo Toledano had spoken openly in government circles about the "danger of American capital," so much so that the president reminded him of the "necessity of the participation of American capital," after which point he modified his views. After having been frozen out of the executive office for a year, Lombardo Toledano jumped at the opportunity to have access again to the president. In Padilla's view, the president believed that he could control and channel Lombardo Toledano's activities if he were still within the governing circle.[24] It is difficult to avoid the conclusion that Mexico's best-known labor leader of the day bartered his views on U.S. investment in postwar Mexico for access to the presidential office. Diplomats certainly doubted his sincerity in his new and moderate attitude toward their investment, for this way of thinking was very far from the Lombardo Toledano of a few years earlier. Speaking at the 1941 Congress of the CTM, he had said, in a much more characteristic mood: "If we are to continue to be squeezed by the great Yankee monopolies as one squeezes an orange, Mexico's advanced social legislation will avail nothing to protect the workman, because the price of the peso will be fixed by the producers, merchants, and bankers of the United States."[25]

The Soviet entry into the war, in June 1941, changed his view completely, as he supported any force that would aid the USSR. Eventually, Lombardo Toledano tried to salvage something from his contradictory statements on foreign investment by maintaining a distinction between "Yankee imperialism," which he said meant speculators who came down to Mexico for a quick killing, as contrasted to investors who increased agricultural and industrial production and would follow the rules of the country. He argued repeatedly that it was the far Right, as typified by Luis Cabrera and Gómez Morín, where the deepest opposition to U.S. investment resided.

For his part he professed great respect for President Franklin D. Roosevelt, Secretary of State Cordell Hull, and labor leaders such as Martin Kyle of the CIO.[26]

Lombardo Toledano accepted the view that Mexico lacked capital to develop industry and agriculture, and he therefore saw U.S. capital as filling that need: "We fight in this stage for the Bourgeois Revolution and not socialism. Personally I believe that one day . . . the entire world will be transformed and a socialist regime will come to all the earth. But because I am a Marxist, I know that the only thing that we Mexicans can do at this stage is to work for the Bourgeois Revolution."[27] This steadfast view made coalitions between nationalistic industrialists and workers possible. After the war, he tried to argue for a continuance of the alliance; however, the moment of need had passed, and his became a forlorn attempt to exclude U.S. capitalists from Mexico, long after his influence was exhausted.

Labor organizations opposing the CTM shared many of the dominant labor organization's attitudes toward the necessity of industrialization. In December 1942 a number of anti-CTM labor organizations held a conference at Bellas Artes under the title "Primer Congreso Nacional de Economía de Guerra del Proletariado Mexicano."[28] Such disparate labor groups as the CROM, CGT, COCM, CPN, and SITTFDS agreed that greater state resources should be channeled into a rapid push for industrialization. In addition to calling for the development of desired industries and greater honesty in general, the conference proposed some specific ideas, urging the development of the Mexican coast, a policy that Adolfo Ruiz Cortines adopted in the 1950s. Above all, they wanted to limit private profits to 10 percent and to keep salaries high. They wanted to limit the consumption of *artículos de lujo* (luxury goods), and they favored postwar planning. In their view the state could counteract the tendency of the private sector to price gouge and abuse the workers and consumers. Interestingly enough, they called for the inclusion of women in the industrialization process at that date.[29]

Similarly, the far more radical Alianza de Uniones y Sindicatos de Artes Gráficas—best known for its brilliant *calaveras* drawings—continued an ongoing campaign against the tendency of CTM officials to connive with bosses and the government to reduce the popular standard of living and thus limit future consumption of the products of industrialization.[30] Even anti-CTM forces within the labor movement thought that their strongest argument with the president focused upon the assertion that the corruption of the CTM *charros* (cowboys) was limiting the nation's industrialization program. In August 1946 the leaders of seven anti-CTM unions addressed a conference with a statement to the president under the title "Programa y Declaración de Principios por la Renovación de la CTM."[31] At the same time, the National University (UNAM) held a major conference on the topic of the postwar industrialization of Mexico, and Josué Sáenz

and Antonio Carrillo Flores were keynote speakers. However, unlike many academic conferences, this one served as a link between academia and government.[32]

Toward the end of the Avila Camacho administration the implementation of the great goal of industrialization had gone so far that there was the formal establishment of the Worker-Employer Pact on April 7, 1945. The pact was in essence an extension of the wartime Pacto Obrero-Industrial agreements, and it was formally supported by President Avila Camacho. Interestingly enough, although the bulk of the pact consisted of an enumeration of the kinds of industry that the petitioners believed necessary, the signatories observed that "we would incur a lamentable error should we use our credit balance to import superfluous luxury goods or articles we could do without instead of using it to purchase the initial machinery necessary to establish plants in which we can make machinery, which is the basis of any true plan of industrialization."[33]

The U.S. embassy's objections to this pact centered upon Section 6, which governed foreign investment, and Section 8, which dealt with "adequate protective tariffs."[34] The signatories of the pact for business were José Cruz y Célis, José Domingo Lavín, and Aurelino Lobatón, all from the Confederación de Cámaras Industriales; for the CTM, Fidel Velázquez; and for the Confederación de Trabajadores de América Latina (CTAL), Lombardo Toledano.

Labor was firmly committed to a rapid push for industrialization, which took precedence over currents of anti-imperialism that usually dominated the rhetoric. Only after Miguel Alemán had mauled the left wing of the labor movement and those to the left of the PRI—by the time of the Marxist Roundtable of 1947—did some independent figures on the left, such as Valentín Campa and Hernán Laborde, express doubts about the frenzy of development.

## Consumers and Industrialization

Consumers wanted the products of industrialization. Their desire, later termed the demonstration effect, ranged from goods we consider to be basic, to the first widely used industrial items such as electric blenders to refrigerators and cars. Occasionally, an example of needs that many today take for granted surfaces. In 1947 the Unión Mexicana de Dentistas Libres had pointed out to President Alemán that there were only 6,000 dentists in all of Mexico, of whom only 1,424 held a degree from a recognized institution. Their request for the importation of modern equipment carried with it a certain poignancy.[35]

There were, however, several serious limitations to the development of domestic industry. The percentage of the population that could afford

industrial goods may have represented as few as 5 to 10 percent of the population, depending upon the item under consideration. In addition, the proximity of the United States was a double-edged sword in terms of the early stages of industrialization. While unending numbers of new products drifted south and whetted appetites, the foreign competition was not necessarily a stimulus. The long border with the United States also encouraged smuggling, and it made some comparisons of relative quality of products invidious to Mexico's early industrialists. This was especially so in the area of electronics. There also was the threat that if a local firm was too successful, it might stimulate a U.S. competitor to enter Mexico's markets. The infant-industry argument was ascendant in Mexico.

The nation's transportation network strained to the breaking point during World War II. Wartime cooperation greatly increased the shipments of strategic materials, thus placing a heavy burden upon both road traffic and railroads. The Department of Foreign and Domestic Commerce kept a photographic record of the state of the roads during this time. To resolve the problem required the products of industry to build roads. Attempts to use manual labor were slow and frustrating.[36]

In spite of the constraints the national passion for industrialization was so strong that many schemes were established to promote industrialization projects. Those came from the highest level of international capital as well as from individuals who might well have specialized in the sale of snake oil a few years before. Perhaps a record for ingenuity went to Gonzalo de la Peña, who ran an operation called Industrias del Hogar, which offered the individual investor no fewer than fifty plans to choose from in order to start one's own industry. De la Peña's promotions told the customer: "Here is the secret of success in life. It is so simple that it scarcely seems to be a secret. Be the owner of your own industry! . . . Establish an industry in your own home."[37] For as little as five pesos, as the initial installment, de la Peña promised the gullible that they, too, could join the country's industrialists in the Bankers' Club. The popular passion for industrialization had its roots in the immediate past.

The general enthusiasm was not merely based upon wishful thinking. Just as the United States had boomed in the nineteenth century, Mexico also had an important success; the Compañía Fundidora de Fierro y Acero de Monterrey S.A. became the largest iron and steel manufacturer south of Birmingham, Alabama. Established in 1900 under the pro-Díaz governor, Bernardo Reyes, in Nuevo León, the company together with a tax-free environment, a friendly government, an emerging business oligarchy, and proximity to the United States produced an example of the liberal dream.

The firm was founded with an authorized capital of 10 million pesos, then worth 5 million dollars, when Monterrey was only a city of about ninety thousand people. The firm's assets had increased to 30.4 million pesos by the 1930s. Business, labor, and government all viewed the experience of

the premier steel plant in Mexico as thoroughly satisfactory. Here was the entrepreneurial dream of something being created from nothing. A new city, Monterrey, grew around the new industry, increasing its population to 155,000 by 1936. Owners profited handsomely, workers found well-remunerated jobs, and the government gained taxes; all seemed right in the North.[38]

## Mexican Industrialization in the 1940s

The kind of success that was stunning in Monterrey was atypical. Of Mexico's 20,000,000 inhabitants, 13,500,000 were on the land, and only 750,000 found jobs in mining, manufacturing, wholesale and retail trade, and transportation. Roughly 5 percent of the employed Mexicans were in industry, compared to 25 percent in the United States, yet 23 percent of the gross national product (GNP) was generated by industry. Even industry sources noted that "the output in mining and oil has been more closely related to foreign needs than to those of Mexico itself; . . . no major national industry is based directly upon the rich mineral resources of the country, with the exception of oil refineries as far as they go."[39]

Interestingly, U.S. capitalists were looking at the development of the domestic Mexican market as the growth area. They made direct comparisons with the relative importance of industrial production as a percentage of total output and concluded that, in terms of Mexico's 1941 national income of 6,971,000 pesos, 3,700,000 pesos, rather than the existing 2,396,000 pesos, should be coming from the industrial sector. The point is not so much to question the validity of these estimates, as to realize that this was the kind of perspective that foreign investors were using to understand Mexico. Industrialists who still remembered the depression of the 1930s looked at the country as a domestic market that was there to develop if the political conditions should be adequate.

When President Avila Camacho in a speech was able to boast, as he did at the end of his term, that since January 1939 some 360 new industries representing 400 million pesos of new investment had started, he received a standing ovation.[40] Enthusiasm for the industrialization project was great, and people assumed that the results they desired would flow from that effort. After the president made this report to the Tercer Congreso de Industriales de México in February 1946, José Colín, Jesús Cruz y Célis, and Antonio Ruiz Galindo followed him onto the podium, and all three claimed that wartime industrialization was helping the poor.[41] Organizations such as the Comisión Nacional de Planeación para la Paz brought together thirty-two figures in industry, finance, government, and labor to plan for the transition from a wartime economy to the postwar industrial push.[42]

Great enthusiasm for industrialism also existed within government circles. In 1947, Minister of the National Economy Ruiz Galindo was injured in an automobile accident, thereby incapacitating him for some time. The American cultural attaché visited him at his home and suggested that he might like to watch some of the movies that the U.S. mission was showing around the country. The minister gladly agreed. After seeing the first propaganda effort, he was so enthusiastic that he set up nightly viewing sessions of such films as *Defense against Invasion, This Plastic Age, Memphis Belle, Battle of Britain*, and *Steel, Man's Servant* to which he invited other cabinet ministers and even the president. In the U.S. cultural attaché's account, these films were received "to the delight and enthusiasm of the assembled audience at the Minister's bedside." As he editorialized, the attaché thought that his office should send "an expensive orchid to Messrs. Fisher, Donnelley et al. [the propaganda officers]."[43]

A convergence, therefore, emerged between a wide spectrum of Mexicans who clearly wanted to industrialize their way out of poverty and U.S. economic planners who saw expansion into Mexico as insurance against another depression. Both groups were not only thinking about industrial modernization; they also were coming to define and measure it in the same way.

## Defining Progress: From Radical
## Nationalism to Orthodox Development

In the 1930s, Mexico's revolution finally seemed to have found a program. Cárdenas unleashed a torrent of reforms, including land reform favoring the collective ejido, state support for a controlled labor movement, socialist education, the nationalization of the petroleum industry and the railroads, experiments with workers' administration, and the mass organization of civil society. Patronized by the state, with all of the limitations that eventually implied, Cárdenas's reforms appeared to be institutionalizing these changes. Moreover, the formation of workers' militias seemed to imply that the revolution was digging in to defend itself against its enemies. Finally, during the 1930s there was a shift in patterns of income distribution in favor of Mexico's poor. Yet a decade after Cárdenas left office only the state apparatus remained of the monumental Cardenista project. In spite of a massive corporativist organization of the population—that which Arnaldo Córdova quite properly calls the *organización de masas*—one of Latin America's most radical experiments in combating underdevelopment was easily disassembled.[44]

The deepest change in the political counterrevolution of the 1940s was perhaps encapsulated in the very way in which Mexico came to define and measure its progress. Adopting the U.S. national income accounting system, as expressed in such measures as the GNP, Mexico shifted its national

goals and priorities. The country dropped concern with economic justice in favor of adopting policies to increase production. Miguel Alemán put the point frequently when he stated that it did not make any sense to talk about income distribution until one had something to distribute. The governments of the 1940s harnessed the state to the process of development, as defined by the single notion of the GNP.

Philosophical debates about the meaning of progress notwithstanding, in the twentieth century the national income accounting system has given us the practical, one might even say the official, meaning of material progress. The GNP, as the very measurement of progress, today seems clearly accepted. The various measurements of national income have become so well internalized that these statistics are reported with the evening news. There is a tendency to accept these measures as though they were an adjunct of natural law, another category, such as kilometers or degrees of temperature, by which nature is measured. The political impact of the national income accounting system is to place economic categories of analysis beyond the pale of discussion and policy formulation. Just as we can do nothing about the weather, there is a tendency to reify national income concepts and turn economic indicators into ends in themselves.

The crowning achievement of orthodox economics in the West is to be found in the quantification of the meaning of progress that is implicit in the national accounting system. Today's measurements of national income actually evolved from a count of the numbers of cattle coming to market until it ultimately purported to become a measure of all production. Yale economist Richard Ruggles begins a 1983 survey (and celebration) of the topic by stating that "the National Income Accounts for the United States and their statistical implementation represent one of the major achievements in economics in the twentieth century."[45]

The United States had been working toward the creation of a national income accounting system for some fifteen years before its formal adoption in 1947. Simon Kuznets had been collaborating with the Department of Commerce since 1933 in developing the methodology he applied to the United States. His book, *National Income and Its Composition, 1919–1938*, represents a semiofficial adoption of his methodology for calculating national income.[46]

The institutionalization of the national income accounting system became located between the Department of Commerce and the National Bureau of Economic Research (NBER). The latter is another highly successful, richly endowed, semi-independent agency, such as the Council on Foreign Relations (CFR) or the Economic Roundtable, that brings together top government figures, suitable academics, and powerful figures from the business community. Some 18 percent of NBER members are also members of the CFR, including Edwin Gay, of the council's first research committee; Wesley Mitchell, who sat on the CFR's board from 1927 to 1934; and later,

Robert Roosa. Just as the CFR network produces secretaries of state, the NBER is a training ground for future members of the U.S. presidents' Council of Economic Advisers. The publications and conferences of the NBER have created the lion's share of technical writing on the national income accounting system. The Department of Commerce then decides which NBER initiatives it will apply.[47]

The enormity of that achievement is perhaps best measured by realizing how deeply ingrained such concepts as the GNP, the gross domestic product (GDP), national income, and personal income have become in the intervening years, and how rarely they are discussed. National income accounting makes the GNP—the sum of all goods and services produced and sold within a year—into the single most important indicator of a society's material progress. More recently, the GNP may be modified to simply the GDP, or even linked to other indicators into that which is now called an index of leading indices; however, the centrality of the GNP is undiminished, and it still dominates government policies, public debate, and even the media coverage of economic news.

It may not have been the wish of the early pioneers in national income accounting to achieve such sovereignty for their index. Certainly, one should be aware that, even as complex mathematical manipulations are carried out on national income data, we are not observing a scientific operation, such as a statistician claiming a .05 level of significance with an analysis of variance. Kuznets himself admitted, in 1942, that his margin of likely error—in measuring the output of what he called the 520 cells that divided forty specific industries into thirteen income and employment categories for calculating the GNP—varied from 5 percent to 80 percent. As economist Oskar Morgenstern has observed, "Even so meticulous an investigator as Kuznets computes a mean of pure guesses to two decimals."[48]

Although four later statistical revisions in the United States (1954, 1958, 1965, and 1976) claim to have reduced the likely range of statistical error, this level of guesswork, upon which so much sophisticated mathematical analysis is based, is truly startling. The most frequent challenges to the absolute dominance of national income accounting have been on technical grounds. Again, Morgenstern writing in 1965 estimated that "the weighted margin of error for the estimate of national income was found to be about 20 percent by this method of 'expert guesses' of the components, and summing."[49]

However shaky the measurement of the GNP may be, it allows politicians, commentators, and the general public to focus upon a single figure as an overall measure of material progress. It is a number that can be studied, turned, examined, and fondled. If the number drops, we frown; if it increases, we smile. Governments have been known to fall on the movement of the GNP, and even cheat on statistics to make their numbers appear more favorable.

There are, however, major deficiencies in this approach to measuring progress that go beyond the technical problems of measurement. Without arguing that production is unimportant, there are a number of glaring deficiencies in the application of the U.S. national income accounting system that became so quickly applied in Mexico. As the GNP is defined—the total amount of all goods and services produced and sold within a year—every word is problematic. Any production that is not sold does not count. Production for use is relegated to a category of activities that are not considered as being important enough to enter into the central measure of material progress. Kuznets himself faced the problem when deciding upon the fundamental elements of the system. He characterized the making of goods and services that were not headed for sale as "acts [which] might be called 'personal,' such as washing, shaving, and playing for amusement on the piano."[50] Women, peasants, and the poor thus found many of their life-sustaining, but nonmarket, efforts removed from the category of economic production by the Nobel laureate.

Even in the highly industrialized countries this shortcoming relegates the work of women in the home and the caring for children to an unpaid category virtually analogous, from an economic viewpoint, to leisure (unless, of course, one actually has to look after young children). The most difficult problem that women's movements face may be the unwillingness of the economists to attribute value to domestic labor within the rules set by national income accounting systems. This situation remains so today even though opportunity cost analysis could easily be applied to the matter.

If the way we calculate national income causes problems when one examines the poor in rich countries, the problem is compounded when examining lesser-developed countries. Production in the peasant sector which is not sold does not enter into a national income accounting calculation. If farmers produce grain, sell the product, and then purchase grain seed for the next crop, at least three transactions are recorded (the wage bill to produce grain, the sale, and the purchase of seed). If, on the other hand, a peasant family produces grain for its own consumption and retains seed for the next planting, then no transactions would be entered on the nation's record of its productive activity.

Some indication of the magnitude of this problem may be seen from the fact that the accumulators of Mexican statistics, by 1947, estimated that of the 23,000,000 Mexicans only 6,777,137 were economically active. Thus, more than sixteen million people were excluded from consideration as being actively involved in the economic life of the country. Economic policies, government intervention, or even the great industrial push, therefore, would not include provisions for that majority; and their number went far beyond the aged and the very young.

There is extreme ingenuity on the part of the poor in Mexico in finding ways to survive in the face of massive poverty and unemployment. A single

family group may expend great effort to subsist. Children may raise rabbits in unwanted spaces, or fathers may watch automobiles for a living; the possibilities are endless, although the remunerations are slight. Even rooftop economics has emerged in Mexico, where maids, servants, and other poor people try to use the undervalued space on the tops of buildings to engage in petty commodity production. Few of a poor family's life-sustaining activities will enter into the national income accounting system. When one adds the hard-working, but largely unpaid, women of Mexico to the peasant sector, to the hard, hustling poor, one is looking at an applied definition of material production that excludes the vast majority of the population.

At the 1971 conference of the Bureau of Economic Analysis some individual economists charged that the GNP calculations ignored the damage caused to the environment. The Department of Commerce was unconvinced. As one of their economists admitted, "The accounts have changed little since 1947 in any fundamental way."[51] Subsequently, many critics have faulted the dominant system, and some have even proposed interesting alternatives.[52] In the 1990s the United Nations started to calculate a fairly rudimentary Human Development Index, yet none of these alternatives has eroded the importance of the national income accounting system for policymakers.[53]

The important point to keep in mind is that as Mexico was embarking on an urgent program of industrial development, as measured by means of the GNP yardstick, the state was setting out to channel massive resources into the modern, industrial sector. All the manifold productive activities that are not included in the national income accounting system were starved of the funds that the state raised through fiscal means or by borrowing. In addition, the banking sector followed suit by directing capital away from peasant and artisan production. It was only assumed, to the degree that decision makers cared, that somehow industrial growth would have the same general effect as it had in such countries as the United States.

Manfred Max-Neef and the "barefoot economists" ultimately adopted a strategy, in the face of the acute repression of military regimes in South America, of trying to develop programs with the rural poor on such a small scale that they become "invisible" from the point of view of national income accounting and fiscal policies. This populist version of the black economy is based upon some sophisticated analysis and some painful experiences in years of development work in the field in Latin America. Max-Neef's conclusion—"if the national systems have learned to circumvent the poor, it is the turn of the poor to circumvent the national systems"[54]—has on the surface a curious similarity to Mario Vargas Llosa's celebration of the black economy. Still, neither of these approaches is remotely compatible with orthodox economics in the West.

The GNP measures short-term sale; as long as a commodity is sold, it counts. The environmental movement and the appropriate technology traditionally have raised fundamental questions that challenge the dominance of

the orthodox national income accounting system.[55] There is no downward adjustment for damage caused in the process of production. As chemical companies sold their products, the sales figures were added to profit statements and ultimately to the GNP. No figures were ever deducted from the GNP for damage caused to the environment, or the depletion of finite resources, or even the expense of cleaning up rotting forty-four-gallon drums of toxic waste.[56] Nor was the cost of the medical care of poisoned workers or residents of the vicinity ever deducted from the annual profit-and-loss statement, unless, of course, a court enforced a judgment in tort law. Indeed, the cost of medical services or cleanup operations would be entered as more sales, more progress, and eventually a higher GNP. A central function of the state would be to transfer these indirect costs of production to the general community: in short, to privatize profits and collectivize losses.

It is a supreme irony that the only kind of economic sales not counted at face value are criminal activities. As the drug business became a major economic activity in the United States and Latin America, it created the embarrassing problem of omitting, in some regions, the largest business from the calculation of national income. Estimates of the magnitude of the cocaine business—"the world's most valuable commodity," as a recent study puts it—stagger the imagination as it is ever more obvious that Latin America is divided into drug-producing networks and zones of economic devastation. There is no logical reason to omit production by criminals from national income accounting, only coyness on the part of the statisticians.

A few years ago to suggest that GNP figures should be negatively adjusted for damage to the environment would have seemed like the most unrealistic madness. John Kenneth Galbraith was one of the first economists to question the absolute tyranny of the criterion of the GNP in his book, *The Affluent Society*. However, Galbraith's work was not so much a critique of the national income accounting system as a plea to juxtapose public needs to private gain. Even his description of private opulence in the face of public squalor was received in the 1950s—in his phrase—as being "deeply eccentric." Orthodox economists sensed that to give an inch on these valid criticisms was to remove a basic building block from the edifice of neoclassical economic analysis. Galbraith did question the way that the orthodox economists place the act of buying commodities at the center of their system. As he put it, "My colleagues rightly recognized that my case that wants were at least partially contrived by those who produced the goods was deeply subversive of the established orthodoxy. As a matter of vested interest if not of truth, they were compelled to resist."[57]

In Mexico it was frequently argued that, within a context of massive poverty, concern for the environment was a luxury for the rich. Indeed, when the country produced its first environmental engineers in the 1970s, some had to go abroad to find work. As Mexico City's environment now tests the physical limits of the planet to absorb pollution, and a single generation's

destruction of finite natural resources continues at a breathtaking pace, these considerations may not seem quite so unrealistic. Perhaps as nuclear mishaps, chemical waste, and other environmental disasters continue to sterilize parts of the planet, we will rethink our criteria of progress. Even if a dramatic spectacle is averted, a constant erosion of the environment is extant. Yet the Western accounting system is lacking as it skips over these problems in favor of equating short-term profits with human material progress.

Years ago the development economist, Dudley Seers, was one who suggested that a better definition of development was quite different from production for production's sake, whatever the cost and the consequences. He argued that the reduction of poverty, unemployment, and the gap between the rich and the poor (a proposition that need not be carried to its theoretical extreme) ought to form our fundamental definition of progress in a material sense.[58] In addition, one might want to strive to create a sustainable production at the same time that we add an improvement in the quality of social relations, greater popular participation in decision making, the end of discrimination, and the protection of the environment as goals that at least must qualify production for its own sake. However attractive this approach may seem, it is important to realize that nothing of the kind is implicit in the national income accounting system.

In Mexico, Presidents Avila Camacho and Alemán reacted against the social concerns evident in the Cárdenas era. Alemán, in particular, was fond of stating that it was pointless to talk of redistributing income even before production existed. Rejecting income redistribution, real land reform, and aid to the poor, Avila Camacho and Alemán tied the state to the privatization of accumulation, frequently in corrupt ways. That approach prevailed beyond the 1940s, and in most ways it still does today. The industrialized countries in Latin America have demonstrated that one can simultaneously have high rates of industrial growth, increasing poverty, destruction of the environment, high unemployment, and rapidly rising coefficients of income inequality. It is not just that the trickle-down theory of development does not work; the reduction of inequality, poverty, and unemployment were no longer at the heart of the state project by the 1940s. Those who thought that the national goals included a greater degree of equity for the people just did not understand the parameters of the mature Mexican Revolution.

The important element to keep in mind is that we are not simply dealing with a point of theory here. The United States placed enormous political pressure on its allies after World War II to adopt the national accounting system. As a point of comparison, it is worth remembering that even in such advanced economic powers as Germany and Japan, there had been no prewar national income calculations. It was only under the rule of General Lucius D. Clay in 1945 that a U.S. team, headed by George Ball, in the process of studying the economic impact of Allied bombing of Germany

during the war, first calculated the prewar GNP figures for Germany and began to reorganize that country's statistical reporting into the U.S. system.[59]

After World War II the adoption of the U.S. accounting system quickly became an absolute requirement for membership to the International Monetary Fund and for participation in the projects of the World Bank. Students of the history of the Cold War may recall that it was the requirement to make its economic statistics public, and in the form demanded by the U.S. national income accounting system, that was the immediate cause of the USSR dropping out of the plans for its participation in the Marshall Plan in April 1945. Other elements in the split between the two erstwhile allies were obviously important; however, it is worth noting that the definition of progress, as embodied in the national accounting system, was central to the emergence of the Cold War.

## Extending National Income Accounting Abroad

A number of economic conferences were held in the United States during the final stages of World War II, the aim of which was to avoid a repetition of the protectionism that, in the consensus of U.S. planners, had been largely responsible for the severity of the Great Depression of the 1930s. The promotion of free trade, the unimpeded flow of capital, the elimination of trade barriers, and the free access of all countries to technology, markets, and raw materials formed the heart of the program of the United States. This is well known. It is, however, somewhat less well known that a parallel series of technical conferences was organized to convince all countries to abandon their statistical measurements in favor of the new U.S. approach. Initially, there were general conferences dealing with broad problems of postwar planning.[60] Then, through the Pan American Union, the United States sponsored continuing technical conferences, and by October 4, 1944, the union agreed that its approach should be made universal.

Gilberto Loyo, director general of statistics within the Ministry of the National Economy, then headed another Mexican delegation to a bilateral statistical conference in Washington, DC, in September 1947. By that time the changes in national income accounting were presented as technical exercises. The statisticians were active. By November 1947, Antonio Ruiz Galindo, minister of the national economy, was again representing Mexico at yet another conference in Washington at the Inter-American Statistical Institute. By that point the push was for a uniform statistical approach to designing the 1950 census.[61]

In part, the chaos of numbers aided the U.S. economic diplomats in bringing the new system to Mexico. Merwin L. Bohan was the most important of these specialists in Mexico City during the Alemán years. He was

able to use the numerical mess to a purpose. By ridiculing new figures on government revenues—incompatible with earlier figures—or by joking that the government's statistics asserted that the economically active population was less in 1930 than in 1910, while the population had grown by 1,500,000, or that the cattle population increased by 80.5 percent between 1926 and 1930, Bohan was able to convince Mexican officials that their statistical effort was in disarray. By offering the services of Department of Commerce statisticians to Mexico City, he was in a position to influence the evolution of the record-keeping. Inevitably, policy was influenced by the very way that the accounts were established.[62] In 1948 another study of Mexico's statistical efforts was made by Alfred Whitney. Formal meetings between top Mexican authorities (Agustín Luna Olmedo, Gilberto Loyo, Federico Bach, and Josué Sáenz) and U.S. embassy personnel oversaw changes in the country's methodology at the same time that they offered help on the technical side of national income accounting.[63]

As a result of these conferences, and other pressures, Mexico changed key policies in ways that were basic to the direction of its economic evolution. In the early 1940s, before it adopted the U.S. manner of measuring progress, the primary source of statistical reporting for the period was the monthly review *Examen de la Situación Económica de México*, published by the Banco Nacional de México and reprinted in the *Anuario Financiero de México,* which was edited by the Asociación de Banqueros de México and published by the Editorial Cultura S.A. in Mexico City. As in the case of most countries, these early measures had originally focused upon agricultural production. By 1943 the estimate of the national income of Mexico was made by Miguel Sánchez de Tagle, who collaborated with the Banco Nacional de México's economic research section and was the financial editor of *El Universal*. In preparing his estimate, Sánchez de Tagle followed the form that Luna Olmedo had used in his study of the balance of payments for 1940, which was published in *El Trimestre Económico*.[64]

In his discussions with U.S. statisticians, Luna Olmedo admitted that the estimate was "very rough" and that it "cannot be relied upon." He confessed that the estimates on gold and capital movements were "pure guesswork." Boasting that he had graduated at the head of his class at the London School of Economics, the Banco de México had just hired Manuel Chavarría, a Costa Rican, to work on an independent estimate so that the Mexican government would no longer be exclusively dependent upon figures from the country's largest commercial bank.[65] Nevertheless, even on so rudimentary an understanding of Mexican economic reality, the government shifted back to an orthodox concern with production for sale as the only criterion around which public development projects would be based.

Within this context of numerical chaos, technical experts in national income accounting began to aid Mexico by molding its statistical reporting into the U.S. pattern. This emerged in a curious way. The U.S. government

and the International Committee of Bankers had acceded to Mexico's decree of December 1942, in which Mexico set up registration points for holders of that country's debt to register their bonds (or else they would be considered held in enemy hands), a maneuver that reduced its foreign debt by 55 percent. By agreeing to this move, U.S. statisticians acquired leverage over the form of reporting on Mexico's international statistics.[66]

By 1944 wartime economic cooperation was spilling over into a redefinition of the terms of progress. August Maffry of the International Economics and Statistics Unit of the Bureau of Foreign and Domestic Commerce wrote to the Mexican Department of Commerce. Referring specifically to Mexico's internal and external debt, he not only requested detailed information about the debt situation but also queried the form in which statistics were being reported.[67] Periodically, Mexico sent more detailed information than was available to its people to the Securities and Exchange Commission and the Committee on Stock Lists, of the New York Stock Exchange. The Mexican Revolution notwithstanding, the country was shifting its policies into line with the demands of U.S. capital.

The ability of the United States to set the international economic agenda grew dramatically after World War II. Thinking of the period as the "American Century" (in *Time* magazine's famous phrase), decision makers used even mundane economic conferences to establish a postwar system for the West. The conference that has attracted the most attention was held at Bretton Woods in the mountains of New Hampshire; yet, at even small technical conferences, large changes emerged. The Department of Commerce and the Treasury Department held an important meeting on August 1, 1945. It was hardly a typical bureaucratic exercise, as top U.S. economic officials agreed on the kind and form of statistical information that would be required of all countries dealing with the World Bank and the International Monetary Fund. In addition to the universalization of its national income accounting system, the American authorities decided to require detailed information on a continuing basis on each country's balance of payments, monetary reserve, international investments, exchange rates, capital markets, and general finance.[68]

Mexico found itself under pressure to abandon its own statistical effort in favor of adopting the U.S. system. With promising young intellectuals Victor Urquidi and Daniel Cosío Villegas representing their country and handling the technical economic discussions, Mexico dropped a series of controversial statistical measures, such as recording the percentage of capital, land, and factories that were owned by foreigners as well as differentiations between the peasant and the farming sectors, for it is a sacred tenet of orthodox national accounting to insist that all production that is sold through the marketplace be valued at the sale price, whether the item produced is so shoddy that it will break the first time it is used or so fine that it will last for centuries.

At the time, the adoption of the U.S. system seemed uncontroversial, since these technical arguments generate little interest in the wider community. Apart from minor objections by Mexico, and more fundamental concerns on the part of Australia at Bretton Woods, the U.S. economic system of accounting was adopted. After all, the economy of the United States was the envy of the world. Between 1941 and 1944 its GNP increased, in 1958 prices, from 264 billion dollars to 360 billion dollars. Of that 360 billion, even at the height of World War II, the government absorbed only 160 billion dollars for the war effort. Given the absence of so many soldiers, the war represented a minimal reduction in living standards for the United States.[69] From 1941 to 1944, in spite of the pitiful preparation for the war, the industrial output increased by two and one-half times.[70] The will for war had created the way to economic growth, and the country that stood at the apex of the Western economic system seemed to have found the route to the industrial utopia for which Mexico longed.

It was not that Simon Kuznets in the United States, Colin Clark in Britain, and the other economists who designed the national income accounting system were overtly trying to please powerful interests.[71] Yet the tradition of orthodox economics from which these pioneers emerged was fundamentally compatible with the interests of capital. By creating a national accounting system that only measured what was produced and sold, they made it difficult even to consider the peasant sector, and it relegated matters of distribution to mere welfare or charity; indirectly, they provided the technique that helped to excise the heart of radical reform projects.

## Lost Worlds: Alternative Measures that Were Dropped

Before these conferences, some of the radical tendencies in the Mexican Revolution had surfaced in the country's economic statistics. The methodologies were certainly flawed and, at times, difficult to work with, although in truth the frequency of change in statistical categories provided the researcher with even more difficulties than the inadequacies of the accounting procedures. Among some of the more interesting items that were dropped as Mexico moved to the U.S. system of national accounting was a detailed distinction between production on collective ejidos as contrasted to the private sector by area and value. That organization made it easier to calculate which sectors were using resources more effectively. Later, the distinction would be dropped, and only the total produced and sold would be estimated at the detailed level of statistical reporting.

In the early industrial reporting there were also categories that were sensitive to the economic nationalism of the Cárdenas period. Percentages of foreign ownership of firms and resources were reported; and detailed

calculations of the domestic and foreign ingredients used in production by the manufacturing industry (as in the *industrias de transformación*), as well as value-added figures, were included. Had these calculations been continued, they would have made it easier to see the degree to which the multiplier effect was being exported. Even investment was subdivided in a way that differentiated between money that went directly into new production, as contrasted to funds spent bidding up existing equity shares or real estate. The terms of the debate over strategies of development would have been powerfully augmented, had these calculations been continued.

Matters of income distribution played a more central role in the early statistical reporting. Employment figures were reported at a detailed level, making the employment generated by national and international industry more visible. Average incomes were reported in each industry, and distinctions were made between *directores, empleados,* and *obreros.* And there even was an attempt to calculate an index of absorption of labor. But many of those distinctions were replaced by less useful aggregate figures as the U.S. national income accounting system was implemented in time for the industrial census of 1945 and 1951.

A final point to keep in mind, in this consideration of the yardstick of progress, is that future governmental intervention and subventions would be essentially tied to this single measure of material production. Ministers, politicians, economists, and commentators would all tend to accept as the criterion of success changes to the national income figures. Nacional Financiera, to take but one important institution, would channel domestic and foreign funds into industries that would increase the country's GNP. The ejido sector, the peasantry, the poor, and the women of the country did not stand a chance of receiving any support, apart from the odd bit of charity. Those groups would not even enjoy a proportional part (to their indirect tax contribution) of the nation's budget, as the central productive use of resources would be placed in the hands of those whose activities added to the country's GNP.

Optimists thought that increases in output would trickle down, as the phrase went, and improve the lot of the entire community. Eduardo Villaseñor, director of the Banco de México, gave a speech at the height of wartime economic cooperation between the two countries in 1943 in which he reassured his audience that development came from "investment in a concrete form, that is to say in the form of new plants, new industries, additional equipment,"[72] and not merely speculation that increased the price of existing assets. He desperately hoped that the Cardenista concerns with redistribution could be compatible with the new GNP approach, and that was not an isolated view.

> One of the fundamental principles of the social upheaval that we know as the Mexican Revolution, has been to raise the standard of living, or in

other words, to increase the purchasing power or the capacity of the population to consume. . . . The improvement in the remuneration of the workers during the period 1936–40 has proved to be a stimulus to industrial production, a growing capitalization of profits thus acquired, and an expansion of production in many branches, especially industrial production. . . . During the two-year period 1941–42, the direct cause of the continued rise in the purchasing power of the Mexican people has been chiefly the government's expenditure on public works.[73]

There are two distinct traditions that Villaseñor drew upon in this statement, both of which were subsequently dropped from mainstream economic analysis after the Cárdenas period. In this instance, there was a strong current of underconsumption analysis, the line of argument that stressed the need to create a domestic demand by increasing wage levels.[74] He also differentiated between production and speculation, a distinction that is ignored by the national income accounting system. But whether or not the Mexican Revolution's goal of improving the lot of the poor was compatible with the new GNP application of orthodox economics, people believed that it was.

## Excitement over Margarine: An Episode

In mid-January 1950, Anderson, Clayton, and Company (A.C.&Co.) opened a large, state-of-the-art, finished oil mill on the outskirts of Monterrey. Today, the opening of a factory that could turn one hundred thousand tons of cotton and sesame seeds into edible oils may not be too exciting. However, the opening of the new plant in Monterrey was a thrilling event in 1950. The company planned a lavish inauguration and chartered special airplanes to bring celebrities and high officials to Monterrey to be entertained by a large troupe of Mexican and U.S. performers. Some six hundred official guests attended an opulent banquet. While it is not surprising to see a company celebrate its success, and A.C.&Co. was the world's largest cotton brokerage firm, the public's response was amazing; an estimated fifteen thousand persons attended the opening festivities. Extra buses were hired to supplement the fleet of A.C.&Co. buses and trucks bringing people out from the center of Monterrey. Special signs were installed in the city center to help drivers find the new factory, and a national radio network brought the inauguration celebrations to the rest of the country. One report stated that the crowds were so much larger and enthusiastic than anticipated that the company had to replant the lawns and gardens around the factory after the opening, so great had been the throng.

In addition to being one of the world's largest and most aggressive agribusiness firms, A.C.&Co. was the personal property of Will L. Clayton, who made a massive fortune in cotton, rice, and land.[75] He had been a dollar-a-year man during the Second World War, eventually rising to the

position of undersecretary of state and other important posts within the Roosevelt administration. The thousands of Mexicans who attended the opening of A.C.&Co.'s new oil mill did not think that they were celebrating the increase in Clayton's personal fortune. As the U.S. consul in Monterrey reported, "Throughout the celebrations and inauguration Anderson, Clayton and Company stressed the Mexican character of the enterprise in this country."[76]

Cotton was booming at the time, and, in 1949, 400 million pesos' worth was being produced in Matamoros alone. A.C.&Co. had built an additional nineteen cotton gins in northern Mexico, including an even larger cotton-seed oil mill in Matamoros. The idea was to take advantage of the high price of cotton, or "white gold" as some were calling it, on the eve of the emergence of synthetic fibers. More important than the immediate boom, many influential Mexicans had come to believe in recent years that by locating factories in the country, even foreign firms were helping to develop Mexico. At a very different level, at roughly the same time, Raul Prebisch of the United Nations' Economic Commission for Latin America was arguing that the region's poverty had reflected poor leverage caused by selling primary products to be refined abroad. It seemed to the crowd in Monterrey that the process was being reversed, and overturning that disadvantage was something to celebrate. The path to progress seemed clear.

## Notes

1. In 1948 the Alemán administration was munificent as it purchased the rights to Ralph Roeder's *Juárez and His Mexico* and awarded him the Aztec Eagle Prize for his effort to show a direct line of descent between earlier reform movements and the project of modernization. Lombardo Toledano proposed the idea for the award, and the president accepted. AGN, RP/MAV, 704/262-A.

2. Report from William K. Ailshie to secretary of state entitled "Reaction to the Announcement of the Abolition of the Presidential Committee for Postwar Planning," December 18, 1944, USNA/RG 59, 812.00/12-1844.

3. Merwin L. Bohan to secretary of state, January 26, 1947, USNA/RG 59, 812.50/1-2947.

4. In studying the economic aspects of the Tuxtepec rebellion, for example, it became clear that the government budget did not reflect the cost of fighting a three-way civil war. Armies lived off the land, and their efforts must have destroyed local production time and again. See Stephen R. Niblo, "The Political Economy of the Early Porfiriato" (Ph.D. diss., Northern Illinois University, 1972), 57–58.

5. The authoritative description of the colonial system of public finance was by Urrita y Fonseca; merely to describe all of the taxes required several volumes. To liberals, such taxes as the *alcabala* (turnover) became symbols of colonial backwardness.

6. Coatsworth, *Growth against Development*, 175–91.

7. Haber, *Industry and Underdevelopment*, 4.

8. Institute members who had been president of the Mexican Bankers' Association include Mario Domínguez, Banco General de Capitalización; Salvador

Ugarte, Banco de Comercio; Luis G. Legorreta, Banco Nacional de México; Aarón Sáenz, Banco de Comercio e Industria; and Raul Bailleres, Banco de Crédito Minero. Long lists of key industrialists and government officials made up the membership.

9. Manuel Hernández to Spruille Braden, January 12, 1946, USNA/RG 59, 812.50/1-1246.

10. See José R. Colín's report on the Tercer Congreso Nacional de Industriales, *Requisitos Fundamentale para la Industrialización de México* (México, D.F.: N.p., October 1945), in AGN, RP/MAC, 523.1/109. In a somewhat forlorn mood, he called for foreign capital to be welcomed to invest in public services but not the manufacturing sector.

11. Mosk, *Industrial Revolution in Mexico*, 27.

12. In his pamphlet, *Materias Primas y Capital Extranjero*, José R. Colín called for the government to guarantee a national chemical industry. It was a move that was closely related to his own business interests. Other publications of similar ilk include *De la Necesidad de Formar la Industria Química Mexicana* (México, D.F., 1943); *Plan Inmediato de Industrialización en México* (México, D.F., 1945); and *La Industria Química Nacional* (México, D.F., 1945), all by José Domingo Lavín. These pamphlets may be found in AGN, RP/MAC, 523.1/109

13. Dionisio Encina to the Comisión Nacional de Planeación para la Paz, November 22, 1944, AGN, RP/MAC, 433/310. Their approach to industrialization was essentially to cite lists of the kinds of industries that the PCM wanted for the country.

14. Walter Thurston to secretary of state, January 8, 1947, USNA/RG 59, 812.51/1-847. The newly irrigated lands increased Mexico's agricultural exports, thus benefiting local landowners, their allies, and the U.S. supermarket chains. Meanwhile, the ejido sector was required to produce staples at fixed prices in order to subsidize urban consumption. For a study of the international nexus in agribusiness see Baird and McCaughan, *Beyond the Border*.

15. See the president's requests for appointments, AGN, RP/MAC, 523/54.

16. Undersecretary of the Economy Germán Parra claimed to U.S. diplomats that he headed a second school within the government, closer to Cárdenas's tradition, that thought that Mexican capital should be fully utilized before allowing U.S. capital into Mexico. Report entitled "Main Currents of Mexican Economic Philosophy According to Undersecretary of Economy Parra," January 29, 1948, USNA/RG 59, 812.50/1-2948.

17. James Henderson to secretary of state, January 11, 1945, USNA/RG 59, 812.00/1-1145.

18. Abelardo Rodríguez seemed to have the first audience with the president on many days when he was in the capital. AGN, RP/MAC, 523.6/7.

19. See, for example, *Voz Patronal* (official organ of the Confederación Patronal de la República Mexicana), May 15, 1946, 4–7. Its confidential *Bulletín #15*, directed to the president, also made that point explicit. June 16, 1941, AGN, RP/MAC, 545.2/7.

20. AGN, RP/MAC, 545.3/17-1 contains a series of petitions against the IMSS levy, from November and December 1944.

21. Report from Ailshie to secretary of state entitled "Conversation with Lic. Alejandro Carrillo, Editor of *El Popular* and Prominent Mexican Labor Leader," September 21, 1944, USNA/RG 59, 812.00/9-2144.

22. *El Popular*, March 24, 1945. Lombardo Toledano also took encouragement in this project from an editorial on March 23, 1945, in *Boletín Financiero y Minero de México*, which was the official organ of the Mexico City stock exchange.

23. George Messersmith to John Willard Carrigan, State Department, April 11, 1945, USNA/RG 59, 812/4-1145.

24. Ailshie, "Memorandum of Conversation with Mr. Lombardo Toledano by a Member of the Staff of the Embassy," April 17, 1944, USNA/RG 59, 812.504/2273.

25. Ibid.

26. Ibid.

27. This view was quoted and fiercely criticized in *Voz Patronal*, May 15, 1946.

28. These conservative groups—with links to the United States—were represented by the 526 delegates, including Confederación Proletaria Nacional, Alfredo Navarrete and Enríque Rangel; Confederación de Obreros y Campesinos de México, Julio López Silva; Confederación Regional Obrera Mexicana, Luis N. Morones; Confederación General de Trabajadores, Carlos Sánchez; Confederación Nacional de Cooperativas, Nicolas G. González; Sindicato Industrial de Trabajadores Textiles de Fibras Duras y Similares, Higinio Esquivel. Interestingly, all of these organizations were still petitioning the president, trying to join the PRM.

29. The conference proceedings were summarized in the pamphlet *Primer Congreso Nacional de Economía de Guerra*, published in November 1942, AGN, RP/MAC, 433/310, and 433/310.1.

30. See their petitions to the president and the pamphlet *La Justicia Social en México*, August 1945, AGN, RP/MAC, 433/544.

31. The unions involved were Sindicato Nacional de Telefonistas, Alianza de Tranviarios de México, Sindicato de Trabajadores Ferrocarrileros de la República Mexicana, Sindicato Industrial de Trabajadores de Artes Gráficas de la República Mexicana, Sindicato Nacional de Trabajadores de Aviación y Similares, and the Sindicato Nacional de Trabajadores de Aguas Gaseosas. AGN, RP/MAC, 542.1-1060.

32. See the letter from Rodolfo Brito Foucher (rector of UNAM) to the president's private secretary, J. Jesús González Gallo, November 28, 1942, AGN, RP/MAC, 433/310-1.

33. *El Nacional*, August 27, 1945.

34. Ailshie to secretary of state, August 30, 1945, USNA/RG 59, 812.504/8-3045.

35. Bohan to secretary of state, August 6, 1947, USNA/RG 59, 812.50/8-647.

36. Department of Foreign and Domestic Commerce, USNA/RG 151, boxes 73 and 74.

37. The promotional material and a request for financial help from the president may be found in Gonzalo de la Peña to the president, June 28, 1943, AGN, RP/MAC, 523/5.

38. U.S. consul general in Monterrey to secretary of state, USNA/RG 59, 812.6511/8; Saragoza, *The Monterrey Elite*; Nuncio, *El Grupo Monterrey*.

39. This material comes from a study ordered by the Inter-American Development Commission, an organization closely tied to the U.S. Chamber of Commerce, "Memorandum of Comments on Reports Submitted by the Comisión Mexicana de Fomento Interamericano," confidential study of Mexican industrialization by Ford, Bacon, and Davis Engineers, October 15, 1943, USNA, RG 59, 812.50/438PS/FP.

40. The report was made before the Tercer Congreso de Industriales de México, in February 1946, AGN, RP/MAC, 523/54. By contrast, see Chapter 5 in this volume for a different analysis of the impact of the war on the standard of living.

41. AGN, RP/MAC, 523/54. For a contrasting view of the effect of the effort see Chapter 3 in this volume.

42. Final report of the commission from Aarón Sáenz to President Avila Camacho, January 26, 1945, AGN, RP/MAC, 433/310-3.

43. Lew B. Clark to secretary of state, May 9, 1947, USNA/RG 59, 812.50/5-947.

44. Córdova, *La formación del poder político en México.*

45. Ruggles, "The United States Income Accounts," 15.

46. Carson, "National Income and Product Accounts," 153–81.

47. Shoup and Minter, *Imperial Brain Trust,* 110.

48. Morgenstern, *On the Accuracy of Economic Observations,* 242–54.

49. Ibid., 225.

50. Kuznets, *National Income and Its Composition,* 6–7.

51. Tice's "Comment on Richard Ruggles," 96–104.

52. One of the interesting attempts to generate an alternative approach is Morris, *Measuring the Condition of the World's Poor.*

53. United Nations, *Human Development Report,* 100–112.

54. Max-Neef, *Experiences in "Barefoot Economics,"* 129–44, 117.

55. See Nash, *Progress as if Survival Mattered*; and Schumacher, *Small Is Beautiful,* which occupied an intermediate position between the Club of Rome and the environmentalists.

56. The orthodox economist, Kenneth Arrow, acknowledges that critics have charged that the U.S. national income accounting system ignores damage to the environment. He simply disagrees without giving any reasons for his opinion. Arrow, "Economic Development," 183–207.

57. Galbraith, *A Life in Our Times,* 352.

58. Seers, "The Meaning of Development," 2–6.

59. Galbraith, *A Life in Our Times,* 214.

60. Subsecretary of the National Economy Gustavo P. Serrán headed Mexico's team at the Interamerican Technical Economic Conference in September 1944. See Padilla to Avila Camacho, AGN, RP/MAC, 433/489.

61. AGN, RP/MA, 433/183.

62. Bohan to secretary of state, March 5, 1947, USNA/RG 59, 812.50/3-547.

63. Memorandum from Alfred Whitney to Bohan, August 3, 1948, USNA/RG 59, 812. 501/8-1848.

64. Olmedo, "Algunos aspectos de la balanza de pagos," 14–52.

65. Report entitled "Mexico's Monthly Balance of Payments," William F. Busser to secretary of state, November 30, 1944, USNA/RG 59, 812.51/11-3044.

66. U.S. attorney general to secretary of state, December 9, 1944, USNA/RG 59, 812.51/12-944.

67. Busser to secretary of state, October 19, 1944, USNA/RG 59, 812.51/10-1944.

68. Memorandum, August 1, 1945, Roman L. Horne Papers, box 2, Truman Library.

69. *Economic Report of the President,* 140–43, as cited in Galbraith, *A Life in Our Times,* 214.

70. Harris, *Problems in Price Controls,* 12–14.

71. Indeed, Colin Clark still cited Cecil A. Pigou's classical definition of the purpose of economic study as including the equalization of income distribution. See Clark, *National Income and Outlay,* 1.

72. Speech delivered by Eduardo Villaseñor, at UNAM, April 10, 1943.

73. Ibid.

74. The conservative newspaper, *El Universal,* also argued this underconsumption position in its editorial, May 9, 1944.

75. It was Clayton's daughter, heir, and biographer, Ellen Garwood, who in 1987, at the time of the Contragate scandal in the Reagan administration, testified to having personally contributed some 2 million dollars to the Nicaraguan contra leaders via Col. Oliver North. Testimony to the Iran-Contragate hearings, May 21, 1987.

76. U.S. consul in Monterrey to secretary of state, January 14 and February 2, 1950, USNA/RG 59, 812.00/1-1650 and 812.00/2-250. Accounts of the events also may be found in *El Norte* from Monterrey.

# 2 The "Good Neighbor" Copes with Cárdenas

The events leading to the nationalization of the petroleum industry are well known. At the heart of the conflict was the issue of national sovereignty. The petroleum companies had taken an absolute view of private property that clashed profoundly with Mexico's revolutionary nationalism. In the industry view, the oil was theirs and no government had the right to regulate their activities. They were playing for the validation of the absolute right of private property, and a precedent that would apply around the world. By contrast, the social program of the Mexican Revolution—as embodied in Article 123 of the 1917 constitution—included the hope of ameliorating living conditions for Mexican workers. The oil companies held that proud showpiece of the revolutionary constitution in contempt. Even then, many Mexicans also resented the extraction of surplus and the environmental destruction that had been wrought to the land in places like Tampico, as the petroleum enterprises pursued their interests.

Conflict ebbed and flowed for decades between Mexican leaders and the oil companies. Even though there was an accommodation between U.S. Ambassador Dwight Morrow and President Plutarco Elías Calles in 1928, the conflict between national sovereignty and property rights still persisted. At the beginning of 1936 the petroleum companies again complained to the State Department that the Mexican Department of the National Economy was slow to reexamine oil concessions, that it delayed issuing new drilling permits, and refused to issue confirmatory titles. On January 31, 1936, the Mexican government issued a ruling that no new permits would be granted unless the petroleum companies paid a royalty. The Cárdenas administration also added some seven million hectares to the national petroleum reserve. The parties were again disputing the property rights by issuing contradictory interpretations of the Morrow statement of March 28, 1928, and, more generally, the Morrow-Calles agreement.[1]

Initially, Ambassador Josephus Daniels was convinced that Mexico was not going to nationalize petroleum.[2] Since Secretary of State Cordell Hull viewed Daniels as being "a little radical at times to suit me," that seemed reassuring to opponents of the Cardenista reforms.[3] During the Cárdenas years the state was growing, not only by creating mass organizations but also by applying a broad body of social legislation to the conditions of labor. There was no more dramatic instance of conflict over social legislation

than in the dispute between the foreign petroleum companies and the labor movement, as labor leaders pressed the foreign enterprises to implement recent changes to the law.

By March 15, 1938, the Supreme Court and the District Court had denied all of the specific points in the oil companies' case against paying higher salaries and benefits, as required by Mexican law. Political negotiations between the companies and Finance Minister Eduardo Suárez and the head of the Labor Department, Antonio Villalobos, had stalled. On that day the ultimatum from the Federal Board of Conciliation and Arbitration expired. The companies had stated their unwillingness to comply with the law, and they were, therefore, considered to be in a state of rebellion under Mexican law.

The Petroleum Workers' Union, the STPRM, became deeply involved in the conflict. Ever since the publication of the massive Silva Herzog report on the petroleum industry in 1937, which identified some forty areas in which the companies were found to be operating in violation of the law and the national interest, the union's hand was strengthened in dealing with them. When the court declared the companies to be in a state of rebellion, the union announced that all work on their property would cease, as of March 18. Events occurred in dramatic succession. An El Aguila Oil Company tanker slipped out of port at Tampico to avoid seizure, even though its cargo was only partially loaded, and at 10:00 P.M. the president spoke to the nation. The following day the decree of nationalization was issued. It affected the property of seventeen foreign petroleum firms.

Troops and workers immediately seized all of the oil companies' installations. Foreign bosses quickly returned to the United States or took refuge in Mexico City. By March 20 reports from all over the country showed that union and government agents were taking over the existing stocks of petroleum for sale and distribution, and on March 21 the government announced the formation of the General Council for Petroleum Administration. To add insult to injury, the new petroleum monopoly moved into the recently finished Mexico City offices of El Aguila on Avenida Juárez. By the last day of the month a new export company, Distribuidora de Petróleos Mexicanos, was formed to distribute the oil, and Petróleos Mexicanos (PEMEX) was placed in charge of production.[4]

It became a national celebration, almost an act of catharsis. The announcement came on one of those dusty March days in Mexico City. The news broke over the radio at about 10:00 P.M. on Saturday, March 18, 1938: first in Spanish and then, surprisingly, in English, "the oil is ours." By March 23 the CTM had organized enormous celebrations on the streets in most major cities. Office workers, unionists, and soldiers joined the throngs in a celebration that lasted for most of the day.

Decades of resentment seemed to have been avenged. No longer would oilmen such as Weetman Pearson, Edward Doheny, and others operate in

Mexico with such impunity. Old grievances were to be settled. Of course, President Lázaro Cárdenas understood that it might be war if his government did not agree immediately to compensate the foreign oil companies. So tables went up in the Palacio de las Bellas Artes. The wife of the president, in the following days, oversaw an effort in which Mexicans of all classes queued up to donate money or their family's jewelry and treasures, often in tiny quantities, to the great cause of economic emancipation, and by the end of May they had collected more than 1 million pesos.[5] For many, it appeared to be the economic equivalent of national emancipation. Old wrongs were to be undone. The super-profits of petroleum were now to belong to the Mexican nation; no more surreptitious deals would siphon off the wealth of the country. No longer would Mexico be a mere pawn in the Achnacarry Castle agreement.[6]

To friends and foes alike, it appeared to be the height of Cárdenas's economic radicalism. Some of his followers on the left hoped that the move might be part of a broader goal of nationalization of the means of production, for the government had also nationalized the railroads and large amounts of land. Taken in conjunction with the militarization of labor, experiments in workers' administration, a program of socialist education, the creation of organizations of mass political support, and strong support for the nation's three thousand cooperatives, President Cárdenas's program seemed radical indeed.[7] Yet it was not only the economic nationalists and the political Left who celebrated, but there was also a strong tradition of conservative nationalism that resented the behavior of the petroleum companies even though that clashed, in this instance, with their belief in private property rights. But for most Mexicans, this recovery of national pride was a crowning achievement of the revolution.[8]

In a strange and unexpected way, however, the very success of the expropriation of the petroleum set off a chain of events that was quite unforeseen. This most radical of Cárdenas's reforms eventually led to both an accommodation between Mexico and the United States and an end to other radical reforms of the period. Soon, President Cárdenas found his popularity soaring, and he used the opportunity to consolidate politically. Calling the state governors together, he persuaded them to support the nationalization of the petroleum, which was easy, and also to redouble their efforts in the area of land reform. He argued that while the goal ideally was to implement all of the grants of land to the collective ejidos, the moment now required consolidation of existing gains. At the same time, he announced the formation of the new Partido Revolucionario Mexicano, the PRM. Ambassador Daniels was fascinated by the way Cárdenas linked the nationalization of oil with a call for an intensification of land reform and the formation of the new party. In his view, the issues that brought all of the state governors into line was the decision to allow them to arm the *ejidatarios*, or peasants, thus allowing the governors to disarm their opponents throughout

the country: "So when you take into account the rapid juxtaposition of the nationalization of the petroleum industry, the formation of the new national party, the PRM, and the very considerable concessions to the state governments at the time of the former events, we then see the full and rich complexity of the President's political strategy."[9] Momentum continued as, on April 28, 1938, the government turned the administration of the nation's railways over to the railroad workers' union, the STFRM.

## A Close Call

It was not entirely clear what the U.S. position would be. The State Department, during this period, was a very different institution from the excessively bureaucratized Foggy Bottom that we have known in recent years. In the first three decades of the twentieth century, it was an exclusive bastion of WASP privilege. Ambassadors were appointed on the basis of their connections and their personal financial resources. An ambassador of a major embassy required a considerable fortune to support wide-ranging social obligations. The Old Guard of the department were usually close to the U.S. establishment and tended to be highly Anglophile.

The old traditions in the State Department were under attack from President Franklin D. Roosevelt, but it was not certain that the New Dealers would prevail. The private correspondence between Daniels and the U.S. ambassador to Spain, Claude Bowers, makes it clear how outnumbered the New Deal diplomats felt in the State Department and, incidentally, how deeply opposed they were to the U.S. policy toward republican Spain. Facing an Old Guard that, at the secondary administrative level, antedated the Roosevelt administration, the New Deal diplomats believed that they had an uphill battle on their hands in implementing the Good Neighbor policy. As events shifted attention toward Mexico, these divisions within the State Department became critical.[10] The difference between Pierre L. de Boal and John H. MacVeagh, in the U.S. embassy in Mexico City, epitomized the difference between the Old Guard in the State Department and the New Dealers.[11]

One account of the U.S. reaction to the nationalization of petroleum is fascinating. Only junior staff members, John MacVeagh and Steve Aguirre, were still on duty in the U.S. embassy when the surprise announcement came over the air. MacVeagh stated that they soon received a telegram from Washington recalling Ambassador Daniels. Moreover, the word was that Sumner Welles, undersecretary of state, was coming down to Mexico to "straighten things out." Given Welles's performance in Cuba in 1933–34, that was ominous indeed. Putting him and Saturnino Cedillo, the rebellious governor of San Luis Potosí, in the same place would have been, in MacVeagh's view, highly provocative and even reminiscent of Welles's relationship with Fulgencio Batista in Cuba. John MacVeagh and his wife

Bobbie went to alert Daniels on the seriousness of the situation. MacVeagh thought that Chargé d'Affaires Pierre de Boal, who had only just arrived back in Mexico City from Cuernavaca, was behind the plan to bring Welles directly into the situation.

In parallel reminiscences Bobbie MacVeagh added further detail. She pointed out that every day in March, Saturnino Cedillo's people were calling the embassy in order to determine the U.S. position in case of a conservative rebellion against the Mexican government. She also noted that Welles's sympathies in the Spanish civil war "were entirely with Franco." Pierre de Boal and Herbert Bursley were in general agreement with Welles's viewpoint, and she recalled that, immediately after the news broke, John MacVeagh had transmitted a message to Daniels in which he was instructed to "deliver to the Mexican Government a note so strong it was almost a severance of relations and to fly back to Washington immediately afterwards."[12]

The MacVeaghs obviously thought that they had stuck their necks out by urging Daniels to oppose Welles's ploy; they noted that Pierre de Boal was not amused. If one accepts this account, it is clear how much depended on the personal views of individuals who were on duty at a key moment. They truly were in a position to make history. In any case, other elements combined to convince the U.S. policymakers to work for accommodation with Mexico.

Today we tend to think of the petroleum expropriation as the great international event of the final years of the Cárdenas presidency. Given the never-ending dependence upon petroleum in recent years, it is easy to lose a sense of proportion on the issue. During the late 1930s petroleum was not viewed, either by U.S. diplomats or Mexican political figures, as the central issue of the period. Agrarian claims against Mexico exceeded the value of the petroleum expropriation. Not only expropriation but also more generally the rules governing foreign landowners were in question. In 1939, for example, the U.S. embassy took up the case of the United Sugar Company at Los Mochis, Sinaloa. Some 87,643 hectares of land had been expropriated to the benefit of fifty-six villages; however, the company retained ownership of the mill. Its control, finance, and milling kept the company in a position of dominance, in spite of the loss of the land. Producers were tied into a five-year contract with the price of sugar fixed at 9.50 pesos per ton. The Cárdenas government was insisting that the price be increased to 12 pesos per ton. William Patrick Briggs took the case to the International Agrarian Claims Commission when President Cárdenas threatened further expropriations if the price were not raised.[13] Many similar cases, including the extensive lands of William Randolph Hearst, made the agrarian claims of the period politically sensitive.

In the business sphere, by the criteria of production and export, the Guggenheim-owned American Smelting and Refining Company (ASARCO)

was of greater significance than oil. Indeed, it was the largest exporter of Mexican minerals, and its production was sent to smelters throughout the United States for processing. ASARCO alone employed about nineteen thousand people, roughly a thousand more than the entire petroleum industry, and by August 1938 some nineteen spontaneous seizures of mines had taken place, including the important ASARCO mines Nueva Rosita and La Noria, as well as the San Rafael and Dos Estrellas mines. The threat of further nationalizations was in the air.

On February 22, 1938, negotiations between the workers and ASARCO over a collective contract broke down and, by March 7, workers in a plant in Monterrey staged rolling sit-down strikes during each shift. Management retaliated by dismissing 266 of the 450 employees. Similar events ensued in Chihuahua plants. The conflict at ASARCO was smoldering when the petroleum expropriation hit the industry. Management feared that Cárdenas might be embarking on a general program of nationalization. Company executives quickly realized how high the price of dogmatic intransigence had been for petroleum executives, and they vowed not to make the same errors.

It is less generally known that the Mexican Department of Labor brought great pressure to bear upon the miners' union to arrive at a quick settlement with ASARCO, since the government realized that, given the battle with the oil companies, the foreign exchange generated by ASARCO was critical to maintain state solvency.

## Cárdenas's Reassurances to the United States

In addition to public statements aimed at reassuring the United States, General Eduardo Hay, the foreign minister, visited Ambassador Daniels at his home on the Sunday after the announcement of the expropriation to assure him that Mexico would pay compensation. Daniels was reassured, for he immediately began to argue against the U.S. decision to suspend silver purchases; figures on both sides were immediately working for accommodation.[14]

On March 22, Daniels met Cárdenas, with Undersecretary of Foreign Affairs Ramón Beteta translating. The president said that he was sorry about the turn of events; however, the decision was irrevocable. It was forced on him, said Cárdenas, by the rebellious attitude of the oil companies, their withdrawal of funds from Mexico, their propaganda against his government, and their efforts to hurt the country economically. Cárdenas immediately reassured the diplomat that he would agree to compensation, perhaps by giving the companies a share of the oil. He shrewdly elevated the issue to the pinnacle of international strategy when he said that he hoped that he could find buyers for the petroleum other than Japan and Germany. However, by raising this issue, he made a subtle threat.[15]

By the end of March, it was clear that the United States would accept the situation.[16] Cárdenas wrote to Daniels that Mexico is celebrating President Roosevelt's policy and that it "is winning for your country the affection of many people of the world."[17] By July, Cárdenas announced that no mining companies would be nationalized, and Roosevelt obviously felt that matters were well enough in hand to visit Magdalena Bay in July and holiday on Cedros Island.

## The Domestic Effects of the Nationalization

After the nationalization, President Cárdenas froze exchange controls. This quickly brought important segments of the retail trade to a standstill. Giant corporations like Westinghouse, International Electric, General Electric, Ford, and General Motors all cut credit lines, reduced production, and, in the case of the automobile industry, increased prices between 20 and 50 percent. Panic convinced price setters throughout the country to raise prices rapidly, anticipating the impact of a likely devaluation. The psychological basis of many of the increases was clear. Even items that had no imported content rose. Beans, for instance, shot up from 12 centavos per kilo at the beginning of March to 31 centavos by the end of the month. Similarly, the price of corn doubled in March.[18]

Other problems abounded. Petroleum had generated considerable tax receipts, nearly 65 million pesos in 1937 or 14.3 percent of the government's revenues. U.S. petroleum officials doubted the government's assurances that domestic sales would cover the wage bill in the industry, estimated to reach about 6 million pesos per month. And that problem threatened the core of Cárdenas's high strategy.

The period of the 1930s and the remarkable reform movement of the Cárdenas administration was, as we have seen, stimulated by a profound desire to catch up in the economic sphere. The distinctive mass organizations formed in the 1930s worked because of the hopes of material improvement on the part of the population. It is important to realize that Cárdenas was not successful at creating mass organizations because he was able to design clever organizational charts. Rather, the intense enthusiasm for development that he tapped enabled the governing party to augment the role of the state in order to solve perceived problems. When the president nationalized land, railroads, or petroleum, or when the government committed the country to a massive steel-making project in as remote a location as Las Truchas, Michoacán, the president carried the country with him because he tapped deep emotions and a profound desire to catch up to the affluence of the United States.

The belief that a crash program of industrialization was imperative was even written into the governing party's Second Five-year Plan, which was

the election program released on November 1, 1939. The plan called for the establishment of an office to survey the status of industry and to evaluate information relating to possible industrial projects. The idea was that this office would employ technical experts to develop, regulate, and protect native industry. Yet, in a curious way, the very success in nationalizing petroleum, without precipitating U.S. intervention, put a brake on the other programs of industrialization.

President Cárdenas tried a number of concrete approaches to stimulate industrialization. The organization of the masses was, in part, aimed at mobilizing human resources to support state development projects, in addition to creating support for the centralizing political project of the period. In spite of the fact that Cárdenas called himself a socialist and patterned some of the political innovations of the era on European corporativist traditions, he recognized that foreign technology was central to the industrial push. In 1937 he approached L. M. Kniffin, a U.S. consulting engineer with the Reconstruction Finance Corporation in Washington, to work on plans for bringing safe water supplies to Mexico. As Kniffin recalled the discussions with President Cárdenas, he recognized that "the basic need on which all of the projects depended was a steel industry that could provide the requirements for agriculture, mining and all types of manufacture." Kniffin, in time, received a commission to survey the location of natural resources that would determine the site for a steel industry. Stocks of iron, coal, and other ingredients were then placed in a federal reserve which would be operated as a national enterprise. Kniffin's report recommended a site near the outlet to Lake Chapala, in Jalisco.

Several cabinet meetings discussed the plan for a national steel industry, and it was initially assumed that the Mexican government would hire a U.S. steel firm to operate the plant. However, that approach had to be dropped. After the expropriation of the petroleum industry, funds were no longer available to build the plant. On June 19, 1940, the Ministry of the National Economy authorized Kniffin to represent Mexico in negotiating with foreign investors. As a letter from Modesto C. Rolland, undersecretary of communications and public works, to Kniffin put it, "You are hereby authorized to represent the Department of Economy in presenting the information and securing attention for organizing such industries. As soon as firm desire is evidenced you are to put such persons in contact with me and assist in completing investigations so that agreements can be concluded as promptly as possible. Please keep me posted in regard to all developments."

According to Kniffin, President Cárdenas recognized that the changing circumstance dictated that the natural resources and the controlling interest in the plant would have to be turned over to the foreign investors who would build the steel mill. The nationalistic approach would not prevail. "The plant that has been started at Monclova, in the State of Coahuila, will not accomplish the objectives of the Cárdenas plan." There also were technical prob-

lems; the location was too remote to generate satellite industries, the water supply was inadequate, and the cost of transporting the iron ore all would make the steel expensive.[19] U.S. diplomats were not displeased when the Altos Hornos project eventually proceeded without Kniffin, since they viewed him as having "personal interests" in what purported to be a technical analysis. This was the moment when the steel mill project moved from being a public project to one in which the state aided the private sector, albeit in less obvious ways.[20]

The Cárdenas administration explored the idea of some other very large industrialization programs. At one point in May 1940, Rolland and the Northern Construction Company of Vancouver explored the possibility of entering into a forty-year industrial development project costing 370 million dollars in gold. The Cárdenas administration paid for the study and approved in principle a wide-ranging plan for the construction of dozens of projects including the building of pipelines, steel and chemical industries, and manufacturing. The plan even included a Tehuantepec canal and was entitled *Industrias Básicas Mexicanas*.[21] Implementation of that undertaking was based upon the projected sale of petroleum, which in turn assumed a rapid settlement of the oil dispute. In reality, the scheme required U.S. capital, and the likelihood of the United States supporting a Canadian construction firm was remote; however, the urgency to industrialize was apparent in the project. Moreover, the depth of the plan shows that the Cárdenas administration was commissioning quite detailed technical studies of the nation's natural resources, and it also was opening technical discussions with industrial engineers aimed at harnessing the state to a rapid industrialization program.

Business disliked the way in which Cárdenas included workers' representatives in tripartite committees, which were also comprised of representatives of business and government. Business leaders, such as the president of the nation's chambers of commerce, Leopoldo H. Palazuelos, strongly opposed labor representation on the various Boards of Conciliation and Arbitration and on the country's 230 chambers of commerce. In their view labor had no right to become involved with the decision-making process on projects of industrialization.[22] Yet financial pressure put these plans in jeopardy.

## International Repercussions

The first act of retaliation was to cut off silver purchases. The Roosevelt administration initially assumed that this was going to hurt the Mexican economy. However, things did not work out that way. A curious chain of events emerged. Mexico's monthly production of silver was normally in excess of 5 million ounces, fully one half of which came from the

ASARCO plant in Monterrey.[23] Before the expropriation, the plant's silver was purchased by the United States at forty-five cents per ounce. After the nationalization, a run on the peso actually created a silver shortage for the government since, under the circumstances, people wanted to hold silver coins rather than paper notes. The Banco de México had about 75 million pesos' worth of minted coins; the run on the silver pesos consumed about 20 million. In spite of the boycott, the government faced a silver shortage and actually entered the market using its gold reserves in the Federal Reserve Bank to buy more silver from sources other than ASARCO, since the plant was on strike. This cleverly notified the United States that the silver boycott was not having the intended effect. However, it cut both ways since without the Monterrey plant's production the Mexican mint could only produce 5 million pesos' worth of coins per month. The silver game could only be a short-term standoff.

Bankers informed the U.S. diplomats that the reserves in the Banco de México had reached an all-time high of 195 million pesos in August 1937, declining to 109 million by the time of the nationalization. Commercial banks borrowed heavily in the wake of the nationalization, and, by March 19–21 alone, the Banco de México had paid out 15 million silver pesos in the redemption of paper currency, thus reducing the reserve of silver coins by nearly 60 million pesos. Moreover, the government was running an 89.3-million-peso overdraft in order to keep its public works programs going. Bankers advised the U.S. government that Mexico could inflate by means of creating bank credit to about 500 million pesos before the public would completely lose confidence in the paper currency. Instead, the government was discouraging further lines of credit and rediscounting was difficult to arrange.

Foreign firms, such as the Fulton Iron Works, complained that the government was running far behind on its payments for work on the Zacatecas sugar mill. The government asked foreign companies, including ASARCO, to prepay taxes for March. ASARCO decided to comply and advanced the government 2 million pesos. It was not going to follow the petroleum companies into exile, although its executives quickly complained that by prepaying their taxes as the peso fell in value, it cost them an extra 50,000 dollars.

The Mexican government's payroll was best seen as comprising three sectors. First, there were the payrolls covering the jobs contracted by the government from private contractors, largely for public works. This sector represented two hundred thousand workers, with a monthly payroll of 8 million pesos. Second, the government's own payroll was 5.2 million pesos for the army of fifty-eight thousand men and 15 million pesos for civilian employees. Third was the petroleum industry with a payroll of 6 million pesos per month. In total the government faced a payroll of 35 million pesos, with an average income of 25 million pesos, plus funds generated by

petroleum sales. With this intelligence, Daniels concluded that Cárdenas could go no further.[24] Indeed, by the summer, Mexico had to suspend a number of road-building projects, so great was the pressure on the government's budget. In short, the financial pressures, although complex, affected both sides and created a powerful logic for accommodation rather than further conflict.

## Fears of U.S. Intervention

On May 20, 1938, soon after the nationalization of the petroleum industry, there was an uprising against the Mexican government led by the former minister of agriculture and caudillo of San Luis Potosí, Saturnino Cedillo. By May 18 the president had traveled to San Luis Potosí to make an open call to the general to stop forming armed groups in the district, and he ordered General Cedillo to take command of the 21st Military District, thus placing him under military discipline. The following day an airfield and the railroad between Tampico and San Luis Potosí were attacked and a section of track was destroyed, apparently by Cedillo's forces. On May 26 the governor of the state went over to the Cedillo side. Other trains were sabotaged, and the next day President Cárdenas accused "foreign interests" of backing Cedillo. The fact that the United Kingdom had broken diplomatic relations with Mexico on May 14 fueled this speculation. For his part, General Cedillo, broadcasting from McAllen, Texas, accused Cárdenas of running a "communist dictatorship." The major oil companies published denials that they were behind the Cedillo revolt.[25]

Although it ended with a battle in which the general and a number of his followers lost their lives, the Cedillo revolt came to very little. In many ways it was a retrospective rebellion, looking back to the nineteenth-century tradition of the *pronunciamiento*, and it was strongly disavowed by the vast majority of the Mexican people; nevertheless, at the state level, Saturnino Cedillo enjoyed an undisputed following.[26] It was, however, the international angle that made the rebellion more ominous. Many Mexicans were prepared to believe that the major oil companies were using Cedillo to intervene in this way to try to save their property, and there were numerous precedents for such an opinion. Even Ambassador Daniels believed that "some of the oil men are predicting a revolution here and some of them are wanting it or would want it if they thought that they could return to conditions here as existed under Díaz or Huerta."[27]

Backers of the Good Neighbor policy were sensitive to this kind of charge, since they knew it was so. Far-sighted New Dealers also remembered that Mexican petroleum was nationalized only a week after the Anschluss. The increase in Germany's power, and the growing likelihood

of war, indirectly argued for accommodation with Mexico. Certainly any policy that pushed Mexico into an alliance with the Axis powers was the worst possible idea. Such a move was credible since in 1937, before the petroleum expropriation, Cárdenas had encouraged German diplomats to build trade links and explore for petroleum in southern Mexico. But German expansion in 1938 quickly brought that possible link to an end.[28]

There were, however, hard-liners in the U.S. bureaucracy who would have supported action against the Cárdenas administration. J. Edgar Hoover, for one, vented his wrath in a letter to Adolf Berle: "President Cardenas [*sic*] has always been Anti-Foreign due to his Indian Antecedents. He has always favored the ignorant 'sandal-footed' Indian-Mexican to the extent that it is known that he has received delegations of that type in his Office while Diplomatic Representatives of foreign countries were awaiting an audience with him."[29] Privately, Berle made fun of the appalling level of understanding of Mexico that Hoover's reports contained. Hoover was concerned about Cárdenas's long friendship with a German merchant in the hardware business in Morelia named Gerard Maier. Amazingly, Hoover believed that "Maier is a rabid Nazi and can assert great influence on Cardenas."[30] In addition to Cárdenas, Hoover thought that most of the Mexican cabinet was pro-German. He believed that it was quite possible to be, simultaneously, a communist and a fascist, a bizarre view that some tried to maintain between 1939 and 1941.

Even Daniels's successor as ambassador to Mexico viewed President Cárdenas as being "unfriendly" (the State Department's code word for anyone who disagreed with its policies) to the United States As George Messersmith put it, "I do know that his [Cárdenas's] feelings against the United States were so strong that they would be controlling over every other consideration."[31] This U.S. hostility was felt within Mexico; it was the possibility that Cedillo might serve as "the natural leader for a fascist *putsch* against the government" that convinced Lombardo Toledano and Francisco Múgica that the Cárdenas administration had no acceptable alternative except to take a hard-line policy against the rebellion. The anti-Cárdenas attitude of U.S. businessmen in Mexico gave the government's position a degree of credibility, even though Romana Falcón and Dudley Ankerson, the most rigorous scholars to study the affair, differ on the degree of support that the petroleum companies offered Cedillo.[32]

At times hard-liners got carried away. In Texas, S. T. Brogan, in announcing his candidacy for governor, called for the U.S. annexation of Mexico.[33] The effort came to little and it seemed exaggerated, even by contemporary standards. More seriously, there was a dominant current of opinion among foreign businessmen to the effect that Cárdenas's presidency was a disaster. That is not surprising since the government was reducing business prerogatives. As William B. Richardson, manager of the National City Bank in Mexico City, explained, "Any of these men [candidates for the

1940 election: Manuel Avila Camacho, Juan Andreu Almazán, or Rafael Sánchez Tapia] cannot but be an improvement on the present incumbent."[34] Furthermore, as Herman H. Horton, manager of Moctezuma Copper Company, a subsidiary of Phelps-Dodge Corporation, said, "As far as operating companies are concerned here in Mexico, I doubt that it makes any difference to them as to who the person is who becomes President, but everyone is anxious to see some change in attitude of the Government towards the industry, which is in a most unfavorable condition."[35] Business interests harbored some hope for improvement; according to American Consul General Blocher, Hearst land interests in Mexico were already relying upon the Avila Camacho faction to prevent expropriation of lands, especially in Chihuahua.[36]

## The New Deal and Cárdenas

Secretary Hull initially responded with hostility to the petroleum expropriation, lecturing the Mexicans on the sacrosanct nature of private property. However, he was quickly brought to heel. Daniels worked hard to convince FDR that although he opposed Cárdenas's policy, it was a great mistake to press Mexico too hard due to the massive public support for the expropriation.[37] Daniels's immediate reassurances and Mexico's memorandum of March 30, stating its willingness to talk about compensation, convinced FDR. The president wrote to a New York businessman (who complained about developments in Mexico): "I cannot help feeling that your friend has obviously been talking principally with the kind of people who would give anything to have old President Díaz reincarnated and restored to power in Mexico. His type of benevolent despotism is, they argue, the only permanent solution for the governing of a lot of ignorant natives. It is largely because of the ownership of Mexico by 'successful businessmen' for so many years that the somewhat unhappy transition period of the last twenty-five years became inevitable."[38] By April 1, recognizing the right of Mexico under international law to expropriate property, Hull shifted to the demand for compensation.[39]

There is an important Memorandum of Conversation between Luis G. Legorreta, president of the Banco Nacional de México, and Herbert Bursley of the U.S. embassy in Mexico City. Meeting on February 26, 1940, Legorreta told the diplomat that business interests were trying to generate support for General Avila Camacho; he gave Bursley "the impression that things would be better in Mexico from the point of view of the foreign investor." Most fascinating of all was an exchange between the two men in which "Mr. Legorreta stated that he had received a letter from Jesse Jones [director of the Reconstruction Finance Corporation] stating that there could be no financial assistance for Mexico so long as American interests were 'harmed' in Mexico."[40] Legorreta responded by saying that he did not see

how any American interests were adversely affected, except for those in the oil industry. The argument that the petroleum issue was unique was gaining in all quarters. In fact, as early as 1936, Ambassador Daniels and the president were moving toward military cooperation.[41] There was a basis for accommodation, and the pressures of the day revitalized that tendency.[42]

## Pressure on Mexico after the Oil Nationalization

A severe financial crisis between February 8 and 13, 1940, forced the government to reassess its economic strategy more broadly. Facing a run on the peso as firms preferred to hold dollars, the Banco de México had to sell to the Federal Reserve Bank 6 metric tons of gold, thus reducing the Banco's stock of gold from 26.5 to 20.5 metric tons. Pressure eased on February 14, due to the decision of the Senate Finance Committee, and especially Senator Alben Barkley, to support the continued purchase of silver from Mexico. The period of crisis had caused Mexican banks to reduce funds for loans. In addition, many companies were forced to sell gold or U.S. dollars rather than to use them as collateral for loans. The fact that Mexico's government entered a lean period from the middle of March to the end of September, in collecting government receipts, added pressure on the administration.[43]

The pressure on Mexico was reduced somewhat by June 1940, the key month of Nazi expansion in Europe. As a result of the invasions of Scandinavia, France, and the Low Countries, there was panic selling of dollars in Mexico—by people who thought the Allies were losing—thus relieving the peso from pressure. On the other hand, mining was adversely affected. Copper, zinc, lead, and other minerals traditionally found markets in Europe. Moreover, U.S. economic pressure was matched by the possibility of its favors. By the end of 1939, Mexico was being treated favorably when purchasing U.S. armaments. In negotiations with the Curtis Wright and Douglas Aircraft companies, Mexico was attempting to buy thirty reconnaissance aircraft, thirty bombers, and another dozen fighter planes.[44] These aircraft, in addition to the purchase of artillery, machine guns, and rifles, acted as a pressure point during the period between the initial oil expropriation and the final settlement. Rather than complicate matters by threatening to withhold the sale of weapons from the Mexicans, the New Deal diplomats not only authorized the sale, but also, in the words of the Mexican ambassador to Washington, "They have given me roughly the same prices on similar materiel that the American Army enjoys."[45]

Two results seem clear. Economic logic was pushing both Mexico and the United States toward accommodation, and the United States was offering political favors, in the form of weapons. The interests of both governments were converging. President Roosevelt immediately worked to

reinforce that accommodation. A few days after the expropriation, FDR had tried, in conversations with Ambassador Francisco Castillo Nájera, to counter the hostility building in the press. In their private conversations, the U.S. president admitted that he had sympathy for President Cárdenas's effort. He noted that landlords such as W. R. Hearst had obtained their land in Mexico for as little as three centavos per hectare. FDR noted that he wanted to work for a "quick political solution" based upon the amount the companies had actually invested, rather that the potential value of the oil, as they desired.[46]

## Cárdenas's Retreat

While most in the Roosevelt administration were working for accommodation, the Mexican government was trimming the more radical experiments of the early 1930s. Cárdenas's experiments with workers' administration had particularly alarmed U.S. businessmen in Mexico, and the State Department viewed the policies as highly objectionable. It was an age in which most bosses viewed the notion of worker participation as an impertinent intrusion into management's prerogatives. In April 1939 a disastrous railroad accident took place, and public opinion quickly polarized. Management in the private sector charged the workers' administration with a lack of discipline. So when, on June 22, 1940, the Administrative Council of the National Railways resigned en masse, and a month later labor leader Juan Gutiérrez followed suit, U.S. officials viewed the change as evidence of Cárdenas's return to a more moderate position.[47]

Perhaps the most important item in the case for Cárdenas's pullback was seen in the settlement of the ASARCO dispute. In the face of declining exports from petroleum, zinc, lead, and copper, the government put pressure on the mining unions to come to an amicable settlement with the country's largest mining firm. Even U.S. diplomats saw the settlement as evidence that the president wanted to reduce conflict with U.S. interests in Mexico.[48] The fact that ASARCO was extending tax advances to the Mexican government to help the state through the tight fiscal situation caused by lower petroleum sales abroad undoubtedly played a large role in determining government policy. It also contributed to Cárdenas's retreat from his most radical reforms.

The labor attaché of the U.S. embassy carefully plotted the rate and intensity of strikes. In April 1939 he first noted that the Mexican Labor Ministry was taking a less favorable line toward strikes, and, by the end of the month, the number of government-backed strikes had decreased so dramatically that there was not a single case before the Federal Board of Conciliation and Arbitration. The most important strike in the country was a jurisdictional dispute within the Bakers' Union, representing a challenge

to the leadership of the CTM leader, Lombardo Toledano. Moreover, the government arrested fifty workers for stealing ore from the seized Real del Monte silver mine in Pachuca.[49] Even support for the ejido movement had tapered off to the point where, by 1938, workers were staging hunger marches through the streets of Torreón. In short, the desire to reassure the United States that the petroleum expropriation was an isolated case merged with financial pressures on the Treasury, caused by reduced exports, to convince the president that the time had come to push no further on the radical reforms. General Hay soon concentrated on currency stabilization, a commodities agreement, and road construction projects.[50] Just as the Cárdenas administration was tempering its radicalism, the great petroleum oligopolies were making a major effort to discredit the Mexican government.

## Behind the Negotiations

The major petroleum companies, known colloquially as the Seven Sisters, had been making a series of important mistakes in Mexico by adhering to a position of absolute intransigence in regard to their properties. They had defied local law and political reality, and precipitated the nationalization of their Mexican properties in 1938.[51] Cárdenas's suggestions that the major petroleum companies had courted treason by aiding the Saturnino Cedillo rebellion against the Mexican government in May 1938 seemed at least plausible.[52] President Roosevelt, however, stopped any such plans by announcing that any pilots who accepted mercenary positions with the Cedillo forces faced cancellation of their U.S. licenses.[53] Whether or not Cárdenas actually believed that the oil companies were fomenting rebellion, or merely used the suggestion in his case against them—and the latter seems more likely—the petroleum companies were running a propaganda campaign against the Mexican government.

Representative Hamilton Fish of New York was active in arguing the case that it was FDR who was "aiding and enacting communist propaganda in Latin America."[54] Similarly, the Hearst press followed this line on the extreme Right in the United States. The orchestrated nature of the press campaign became clear when on June 24, 1938, three Washington newspapers—Hearst's *Washington Times,* the *Evening Star*, and the *Washington Daily News*—all published similar articles on Mexico, and the next day the *New York Times* joined in with an article entitled "The Problem with Mexico." When Lombardo Toledano visited Washington in June, the conservative press became alarmed. The *New York Herald Tribune* even announced that there was to be a new 12 percent tax on exports to the United States.[55] Columnist Frank L. Kluckhohn maintained a vituperative campaign against the Mexican government in the pages of the *New York Times*.

Another line that the oil companies appeared to like, perhaps in a spirit of psychological projection, was that Mexico's oil expropriation placed the country in the Axis camp. The *Washington Daily News* informed its readers that "Spies of Foreign Countries Find U.S. an Easy Mark; West Coast Vulnerable" or that "Mexico Oil Deals Would Give Japanese a Sure Footing Near American Border." The *New York Times* reported the incredible claim that fifteen hundred German officers were training the Mexican Army, and *Newsweek* reported: "Mexico: Friendship with the U.S. Seriously Jeopardized."[56] Standard Oil even brought out a book entitled *Mexico at the Bar of Public Opinion.*

The Foreign Relations Ministry in Mexico City kept close track of the press campaign in the United States, and diplomats thought they had evidence that the petroleum companies were behind the campaign directly. Well-informed and balanced articles, like those by Carleton Beals, were definitely the exception in the summer of 1938.[57] The Mexican diplomats did try to counter the propaganda campaign. When Senator Dennis Chávez of New Mexico gave a speech praising good relations between the two countries, the Mexican embassy in Washington printed and distributed five thousand copies of the talk. However, such efforts scarcely offset that which the companies were able to achieve.

By the autumn of 1938 it had become clear that President Roosevelt was not going to save the petroleum companies. In spite of the propaganda campaign waged in the U.S. media over the major oil companies' charge of "stolen oil," the logic in favor of negotiating increased. Standard Oil officials were frustrated with the State Department for not helping them sufficiently. In addition, several minor oil operators broke ranks with the Seven Sisters in seeing opportunity in Mexico's nationalization. Sinclair Oil contracted Patrick J. Hurley to represent them in negotiating with the Cárdenas administration. Hurley was a lawyer and former assistant secretary of war in the Hoover administration, where he had turned repression of the Bonus Army into a career. At the same time, Standard Oil hired the New Dealer, Donald R. Richberg, to represent its interests. At first the two men combined their efforts; however, by March 1939, Standard Oil instructed Richberg to act individually. As negotiations with Standard Oil bogged down, Hurley and Cárdenas arranged a separate deal. By dropping the theoretical issues associated with private property from the agenda, Sinclair Oil and Mexico, in April 1940, agreed to a cash settlement of 8.5 million dollars, paid over three years, and a discount of between 20 to 30 cents on the sale of petroleum to Sinclair Oil for four years.[58]

Mexico, in addition to convincing this company to break ranks with the majors, found some formidable outlets for the sale of the crude petroleum that formerly had been going to the United States and Britain. For example, Mexico bartered oil with Italy for rayon yarn. Suárez took pains to show

U.S. officials that his country was successfully selling oil and accumulating the dollars with which to compensate the oil companies for the expropriation of the oil fields. This amounted to a warning not to push Mexico too far into Axis hands.[59] By turning to William Rhodes Davis, another independent oil operator, to break the major companies' boycott, Mexican leaders threw the issue into an entirely new category of high international politics, a story to which we shall turn in the next chapter.

The New Deal had to resist considerable domestic opposition to the Cárdenas administration. In the Senate, Texans Tom Connally and Morris Sheppard worked for a bill to exclude Mexican products from the United States, and at one point the secretary of the navy rejected low bids from Sinclair Oil to punish Mexico. Adolf Berle eventually convinced the State Department not to back these moves.[60] And other businessmen like Curtis E. Calder, president of American and Foreign Power Company, agreed with Ambassador Daniels that there was no danger of expropriation of their industries.[61]

In spite of countervailing pressures, the two countries moved toward an accommodation for a number of reasons. The New Deal diplomats calculated that accommodation was better than confrontation on the eve of war. They knew that to push too hard for the interests of the major oil companies would jeopardize other investments in Mexico, most notably the mining interests, which were more important than the petroleum interests. In addition, there was a domestic reason to downplay the major oil companies' concerns. Not only were many of the New Dealers opposed to the oil majors but also during the 1940 election, in which FDR faced his most serious challenge, the Democratic party found that a young congressman from Texas, Lyndon B. Johnson, was useful in tapping funds from the independent oil and construction interests.[62] Therefore, a policy that offended the Seven Sisters was not a tragedy to New Dealers such as Henry Morgenthau, Jr., and Harold Ickes, especially since it was in line with President Roosevelt's thinking.

Ultimately, the Roosevelt administration was less interested in helping the major oil companies than in securing a firm southern flank in the event of war. However, there was a long period of negotiations before the final settlement was achieved. On the Mexican side, Cárdenas played a well-conceived hand. He used the anti-Mexican press campaign, all the while realizing that it mattered little. He believed that Roosevelt could bring the campaign to an end if he so desired, but that FDR allowed it to go on to increase his bargaining position.[63] Ramón Beteta kept a list of U.S. firms that openly opposed Mexican policy so that business could be directed away from them.

Cárdenas's negotiations with the petroleum companies dragged on for over three years. A reading of the seemingly interminable negotiations makes

it clear that formal and informal channels all proved to be barren of results.[64] These negotiations ultimately failed because the oil companies were unwilling to settle for mere money. Spokesmen for the petroleum industry wanted a percentage of future production, administrative control of the industry, and reduced output. By contrast, Cárdenas was fighting for economic sovereignty. He insisted that control should be solely in Mexican hands and that the settlement be based upon a fixed cash payment exclusively.[65] The major companies were willing to allow the negotiations to drag on, in part because lower Mexican production and sales took pressure off the supply side of the industry and in part because the issue of control of petroleum policies was at stake. The oil companies were outraged that Cardenista policies meant that petroleum profits were being shared by the government and the workers.[66]

Cárdenas played the role of chief negotiator effectively. He was absolutely in control on the Mexican side, and Castillo Nájera enjoyed no latitude in the negotiations. Each and every position had to be cleared with the Mexican leader, and time was on his side. In fact, Castillo Nájera constantly pleaded for more time to communicate with the president, even using his travel to remote regions in Chiapas as a pretext for further delays.

Yet even as the world focused upon the radical nature of the petroleum nationalization, Cárdenas was preparing for a settlement. In a revealing relationship with private banker Luis G. Legorreta, the president asked him to study Mexico's capacity to pay. Legorreta concluded that the country's existing production of forty thousand barrels per day could be increased to ninety thousand. He argued that the "labor problem" had not yet been solved and that production had not yet equalled pre-expropriation levels, "in spite of all that has been said to the contrary." Legorreta concluded in his confidential study for the president that experiments in workers' administration would have to be terminated if the country were to refurbish its oil industry and compensate the previous owners.[67] By adopting the banker's suggestions, Cárdenas made it clear that he was not as radical as many of his supporters believed.

On the U.S. side, Roosevelt maintained a general level of sympathy for the Mexican government, and he resisted pressure for serious retaliation from W. S. Farish, president of Standard Oil of New Jersey; however, the president became quite impatient as the negotiations dragged on for more than a year.[68] Hull followed FDR but was more bothered by the issue of private property; and Welles's efforts were, in effect, counterproductive as he interjected land issues into the negotiations, thus making a settlement more difficult. It is fairly clear, from the surviving records, that it was FDR who sustained the desire for a settlement.[69] By contrast to more recent periods of U.S.-Latin American relations, it seems that these two governments achieved a political settlement because both presidents wanted such an

accommodation. The timing was impeccable. The two countries actually signed a general settlement of outstanding grievances merely seventeen days before the Japanese attack on Pearl Harbor.

## The Settlement

President Cárdenas defused the crisis after nationalizing the petroleum industry by reassuring the United States that this was not merely the first step in a general program of nationalization of its assets and by agreeing to compensate the companies for their loss. He repeatedly reassured FDR that Mexico was a reliable ally in case of war. Petroleum sales to the Axis powers were used as a reminder that Mexico could not be ostracized with impunity. Yet that sanguine view from the political heights was not widely shared in the business community, and petroleum was only part of the picture. From the point of view of the bondholders, the situation was at a low ebb. Porfirio Díaz's reputation for paying foreign creditors lasted until the collapse of 1914; however, it took some years before international financiers realized how precarious their Mexican investments were. In the late 1920s, Mexican bonds were still selling for between 40 and 50 percent of their face value in New York. The radical features of the Cardenista period changed that. By 1938 to 1940, a 1,000-dollar bond sold for 5 dollars, little more than the brokerage fee. Wall Street speculators even shied away from Mexican paper due to the bulk storage problems. Added to the complexity of the nationalization of the railroads in 1937, which affected some fifteen additional loans, the petroleum expropriation and land reform seizures all added to defaults by 1940. The possibility of arbitration was rejected by Mexico, especially since the historical precedents for the U.S. compliance were not encouraging.[70]

A general agreement between the two countries was signed on November 19, 1941, resolving a number of immediate and long-standing issues. Mexico committed itself to paying a first installment of 40 million dollars, of which 6 million was already paid, to settle all outstanding claims except petroleum. Before the general settlement, an agreement on the outstanding debt took place and then a reciprocal trade treaty and a currency stabilization agreement were negotiated, implying that the United States would resume its silver purchases from Mexico. The United States agreed to give advances through the Export-Import Bank for raw material purchases.

Finally, in the wake of Sinclair Oil's private settlement of its claim against Mexico for 8.5 million dollars, the Joint Commission, made up of Morris L. Cooke for the United States and Manuel J. Zevada for Mexico, was established to determine the amount of the petroleum debt. The commission settled upon the value of the oil properties as being just under 24 million dollars; the payments were liquidated punctually by 1949.[71] The

large British settlement was not arranged until 1947, but from a political perspective the petroleum issue was essentially over by 1941.

The complexity of the debt issue was enormous. Some bonds under dispute went back to the *porfiriato*. By October 1940, Antonio Espinosa de los Monteros, undersecretary of the treasury, was engaged in serious negotiations with Laurence Duggan and Pete Collado of the State Department, and U.S. Treasury officials were beginning to take a crucial role in casting Washington's position. Espinosa de los Monteros opened, calling for an overall settlement, and mentioned a figure of 10 million dollars. U.S. negotiators responded that an overall figure of 30 to 35 million might be in order. Officials added a sweetener by suggesting that the Treasury might approve a line of credit of up to 60 million dollars, which effectively meant that half would be unsecured since the Banco de México had gold reserves of 30 million. There would be an initial payment of 12 million dollars, of which 9 million would represent oil payments. Mexico's negotiator also wanted a currency stabilization fund established.[72]

President Roosevelt used the semiautonomous International Committee of Bankers, headed by Thomas Lamont, of the House of Morgan, which had been handling debt negotiations with Mexico since it was established by President Woodrow Wilson. The International Committee of Bondholders had been trying to collect Mexican debts for years. The de la Huerta-Lamont agreement of 1922, covering both government and railways debt, was effectively eradicated by the de la Huerta rebellion. The Pani-Lamont agreement of 1925 broke down after a few years, although it relieved the government of responsibility for the railways debt. The Montes de Oca-Lamont agreement of 1930 was never ratified by the Mexican Congress and matters had been in abeyance ever since, although Mexico did deposit the equivalent of 7 million dollars as a first payment. Those funds were then tied up in litigation. The committee sent agents to Mexico who spent years there negotiating with nothing to show for their efforts. The committee kept tabs on the total amount owed to the bondholders, and they calculated that it had reached 511 million dollars by January 1938, before the oil expropriation. The net effect was to create something of a softening-up process. Moreover, there were lawsuits in both countries relating to the question of legal jurisdiction, the most important being the *Lamont vs. Travelers Insurance* case in New York. In addition, fluctuating exchange rates complicated the matter. Clearly, the debt problem demanded a political solution. With the approach of war clouds, the political will for a solution appeared.

A 1938 draft agreement was proposed to cover 250 million dollars of direct government debt and an equal amount of interest to be covered by a new bond issue at a fixed exchange rate, to be paid by the Mexican government from tax revenues; however, it failed when Mexico calculated that the ongoing tax burden would be too great. The committee responded by offering a series of combinations of cash payment claims on the tax receipts.

Negotiations reopened in February 1941 and the committee held out for a settlement price of 75 million dollars. By September 1941 the committee was offering a reduction of 85 percent on their maximum figure, and the Mexican government was holding out for a 90 percent reduction.[73]

The agreement covered fifteen bond issues, going back to 1885, of which six were sterling loans, two were dollar issues, and seven were peso agreements. The total debt was calculated to be about 10 percent of that which the bondholders claimed, or 230.6 million dollars. Mexico agreed to annual payments of 10 million pesos. Depending on the issue, interest rates were reduced to as little as 0.63 percent. Mexico would pay an annual annuity of 10 million pesos in semiannual installments, starting on January 1, 1943. At the end of the fifth year, 5 million pesos would be retired annually until the debt was discharged in 1963. The Suárez-Lamont agreement included a fixed exchange rate and was in every sense favorable to Mexico, as that country's negotiators proudly recognized.[74] Thomas Lamont said: "The securities that are revalidated and upon which service is to be paid will approximate roughly 10 percent instead of the 15 percent of the claims. If we had tried to stick it out for the former figure, we should have had at the best a long and interminable wrangle."[75]

So the bankers accepted the inevitable.[76] State Department adviser and historian Herbert Feis and the House of Morgan's Arthur M. Anderson arranged the mechanism relating to this compensation in Mexico's favor by allowing the registering of these outstanding obligations only in Mexico City, New York, and London. Moreover, the agreement allowed only sixty days for any claims to be so filed.[77] Bonds not registered were presumed to be held in enemy hands and were vested in Nacional Financiera, a position that the United States did not support, preferring to protect the property of individuals in enemy territory over Mexico's desire to assume unregistered bonds. By June 1943 only some 45 percent of the bondholders had accepted the offer; the bonds held in Germany, Holland, and France were largely written off. It took until 1946 to make a similar settlement on the railroad bonds. The two sides agreed to finalize the railroad bonds issue within six months of the agreement.[78]

The settlement of Mexico's debt formed part of a general agreement that linked debt to high politics. By comparison with the country's catastrophic slide into the debt trap under Presidents Luis Echeverría and Miguel de la Madrid, the 1941 settlement shows how much debt can be subject to bargaining. Mexico had some leverage over the United States due to the approach of war. Therefore, a settlement in which it reduced a maximum claim from 1,066,600,000 dollars to 116,900,000 dollars was realistic in a way that seems to be impossible today.[79]

President Roosevelt used Thomas Lamont of the House of Morgan, the most powerful and prestigious center of U.S. capitalism, to tell bondholders to take the deal or get nothing. Facing opposition from government and

the pinnacle of the U.S. establishment, most creditors concluded that this was their last moment to salvage anything from their Mexican investments. As a result, the Avila Camacho administration faced the most favorable debt situation of any government in Mexico since the 1820s.

There were continuing voices of opposition in Mexico. Pedro Merla spoke out in the pages of *La República.* He argued that the government should refuse to deal with Lamont's committee and deal directly with the bondholders, on the grounds that the House of Morgan banker had acted improperly in seizing Mexican funds in the 1930s and that the committee had included exorbitant charges. He thought that his country should pay only the stock market quotations on the bonds, which is to say, very little. Trying to rally support, he also pointed out, erroneously, that one of the Morgan partners had just been carried off to Sing Sing prison in New York State. Merla confused George Whitney, the Morgan partner, with his brother Richard Whitney, who had misused investors' funds—while president of the New York Stock Exchange—and been incarcerated from 1938 to 1941. George had, however, loaned millions to Richard for his speculation.[80] Although nationalist spirit was strong in Mexico, the government was also committed to a settlement.

The Good Neighbor policy prevailed in the case of U.S.-Mexican relations. In spite of internal divisions within the State Department and hostilities within the business community, the Roosevelt administration took a subtle approach toward dealing with the radical nationalism of the Cárdenas administration. Given the rapid succession of events that followed the agreement between the two countries, that approach served the United States well.

## Notes

1. Association of Petroleum Producers in Mexico to secretary of state, January 31, 1936, Library of Congress, Daniels Papers (hereafter cited as LC/Daniels), B675.

2. Memorandum of conversation between Ambassador Josephus Daniels and President Lázaro Cárdenas, December 15, 1936, LC/Daniels, B647.

3. Hull, *Memoirs,* 182.

4. The best account of the petroleum expropriation is Meyer, *México y los Estados Unidos en el conflicto petrolero,* 198–222.

5. For a study that communicates the depth of the contemporary emotion that the petroleum workers felt see Antonio Rodríguez, *El Rescate de Petróleo,* 100–105.

6. Achnacarry Castle was the venue of a meeting in 1928 between Sir John Cadman of British Petroleum, Walter Teagle of Standard Oil Co., and Sir Henri Deterding of Royal Dutch-Shell at which, after hunting in the Scottish Highlands, the oil magnates sat down and divided up the world's oil markets and reserves. They also tried to agree on operating principles for the industry. Mexico went to Standard Oil; however, there were other firms such as Sinclair that challenged the majors. See Sampson, *The Seven Sisters,* 85–89.

7. For a recent favorable treatment of the Cárdenas era see León and Marván, *En el Cardenismo*. For an example of a more critical treatment that focuses upon the state's domination and subordination of organized labor see Córdova, *La política de masas del Cardenismo*.

8. The economic nationalists of the 1940s were quick to differentiate their position from autarchy.

9. Daniels to Hull, April 15, 1938, USNA/RG 59, 812.00/30559.

10. Henry Wallace recorded that "there is no question but that the President has it in for the State Department and at the right time will move in on them." Wallace, *The Price of Vision,* 91. Roosevelt viewed Daniels as an old ally and George Messersmith as an example of the kind of young, competent diplomat—who significantly emerged from the consular side—with whom to combat the State Department "mandarins."

11. John H. MacVeagh to Daniels, March 12, 1946, LC/Daniels B657.

12. Bobbie MacVeagh to Daniels, March 15, 1946, ibid.

13. U.S. embassy to Secretaría de Relaciones Exteriores, July 19, 1939, SRE, III-1707-3. In this case as well, Daniels stressed compensation rather than the right to expropriate. Daniels to Eduardo Hay, September 9, 1939, ibid.

14. Daniels to Hull, March 27, 1938, LC/Daniels, B675.

15. Memorandum of conversation between President Cárdenas and Daniels, March 22, 1938, LC/Daniels B674. Subsequent correspondence in April also gently mentioned overtures from the Axis powers.

16. This position was made clear to the Mexican president in his private correspondence with his ambassador to Washington, Francisco Castillo Nájera. SRE, 39-10-2.

17. Cárdenas to Daniels, March 31, 1938, LC/Daniels, B645.

18. Daniels to Hull, April 15, 1938, USNA/RG 59, 812.00/30559.

19. L. M. Kniffin to secretary of state, May 3, 1940, and Modesto C. Rolland to Kniffin, June 19, 1940, USNA/RG 59, 812.6511/5-345.

20. Charles A. Bay to secretary of state, June 1, 1945, USNA/RG 59, 812.6511/6-145.

21. Cárdenas to the Northern Construction Company, May 30, 1940, USNA/RG 59, 812.602/93.

22. Leopoldo H. Palazuelos (president of the Confederación de Cámaras Nacionales de Comercio e Industria) to the president, February 18, 1941, AGN, RP/MAC 545.2/7.

23. In addition, there were about two hundred fifty small silver mines that operated with an average of only fifty employees. Many of those workers were stood down immediately after the United States suspended silver purchases. Memorandum of conversation with Ned Woodul, general manager of ASARCO, March 30, 1938, LC/Daniels, B675.

24. Ibid.

25. *Novedades*, May 20, 1938. Other newspapers carried the denial a few days later.

26. For a view that argues that Cedillo was forced into rebellion as a by-product of the centralism of the Cárdenas government see Ankerson, *Agrarian Warlord*, 193–99. See also Falcón, *Revolución y caciquismo*.

27. Daniels to secretary of state, April 16, 1938, LC/Daniels, B675.

28. Schuller, "Cardenismo Revisited," 60–68.

29. J. Edgar Hoover (director of the FBI) to Adolf A. Berle, Jr. (assistant secretary of state), November 7, 1939, USNA/RG 59, 812.00/30886.

30. Ibid.

31. GSM papers, memoirs, vol. 2, no. 15. Messersmith did not approve of Cárdenas's friendship with Professor Frank Tannenbaum; moreover, he was delighted to point out to the State Department that Cárdenas paid for Tannenbaum's annual research trips to Mexico.

32. Falcón, *Revolución y caciquismo*, 234–35; Ankerson, *Agrarian Warlord*, 181.

33. *Valley Morning Star* (Brownsville, TX), July 16, 1938.

34. W. B. Richardson to W. W. Lancaster, Sherman and Sterling, Wall Street, May 14, 1940, USNA/RG 59, 812.00/31055.

35. Lewis V. Boyle (American consul in Agua Prieta) to secretary of state, June 3, 1940, USNA/RG 59, 812.00/31069.

36. Herbert Bursley to Laurence Duggan, March 8, 1940, USNA/RG 59, 812.00/30956.

37. Daniels to Roosevelt, March 24, 1938, Roosevelt Library, PPF 86.

38. FDR to George T. Bye of George T. Bye Company, 535 Fifth Avenue, New York City, March 7, 1939, Roosevelt Library, PPF 2865.

39. Hull's statement of April 1, 1938, LC/Daniels, B675.

40. Bursley to Duggan, memorandum of conversation with Luis G. Legorreta, March 7, 1940, USNA/RG 59, 812.00/30968.

41. Memorandum of conversation between Cárdenas and Daniels, October 7, 1936, LC/Daniels, B647.

42. Revealing of the mood of accommodation is the fact that Secretary of State Hull devoted only two descriptive paragraphs to the Mexican oil expropriation in his memoirs. See Hull, *Memoirs,* 2:610.

43. Daniels to Hull, February 16, 1940, USNA/RG 59, 812.5151/283.

44. Memorandum from Mexican embassy in Washington to Secretaría de Relaciones Exteriores, December 21, 1939, SRE, 39-10-12.

45. Francisco Castillo Nájera to Cárdenas, December 11, 1939, ibid.

46. Memorandum of conversation between FDR and Castillo Nájera, April 5, 1938, SRE, 30-3-10. Cárdenas was also assured privately of FDR's support in the Richberg negotiations in the first months of 1939. Castillo Nájera to Cárdenas, February 4, 1939, SRE, 39-10-2.

47. Daniels to Hull, July 25, 1940, USNA/RG 59, 812.504/1962. Daniels did note that the workers' administration demanded that they not be forced to contribute the 50 million pesos that the government had taken from the railroads to go to general revenues. Businessmen saw the development as evidence of managerial incompetence.

48. James B. Stewart (American consul in Mexico City) to secretary of state, April 11, 1939, USNA/RG 59, 812.00/30716.

49. James B. Stewart to secretary of state, May 9, 1939, USNA/RG 59, 812.00/30739; Peláez, "Un año decisivo," 177.

50. SRE, 39-10-7, 1940 background papers for Secretary Hay.

51. Meyer, *México y los Estados Unidos en el conflicto petrolero*, 205–22.

52. The main investigators who have examined this issue agree that no evidence has been found linking the petroleum companies to the Cedillo revolt. See Meyer, *México y los Estados Unidos en el conflicto petrolero,* 363; and Ankerson, *Agrarian Warlord,* 179.

53. *Washington Post,* June 8, 1938.

54. Ibid., June 19, 1938.

55. Ibid.; *Washington Times,* June 24, 1938; *Evening Star*, June 24, 1938; *Washington Daily News*, June 24, 1938; *New York Times,* June 25, 1938; *New York Herald Tribune,* July 2, 1938.

56. *Washington Daily News*, April 11–13, 1938. For the same line see *Washington Herald*, August 15, 1938; *New York Times*, August 14 and 15, 1938; and *Newsweek*, August 15, 1938.

57. See Beals, "Army Action Lessens Cedillo Peril."

58. Buhite, *Hurley and American Foreign Policy*, 88–99.

59. Report entitled "W. R. Davis: Barter of Mexican Oil for Machinery and Goods," from Daniels to secretary of state, December 8, 1938, USNA/RG 59, 812.6363 Davis and Company/152.

60. Buhite, *Hurley and American Foreign Policy*, 96–97.

61. Daniels to secretary of state, December 6, 1938, USNA/RG 59, 812.6463 Electric Bond and Share Company/37.

62. Caro, *The Path to Power*, 606–17.

63. Cárdenas to Castillo Nájera, February 8, 1939, SRE, 39-10-2.

64. The record of a telephone tap reveals that President Cárdenas used historians Ernest Gruening and Howard Cline to try to open channels for negotiations with the major oil companies. Ibid., two telephone intercepts of March 8, 1939.

65. Richberg's proposal of March 15, 1939, for a share of future production met with absolute intransigence from Mexico. Cárdenas to Castillo Nájera, April 29, 1939, and June 23, 1939, SRE, 39-10-2.

66. It was only after Hurley dropped a similar demand for a co-ownership arrangement that the Sinclair settlement went through. J. Silva Herzog to Cárdenas, April 9, 1940, SRE, 39-10-2 (III).

67. Luis G. Legorreta to Cárdenas, April 1940, SRE, 39-10-3 (I).

68. Memorandum of conversation between Castillo Nájera and Roosevelt, June 15, 1939, SRE, 39-10-2.

69. FDR's personal correspondence with Cárdenas, after the final failure of the direct negotiations with the petroleum companies, was critical to the final settlement. Roosevelt to Cárdenas, August 31, 1939, SRE, 39-10-3.

70. The historical case was made in *Excélsior*, August 29, 1938.

71. Cline, *The United States and Mexico,* 245–48.

72. Memorandum of conversation between Antonio Espinosa de los Monteros and Emilio "Pete" Collado, October 1, 1940, USNA/RG 59, 812.51/2460.

73. Draft memorandum, "Mexican Foreign Debt," n.d., USNA/RG 59, 812.51/2623.

74. Avila Camacho to Thomas Lamont, November 5 and December 29, 1942, AGN, RP/MAC, 545.22/179.

75. Lamont to Hull, October 21, 1942, USNA/RG 59, 812.51/2637.

76. These agreements can be found in USNA/RG 59, 812.51/2635 and 812.51/2360.

77. *Diario Oficial*, December 8 and 24, 1942.

78. Hull to U.S. embassy, November 7, 1942, USNA/RG 59, 812.50/306A.

79. Zorilla, *Historia de las relaciones,* 2:499.

80. Pedro Merla, "El Convenio Suárez Lamont," *La República*, December 26, 1942.

# II WARTIME COOPERATION

# 3 Mexico's Entry into World War II

## Mexico and the Great Powers
## before Pearl Harbor

Even before the bombs had fallen on Pearl Harbor on that formidable Sunday in December 1941, the government of Mexico had made its decision. Support for the U.S. war effort would be offered at the maximum level politically acceptable in Mexico. There was to be no neutrality, much less any attempt to use the northern neighbor's problems to avenge old wrongs. The speed and depth of the country's international commitment were remarkable.

People who came of age after the war had grown up in only a bipolar world, in which Third World countries were overwhelmed by the conflict between the United States and the USSR. Students of the Cold War have frequently been frustrated by the Great Powers' crude reductionism in their treatment of other nations. After World War II, U.S. relations with major powers in the region such as Mexico and Brazil seemed to have become less important because, at least until the Cuban Revolution of 1959, the United States faced only minor challenges to its hegemonic position in the hemisphere. Merwin L. Bohan, the top economic officer in the U.S. embassy in Mexico City after World War II, reported that, under President Dwight D. Eisenhower, the State Department simply did not need to pay much attention to Latin America and that it was Secretary of the Treasury George Humphrey (as a result of his business career managing Hanna Industries) who virtually ran U.S. policy toward Latin America.[1]

It is important not to project that postwar situation, which assumed that Latin America played a small role in world affairs, back into the period before Pearl Harbor. Before World War II there was a three-sided ideological conflict between the Great Powers of the day, and Latin America was seen by Washington as part of the front line against fascist expansion. The Allies opposed communism and fascism; however, the latter was the more immediate threat in the hemisphere. New Deal diplomats hated the outrages perpetrated as Germany, Italy, and Japan expanded. The very day that Secretary of State Hull and the U.S. delegation arrived at the 1936 Pan American Conference in Buenos Aires, Adolf Hitler announced the

Anti-Comintern Pact with Japan. President Roosevelt and Secretary Hull viewed a strengthened Pan American system as a response to events in Berlin.

The Pan American Conference in Lima at the end of 1938 went even further. Parties identified as being akin to the National Socialist Party in Germany, caches of German arms, Axis propaganda efforts, and German barter-based trade deals were all viewed by U.S. diplomats as "Axis penetration" and part of a grand design to convert the Latin American republics into "virtual dependencies" of the Axis powers.[2] The United States intended to cooperate at these conferences to sever financial links between the fascist powers and business interests in the countries south of its border. Moreover, German, Italian, and Japanese populations in Latin America created an ethnic base for the fascist powers, in a way that no parallel business or ethnic base existed for Soviet influence.

A Pan American Conference in Panama in September 1940, after the war in Europe began, issued a call for further action including: the prohibition of the use of American territory by belligerents, a 300-to-1,000-mile zone of maritime neutrality, the forbidding of Axis radio stations, economic cooperation to offset the disruption of trade from war zones, and the closer cooperation of intelligence efforts. Many Latin Americans as well as U.S. officials took the Axis threat seriously.[3]

U.S. policymakers also remembered their long-term interests. The Council on Foreign Relations (CFR) was active in planning for the postwar period, even in the early stages of World War II. The council had been formed as a think tank for foreign policy after U.S. diplomats floundered in Paris in the complexity of the settlement of the Great War, 1914–1918. As historians of the CFR explained, "Less than two weeks after the outbreak of the war, Hamilton Fish Armstrong, editor of *Foreign Affairs*, and Walter H. Mallory, the executive director of the council, traveled to Washington D.C., meeting with assistant secretary of state and council member George S. Messersmith on September 12, 1939. They outlined a long-range planning project which would assure close CFR-Department of State collaboration in the critical period which had just begun."[4]

Under the guiding eye of President Roosevelt, several study groups were initiated. Hull and Undersecretary of State Sumner Welles were active, and the group arranged for a Rockefeller Foundation grant to support detailed work.[5] So immediate issues and opportunities arising from the war were to be kept within the perspective of long-term U.S. interests. Furthermore, in the immediate wake of the outbreak of conflict in Europe, the president stated that he intended to create a 2-billion-dollar cartel to stockpile commodities from Latin America in case of war. After some opposition from Senator William Borah, Roosevelt turned to Jesse Jones of the RFC to oversee the effort. Jones believed that it was necessary to expand the Export-Import Bank's role (the original idea in 1934 was to trade only with the

USSR; however, the bank's charter had been rewritten after two months when that trade proved to be illusory). After the outbreak of war, the RFC and the Export-Import Bank further expanded their roles to include loans to governments. Still, there was a tension between the president's idea of using loans as a mechanism to ensure stockpiling and the RFC's commitment to a policy of "Business, not Santa Claus, in South America," as Jones wrote in his memoirs.[6]

## Strategy and Vested Interests, 1938–1941

The great settlement between the United States and Mexico on the eve of Pearl Harbor had ameliorated the old divisive issues of oil, debt, and the nationalization of property. A rapidly changing world order emerged as the prospect of global war became ever more obvious. Mexico assumed a new importance as the logic of accommodation grew. Fear that the long and painful history of relations between the two countries might generate an alliance between Mexico and the Axis powers, especially if the petroleum conflict escalated too far, led the United States to temper its attitude toward its neighbor.

Germany had enjoyed a greater degree of influence in Mexico earlier in the century, and memories of the Zimmerman Telegram conspiracy made policymakers ponder the relationship between those two nations. Moreover, there still were significant German business communities in Mexico City and Monterrey. Important German firms dominated the chemical and pharmaceutical industries.[7] In some industries, the impact of a break with the Axis powers would be harsh.[8] The Mexican government wanted to control German nationals and capital without destroying important production.[9] The Ministry of the Interior (*gobernación*) estimated that there were about 6,500 Germans, 6,900 Italians, and 4,300 Japanese citizens living in Mexico on the eve of the war, many of whom held important positions in business.

When President Roosevelt designated Vice President Henry A. Wallace as his representative to the inauguration of Manuel Avila Camacho, in December 1940, he chose a member of his administration with an established interest in Mexico. The most pressing item of business that Wallace was to conduct at that event was to facilitate the Joint U.S.-Mexican Defense Commission. At the same time, he informed his government that the new administration was convinced that President Cárdenas had moved too far, too fast, on its reforms. Wallace reported to FDR that the new Mexican president was steering a middle course between Cárdenas and the capitalists: "I am convinced from talking with Avila Camacho that he is fully aware of the economic and political importance of the United States to Mexico and that he is anxious to move in our direction as fast as political necessities permit him to do so."[10]

The vice president soon became aware that there was German influence in Mexico. German business interests were significant in such areas as iron hardware, chemicals, aviation, and electrical equipment. Noting that the evening newspaper, *Ultimas Noticias*, was virtually an organ of German propaganda, he suggested that the United States use the power of its advertising to shift the newspaper's attitude and, to a lesser degree, the parent publication, *Excélsior*, toward the Allied cause. This aspect of his report foreshadowed the wartime propaganda effort that young Nelson Rockefeller, as coordinator of the Office of Inter-American Affairs, would mount. Moreover, Wallace was already talking about plans for agricultural cooperation between the two countries.[11]

As members of the U.S. Chamber of Commerce in Mexico explained to the vice president, North American businessmen were suffering from German competition. The most immediate problems they needed to address were a stabilized exchange rate, the overrepresentation of U.S. firms in Mexico by German nationals, and increased access to additional capital. The problem, according to the Chamber, was that German capitalists had access to currency from the Reichbank and were able to mobilize their funds quickly and effectively through the German bank in Mexico City. In contrast, U.S. banks suffered from the extreme reticence of bankers to lend money to firms operating in Mexico for longer than ninety days, especially after the petroleum expropriation and given the possibility of a European war.[12]

Wallace reported to the president that the lack of investment capital in Mexico was a severe problem. If the United States was not helpful in providing investment funds for its neighbor, then Nazi investors would be forthcoming. He suggested that the role of the Export-Import Bank be expanded beyond merely financing sales to provide capital. Wallace's report was prophetic in identifying approaches that would characterize the cooperation between the two countries during World War II. It is important to realize how competition with Germany for advantage in Mexico motivated his analysis.[13]

In the United States there were fears that Axis secret agents were operating in Mexico. J. Edgar Hoover produced a stream of alarmist reports purporting to see Axis agents in many quarters.[14] He entertained fears of the Mexican Right cooperating with Germany. In one report he stated that a revolution led by General Juan Andreu Almazán and "most of the army officers of the Mexican Army" was "likely to break out at any moment" to keep petroleum from reaching the Allies or even to obtain that resource for the Axis powers. The top crime fighter in the United States passed along undigested rumors from businessmen operating in Mexico. Hoover reported the alarming news that not only was a new revolution brewing in that country, but also that the Mexican Army was about to attack the British Empire: "This confidential source also indicates that information has previously been

obtained that there is a large concentration of [Mexican] troops on the British Honduran border and it has been suggested that this is synchronized with the [German] attack on Scandinavia."[15]

Hoover's reports were full of factual errors (FBI agents frequently confused the names of individuals and places) and replete with hearsay. The great G-man became the object of jest among such State Department figures as Adolf Berle, Laurence Duggan, and others who were familiar with Mexico.[16] At one point, Hoover passed along a report from the postmaster of Cottonwood, Arizona, who, when on holiday at Guaymas in 1938, was told by an acquaintance that the Japanese had been fortifying a hill near Empalme and would not allow Mexicans near the place. Apparently, in the intervening two years, Hoover had not sent agents to check on the Japanese forces. However, that too became classified intelligence information.[17]

If there was a grain of truth behind the FBI's alarming intelligence reports, it was due to resentment of the long history of U.S. and, to a lesser degree, British intervention in Mexico. There was a residue of sympathy there for the enemies of one's enemies. When Adolfo León Osorio and others founded the Pro-Neutrality Patriotic Committee, it tapped, in addition to support from the German embassy, an understandable current of opinion. As the American consul in Mexico City explained, "There appears to be no doubt that up until two months ago public opinion was, to say the least, decidedly influenced by German sympathy, probably the result of subtle and effective German propaganda in Mexico and a natural anti-American attitude. However, there now appears to be no doubt that the attitude of the administration and the army as such in endeavoring to follow the policy of Washington in support of Great Britain and her allies is causing an apparent swing of attitude in favor of the last-mentioned powers."[18]

About two dozen German agents were operating in Mexico. Rather than relying upon solid intelligence information, Hoover reflected fears generally extant within the United States. Friedrich Schuller, the most recent scholar to examine the German effort in Mexico, argues convincingly that Axis intelligence agents were overrated, and they produced less valuable intelligence than the shipping schedules from Tampico.[19] Nevertheless, the fear of German spies in that country merged with other forms of mythology. Scrap iron, for example, provided a comfortable explanation for the enemy's strength in the early stages of World War II, since a few years earlier, U.S. suppliers had sold major quantities of that material to Japan. It was a convenient belief that this error had enabled the Japanese, and to a lesser degree the Germans, to threaten the Allies so effectively. Thus, reports of the sale of scrap iron from Mexico to the Axis powers not only reflected former business practices but also confirmed U.S. fears.

Fear of conspiracies abounded on the left as well as on the right. Hoover processed rumors from Joe W. Mayberry and William L. Brunt of the Metals Conservation Corporation in Seattle to the effect that Fred Olney,

whom Hoover identified as an American communist, was working with the PCM to prepare a communist revolt in Mexico: "Olney also gave Mr. Mayberry the impression that the Communists were storing munitions in Mexico to be used against the United States at the proper time."[20]

While there were some significant German interests in Mexico, some branches of U.S. intelligence seriously overrated the threat. Military intelligence was even less sophisticated about the country than the FBI. As World War II approached, the State Department maintained a much better sense of proportion on Axis influence in Mexico. Those prone to seeing secret agents everywhere even pointed to a Japanese exhibition of art at the German Casino in Mexico City, in October 1939, to support their fears.[21]

Japan did have some economic interests in Mexico. According to William B. Richardson, head of the National City Bank in Mexico City, Japanese investments were concentrated in three firms, one of which was the Compañía Mexicana de Petróleos "La Laguna" S.A., formed in 1935. On its board were Carlos Almazán, president; and Kisso Tsuru, Agustín González Palavicini, Jesús M. Villaseñor, and Pablo O. Alarcón, directors. A close political ally of Emilio Portes Gil, Carlos Almazán had been mayor of Tampico and also a congressman. No relation to General Juan Andreu Almazán, he entertained lavishly at a residence rented for him by the Japanese in the posh Mexico City suburb of Lomas.

The second center of Japanese investment was the Compañía Petrolera Veracruzana S.A., formed in 1934, with a board of directors consisting of Modesto C. Rolland, president and general manager; Rafael Murillo, treasurer; Rafael Pous Cházaro, secretary; and Luis Flores Esponda, comptroller. The board was reorganized in 1937 with Kisso Tsuru added as a director when the Compañía Mexicana de Petróleos "La Laguna" S.A. ceded the rights to drill on 1,454 hectares at Puerto México, and at Panuco, Veracruz, to the Compañía Petrolera Veracruzana S.A. The fact that Rolland was undersecretary of the Ministry of the National Economy in the Avila Camacho administration caused concern. Richardson believed that the Japanese were paying Rolland and General Juan Barragán 800 pesos per month "for obvious reasons."

The issue of the transisthmian oil pipeline assumed strategic importance on the eve of U.S. entry into World War II. John A. McCone, the future director of the CIA, had worked his way up from being a sales manager in the Llewellen Iron Works of Los Angeles in 1931 to a partner in the Bechtel-McCone Corporation by 1937. (The firm began to put together complete construction packages for petroleum refineries.[22]) McCone's company had been a member of a consortium called International Contractors, under the direction of Maxwell M. Upson, president of Raymond Concrete Pile Company. McCone reported that the consortium had built a pipeline of over one hundred miles in Veracruz. The consortium then had been approached by an entrepreneur named Gregory Linder (who had established himself in

Mexican circles by means of a letter of introduction from U.S. Senator Robert R. Reynolds of the Committee on Military Affairs) to organize a twenty-inch pipeline from Minatitlán to Salina Cruz, thereby making it possible to export Mexican crude to Japan.

Linder, a promoter and banker, had been living in Mexico City for five years, although he maintained offices in Hollywood. He had been unable to complete the pipeline project, in spite of Vicente Lombardo Toledano's help. He stated that "he has a lot of dealings with these lawyers [the Lombardo Toledano brothers]; that the association has been lucrative for them all." However, the problem was not on the Mexican side, in spite of the fact that Finance Minister Eduardo Suárez would not accept his bribes. Linder had tried to buy steel from U.S. Steel, Bethlehem Steel, and Youngstown Steel, but none of these would sell to the consortium since they viewed the Mexicans as paying in "stolen oil."

It was proposed that the new pipeline should be financed by selling scrap Mexican steel to the Houston firm of Deitcher Brothers, after which new pipes would be shipped back across the border. Suárez had just commissioned a study showing that there were 200,000 tons of good scrap iron that could be exported. The fact that Linder had married the niece of Manuel Avila Camacho did not seem to be hurting McCone's project.[23] J. Edgar Hoover already reported the signing of a contract between Mexico and Japan in May 1940 for two million barrels of crude oil at prices below those in California.[24] In short, the episode neatly highlighted the ambiguities of the period. By treating Mexico as an outlaw nation for having confiscated the petroleum industry, U.S. corporations created conditions that pushed that country toward the oil-hungry Axis powers.

U.S. diplomats periodically worried that the Japanese engineers associated with the oil companies appeared to be unfamiliar with petroleum engineering. Speculation was rife that these firms were really trying to prepare the ground for Japanese bases in northwestern Mexico.[25] Among other Japanese enterprises directly active in Mexico was the Compañía Internacional de Drogas S.A., an offshoot of Kokasai Seiyaku Kabushiki Kaisha of Toyama, Japan. With Kisso Tsuru as president and general manager, it soon was renamed the Compañía Internacional de Comercio S.A. The firm became active in trying to buy Mexican mercury, another product of wartime significance in short supply in Japan. Furthermore, Japanese interests dominated fishing off the west coast of Mexico before the war, and this created concern within the intelligence community since fishing boats could easily be used for military intelligence.

With the fall of France and the rapid Nazi gains across the continent, some feared that the Axis powers might gain control of Mexican institutions through assets held in conquered Europe. Josephus Daniels reported that French holdings in Mexican firms amounted to 160 million pesos. French investors owned eight commercial houses, seven factories, and a bank (Banco

Nacional de México, now called BANAMEX). In all cases other than BANAMEX and El Boleo Copper Company in Baja California, effective control rested in Mexico. The embassy's information was that, even in these cases, the controlling shares had been removed from France before the Nazi conquest. In any case Mexican banks did not deal in conquered currencies; only by trading in Swiss francs via New York could Mexican firms do business with conquered Europe.

Similarly, almost all Dutch investments in Mexico had been in the Compañía Mexicana de Petróleos El Aguila S.A., which had been expropriated in 1938. Most of the stock was in England and was owned by Royal Dutch-Shell, 17 percent, and Viscount Pearson, 18 percent, with 60 percent scattered among private investors in the United States, the United Kingdom, and Holland. Only 5 percent was in France.

Belgian investment in Mexico was confined to the Mexican Light and Power Company (MEXLIGHT). No direct dividends had been paid by the company since 1913, but that much-publicized fact did not include interest that had been paid regularly on first- and second-mortgage bonds held by the parent Belgian company, SOFINA. The firm moved out of Belgium before the occupation and was relocating in Toronto, so Daniels did not believe that significant funds would be shifted from Mexican investments back to Germany. He counted on friendly banks to continue to monitor the situation closely.[26]

## Mexico's Leverage: W. R. Davis and Company

Discussions of Mexico's experience after nationalizing its petroleum resources have frequently centered upon the issue of the settlement of claims with the United States, in November 1941, and later with the United Kingdom. Alternatively, from an industry perspective, the question of Mexico's efficiency in processing its petroleum has received attention. Yet it may well be that the petroleum issue was most important in increasing that country's bargaining position vis-à-vis the United States. Immediately after the nationalization of petroleum, the major oil companies initiated a boycott. They tried to use their clout to convince other corporations and the U.S. government to punish Mexico and force a favorable settlement of outstanding claims. Secretary Hull at first took a hard line against the Mexican expropriation, and Daniels worked to soften his approach.

In spite of their profoundly different ideological orientation, there was a logic of rapprochement between Germany and Mexico. Indeed, President Cárdenas and German Minister Rüdt von Collenberg explored the possibility of improved relations and petroleum sales.[27] The Mexican president was keeping this avenue open should the U.S. government adopt too hard a line.

In addition to their errors in Mexico, the Seven Sisters had also made mistakes north of the border. Firm in their belief, in the second and third

decades of this century, that there was no oil in Texas or Oklahoma, they allowed a number of independent speculators, or wildcatters, to establish themselves in what might have been expected to be a preserve of the majors. Famous Texas oilmen such as Clint W. Murchison, Sid Richardson, J. Paul Getty, and many others shared with Mexico a mixture of fear and contempt for the great oil companies.[28]

Mexico's problems with petroleum, however, went considerably beyond the immediate dislocation caused by the nationalization and even the problem of debt. In the oil business, supply and demand only influence price levels to a degree. In an industry dominated by oligopoly, existing patterns of distribution and supply can tie up markets. Such was the case with petroleum. The oil majors wanted to boycott the sale of Mexican crude as punishment for nationalization, and they controlled many traditional markets. The Allies' problem was that there were three important energy-poor, but recrudescent, powers on the eve of World War II (Germany, Italy, and Japan) and one source of uncommitted petroleum (Mexico). There was a natural tendency for these powers to draw together.

W. D. Crampton, vice president of the French branch of Standard Oil, provided an account of the major oil companies' response to early Mexican efforts to sell its newly nationalized product. He reported how high-quality petroleum was being sold to independents in France for low prices. As Crampton described the working of market forces, "at our next Commission Paritaire Meeting, October 1st, the Mexican competition will be taken into account in the figuration [*sic*] of the October selling prices and this in itself may have a direct tendency to lower prices on the French market to the detriment of the distributing companies in France."[29]

Standard Oil officials were frustrated with the State Department for not helping them enough. Even though some outlets for its crude existed, Mexico still found it difficult to sell all of the petroleum that formerly had been going to the United States and Britain. Consequently, in the wake of the disruption to the Mexican petroleum industry that inevitably followed the expulsion of the foreign oil companies, it was to one of the independent operators that the Cárdenas administration turned.

William Rhodes Davis, who claimed direct descent from Cecil Rhodes and Jefferson Davis, was a minor wildcatter who got his start in the oil business in 1929 when Standard Oil and Peru were in conflict. By the eve of World War II, Davis owned only fifty oil wells in the United States but, more important, he had acquired pipelines, terminals, storage tanks, and refineries in Texas and Louisiana. In addition to minority interests in Poza Rica in Mexico, he also owned a refinery in Hamburg, an oil storage ter-minal in Malmo, Sweden, and distribution facilities in Sweden, Norway, Denmark, and Finland, the latter transshipping to the Baltic states. Thus, Davis was well positioned to take advantage of the events of March 1938.

Using his friendship with John L. Lewis to gain a favorable introduction to Lombardo Toledano, Davis again prospered in the wake of Standard Oil's troubles by offering market outlets for Mexican oil.[30] After first trying to undercut the oligopolistic price of petroleum in Europe with only minor success, Davis began to deal with Germany, Italy, and Japan. By the end of September 1938 he arranged a series of sales of Mexican petroleum to Japan's Department of the Navy by way of Mitsui and Company, Asando Bussan Kabushiki Kaisha, and the Mexican Export Oil Company, which the State Department suspected to be a front operation.[31] Davis tapped a 3-million-dollar line of credit from the Reichbank to export petroleum from Mexico to Germany.[32] He tried to cover the politically sensitive nature of his business by claiming that he was friendly with President Roosevelt. He even boasted of having lunch with him, thus implying FDR's imprimatur in his business dealings, something that U.S. officials vehemently denied.[33]

The U.S. consulate general in Hamburg discovered that, immediately after the Mexican expropriation of petroleum, the major British and U.S. oil companies were able to cut off the supply of Mexican oil to Deutsch-Amerikanische Petroleum, a German subsidiary of Standard Oil of New Jersey.[34] State Department functionaries were worried that this oil, cut off from the commercial market, was finding its way into the new German Navy's reserve storage tanks at Nordenham and Bremerhaven. Those tanks were not for the use of commercial shipping, and their importance to Germany in case of war was great.

According to one source in the Swedish petroleum business, the outbreak of war in Europe was followed by a number of rapid deals in the European oil industry. Davis sold his English and Irish oil interests and, in conjunction with his interests in the Eastern States Petroleum Company of Houston, Texas, entered into an agreement with the Mexican government to barter ten million dollars' worth of Mexican oil in Germany in return for manufactured goods to be sold in Mexico or elsewhere. Davis enjoyed a monopoly on the sale of Mexican oil to Germany, Scandinavia, the Baltic countries, and Czechoslovakia at the end of 1938. Describing his Eurotank operations in Germany as "a perfect dream for a money maker," one Swedish oilman reported that Davis was buying Mexican oil at rock-bottom prices and making massive profits by taking German industrial products in return. Davis then secured a contract from the Mexican government to produce petroleum products for northern Mexico through his Eastern States Petroleum Company. Therefore, oil from Veracruz was being supplied to the new, efficient Eurotank Refinery in Germany, which had been built by engineers from Wichita, Kansas, in 1934–35 for the German Navy.[35]

The broad outline of these events was generally confirmed to the U.S. government by Finance Minister Suárez. Davis had a contract to sell nineteen million barrels of Mexican crude in 1939 for which 15 million dollars of credit would be provided overseas. Davis would bring in German equip-

ment in order to renovate a Mexican refinery, and he was also arranging sales of Mexican petroleum to the Azienda Generale Italiana Petroli S.A. in exchange for heavy tankers. The U.S. government was subjecting the Eastern States Petroleum Company to antidumping investigations, a ploy that was "about to strangle the company financially." Furthermore, Mexico bartered its oil with Italy for rayon yarn. Suárez took pains to show U.S. officials that his country was successfully selling its oil and accumulating the dollars with which to compensate the oil companies for the expropriation of the oil fields, and also as a warning not to push Mexico too far into Axis hands.[36]

Davis expanded his role as intermediary considerably by offering to facilitate trade and by working to increase German exports to Mexico. Having signed an agreement with Germany, and boasting of his relationship with Dr. J. G. A. Hertslet of the Economic Ministry in Berlin and Eugen Brieschke of the German Oil Import Board, Davis proceeded by offering firms, including General Motors and British American Tobacco Company, cash rebates if they would funnel their business with Mexico through him. In effect, Davis was offering a 3 percent rebate to any firm that would help him get his petroleum credits out of Germany by purchasing German equipment.[37]

However, a less sympathetic interpretation of the matter emerged from Drew Pearson's column, "The Washington Merry-Go-Round," when the journalist charged Davis with "selling oil to Hitler."[38] John L. Lewis reacted to the adverse publicity by calling on President Roosevelt for action, and the British detained Davis in Bermuda. When Davis was stopped by the FBI on his return to Washington, he was found with correspondence from Hitler in his possession. Clearly, the sensitive nature of Davis's business emphasized the importance of Mexican petroleum and undercut Standard Oil's desire to have the United States implement the National Stolen Property Act against Mexico.[39] Ambassador Daniels also worried that Mexico would build a pipeline across the Tehuantepec Isthmus to supply petroleum to the Pacific coast. To get petroleum products to the west coast, it had been necessary to load vessels at Minatitlán and to proceed through the Panama Canal. Storage tanks were being built at Salina Cruz, but Daniels thought that this might be the forerunner of sales to Japan when Davis reported that he was negotiating with Mexico on the construction of such a pipeline.

After war started in Europe, W. R. Davis and Company found its position more difficult. In discussions with PEMEX, the company claimed that Davis had a personal investment of 50 million marks in Germany, of which 10 million was in cash and was lost. He claimed that the fifty thousand dollars' worth of refinery machinery he had ordered for Mexico's account was now lost with the outbreak of war. Davis immediately inquired of Suárez if German ships in Mexican waters could be seized in lieu of payment, but

the United States and Mexico viewed that action as incompatible with international law.[40]

There were even rumors that a German-Mexican treaty was possible.[41] At one point, Hertslet and Brieschke visited Mexico. U.S. diplomats viewed Hertslet as the "right-hand man of Hitler" in economic and trade matters. Discussions ranged widely and covered such topics as petroleum, chemical industries, and finance. Suárez was at pains to deny to Daniels that his country would enter into formal agreements. However, the possibility of German-Mexican cooperation was suggested,[42] and President Roosevelt, sufficiently concerned about such a possibility, called a joint session of Congress in May 1940. At the conference he warned that, in the event of war, Mexico might fall under German influence. As he reminded his listeners, "Tampico is only two and a quarter hours away [by air] from Saint Louis, Kansas City and Omaha."[43]

The British kept track of Mexican sales to the Axis forces. N. K. Butler, counselor of the British embassy in Washington, and A. K. Helm, the first secretary, complained to Berle in the State Department that W. R. Davis and Company was selling oil to Spain even after the outbreak of World War II. The tanker *Spencer Kellogg* was scheduled to sail from Brownsville with sixty-five hundred tons of oil, with another ten thousand tons to follow at the end of June, ultimately bound for Italy or Germany by way of Spain.[44] Davis avoided the U.S. Maritime Commission's regulations on shipping to Spain by chartering foreign vessels in his own name. Needless to say, Roosevelt's State Department was sensitive to criticism over policy toward Spain. Davis eventually died in mysterious circumstances in June 1941. Most serious students of the wartime espionage networks think there is at least a significant chance that William Stephenson's agents of the British Security Coordination "may have acted to quicken Davis' journey into the next life."[45] Whereas Davis's death solved a strategic problem for the Alllies, his career aided Mexico in its strategic bargaining with the United States.

Mexico's position also was aided by the fact that many U.S. firms were favorably disposed toward the Nazis before Pearl Harbor. Spruille Braden, the extremely conservative U.S. diplomat and heir to a copper corporation in Chile, complained about the pro-Nazi disposition of firms such as International Harvester (IH). For ideological reasons, and in defense of their 17-million-dollar plant in Germany, IH was not cooperating with U.S. measures to reduce Nazi influence in Latin America. As Braden explained, "In many of these cases I do not know whether I am more shocked by the lack of patriotism or the dangerous shortsightedness."[46]

## Military Relations

If commercial relationships were a problem for Washington, an examination of military interactions between the United States and Mexico

shows a quite different pattern from that of the more stressful petroleum relationship, and probably offers the best barometer of the overall situation between the two countries. At no time during the Cárdenas administration, even after the expropriation of petroleum, were political-military links severed. By June 1940, Ambassador Castillo Nájera was holding out the possibility of further military cooperation with the United States to Undersecretary Sumner Welles: "President Cárdenas was entirely favorable to the suggestion of this government that the secret conversations between appropriate military and naval officers of the two governments should be undertaken in order to determine what precise measures of cooperation both governments could take in the event of emergency."[47]

Cárdenas assured Welles that "in the event of any controversy resulting from any act of aggression against the American continent which brought the United States into war, the United States could count on full military and naval cooperation from Mexico in addition to the use of Mexican territory and Mexican naval bases for American forces."[48] President Cárdenas also let it be known to U.S. officials that he had recently received overtures from the Italian government to send an aviation mission to Mexico, an offer that he had refused. In return he asked if the U.S. Air Corps could train Mexican flyers. This ploy made Secretary Hull think again about lecturing Mexico on taking other people's property, as he had done immediately after the nationalization of petroleum, in the summer of 1938. It also neutralized any possible U.S. interference in the 1940 election, since General Almazán could offer nothing more.

The general agreement signed between the two countries solved a number of long-standing issues and facilitated the ongoing military alliance.[49] It was highlighted by the understanding that Mexico would totally support the United States in the likely event of war. The central economic decision was announced on July 10, 1941, after talks between the two countries. Mexico stated that it was henceforth prohibiting the export of all "basic and strategic" materials to *"all non-American countries"* and to any American country that *"had not established export limitations similar to those sought by the decree."* A few days later, on July 15, 1941, Mexico announced a further agreement with the Federal Loan Agency providing that the Metals Reserve Company and the Defense Supplies Corporation would, for eighteen months, purchase up to 25 percent more than the average Mexican export of commodities at a negotiated price. In other words, Mexico entirely tied its export economy to the U.S. war effort as it virtually established a monopsonist position.[50] These measures antedated the U.S. entry into World War II.

Mexico was thus firmly committed to the U.S. side on the eve of war. Years of military cooperation had set the basis for that. President Cárdenas turned his efforts to preventing military cooperation from leading to an erosion of national sovereignty. In 1939 the United States asked for

permission to send surveillance aircraft over the border. Cárdenas resisted that proposal, fearing that such aircraft would become accustomed to operating independently in Mexico.[51] Furthermore, as the president instructed his foreign minister, "the government of Mexico cannot accept in any way, that any part of its territory might be occupied, temporarily or permanently, by a foreign power." [52] The president would not even allow work to be done on military bases unless it was carried out by Mexican engineers and personnel.

The Mexican government's commitment to the Allies was clear, even before the war came to the Americas. President Cárdenas insisted that the alliance should be "definitive" rather than a mere reaction to a state of emergency. It should provide for the defense of the American continent against imperialism from whatever source, and it should be based upon policies leading toward the industrialization of the country.[53] Given the adverse impact that wartime cooperation had on so many aspects of revolutionary nationalism in Mexico, it is natural to wonder about the Cárdenas administration's reasons for making such a firm commitment. The fact that Lázaro Cárdenas was a military man, and that U.S. arms were so central to the Mexican Army, provides one reason for such a policy.

President Cárdenas had another reason to support the alliance with the United States. In a personal letter to Elena Vázquez Gómez, who was visiting Havana in the summer of 1940, he set forth his country's position: "The fundamental explanation of the policy followed by Mexico is to be found in the experience of the weak countries of Europe which, by trying to maintain a self-centered attitude of neutrality and indifference to the major fight, had to suffer the invasion of their territories, and then found themselves in the midst of modern combat."[54] Like it or not, Cárdenas viewed Mexico as being inexorably linked to the United States for reasons of security. He saw cooperation with his northern neighbor as essential if Mexico was to avoid the fate of small countries conquered in Europe, Asia, and Africa. Additionally, the desire to combat the evil of fascism gave a moral dimension to his policy.

There was significant opposition to the policy of complete support for the Allies within Mexico and even within government circles. Isidro Fabela, the diplomat and legal scholar, presented President Cárdenas with a strategic study in 1939. He argued that any alliance between a strong and a weak power is inherently dangerous, and he anticipated that the United States would want naval and air bases, free transportation privileges for troops and airplanes, unlimited access to the Mexican coast, and the right to train Mexican military units. These policies, initiated in the moment of crisis, could easily lead to the military occupation of the country and create "another Veracruz." For these reasons Fabela counseled against a firm alliance with the United States.[55] While clearly aware of the dangers posed by what he called "imperialist sectors in the United States," Cárdenas thought that

close cooperation was the best way to protect national sovereignty from fascist conquest, and he accepted that Mexico might have to consider obligatory military service in the emerging world crisis.

## Mexico's Response to Pearl Harbor

The change of administrations from Cárdenas to Manuel Avila Camacho implied no change in policy toward the U.S. alliance. Avila Camacho had denounced the Axis powers as dictatorial, as early as April 1941, so there was no surprise when he reacted swiftly after the Japanese bombing of Hawaii. The Foreign Ministry, on December 8, and the president in his speech of December 9, broke off relations with Japan and completely committed the country to a U.S. pact.[56] Four days later German and Japanese assets were frozen. The Ministry of the Interior quickly forbade sending any messages in a language other than Spanish or English and ordered Axis nationals out of coastal and defense areas.[57] The export of strategic raw materials without governmental approval was prohibited.[58]

Today it is easy to underestimate the degree to which the unknown affected thinking after the Japanese attack on Pearl Harbor. We know that the Japanese continued to press on in the Pacific toward Southeast Asia and Australia; however, that was not clear in December 1941. There was a general fear that the west coast of North America was exposed to further attack. Indeed, after Pearl Harbor many San Francisco residents went to the beach to stare out over the Pacific Ocean to see if the Japanese would arrive, and college football authorities switched the Rose Bowl game from Pasadena to North Carolina to protect it from enemy attack.[60] When Germany, in a fit of enthusiasm, declared war on the United States in response to Japan's bombing of Pearl Harbor, even though it was not so bound by its treaty with Tokyo, U.S. involvement in a war in Europe as well as in the Pacific was ensured. Mexico quickly severed diplomatic relations with Germany and Italy on December 11, 1941.[60] U.S. and Mexican military establishments soon realized the vulnerability of their western flank. Responding to that fear in Mexico, General and former President Lázaro Cárdenas was recalled to active service and placed in charge of the newly organized Pacific Military Zone.[61] In January the two governments announced the formation of the Joint Mexican-United States Defense Commission.[62]

It is frequently forgotten how close the submarine warfare in the Atlantic and the Caribbean came to Mexico and the United States in 1942–43. On the Gulf Coast of Mexico, shipping was seriously disrupted, and the segments of the economy tied to maritime activities went into an acute decline. In the United States the threat was so great that coal shipments from Hampton Roads, Virginia, destined for the northeastern steel-making factories, usually shipped by ocean-going colliers, had to be transferred overland as a result of Axis submarine activity.[63]

On May 13, 1942, a Mexican ship, the *Potrero del Llano*, was sunk in the Gulf of Mexico by German submarines, killing five crewmen. Reaction in Mexico was immediate. The Right was divided. Some prominent figures momentarily hinted that the United States or Britain might have sunk the ship in order to draw the country into the war, while others were apathetic. The CTM, by contrast, immediately organized major rallies and demanded that the workers' militia be given additional arms for defending the country. Within the government, Foreign Minister Padilla pressed for war. After the sinking of the *Potrero del Llano*, he delivered a demand for compensation to the German Foreign Office, through Sweden. According to one U.S. diplomat, between the first and third draft of the note, the time given for the Germans to respond was reduced from two weeks to one week.[64]

The Foreign Office declined to accept the note, and on May 21 a second ship, the *Faja de Oro,* was sunk, killing seven more Mexicans. In response, President Avila Camacho stated that this meant war. Finally, on May 25, he called Congress into special session to declare war upon the Axis powers.[65] The president set up the Consejo Supremo de la Defensa Nacional over which he presided, with General Cárdenas in charge of military matters and Eduardo Suárez as the highest economic authority. Former President Rodríguez was put in charge of national production.[66]

U.S. diplomats played a restrained game during this moment of crisis. Ambassador Messersmith was in Undersecretary Torres Bodet's office when the news of the sinking of the *Potrero del Llano* came through. Mexico's only source of information was its consulate in Miami, Florida. Messersmith limited his role to providing additional information and let the Mexican leaders come to their own conclusions. Indeed, he believed that they would make the right decision "if there is no intimation, or slight pressure from us, from any direction, of any kind."[67] And so it was. The sinking of the *Potrero del Llano* and the *Faja de Oro* was crucial. Support for the Allied cause grew massively, and opponents of wartime cooperation with the Allies faced the onslaught of nationalistic sentiment.

Although Minister of the Interior Miguel Alemán and Secretary of the Navy General Jara were widely understood to oppose the war, neither of them expressed any public dissent. Those on the right, such as General Nicolas Rodríguez (the old Villista general who had founded the Camisas Doradas), the Marqués de Castellón (the Spanish spokesman for the Falange in Mexico), the UNS, and others sympathetic to the Axis, regarded their position as untenable. Surprisingly, the CTM, the PCM, and the broad Left found their views in line with patriotic sentiment.

The greatest beneficiary of the declaration of war was the Mexican president. Before the war, Avila Camacho was continuously trying to hold the PRM factions together. Even though the great mass of the people was indifferent toward the war in the initial stages, the president quickly assumed the dignified stance of a wartime statesman. The political generals—

Cárdenas, Calles, and Rodríguez—as well as other politicians rallied to the support of the government. Twice in the first week after the declaration of war the president assumed direct command of aerial exercises in the skies over Mexico City. The cabinet was alerted to the possibility of sabotage, and major labor organizations, including the CTM, CROM, CGT, and CPN, signaled their willingness to relinquish the weapon of the strike if guarantees were given that their interests would be respected.[68] One foreign diplomat stated that "there is no doubt that he [Avila Camacho] had achieved the almost unanimous support of the Mexican people even if he had led them into a war which they would have generally chosen to avoid."[69]

Some figures in Washington pressed hard and fast. Secretary of War Henry Stimson immediately urged Avila Camacho to allow thirty U.S. military personnel, "not in uniform and in automobiles," to go into Baja California and Sonora to search for secret Japanese landing fields. Stimson imagined that a Japanese carrier force was planning the equivalent of the Doolittle bombing raid on Tokyo against the United States by using secret airfields in Mexico. It was only the intervention of General Cárdenas that convinced Avila Camacho that such airfields did not exist. The Mexicans agreed, however, to allow three teams of radar monitors into Baja California to scan the Pacific Ocean. Messersmith bucked Stimson over his displeasure with Avila Camacho's decision, stating, "I am still of the opinion that the President of Mexico is a better judge of what is feasible and desirable and possible in Mexico than our Army officials."[70]

Mexico refused to allow the United States to establish submarine bases in Yucatán. Ambassador Messersmith also intervened with Pan American Airways to stop the company from replacing all Mexican radio officers, code clerks, pilots, and managers with U.S. personnel.[71] Moreover, he and the president agreed that it was important to bring the country into the war effort "step by step" in order to overcome latent opposition to Mexico's participation by considerable segments of the community.[72] In a subtle vein, U.S. diplomats were convinced that it was vital to have Latin America's military defend its own territory in order to bring it more deeply into the war effort. By mid-July, the American ambassador reported to Washington that the Mexican newspapers were cooperating with the endeavor "one hundred percent." He added, "They publish anything we give them and their attitude is all that we could wish and we are not giving them any subsidies of any kind."[73] Similarly, the Allies could direct the wire services to put anything they wanted on the radio. Embassy secretary Guy Ray liaised with the Mexican media. His effort was important in putting popular opinion on the side of the war effort and in gaining a foothold for U.S. media corporations after the war.[74]

Washington's strategy was to avoid direct confrontation with the church and the far right. Recognizing that the clergy's attitude toward Mexico's participation in the war was "luke warm" and strongly pacifist, U.S.

officials tried to stress the theme that Catholics in occupied Europe were suffering enormously at the hands of the Nazis. Propaganda officials relied on events to silence the Catholic Right.

Emergency powers were granted to the president by Congress on June 1, 1942.[75] Avila Camacho vowed to use those powers sparingly, a promise that he kept. On June 11 a decree outlawed work stoppages that were not legally recognized strikes. In other words, unless strikers had the approval of the Board of Conciliation and Arbitration for their strike, their action was illegal. Fidel Velázquez, ever keen to find a legal distinction enabling the CTM to support the government, tried to distinguish between the emergency decrees suspending only individual, and not collective, rights. Given the fact that wages had been frozen in the face of rapidly rising prices, these were severe measures.[76]

## Manuel Avila Camacho and the Allies

Economic warfare also came to Mexico. When war broke out in Europe in 1939, the country suffered a series of immediate losses. Some 19 million marks in credit, for the sale of petroleum through William Davis, had accumulated in Mexican accounts in Germany. A number of ships were rerouted from Northern Europe to Land's End in the United Kingdom. The declaration of war was quickly followed, on June 13, by a decree prohibiting trade with the enemy, and Mexico took over forty-three Axis-owned enterprises at once. On November 26, 1942, the president signed a decree naming the Banco de México as trustee for Mexican bonds held in enemy hands. This measure was quite sweeping as it covered bonds and securities held either in Axis or conquered countries, regardless of the nationality of the bondholders; moreover, there was a requirement that such holdings be registered in Mexico within thirty days or be treated as "enemy shares."[77]

President Avila Camacho's geopolitical view of the coming world war merged neatly with his economic strategy. His pro-Allied sentiments led him to oppose the exclusive trade blocs that were being developed by Germany and Japan. In a speech in 1942 he said that "the principle of autarky is not a democratic principle, because it stems from a premise that excludes voluntary international collaboration, which is the primordial law of democracy, and because it presumes, in effect, the imposition of the State which leads to dictatorship and from there directly to war."[78] Washington totally agreed with this position and, therefore, extremely close collaboration with Mexico City followed.

The mere suggestion that Mexico might favor the Axis powers infuriated its officials. Cornelius Vanderbilt visited the republic and wrote an article in the magazine *Liberty*, entitled "Is Hitler Militarizing Mexico?" He asserted that the country was drawing close to Germany and, as evi-

dence of opposition to its pro-German stance, he even claimed to have seen a massacre in the capital on the Paseo de la Reforma during an anti-Avila Camacho rally: "Scores bit the dust. Shots went wild. I saw a man two stories up in an office building reel over and slide off the railing and fall headlong into the street."[79] There were minor election riots; however, Vanderbilt's article was pure fiction. Ambassador Daniels took great pleasure in establishing that Vanderbilt had actually left Mexico City four days before the election. But the interesting aspect of the episode was the reaction of local officials to that report. "I have rarely known Mexican officials to express themselves as so incensed over any article as over the article in *Liberty*."[80]

Avila Camacho's administration showed the depth of its commitment to the Allied cause in an open exchange in the press between the president and Vicente Lombardo Toledano in which the labor leader asked the president a series of open questions: Were there any secret pacts between the United States and Mexico? Had any Mexican territory been ceded for U.S. bases? Had other secret promises been made? The president answered Lombardo Toledano scornfully.[81]

In fact, Avila Camacho wanted to cooperate with the Allies more than his country was prepared to tolerate. At least that is what he told the U.S. ambassador. Messersmith was informed that a number of Mexican generals proposed training troops for battle with the Allied forces. He quoted Avila Camacho: "He said that he could not openly give approval to this measure at this time, but that he was certainly not discouraging it."[82] Indeed, the president wanted to change Mexican law so that troops could be deployed outside the country.

An enormous change had taken place as a number of disparate groups had come together in support of the war. For Mexicans on the left, the end of the Nazi-Soviet pact meant that all support could be given to the war effort. On the right, however, war was more problematic. Intellectuals such as José Vasconcelos, Luis Cabrera, and Agustín Aragón or newspapers such as *Excélsior* had been fairly open about viewing Germany as a shield against the Soviet Union. To them, as to the men of Munich, the reality of Germany turning west in 1940 rather than continuing on toward conflict with the USSR was shattering. In addition, it was tempting to focus upon the Acción Nacional and the Sinarquistas, who were unfriendly toward the United States. Yet it is important not to equate this segment of the far right with the business community in general. With the outbreak of war, Mexican businessmen in large numbers rallied to the defense of the country. In the first two years of the war the *sector patronal* contributed 250,000 pesos to the civil defense effort; by comparison the government put up only 100,000 pesos. (It was only by 1944 that the employers had second thoughts about the effectiveness of civil defense, and they began to see their contributions to it as indirect support of the workers' militias.)[83]

Within the governing PRM, most conservatives received the message and went along with the declaration of war. The old Calles clique was believed to be pro-Axis.[84] However, those of similar persuasion such as Maximino Avila Camacho and Octavio Véjar Vásquez, the minister of education, began to play down their position. Maximino was content to administer his interests from within the cabinet—although his business dealings tied him to Axis sympathizers—and Véjar Vásquez tried to lead a purge of people on the left from within the cabinet. So neither was going to risk much for the fascist movement after Mexico entered World War II. The United States had sent what State Department economic planner Emilio G. Collado called "a discrete small technical group to work with General Rodríguez" to find ways to link industry in Mexico to war production.[85] Secretary Hull called this move "imperative."

The property of German, Italian, and Japanese nationals in Mexico was quickly embargoed and placed under a committee, headed by Luis Cabrera (by then an old man of the right), to administer it during the war years.[86] The U.S. agencies created a blacklist of firms controlled by Axis citizens, and the Mexican commission worked in tandem with U.S. authorities.

For most Mexican politicians, the declaration of war represented something of a political truce. Wartime cooperation meant that people who formerly had little to do with each other became comrades. Photographs of the huge prowar rally on June 1, 1942, after another Mexican ship was torpedoed, showed the CTM and PCM banners to be dominant. Following Mexico's declaration of war, attempts were made to generate a climate of enthusiasm for the crusade. On August 18 the Electrical Workers' Union held a mass meeting to emphasize the unity of workers behind the war effort and also to urge the Allies to open up a second front in Europe, as the Soviets were demanding. On the platform sat Lombardo Toledano, eminent Chilean poet Pablo Neruda (then Chilean consul in Mexico City), as well as representatives of the CTM, FSTSE, and PCM. These were the days when Angel Olivo of the PCM openly praised the CTM and argued that Fidel Velázquez represented the best traditions of working-class unity. As Lombardo Toledano spoke, Orson Welles and the film actress Dolores del Río came onto the platform; they had just announced their engagement, and the crowd went wild.[87]

Lombardo Toledano moved into new circles by giving a speech at a well-attended luncheon in a private club on June 1, 1943. Not only old comrades such as Alejandro Carrillo attended, but also ministers on the right such as Foreign Minister Padilla and Interior Minister Alemán were there to salute Lombardo Toledano's call for wartime unity. Dolores del Río and other movie stars, orchestra leader Carlos Chávez, and artist Miguel Covarrubias applauded. Even a number of important industrialists nodded approvingly as don Vicente called for the collective defense of democracy,

whether traditional or proletarian. He also asked for collaboration with liberal Catholics, a group not yet included in his constituency. Trying to be all things to all people, Lombardo Toledano defended former President Cárdenas's program while simultaneously arguing that President Avila Camacho's program was necessary because of the times.[88] U.S. diplomats doubted that Lombardo Toledano's change of position represented anything other than wartime expediency; however, they observed that many revolutionaries of 1910 had become prosperous and moderate and had achieved "something resembling middle class status."[89] And with few exceptions, these leaders supported the war effort.

## An Unpopular War

Although the leaders had committed their nation to the Allied cause in World War II, the Mexican people were unconvinced. The war was brought home quickly to them, as electricity was rationed by means of reduced voltage and a two-hour-per-day decrease in the supply of current.[90] Recognizing that the opposition related more to internal political dynamics than to Great Power rivalries, one British propagandist operating in Mexico observed that, for the vast majority of Mexicans, this was a distant event about which they knew very little. I. D. Davidson represented the expropriated British petroleum interests in Mexico after relations were severed. He argued that, in 1940, public opinion "that mattered" was held by perhaps 2 percent of the population, half of whom lived in the Federal District. He asserted that fully half of the rest of the population did not know that a war was going on.[91]

There even were places where popular sympathy seemed to be on the German side. In Ciudad Madero in 1942 moviegoers at the Cine Alcazar reacted rudely to news footage of President Roosevelt and Prime Minister Winston Churchill. The report to the president said that "they were manifestly ridiculed by the majority of the audience."[92] That attitude probably reflected the pro-German orientation of the local newspaper *El Mundo*. As late as 1942, British diplomats were writing back to London: "Little popular zeal was shewn for the cause [the declaration of war] Mexico has espoused."[93] Again, in September, a diplomat still bemoaned "the average Mexican's apathy toward the war and his dislike and suspicion of the United States." Enthusiasm was restricted, in that view, to a "small circle" in the capital.[94] British diplomats and businessmen mounted a propaganda effort aimed at changing Mexican public opinion and keeping Britain involved in the economy after the war.

It was only in June 1941 that George P. Shaw, the U.S. consul in Mexico City, thought that the government's efforts in support of the Allied cause

were bearing fruit. Until that time, pro-German sympathies prevailed: "There appears to be no doubt that up until two months ago public opinion was, to say the least, decidedly influenced by German sympathy, probably the result of subtle and effective German propaganda in Mexico and a natural anti-American attitude. However, there now appears to be no doubt that the attitude of the administration and the army as such in endeavoring to follow the policy of Washington in support of Great Britain and her allies is causing an apparent swing in favor of the last-mentioned powers."[95] It should be kept in mind that what Shaw called "public opinion" referred to narrow political circles in the capital. At the extreme, some enthusiastic officials such as Graciano Sánchez, secretary-general of the CNC, wrote to the president urging him to have all citizens of Germany, Italy, and Japan "without exception" placed in concentration camps.[96]

The U.S. pulp magazines tried to whip up enthusiasm for the war. Even *Reader's Digest*, in its Spanish-language edition, ran articles such as "Como Atacar el Submarino" and "La Atración Sexual como Arma de los Nazis."[97] As late as 1943, George Messersmith wrote confidentially to Cordell Hull. The ambassador, smarting under the combination of inflationary pressures being attributed to cooperation with the United States and insensitive and racist attitudes on the part of many wartime officials when dealing with Mexico, complained: "Some of our people have never realized that the declaration of war by Mexico was not an act of the Mexican people, but of its government. It is true that the people have acquiesced and are steadily and continuously more understanding of the meaning of war to them. This does not mean, however, that the government does not have its problems and I can assure [you] that these problems are very real."[98]

In short, Mexico followed the United States into World War II as a result of the orientation of its government. President Avila Camacho, a general fascinated by the political and military events developing in Europe, found that cooperation with the war effort of the Allies was of immense use in carving out an independent space in the Mexican political scene. As a war leader, his role increased and many policies became possible that would have been unthinkable in times of peace. A reading of the historical documentation of the period makes it quite clear that this motivation was at the core of the Avila Camacho policies of wartime cooperation with the Allies. The Mexican government was able to use the approach of war to negotiate the most successful settlement in history of outstanding issues with the United States.

Although the war was not popular with the vast majority of the Mexican people, especially in its early stages, the fact that the Mexican Left also wanted to support the war effort created an unusual alliance between a government committed to shifting the course of the Mexican Revolution to the right and parties of the left. The forces of the right, although tepid in their support of the Allied cause, accepted the inevitable. However, in 1941–42,

few people had any idea of the depth of change that would result from Mexico's entry into World War II.

## Notes

1. Oral History Interview with Merwin L. Bohan, February 1977, p. 84, Truman Library.
2. Hull, *Memoirs*, 2:601, 814.
3. Francisco Castillo Nájera was regularly sending reports on the Axis influence in the region to President Lázaro Cárdenas by 1938. SRE, 30-3-10 (I), April 1938.
4. Shoup and Minter, *Imperial Brain Trust,* 119.
5. Some of the individuals involved in postwar planning included Cordell Hull, Sumner Welles, Lauchlin Currie, and George Messersmith at the State Department; John Foster Dulles and Allen Dulles, corporate lawyers already with close ties to the intelligence community; economists Alvin H. Hansen and Jacob Viner; historians William L. Langer, Crane Brinton, A. Whitney, and R. Griswald; and businessman Whitney H. Shepardson, who had advised President Wilson at Versailles. There also were key lawyers, financiers, military figures, and journalists.
6. Jones, *Fifty Billion Dollars*, 220, 225–29.
7. Among the more important German firms were Beick Felix y Compañía, Casa Bayer S.A., Merck-México S.A., Instituto Behring, Laboratorios Codex S.A., Química Schering Mexicana, Gran Drogería del Refugio, Casa Carlos Stein y Compañía, Drogería Stein, Compañía General de Anilinas, Casa Lammers S.A., Compañía Explotadora de Gas Carbónico, Unión Química S.A., and Gas Carbónico S.A. AGN, RP/MAV, 705.1/108.
8. According to one Mexican estimate, a break with Japan would hurt a number of textile firms including Seda Natural, Textiles Lyon, Hilos Torcidos, and Mafisa. Castillo Nájera to Ezequiel Padilla, May 12, 1941, SRE, 29-30-6.
9. The administration was especially concerned with such German firms as Casa Bayer and Casa Carlos Stein y Compañía, AGN, RP/MAC, 434.1/624.
10. Henry Wallace to Hull, December 16, 1940, USNA/RG 59, 812.001.
11. Castillo Nájera to Padilla, January 16, 1941, SRE, 29-30-6.
12. Memorandum from the U.S. Chamber of Commerce in Mexico City to Vice President Wallace entitled "Camacho, Manuel A.," December 6, 1940, USNA/RG 59, 812.001.
13. One of the most useful examinations of Mexico's position as the war started was a confidential study by the Board of Economic Warfare, *The Mexican Economy*.
14. Hoover's reports actually read like the television series of the 1950s dealing with the FBI; for example: J. Edgar Hoover to Adolf A. Berle, Jr., USNA/RG 59, 812.00/31065-1/2.
15. J. Edgar Hoover to Assistant Secretary of State Berle, April 29, 1940, USNA/RG 59, 812.00/31011-1/2.
16. Berle observed: "He [Hoover] transmits to us anything that comes along, good, bad, and indifferent." Berle to Hull, October 17, 1940, USNA/RG 59, 812.00/31504-1/2.
17. Hoover to Berle, July 26, 1949, USNA/RG 59, 812.00/31263.
18. Report from George Shaw to secretary of state, "Resume of the Political Situation in Mexico City . . . during June 1941," June 28, 1941, USNA/RG 59, 812.00/31715.

19. Schuller, "Cardenismo Revisited," 234–39.

20. Shaw to secretary of state, "Resume of the Political Situation in Mexico City," June 28, 1941, USNA/RG 59, 812.00/31715.

21. *Novedades,* October 6, 1939. After the outbreak of war the German Casino was turned over to the CNC to use as its headquarters. *Diario Oficial,* September 11, 1942.

22. McCartney, *The Bechtel Story,* 51–55.

23. Pierre de Boal, chargé d'affaires ad interim, to Secretary Hull, May 17, 1940, USNA/RG 59, 812.00/31073. John McCone continued to provide a link between Bechtel Construction Corporation and the intelligence community throughout the war. In 1946 a congressional committee investigating Ralph Casey of the General Accounting Office revealed that McCone's shipbuilding interests had earned 44 million dollars on an investment of 100,000 dollars. Halberstam, *The Best and the Brightest,* 189–90.

24. Hoover to Berle, May 28, 1940, USNA/RG 59, 812.00/31065.

25. Report from Josephus Daniels to secretary of state, "Japanese Interests in Four Companies Registered in Mexico," October 25, 1940, USNA/RG 59, 812.5034/147.

26. Report from Josephus Daniels to secretary of state, "Stocks and Bonds of Companies Held in Mexico which are Held in Countries Overrun by Germany," July 23, 1940, USNA/RG 59, 812.5034/144.

27. Blasier, *The Hovering Giant,* 125.

28. Sampson, *The Seven Sisters,* 36–40.

29. W. D. Crampton, vice president of Standard Française des Pétroles, to Edwin C. Wildon, counselor of the American embassy in Paris, September 21, 1938, USNA/RG 59, 812.6363 Davis and Company/133.

30. *New York Times,* August 2, 1941. W. R. Davis was the father of Myron Davis, the oilman and media magnate (television's "Dynasty," etc.) of the 1980s.

31. Joseph C. Grew, American embassy in Tokyo, to secretary of state, "Mexican Oil Activities of W. R. Davis," September 21, 1938, USNA/RG 59, 812.6363 Davis and Company/134.

32. Rout and Bratzel, *The Shadow War,* 53.

33. Laurence Duggan to Sumner Welles, October 29, 1938, USNA/RG 59, 812.6363 Davis and Company/145.

34. Petroleum exports to Germany fell from 168,000 metric tons in the first half of 1937 to 90,518 tons for the same period in 1939. Report from Wilbur Keblinger, American consul general in Hamburg, to secretary of state, entitled "German Imports of Mexican Oil," September 21, 1938, USNA/RG 59, 812.6363 Davis and Company/135 .

35. Wilbur Keblinger, American consul general in Hamburg, to secretary of state, October 28, 1938, USNA/RG 59, 812.6363 Davis and Company/148. The industry source of this information was J. Holger Graffman, managing director of the oil company, Transfer A.B., in Stockholm.

36. Josephus Daniels to secretary of state, report entitled "W. R. Davis: Barter of Mexican Oil for Machinery and Goods," December 8, 1938, USNA/RG 59, 812.6363 Davis and Company/152.

37. Daniels to secretary of state, "Practices on the Part of W. R. Davis and Company." June 17, 1939, USNA/RG 59, 812.6363 Davis and Company/186.

38. *Washington Times-Herald,* February 18, 1940.

39. Davis's role was becoming a public scandal. The *New York Post,* for example, reported these events under the banner "Davis Firm Sold Nazi Goods," Janu-

ary 6, 1941; and Henry Wallace delivered a speech linking Davis to Nazi agents, *Washington Times-Herald*, January 1, 1941.

40. Telegram from PEMEX to secretary of state, September 5, 1939, USNA/ RG 59, 812.6363 Davis and Company/201.

41. Daniels to secretary of state, August 8, 1938, USNA/RG 59, 812.6363 Davis and Company/194.

42. Daniels to secretary of state, August 23, 1939, USNA/RG 59, 812.6363 Davis and Company/199.

43. *Congressional Record* 86 (May 16, 1940): 6, 234.

44. Memorandum of conversation between Butler, Helm, and Berle, June 18, 1940, USNA/RG 59, 812.6363 Davis and Company/264.

45. Rout and Bratzel, *The Shadow War*, 55.

46. Spruille Braden to Adolf Berle, March 4, 1941, Columbia University Manuscript Collection, Braden Manuscripts.

47. Memorandum of conversation between Castillo Nájera and Sumner Welles, June 4, 1940, USNA/RG 59, 812.00/31072.

48. Ibid.

49. For a summary of claims see Blasier, *The Hovering Giant*, 76–77.

50. Board of Economic Warfare, *The Mexican Economy*, 7 (emphasis mine).

51. Cárdenas to Castillo Nájera, October 28, 1939, SRE, 39-10-2.

52. Cárdenas to Hay, December 11, 1940, SRE, 39-10-8.

53. Cárdenas to Castillo Nájera, June 16, 1940, SRE, 39-10-2.

54. President Cárdenas to Elena Vásquez Gómez, June 21, 1940, SRE, 39-10-10. This letter probably provides the best source on Cárdenas's thinking since it was directed to a doubtful member of the "revolutionary family" and was not intended for wider distribution.

55. Isidro Fabela's study was called "Alianza Político-Militár de Cualesquiera de las Naciones Hispano-Americanos con los Estados Unidos de Norte América," Fabela to Cárdenas, June 25, 1940, SRE, 39-10-15.

56. *El Universal*, December 9, 1941.

57. *Diario Oficial,* December 17, 1941.

58. Ibid., December 19, 1941.

59. Wills, *Reagan's America,* 167.

60. *El Universal*, December 12, 1941.

61. Ibid.

62. Ibid., January 13, 1941; State Department *Bulletin,* January 17, 1942.

63. Galbraith, *A Life in Our Times,* 180.

64. Harold D. Finley to secretary of state, June 30, 1942, USNA/RG 59, 812.00/ 32001.

65. *Diario Oficial,* May 27, 1942.

66. AGN, RP/MAC, 550/44-20-8.

67. Messersmith to Hull, May 20, 1942, GSM Papers. It was not until June 15 that Messersmith spoke to the nation over radio station XEQ in Mexico City for one-half hour on the declaration of war.

68. *El Nacional*, June 28, 1942; *Excélsior* and *La Prensa*, June 29, 1942.

69. Finley to secretary of state, June 30, 1942, USNA/RG 59, 812.00/32001.

70. Messersmith to Hull, May 29, 1942, GSM Papers.

71. Messersmith to Welles, June 3, 1942, GSM Papers. U.S. Air Corps officers estimated that Mexico had three hundred top aviators, and U.S. officials wanted to use them.

72. Messersmith to Welles, June 3, 1942, GSM Papers.

73. Messersmith to Duggan, July 19, 1942, GSM Papers.

74. Messersmith to Duggan, July 27, 1942, GSM Papers. See also Niblo, "British Propaganda in Mexico," 114–26.

75. See *Diario Oficial*, June 2, 1942, for the formal declaration of war and the suspension of constitutional guarantees.

76. Ibid., September 20, 1943.

77. Ibid., December 8, 1942.

78. *El Nacional*, September 25, 1942.

79. *Liberty*, September 14, 1940.

80. Daniels to Hull, September 10, 1940, USNA/RG 59, 812.00/31387.

81. For Vicente Lombardo Toledano's questions see *El Nacional,* May 31, 1941. The president's denials are in *El Universal*, June 1, 1941.

82. Messersmith to Roosevelt, July 10, 1942, USNA/RG 59, 812.00/32007.

83. Francisco Herrera, president of the VII Committee of Civil Defense, to the president, February 23, 1944, AGN, RP/MAC, 550/44-20-8. There was a proliferation of antifascist committees comprising people from most political persuasions. AGN, RP/MAC, 550/44-20.

84. Hoover to Berle, April 18, 1942, USNA/RG 59, 812.00/31966.

85. Emilio "Pete" Collado to Messersmith, November 4, 1942, USNA/RG 59, 812.60/21A.

86. For the terms of the relationship between the junta and the German colony, see AGN, RP/MAC, 550.9-15.

87. *El Popular*, August 19, 1942.

88. Ibid., June 2, 1943.

89. Finley to secretary of state, June 5, 1943, USNA/RG 59, 812.504/2204.

90. Fidel Velázquez to the president, May 2, 1941, AGN, RP/MAC, 523.4/2.

91. I. D. Davidson to F. Goodbar, January 4, 1940, PRO, FO/371, 24217.

92. Report to the president, January 15, 1942, AGN, RP/MAC, 561.1.

93. Annual Report, March 31, 1942, PRO, FO/371, 24217.

94. Foreign Office Internal Report, September 15, 1942, PRO, FO/371, 24217.

95. George P. Shaw to secretary of state, June 28, 1941, USNA/RG 59, 812.00/ 31715.

96. Graciano Sánchez to the president, August 28, 1942, AGN, RP/MAC, 550.67.

97. *Selecciones de Reader's Digest*, December 1942.

98. Confidential letter from Messersmith to Hull, April 14, 1943, USNA/RG 59, 812.51/2691.

# 4  Politics and Wartime Cooperation

## Strategic Aspects of the Alliance

As war clouds drew close, high officials in the United States were on the radio regularly to prepare the general population for the coming conflagration. They frequently identified Latin America's role in the coming struggle as supplying raw materials for the war effort.[1] It became clear that Mexico's place in the international arena had shifted definitively. No longer primarily a country that had nationalized the property of major U.S. and British corporations, Mexico now occupied the southern flank of a nation engaged elsewhere in a two-front war. A treasure house of nonferrous metals and an agricultural producer of significance, it began to take on a new importance. As one diplomat put it, "Mexico is perhaps the country of the American Republic to which we shall have to look most for many materials during the war, and perhaps afterwards . . . when looking for raw materials the transport problem will be a primary factor in determining the source."[2]

As an indication of the increased importance of Mexico at the beginning of 1942, the United States sent a top diplomat to Mexico City to replace aging Ambassador Josephus Daniels. George S. Messersmith, who arrived there in February, brought an impressive array of credentials to the job. He had risen through the State Department in the Caribbean and Europe, and while in Berlin he clashed openly with Adolf Hitler. Messersmith was the U.S. ambassador to Austria during the Anschluss. As undersecretary of state from 1937 to 1940, he was charged with implementing Sumner Welles's reorganization of the Foreign Service.[3]

Messersmith was involved in high-level planning. He was well connected as a result of his marriage to Marion, the daughter of Lewis Mustard. Close to the Du Pont family, he was one of the three or four diplomats (Daniels was another) who could write FDR directly—a fact that was not lost on his superiors in the State Department—and he even stayed with the Roosevelts on some visits to the United States. He was extremely competent, and he maintained an overall vision of American economic expansion, not through the clumsy techniques of direct intervention but rather through subtle and indirect forms of influence.

It is generally forgotten today how massive was the Mexican wartime cooperation with the United States. Messersmith recalled that when he

arrived in Mexico City in 1942 "there must have been between 400 and 500 altogether on the staff of the embassy in Mexico City," and that figure grew to eight hundred at the height of the war effort.[4] The two countries, according to his count, negotiated "fifty-two or fifty-three" major contracts covering all essential raw materials to support the war effort. Charged with implementing the maze of wartime regulations that touched Mexico, he worked hard at the job. He produced a prodigious volume of correspondence and earned the nickname "Forty-page George" from colleagues on the Mexican desk of the State Department.[5] His confidence within the high circles of government was strengthened by the numerous friends he had on Capitol Hill, although he made an enemy by blocking Dean Acheson's choice for his assistant in favor of Mexico City businessman Floyd Ransom; in the end he paid dearly for that friction. Yet, as long as FDR was in office, his position was firm and there was an open channel between Mexico City and Washington. The president made the importance of Mexico explicit to Ambassador Messersmith as he began his assignment: "The outstanding example of national leadership which President Avila Camacho is now giving to the Mexican people is a tremendously important contribution to our cause at this time."[6] Furthermore, as FDR explained in a letter to Justice Frank Murphy of the Supreme Court, his administration worked toward "the strengthening of the inter-American concept on the broad hemispheric basis that has been opposed to regional groupings within the Western Hemisphere, either political or economic."[7]

Messersmith's ambassadorship was fundamentally different from that of other emissaries from Washington. The diplomatic history of the two countries is replete with U.S. ambassadors who were eager to tell Mexicans what to do. However, no other ambassador to Mexico had such integral functions to perform for the internal functioning of that country's economy. Messersmith's job was to administer Mexico's contribution to World War II. Moreover, since the Avila Camacho government was following a high strategy of using the wartime cooperation to industrialize the country, Messersmith's help with wartime regulations was wanted. No other U.S. ambassador ever held so many levers in his hands, and few others have been so laudatory toward their Mexican counterparts. Messersmith described the economic ministers, Eduardo Suárez and Francisco Javier Gaxiola, as "collaborating to the fullest extent possible." As he later reflected, "I do not recall a single instance when the Mexican government endeavored to take advantage of the war situation and enter into contracts providing for prices which were higher than those that should be properly paid."[8]

Messersmith was able to operate at a number of levels of Mexican society in ways that would be unimaginable for a U.S. ambassador today. He maintained contacts with labor and radical leaders and was welcome to give talks, from time to time, at the National University and the Universidad Politécnica. He maintained a cordial relationship with people with whom

he disagreed, such as Alejandro Carrillo, and even arranged for a member of his staff, Videl Poodevan, to spend her leave of absence assisting Diego Rivera, for which the great communist artist was grateful.[9]

## Economic Policy of the Alliance

The most important wartime measure antedated Pearl Harbor. On July 10, 1941, Mexico prohibited the exportation of "basic and strategic materials" to all non-American countries as well as to any country that had not established similar export restrictions. The enormity of that decision for the future of Mexican development should not be underestimated.[10] As early as June 1941, Harry Hopkins concluded that it was in the interest of the United States to try to increase the steel production of the Compañía Fundidora de Fierro y Acero de Monterrey in order to gain an additional source of supply and also to reduce Mexico's purchases in the United States in the event of war.[11] The Allies viewed Mexico's raw materials as being of particular importance to the emerging role of the United States as the "arsenal of democracy," in FDR's phrase. Since the traditional supply lines to many parts of Europe, Asia, and Africa had been interrupted by the war at sea, the long and secure border between the United States and Mexico meant that raw materials could be safely transported north.

Both countries entered into an agreement on the stabilization of the peso-to-dollar ratio. Essentially the Banco de México and the Federal Reserve Bank agreed to work together to maintain the value of the two currencies. Even guaranteeing each other six months' notice on any proposed changes in the relative prices of currencies, the two central banks effectively ensured price stability for the period of the war, although Mexico earned only 1.5 percent interest on the funds deposited in its account in the Federal Reserve Bank.[12] This first financial step made other cooperation possible.

An Inter-American Conference on the Systems of Economic and Financial Control was held in Washington from June 30 to July 10, 1942. The top officials in the respective ministries of finance and treasury, the central banks, and other high economic institutions met quietly—hardly a media event—to coordinate measures of economic warfare. Since there had been a general settlement of the outstanding issues between the two countries, a broad range of cooperative activities emerged, centering, in the first instance, on strategic raw materials.

## Minerals and Mining

The Army and Navy Munitions Board drew up a detailed report entitled "Strictly Confidential Report on the Mexican Mining Industry" on

the eve of World War II. It classified the most important metals for the war effort as strategic (aluminum, antimony, chromium, manganese, mica, nickel, quartz crystals, mercury, tin, and tungsten) and others as critical (asbestos, cadmium, cryolite, fluorspar, graphite, iodine, platinum, titanium, toluol, and vanadium). The board noted that only in the case of five of the twenty vital metals was Mexico not considered an important producer (aluminum, iodine, nickel, platinum, and titanium). For all the other strategic and critical minerals, its supplies had a double importance. Mineral resources were already significant, and the report stated that, in most cases, the production could be dramatically increased since "Mexico's mineral resources are almost unexplored." In addition, immediate and secure transportation from primarily U.S.-owned mines in Mexico guaranteed the supply for the war effort.[13]

By World War II it was the nonferrous and nonprecious metals that commanded strategic attention. Although the mining industry employed no more than eighty thousand workers, it was a primary source of government revenue, estimated by sources within the mining industry to have contributed between 35 and 37 percent of the federal government's total income. ASARCO was the largest mining company in Mexico, and its ownership by the Guggenheim family assured diplomats that it was a safe source of supply.[14]

The main wartime agreement between the two countries was that of Suárez-Bateman in 1942, which was quickly followed by a plethora of others. In April 1942 an agreement on lead and zinc was signed between Finance Minister Eduardo Suárez and Alan M. Bateman of the Metals Reserve Corporation for the United States. Mexico gained a 25 percent price increase, to be taken as a tax, for those metals in return for selling all output to the United States. The base price of lead was to be 11 percent above the then current price.[15] This agreement created a precedent for other industries.

A major effort was made to increase wartime mineral production, and concomitantly the taxes also increased. ASARCO produced the following figures:

|  | *1940* | *1943* | *%∑* |
|---|---|---|---|
| Lead (metric tons) | 60,726 | 94,983 | +56.4 |
| Copper | 5,628 | 6,499 | +15.5 |
| Zinc | 56,750 | 101,499 | +64.9 |
| Taxes Paid | U.S.$19,171,500 | U.S.$55,983,306 | +192.0 |

The company managed to increase its output of these base metals so rapidly by acquiring nonworked mines: Xichú, Guanajuato; Taxco, Guerrero; La Bufa, San Luis Potosí; and Santa Eulalia, San Carlos, Plomosas, and Los Colorados in Chihuahua.[16]

## Agriculture

The reorganization of Mexican agriculture for war —from subsistence agriculture toward agribusiness production—was the next most important form of economic cooperation. The production of edible oils, hard fibers, and other items for the war effort created a dichotomy in the country's agriculture that many orthodox observers were to call, in quite misleading nomenclature, the traditional and the modern sectors. Surprising importance was attached to the production of a number of commodities that might be viewed as mundane. The Allies "regard sisal and binder twine (including henequen) as constituting one of the principal deficiencies" [for war production]. Planners thought that German agriculture might be crimped by strictly controlling the export of these fibers from Mexico, as well as British East Africa, the Netherlands East Indies, and the Portuguese colonies.[17]

Mexico agreed by 1943 to increase the land under cultivation by 3,300,000 acres to provide food and agricultural material for the war effort. This implied allocation of trucks, tractors, and support for irrigation projects. The most obvious target was the El Palmito Dam, which was already 90 percent completed.[18] The origin of that change came from wartime projects aimed at solving one or another shortage in agriculture.

With the Japanese moves into Southeast Asia, shortages of rubber took on a considerable wartime significance, as was demonstrated by the rationing of tires. Secretary of Agriculture Claude Wickard and Mexican Minister of Agriculture Marte Gómez announced a joint project to develop rubber plantations in Mexico to supply that needed substance. A 1,500-hectare plantation at El Palmar, Veracruz, was the first of many over the next eight years. Technical support of rubber production in Mexico was described by U.S. Department of Agriculture (USDA) experts who viewed the project as "highly encouraging."[19]

Another industry that suffered from shortages of raw materials was industrial oils. U.S. attempts to replace foreign drying seeds with flaxseed had partially failed, and recent antimarijuana legislation also undercut another source for drying power for oils. The military applications of oils made the problem serious. Castor seeds were used in the manufacture of hydraulic fluid for jacks and brakes in war machines as well as paint solvent, and rapeseed oil was used as a protective coating for airplane motors.

No substitute was then known for that purpose. The lauric acid in a group of oil-rich nuts was used to make explosives as well as plasticizers, and to reduce the brittleness in soap and synthetic rubber. Cashew-nut oil was used for toughening brake linings and for magneto harness coverings. Palm oil was indispensable for making tinplate, and some maritime engines used it as a lubricant. War planners discovered an old report on a unique variety of chia seed, a species of salvia that grew wild in Mexico. Agricultural experts viewed it as superior even to linseed or perilla oil. Estimates were that it could be profitably cultivated to solve the problem, so another project for Mexican agriculture was organized.[20]

Sugar was in short supply during the war. In 1942 the United States faced a 1,900,000-ton sugar deficit, of which Mexico promised to supply 25,000 tons, in spite of a domestic shortfall of its own. U.S. officials worked to block a deal between Pepsi-Cola Company and Azúcar S.A. to bottle syrup in Mexico for export to the United States. Officials viewed that deal, in effect, as a way of trying to divert sugar from the war effort. As in other areas, increased production in Mexico became a trade-off with the import of industrial equipment from the United States.

To support these projects the United States became involved in building dams in order to increase agricultural output. One was at El Palmito in the Laguna region. It had been started in 1937 but was intensively worked on since 1941 and represented a 25-million-dollar investment aimed at irrigating one hundred thousand acres and also generating thirty-five thousand kilovolts per year of electricity. The other was a project to irrigate sixty thousand hectares of land at El Azúcar, along the San Juan River in Veracruz. In addition, two irrigation projects in Padilla, Tamaulipas (five thousand hectares) and at Xicoténcatl, also in Tamaulipas (fifteen thousand hectares), were started after the outbreak of hostilities.[21] In each case, hydroelectric and irrigation equipment had to be allocated from war production.

In a number of other areas Mexico agreed to provide substantial production for the war effort. There was a contract (July 15, 1942) for all of the exportable surplus of alcohol, some six million gallons. Garbanzos, tomatoes, and tomato juice were purchased by the CCC. In the case of oranges and mangoes, the fruit fly created a problem.[22] The U.S. Army also developed an interest in Mexican *barbasco*, a group of plants whose roots produced rotenone, which served as an insecticide. The annual importation of several hundred thousand dollars' worth from the Far East had been cut off, and the military importance of insecticide was significant.[23]

At times, Mexico gained considerably less for wartime production than the market would have adjudged. It sold virtually its entire crop of henequen through the organization Henequeneros de Yucatán. Since henequen was in abundant supply before World War II, Mexico agreed to sell the entire exportable surplus at prices ranging from 8.5 to 9.125 cents per pound.

(The price had hit 19.5 cents during World War I but had fallen slightly above the contract level before the outbreak of World War II.) The United States agreed to purchase all the henequen that Mexico could supply in order "to produce maximum quantities of desperately needed fibre." As Lauchlin Currie, deputy administrator of the Foreign Economic Administration, wrote, "In fact, our problem has been to prevent buyers of other countries from bidding and obtaining some of the henequen at black market prices ranging from 50 percent to as much as 300 percent above our contract prices."[24]

An interesting perspective on the importance of this kind of contribution to the war effort is seen in Secretary of State Hull's answer to complaints from Representative Paul H. Maloney in 1944 that the United States was shipping scarce food to Mexico at the height of the war. He told him that Mexico's production of rubber, industrial alcohol, mahogany (for PT boats), sisal, and other hard fibers (for webbing and military equipment as well as binder twine) and contributions of manpower were all extremely important to the war effort, and therefore justified diversion of crops to that country, even under conditions of wartime rationing.[25]

## Railroads

Transportation was vital and controversial. Set against a backdrop of nationalization and workers' administration, no sector so inflamed ideological predispositions, apart from petroleum. The security of transportation made Mexico's minerals and agricultural products strategic. Therefore, from the earliest date the United States-Mexican Commission for Wartime Cooperation made support for Mexico's railroad system a high priority. War planners allocated rolling stock, parts, and repair machinery to sustain the system.[26]

A technical railroad mission was initiated at once, and it was exceedingly active in trying to keep the overburdened network running throughout the war. Oliver Stevens, of the Missouri Pacific Railroad, headed a group of over forty technical experts. The Mexican railways were headed by General Enrique Estrada, a man then in his dotage. The problem was that Avila Camacho credited Estrada with having saved his life in battle in Morelia in 1923. It took a while to move him out; however, eventually Stevens's mission strengthened the railroad system even though it was under great strain. In Messersmith's view, "I doubt if anything more constructive or helpful had been done at less cost and with more effect under the Point Four Program than what was done by the U.S. Railway Mission in Mexico during the period of the war."[27] In addition to the transport of strategic products for the war effort, the railroads were also of potential importance to the military effort.

## The Military

At the beginning of World War II, Mexico's military was small. The army consisted of seventy thousand men and sixty-five thousand trained reservists. In addition, there were another twenty thousand CTM unionists who had received military training by the army. The basic unit was a squad of nine men, eight of whom had Mauser-type *musquetón* rifles manufactured in the National Arms Factory in the Federal District. The ninth man had a light Mendoza machine gun, which had been designed by a Mexican inventor. Three squads comprised a platoon, and three platoons equaled a company.[28] Since both countries were facing a two-front war, the naval situation became central. In all of Latin America there were only 75 ships of war; by contrast, the United States had 392 ships. The Mexican Navy was minuscule, comprising only three gunboats, ten armored coast-guard vessels, several transport ships, and fourteen hundred men. The air force, however, had three hundred planes. After FDR had publicly mentioned Tampico as a possible location for an Axis invasion, the Mexican armed forces took on greater importance.[29]

On January 12, 1942, Mexico and the United States announced the formation of the Joint Mexican-United States Defense Commission. The U.S. members were Major General Stanley Dunbar Embick and Vice Admiral Alfred Wilkinson Johnson; for Mexico the members were Brigadier General Miguel S. González Cadena and Tomás Sánchez Hernández. The two presidents signed the military pact on February 27, 1942, and by the end of March, Lend-Lease programs were in place for Mexico.

There were fears of sabotage by the population of German descent and the possibility of a raid on the Panama Canal.[30] Defense planners also were concerned about the vulnerable naval base and aircraft factories in San Diego; therefore, they wanted to build airfields and a military road in Baja California. Accordingly, Vice Admiral Johnson agreed with General Cárdenas and General John DeWitt that airfields be set up at Ensenada, La Ventura, and San Antonio del Mar with advanced airdromes at Rosario and Magdalena Bay. These bases would allow U.S. combat aircraft to extend their range in order to protect San Diego and Ensenada. To finance the construction of the military road between Ensenada and La Paz, Warren Lee Pierson, head of the Export-Import Bank, went to Mexico to evaluate the projects. Although Sumner Welles and Castillo Nájera eventually dropped the idea after the Japanese Navy was defeated at Midway in June, the EXIMBANK took up other projects.[31]

Mexico entered into the spirit of wartime preparation to a significant degree. After the declaration of war, the Avila Camacho administration created a Supreme Council of National Defense and the government initiated a civilian-military training system. There was a promulgation of obligatory military service, and local councils of civilian defense were established;

men between ages eighteen and forty-five were registered, paraded, and drilled.[32] In Mexico City, there were blackouts in anticipation of enemy air raids, although it was never explained where any enemy aircraft likely to attack the country would be based. Finally, the U.S. Army enthusiastically cooperated in forming a completely mechanized division of the Mexican Army. Even at less strategic levels, the spirit of wartime cooperation prevailed. The chief of police of the Federal District, General Ramón Jimenez Delgado, was able to send policemen to the FBI training school in the United States.[33]

The government staged a rally in support of the war effort on September 15, 1942, that included all six living former presidents of Mexico (Lázaro Cárdenas, Plutarco Elías Calles, Abelardo Rodríguez, Adolfo de la Huerta, Pascual Ortíz Rubio, and Emilio Portes Gil). It was no mean feat to get Cárdenas and Calles on the same platform. Such was the power of patriotism in time of war. In addition to these symbols, there also were some significant matters of substance that began to change.

President Avila Camacho found that wartime exigencies enabled him to streamline the command of the army, and he used the situation to retire more than three hundred generals.[34] Near the end of the war, his desire for direct military participation reached a sense of urgency. Indeed, Messersmith in his memoirs recalled, "There was a good deal of sentiment privately among some of the high officials of the government, as well as some of the military men such as General Rodríguez, that there should be active participation by Mexico at the front."[35] However, public opinion in Mexico was far from being ready to tolerate direct participation.[36] Moreover, in the view of U.S. officers, the language barrier proved too great an obstacle to the integration of forces in the field, although Mexican officers were given English lessons in case the situation changed. General George C. Marshall did not favor Mexican contingents participating in the war; however, General Henry "Hap" Arnold thought that the idea was "feasible and desirable."[37]

Avila Camacho urged Roosevelt to intervene with General Arnold, head of the Army Air Corps, to ensure that a Mexican air squadron would in fact be used in the Pacific theater. Avila Camacho wanted that involvement as Mexico's minimum military participation.[38] By March 5, 1944, major air maneuvers were held in Mexico City, followed by a speech by the president at the Casino Militar two days later. A public relations campaign climaxed with the announcement that there was one unit participating in the war directly.[39]

Mexico's 201st Air Squadron, armed and equipped through a Lend-Lease program, was eventually sent to the Philippines, where it took part in the final moments of the war in 1945. There was a parade and a big celebration when the 201st returned at the end of the war; a *corrido* (popular song) commemorated the event. Of course, direct military participation was not Mexico's main contribution to World War II.[40] As Ambassador Messersmith

explained, "In the military field we must not press them too much, for they have an internal problem still to deal with. In the political and economic field I think they are prepared to cooperate to the limit, and the more rapidly we develop the economic cooperation, the more easy we make it for the Mexican Government to cooperate in other fields."[41] By the end of the war, U.S. officials thought that the country had come a long way. As General Marshall said, after reviewing Mexico's forces, "it is a first class army and they carry themselves like a real army."[42]

## U.S. Recruitment of Mexicans

The Selective Service Act required all males in the United States between eighteen and forty-five to register for the draft; as we know, Mexico passed a similar measure after declaring war on the Axis powers. In the Federal District alone, some 120,000 men reported to various locations for weekly military drills. These measures generated support for the war effort. It was in September 1942, for the first time, that British Chargé d'Affaires C. H. Bateman first reported to his government that there was beginning to be evidence of popular support rather than apathy.[43]

One of Mexico's most striking concessions to the war effort was the decision to allow the United States to draft Mexican residents in its country to serve in its armed forces. The Avila Camacho administration signed an agreement, on Christmas Eve, 1942, allowing the conscription of Mexicans in the United States to proceed. The Mexican consulates in San Antonio and Chicago immediately implemented that agreement.[44] Mexico allowed its citizens who were living abroad to be drafted without reciprocal rights applying to U.S. citizens living south of the border; the United States was even allowed to set up recruiting stations throughout Mexico.[45] Estimates have suggested that as many as 250,000 Mexicans, and possibly another million Chicanos, served in the U.S. armed forces during World War II.[46]

The U.S. Army agreed to send a monthly list of the draftees' names to Mexico City and gave a general reassurance that Mexicans would be treated equally in the army.[47] In fact, Mexicans who served during World War II had a difficult time. They were frequently forbidden to speak in Spanish, and the combination of dealing simultaneously with military discipline and a foreign culture was formidable. Charges of discrimination, problems associated with migratory documents, payments to relatives, and questions related to benefits, insurance, and pensions kept the Mexican consulates in the United States busy.[48] However, it must be added that many Mexicans saw participation in the U.S. armed forces as a positive alternative to be pursued, for ideological reasons or economic opportunity. For many, the private's pay of thirty-seven dollars per month was attractive, and even doctors, nurses, engineers, and veterinarians tried to join the war effort.

Mexican officials were keen to receive news of their nationals who served with distinction.[49]

This infringement of sovereignty attracted a certain degree of resentment, much of which was directed at Foreign Minister Ezequiel Padilla, the statesman most closely associated with the policy of cooperation with the United States. Two articles in *Hoy* in November 1942 criticized the Mexican government's compliance with U.S. conscription policies. In a lead editorial, "Not With But Under," probably written by Nemesio García Naranjo, and an article by the historian and journalist José C. Valadés entitled "Mexican Resentment," the attacks were especially critical, asserting that Padilla's policies were obsequious.[50] It was difficult to understand the politics behind the attacks over U.S. conscription of Mexicans in the magazines *Hoy*, *La Nación*, and *Así*, since those publications were partially controlled by Manuel Suárez, an entrepreneur close to the president and Maximino Avila Camacho, the minister of transportation and communications who fancied himself a candidate for the 1946 party nomination. The Catholic Right had never forgiven Padilla for his former role as prosecutor of the assassin of Alvaro Obregón. These articles simply may have tapped a deep resentment against conscription of Mexicans by a foreign power as well as bitterness over U.S. racist attitudes toward Mexicans.

## Reorganization of the Military

In striking contrast to the modest direct military contribution that Mexico made to the Allies in World War II, the impact of wartime cooperation on the country's army was massive. Before the war, the officer corps was, to a significant degree, radical and supportive of the Cárdenas wing of the governing party. The army was open in its defense of the revolution, and officers even collaborated in the training of the workers' militia. By any conceivable measure, the Mexican Army was the most radical military force in Latin America during the 1930s.

Through the process of wartime cooperation with the U.S. military there was an important shift away from that politicized stance. The code words were "modernization" and "professionalization," which meant not depoliticization but merely the diminution of radical positions within the army. By the end of the war Ambassador Messersmith could scarcely contain his enthusiasm. A plan in 1945 for modernization was put forth: "It means that the Mexican Army is to be reorganized on completely modern lines and it means that the organization will follow in a very large extent the organization of our own Army, Navy and Air Force."[51]

Moreover, planning for the United Nations, in the early stages, included a military force, and the Avila Camacho administration had given every indication that it supported that plan. The United States used the argument

that if Mexico were to be part of that force it would have to organize its military along U.S. lines: "The plan is that the Mexican Army shall be organized along the same lines as our own, with the thought that in this Hemisphere or elsewhere, when Mexican forces will be operating under a mandate of the United Nations, they will be operating principally with our armed forces."[52]

It was a subtle process by which Washington made modern arms available to the Mexican military and urged them to develop in a manner similar to the U.S. Army—here the compatibility of communications equipment was important in shifting the Mexican Army into the U.S. mold—and above all to remove much of the political content from their internal operations. It is extremely interesting to note that the U.S. ambassador viewed President Avila Camacho and former President Cárdenas as both moving in the same direction in supporting these military initiatives. This provides further evidence of Cárdenas's retreat from earlier radical stances. Conservative publications such as *Excélsior* ran an ongoing campaign lambasting the army for being overstaffed at the level of generals and colonels, which probably was true but which also had the effect of increasing pressure on the army. That newspaper, for example, estimated that only 7 percent of its three thousand officers had any real military training or experience by 1945.[53]

## Labor Shortages and the Braceros

There were wartime agreements, from August 1942, that brought Mexican agricultural workers—braceros—to the United States. (War had shifted conditions from the unemployment of the 1930s to a labor shortage in the 1940s.) The idea was to bring Mexican workers to the United States to free its own farm laborers for military service. Although the total numbers of braceros varied at any given time, since there were annual and seasonal variations, the Immigration and Naturalization Service authorized 30,000 Mexicans to work in 1941, and that number grew each year of the war, reaching a maximum of about 75,000 in 1944, for a total of about 220,000 workers.[54] Of course, many more Mexicans simply crossed the border and found work outside of the formal agreement. U.S. growers preferred the unofficial workers, since they objected to the thirty-cents-per-hour wage negotiated between the two governments.

The importance of this Mexican labor grew over the years and raised issues of racism, discrimination, the rights of undocumented or precariously documented workers, and the treatment of Mexicans and Chicanos in the United States. Poor Mexicans continued to go north in the hope of earning enough to buy a plot of land or help their families upon their return; for that goal, racism and miserable conditions were tolerated. Incidents of racism against Mexicans abounded, such as the Sleepy Lagoon case (1942), the Zoot-Suit Riots (1943), or the beating of Sergeant Macario García, winner

of the Congressional Medal of Honor, outside a café in Richmond, California. From 1943 to 1947 the Mexican government withdrew braceros from Texas in protest over similar incidents.[55] Even some highly placed Mexican politicians had experienced discrimination. Ramón Beteta, in spite of being married to an American woman, harbored deep resentment over racist treatment while he was a student at the University of Texas, a view his wife shared. Even well-intended Anglos in the Southwest instructed their children that it was more polite to call these people Spanish-Americans rather than Mexicans.

It is important to remember that, even after the war, it was U.S. officials who most wanted the program to continue. Indeed, U.S. diplomats took quite seriously threats from the Mexican left to blow the whistle on mistreatment of these workers and thus place the program in jeopardy.[56] There also was a program that brought some sixty-seven thousand semi-skilled workers into the United States to alleviate labor shortages in railroad construction caused by the war. Mexican railroad crews were used to free U.S. railway workers for service in the military. That program generated a long conflict between the Mexican government and the Railroad Retirement Board over the Mexicans' obligatory contributions to the retirement fund. Few, if any, of the Mexican workers were allowed to stay on after the war and eventually claim a railroad pension. Millions of dollars were at stake, and Mexican diplomats faced an impossible task after the war in trying to claim those funds.

To sum up, Mexico's initial commitment to the Allied cause carried with it an internal logic as generated by the war effort. Matters of high strategy demanded cooperation on the economic, military, transportation, and manpower fronts. The depth of commitment to the war effort in both countries created an irresistible political strength of purpose. Beyond that, the forms of wartime cooperation were molded by specific interests.

## Anti-Axis Efforts: The Blacklist

The United States expected Mexico to join its endeavor to reduce the power and influence of Axis citizens in its economic, political, and covert arenas. On July 17, 1941, Washington had issued a blacklist of eighteen hundred individuals and firms who were seen to be acting in the interests of Germany, Japan, or Italy. The sympathetic nations in the Western Hemisphere were expected to coordinate their efforts against people and companies included on the list. On August 22, Mexico broke off economic relations with Germany, and the two countries closed their respective consulates.

Real concern about Axis agents operating in Mexico was manifested in responsible circles. For example, Eduardo Villaseñor, president of the Banco de México, tapped financial intelligence and reported to the president on

the likely targets of Axis agents operating in the country.[57] In March 1940 the Cárdenas administration closed down the pro-Nazi newspaper *Diario de la Guerra*.[58] By early 1941 the pro-German tabloid *Ultimas Noticias* had switched its line to mildly pro-Ally. Advertising and government pressures combined to effect the change, which required placing editor Miguel Odorica on extended leave.

In the months after the declaration of war individual citizens and descendants of citizens of the Axis countries were targeted. In August at Nueva Rosita, Coahuila, seventy German, Italian, and Japanese families were removed from the area. Mazatlán was thought to be vulnerable to the sabotage of shipping, so another twenty-six aliens were forced to leave the city. The establishment of internment camps did not proceed as far as it did in California; however, many individuals were caught in these initiatives. Still, there was scarcely an inquisitional spirit in the land. The rector of UNAM, Rodolfo Brito Foucher, continued to feel free to make speeches in September, in which he upheld Germany as a model for Mexico to follow. He saw his own country as a province of the Hispanic world, which was to be dominated by Francisco Franco's Falangist model in Spain.[59]

U.S. agents pressured Mexico to act against individuals on the blacklist, but their efforts met with only mixed results. As Ambassador Messersmith related, "It became necessary to isolate or confine or deport Germans, Japs, and Italians." President Avila Camacho was willing to cooperate, but U.S. officials were frustrated by the attitude and inaction of the Ministry of the Interior. Messersmith continued: "Our people collaborated very closely with the Mexican authorities in giving information concerning dangerous enemy aliens. Usually when we gave such information, the man was picked up and sent to prison or detention camp, or other appropriate measures were taken. To our consternation from time to time some of the most dangerous of these aliens, usually Germans, were soon at liberty again. The orders for liberation came from *Gobernación*. The general impression was, and I think it was well founded, that these people bought their way out."[60]

Ambassador Messersmith harbored few illusions about the responsibility for this situation. In his view, Miguel Alemán had little interest in foreign affairs and was motivated by his prewar connections with a number of important German businessmen: "I should not like to think that he profited financially and I do not know that he did but we cannot forget that informed people think that he did and at least they hold him responsible, for he was the responsible head of the Ministry."[61] Alemán also had a mistress, Hilda Krüger, who was a German actress, and it worried U.S. intelligence agents that she was working for the Abwehr.

The most authoritative study of the German intelligence networks in Mexico demonstrates that the early sale of petroleum to Germany produced a climate in which that country's intelligence agents gained a measure of

toleration. Mexico was reluctant to close down the two dozen agents operating in the country. Staffing a listening post, top Axis agents such as Friedrich Karl von Schleebrugge and Karl Rüge lived opulent life-styles and maintained a high profile. Information from U.S. publications, some shipping schedules, and a few documents of value appear to have been collected before the U.S. counterintelligence effort, under FBI agent Gus T. Jones, successfully infiltrated the German network. Teresa Quintanilla, the sister of diplomat Luis Quintanilla, eventually became the most valuable source of Allied information on the Germans after Nazi agent Georg Nicolaus ended an eight-month affair with her in April 1941. Even after those developments the Avila Camacho administration did not expel the known Axis agents until July 30, 1946.[62]

There was the question of the disposition of confiscated Axis properties, some 346 of which had been seized at the start of the war and placed under the control of the Junta de Administración y Vigilancia de la Propiedad Extranjera. President Avila Camacho wanted to hold those assets as compensation for claims against Germany for sinking Mexican ships and other acts. Pressure on Luis Cabrera, as the head of the Board for Seized Axis Properties, for the return of confiscated properties to the German owners "comes from *Gobernación* and I am informed through a very reliable source, from Alemán himself."[63] Eventually, of these properties, which earned an average 16.55 percent profit per annum during the war, 59 were divested of their owners, 38 were sold, and 249 were controlled by the junta led by Cabrera.[64] Avila Camacho followed the U.S. lead and froze assets belonging not only to Axis citizens but also to continental firms in countries under German occupation.

The seizure of blacklisted properties and businesses expanded to include the question of shares in Mexican firms held in conquered Europe. In June 1943 the National City Bank of New York applied to the U.S. Treasury, on behalf of Mexican clients, to purchase 500,000 Swiss francs to buy back securities held in Switzerland. The Treasury turned down the application, after consulting British diplomats who wanted to link Mexico's request to its debt negotiations with the United Kingdom.

On June 2 entrepreneur Luis de Iturbe applied through Eduardo Suárez, the minister of finance, and Thomas H. Lockett, economic counselor of the U.S. embassy in Mexico City, to buy securities in the brewery Cervecería Moctezuma that were held in Europe. Suárez and Eduardo Villaseñor argued that it was not the government but a private investor who wanted to buy the Swiss francs. In the formal U.S. response the Treasury required that the Swiss Bankers' Association provide an affidavit to the effect that the shares had been held by the present owners since April 8, 1940 (to demonstrate that the Nazis were not using the ploy to finance their war effort by means of the sale of these securities), and to prove that no individual on the blacklist would benefit.

In the U.S. ambassador's private note to Secretary of State Hull, however, it is clear that the obstacles placed in the way of the purchase of shares were linked to the Mexican position on a series of controversial policies of which the United States disapproved: adopting price controls; overcoming the position of economic nationalism argued by Villaseñor in his speech of April 6, 1943; and opening access to Mexico for U.S. investors.[65]

Apart from internment and direct seizure of Axis properties, other approaches were used to combat the influence of the Axis powers in Mexico. In its attempt to build opposition to the Nazis within the traditional conservative factions, the visit of Bishop (later Cardinal) John O'Hara of New York was viewed by some diplomats as being important. As Spruille Braden explained, his visit "will go a long way towards eliminating recriminations for the Panama incident [an understated reference to Theodore Roosevelt's seizure of the Canal Zone] and our old 'imperialism' especially in Church and conservative circles."[66] The Mexican government was therefore mobilized against the Axis powers on a number of fronts. Pressure was applied to bring Mexico's security forces into the war effort, and the seizure of Axis assets put some valuable property up for grabs.

## A Sensitive Entry

One man on the blacklist proved to be an embarrassment to the two governments. A number of groups had formed to fill the economic vacuum left by the petroleum expropriation. Former New York State Senator John A. Hastings promoted a series of projects in association with Frank A. Fageol, whose Wall Street firm, Houston and Jolles, Industrial Engineers and Accountants, claimed to have spent some 65,000 dollars working on a "Mexican program." William O'Neill of General Tires in Akron, Ohio, and George Creel of San Francisco and John R. O'Connor of Mexico City, who had been associated with Standard Oil interests, were also involved in the project. Press reports stated that the group had as much as 100 million dollars to invest in Mexico. U.S. diplomats, however, did not view the group as legitimate. They denied that these figures commanded any such sum of capital. J. Edgar Hoover had kept a large file on Hastings since the senator had represented Brooklyn from 1922 to 1932. That career came to an end when he was exposed as a "fixer" for Tammany Hall, collecting protection money for the local political machine.

In Mexico City, Hastings met General and Governor (of Puebla) Maximino Avila Camacho (the president's brother) in 1940–41. A degree of notoriety emerged at one point when the senator and the general argued publicly over a 20,000-peso bill at the Hotel Reforma. As Hoover's report related, "The sum was used by Hastings in entertaining officers of the Mexican Presidential Staff and other Mexicans in influential circles."[67] The plot thickened in November 1941 when the senator introduced Maximino to

Swedish businessman Axel Wenner Gren to help finance Siderurgia Veracruzana, a plan to make steel from the iron ore deposits in Las Vegas, Veracruz. J. Paul Getty, the oilman, also was included in the project. A close friend of General Juan Andreu Almazán, he had many interests in Mexico. As the FBI reported, "Getty has been interested in many business promotion schemes in Mexico and is known to have associated with Hilda Krüger, a suspected Nazi agent and associate of several known Nazi agents in Mexico."[68] Not only was Senator Hastings close to several Axis agents and businessmen, but he also was supported by Father Charles E. Coughlin and his National Union for Justice, which was frequently viewed as a form of native fascism in the United States.

When Wenner Gren was placed on the blacklist as an agent of German interests, it threatened the Hastings-Maximino partnership. For the Mexican president's brother to be so involved created a sensitive situation. It was even more shocking when General Maximino, by then in the cabinet, spoke out in support of Wenner Gren in the hope of convincing U.S. authorities to remove him from the blacklist.[69] The Hastings group was only one element in the business community that saw opportunity in Mexico's contribution to the war effort.

## To Buy without Selling

The U.S. government became deeply involved in the management of the Mexican economy. In 1945 alone the economic section of the embassy in Mexico City produced 132 volumes of studies and correspondence relating to practical problems of Mexico's wartime economy, plus two additional volumes on the problems of the railroads. This formed an unprecedented level of awareness and intervention in the affairs of a neighboring state. Unlike earlier military interventions that generated deep patriotic opposition, this indirect and almost invisible intervention, in the name of the war effort, commanded broad support from most segments of the political spectrum within Mexico.

With the political will in place, the country changed its political agenda, reorganized its military, and dedicated its economic life to the requirements of the Allied cause. Some benefits flowed immediately to Mexico, including an increase in business activity, a highly favorable settlement of the outstanding debt with the United States, and access to modern industrial knowledge. Nevertheless, an unusual problem emerged. Since the United States purchased enormous quantities of raw materials for the war effort and its economy was tightly controlled to channel all possible production into that endeavor, the question of how the nation would pay for its imports became central. It was at this point that leaders had to find political alternatives for what would have been normal purchases in peacetime.

Warren Lee Pierson, president of the Export-Import Bank, accepted an invitation to visit Mexico in August 1943 to study various project proposals that would absorb that country's growing dollar reserves. Plans at that stage were for the completion of the Kansas City and Orient Railway, construction of a dam and irrigation system on the Fuerte River, and adapting a natural harbor at Topolobampo as a terminal for the railway. Mexico anticipated that the United States might find these projects of mutual interest, and later on the EXIMBANK might continue to finance them; in any case, Pierson's visit might help Mexican projects move up on the list of wartime priorities.

Mexico had settled its conflict with the United States over the petroleum expropriation on November 19, 1941, shortly before Pearl Harbor. The fortuitous timing of that settlement opened the way for a 1941 agreement on road projects, such as the Export-Import Bank's purchase of 10 million dollars' worth of Mexican road bonds at 3.6 percent, a price considerably below prevailing market rates, in order to improve transportation between the two countries.[70] By January 1942 three additional projects were being funded: 91 million dollars were to be spent on the Pan American highway bonds; 13.5 million dollars purchased railroad bonds, with further financing forthcoming on the electrical industry (10.5 million); and irrigation projects (67 million) to support agricultural production for the war effort.

At the same time, another solution began to emerge. Presidents Roosevelt and Avila Camacho agreed to form a Mexican-American Commission for Economic Cooperation to address the problem of remuneration for sales of raw materials to the United States. Some indication of the importance given to the project can be seen from the choice of individuals to represent their respective countries in economic negotiations. Secretary Hull's first preference to head the U.S. committee was Eric A. Johnston, president of the U.S. Chamber of Commerce and president of the United States Inter-American Development Commission. However, Johnston was unavailable because of commitments outside Washington. Therefore, Hull recommended Thomas B. McCabe, who had been acting Lend-Lease administrator, and who was the chairman of the Federal Reserve Bank of Philadelphia and formerly the president of Scott Paper Company.[71]

Revealing deep divisions between the business community and the New Dealers during the Roosevelt administration, McCabe was unwilling to serve on this committee since the president was committed to Harry Dexter White, assistant to the secretary of the treasury, as the other U.S. representative.[72] On May 19, 1943, the president announced the appointment of Wayne Chatfield Taylor, the undersecretary of commerce, and White as the U.S. representatives to the committee. By the end of the war, Will Clayton also had joined the committee.

The question of who was to speak for Mexico was central to the administration's grand strategy of using wartime cooperation with the United

States to achieve its historic goal of industrialization. President Avila Camacho chose an old school friend, a mining engineer and director of Cities Service Oil Company in Mexico, Valentín R. Garfías, as a member of the committee. The president had used him once before to study the Mexican takeover of the German chemical and drug companies as Mexico entered World War II. In that instance, Garfías recommended that the government enter into a contract with American Cyanamid Company, a proposal that was accepted and became a controversial issue of the day.[73]

Avila Camacho selected Evaristo Araiza, general manager of the Monterrey Steel Works (Compañía Fundidora de Fierro y Acero de Monterrey S.A.), as Mexico's other representative to identify the most important projects in the nation's interest. Araiza served as the link between the Monterrey Group and the U.S. steel giant ARMCO International Corporation. The Monterrey Group's support for the president in the 1940 election was paying rich dividends. Not since the *porfiriato* had the powerful Monterrey capitalists had their men in such a central economic position at the national level. As a result of the campaign Araiza became an ever-closer economic adviser to the president.

Initially, former president and industrialist Abelardo Rodríguez headed the Consejo de Coordinación y Fomento de la Producción, an ad hoc governmental group set up to coordinate and stimulate wartime measures to aid industrialization. The president's private secretary, Primo Villa Michel, was installed as the head of the Comité Coordinador de las Importaciones. On April 1, 1943, he also took over Rodríguez's committee when the latter resigned to run for the governorship of Sonora.

Abelardo Rodríguez was an important figure on the right wing of the PRM, and he emerged as perhaps the best example of the revolutionary industrialist. He was director of the Altos Hornos S.A. steel project, although he claimed in a conversation with U.S. diplomats that he was "not instrumental in the promotion of the project."[74] Rodríguez may have been far too modest in this assertion, for many contacts were made that eventually channeled Mexico's claims on U.S. industry into projects in which he had a stake, such as the improvement of the open hearth, the rolling mill, and the refractory brick plant for the Compañía Fundidora de Fierro y Acero de Monterrey. Such links were not diminished as Garfías and Araiza took over the representation of their country from Rodríguez.

In Mexico, the press reaction to the projects of the Joint Mexican-American Commission for Economic Cooperation was quite favorable. All newspapers in Mexico City enthusiastically reported the approved projects as they were released on July 18, 1943. *La Prensa* and *Excélsior* treated the announcements of the projects as a refutation of charges of economic imperialism, and the latter newspaper interpreted the development as a demonstration that Villaseñor's approach was incorrect. *Novedades* saw great opportunity and nothing adverse in the proposals. *El Popular* focused upon

the development as recognition of Mexico's contribution to the war effort.[75] Interestingly, the annexes to the study, which discussed the participation of U.S. firms in the many projects, were not released.[76] Even on the left, most people chose to interpret these developments as Mexico thwarting the U.S. desire to prevent the country from industrializing, rather than U.S. firms gaining reentry to Mexico with support from both governments. Mexican officials found great satisfaction in being able to call upon high U.S. officials to convince recalcitrant functionaries to support their projects.[77] The wartime euphoria could be sensed, even at UNAM, when on September 20, U.S. Attorney General Francis Biddle addressed a large and enthusiastic audience, saying that "Mexico must be developed for the Mexicans."[78]

As a result of these pressures, a plan emerged to institute a system of industrial barters to absorb growing dollar balances in the Banco de México even though Messersmith held firm to the U.S. position that no more matériel could be shipped to Mexico, due to the exigencies of wartime production. In addition, he was opposed to a revaluation of the Mexican peso since the cost of wartime production would increase, and it also would establish a precedent for all countries in Latin America. President Avila Camacho was indelibly committed to complete wartime cooperation.

By September 1943 the Mexican-American Industrial Subcommission held its first meetings in Washington in "the highest spirit of cordiality and earnestness," in the phrase of the U.S. record. Mexico's spokesman, Villa Michel, urged that the role of the commission be broadened and the name changed to the Mexican-American Commission for Economic Cooperation so that it could deal with all economic matters, and it was thus known for the remainder of the war. The idea was for this committee of industry experts to access the various projects that Mexico would support in order to make wartime allocations of machinery and equipment. Immediately the subcommission designed forms, to be issued by the U.S. embassy in Mexico City, for proposals.[79] The commission would be vital in speeding the clearance of Mexican requests to purchase matériel from the United States. By this time, Villa Michel (chairman of the commission) and Evaristo Araiza (Monterrey Group) were the Mexican commissioners, assisted by Armando C. Amador, Fernando J. Rosenbleuth, G. A. Rohen y Galvez, Federico Bach, Mario Javier Hoyo, Gonzalo Robles, and Josué Sáenz (son of Aarón Sáenz). The U.S. commissioners were Wayne C. Taylor, Nelson Rockefeller (vice president of the commission), and Thomas H. Lockett (of the U.S. embassy in Mexico City).[80]

The commission assessed Mexican requests to purchase U.S. machinery and equipment. Generally, Mexican proposals, such as a plan to buy three thousand tractors to increase the products of agribusiness for the war effort, were pruned back considerably. Given that the impact of inflation was straining the alliance between the two countries, something had to be done. Suárez suggested that if unused manufacturing plants in the United

States could be transferred to Mexico, that might relieve pressures. Messersmith promised that a U.S. planning expert on the unused plants would soon visit Mexico and pursue the idea further.[81] Since Villaseñor's speech criticizing the U.S. war effort was delivered a few days after the Suárez-Messersmith conversation, a sense of urgency grew, especially within U.S. circles.

By 1943 it was clear that Mexico was receiving far less in the way of industrial development than had been initially promised. In every case when the wartime planners in Washington looked at the possibility of tying Mexico directly into industrial war production, they found that it would not work. At one time or another, projects existed for the production of munitions, machine guns, ships, and other items in support of the war effort; in every case they were dropped for practical reasons. As the U.S. ambassador explained in a letter opposing further Board of Economic Warfare involvement in postwar industrial planning for Mexico, "One of our principal occupations these days is to explain to the Mexican Government, in Washington and here, why we cannot do some things in the way of industrial development—unfortunately some of which were promised to Padilla and others in conversations in Washington."[82]

## Industrial Barter

Mexico was exporting at such a rate that, even after having reduced the external foreign debt, the country continued to accumulate over 20 million dollars per month in 1942–43. Since all exports were subject to wartime regulations, a variety of industrial barter plans emerged. The idea was to search the United States for factories that were standing idle as a result of wartime planning decisions. These factories would be dismantled and shipped to Mexico as payment for the minerals and agricultural products. It was at this point that the composition of the U.S.-Mexican committees of cooperation became vital, since their members would decide who in Mexico would be rewarded for sacrifices in support of the war effort.

One such project was established when the Cervecería La Laguna S.A. spotted a used brewery that stood idle in Pennsylvania and wanted to install it in Torreón, Coahuila. The brewery was estimated to have been worth slightly more than 250,000 dollars, and the company was able to acquire the plant for 10 percent down. The key to the project was the transportation necessary to move it to Mexico.[83] Or again, in October 1944, the War Production Board (WPB) approved the shipment of a secondhand tin-can plant for the Grey International Corporation in the State of Mexico. Since the latter planned to form a Mexican corporation to run the factory, it would qualify on the Mexican list. Similarly, the Atoyac Textile Mill received equipment under this plan.[84]

In some cases the use of wartime surplus equipment represented profound intervention in the Mexican socioeconomic scene. Anderson, Clayton,
and Company, the world's largest cotton brokerage firm and the personal
property of Undersecretary of State Will Clayton, was able to use an application for electrical generating equipment for the Comisión Federal de
Electricidad (CFE) in the Laguna to continue to tie the ejidal producers to
cotton rather than to the other crops that the farmers wanted to grow.[85]

In the petroleum industry this program inadvertently created an opening for foreign capital. Harold Ickes, head of the Petroleum Administration
for the War (PAW), was no friend of the oil companies, but he sent out a
mission to survey petroleum reserves that might be needed for the war effort. Under C. Stribling Snodgrass, head of the PAW's Foreign Operations
Division, the industry spotted an opening. The Degolyer mission, as it was
known, was staffed by dollar-a-year men close to the industry (John McCone
of Bechtel, Ralph Davies of Socal, James T. Duce of Texas Oil, and Earle E.
Garde of Union Oil). The mission arrived in Mexico City in August 1942.
Ambassador Messersmith immediately put it in contact with decision makers and organized a study of the state of the Mexican oil fields, a report that
he sent to both Cordell Hull and Steve Bechtel, the latter setting up a dummy
corporation—Compañía Petrolera La Nacional S.A.—run by a single lawyer who operated out of the Shoreham Hotel in Washington. The United
States granted 20,800,000 dollars for Bechtel to build a new refinery and
pipeline, and Snodgrass shifted out of PAW to represent Bechtel interests in
Washington. This was the first penetration of U.S. corporations into the
domestic side of the Mexican petroleum industry since the expropriation.[86]

Other U.S. corporations also found the war helpful. Sosa Texcoco S.A.
had applied for conversion equipment for the manufacture of soda ash and
caustic soda. The firm was a subsidiary of American Cyanamid, but its interests were rejected by the Chemical Branch of the WPB. In this instance,
G. I. Seybold of American Cyanamid successfully appealed the ruling.[87]
Juan A. Meana, representing the Compañía Mexicana de Malta S.A. of Baja
California, applied to export a used brewery from Akron, Ohio. The Office
of Economic Warfare approved the plan.[88] Furthermore, ARMCO, in its association with Nacional Financiera and the Altos Hornos steel mill at
Monclova, Coahuila, arranged for the purchase of a used forty-four-inch
cold mill. This used equipment was found in Detroit.[89] Still, the number of
cases where factories could be shipped directly to Mexico was limited.

## The Wartime Projects

In early 1942, Sumner Welles reacted to a series of ad hoc proposals by Foreign Minister Padilla by suggesting that an overall survey of
the requirements of Mexican industry was needed so that the United States,
in return for economic cooperation, could commit itself to a broad plan to

aid Mexican industrialization. That suggestion touched heartfelt sentiments in Mexico. However, the proposal stated that there should be a combined presentation to Donald Nelson, head of the WPB, and to the Board of Economic Warfare and the Army and Navy Munitions Board. Each project should have a letter stating its importance to the war effort.

At that time the most important industrial project was the construction of the joint Mexican-ARMCO integrated steel mill at Monclova. Although primarily built with secondhand equipment, the mill represented an allocation of two million dollars' worth of new equipment. Wartime planners thought that the project represented a "direct interference with the steel expansion program of this country [the United States]."

Other undertakings that had been proposed by the Mexican government or by entrepreneurs with the support of that government were the Atenquique Industrial Development project, which was opposed on the criterion of the war effort; the 350,000-dollar expansion of the San Rafael paper mill, which was designed to stimulate the output of kraft paper in Mexico; a 500,000-dollar proposal by the Reynolds Metal Company of Richmond, Virginia, to build a metal foil plant; and a proposal by Anderson, Clayton, and Company to construct a vegetable oil-hydrogenating plant at a cost of 650,000 dollars. Amitas Limited of New York had proposed the expansion of the existing Nonoalco thermoelectric plant of Mexico Light and Power in Mexico City. The Celanese Corporation of America wanted to build a rayon plant. Proposals existed to renovate the Tehuantepc Railroad, the ports at Salina Cruz and Coatzacoalcos, and new dry docks at Salina Cruz, Coatzacoalcos, and Manzanillo. The growth of truck transportation, the increased use of the automobile, and military defense projects combined to create pressure for road construction projects, especially the Pan American highway. Soon demand also grew for tires, tubes, parts factories, and road maintenance equipment. At that point the WPB's priorities were, in order of their importance, the ARMCO steel mill, reconstruction of the Tehuantepec Railroad, port rehabilitation, construction of a basic acids plant, dry docks, rehabilitation of the national railways, expansion of the Mexican Light and Power plant, and the Pan American highway.[90]

Little by little the two countries realized that new structures would be required to deal with this unusual problem. Avila Camacho initially approached the Roosevelt administration on a project-by-project basis, such as pressuring the WPB to grant export licenses for eight hundred thousand dollars' worth of new equipment for the Altos Hornos steel mill.

A rayon factory, built by the Celanese Corporation of America, was also high on the Mexican shopping list, as well as the construction of shipyards, requiring the export of 3 million dollars' worth of used machinery and 1 million dollars' worth of new equipment. As Eduardo Suárez and Espinosa de los Monteros negotiated Mexico's position at the height of its historic bargaining power, Suárez commented to U.S. officials how "tremendously

pleased" he was over his reception in financial circles in New York and how much that had changed in the year after October 1941.[91]

The U.S. response to specific Mexican requests to spend their funds was frequently slow to develop. Virtually all purchases required a governmental decision, slowly made by war planners who had little interest in Mexico. In some cases, racist attitudes emerged. Only at the highest level of the U.S. government was there recognition of the strategic importance of Mexican exports. Frequently, these planners concluded that the war effort would not be served by such a sale, as when the WPB agreed to study the project to establish shipyards and the rayon plant proposal from the Celanese Corporation of America; in both cases the decision was negative. In the first case, war planners in the Iron and Steel Branch of the WPB concluded that Mexico did not have the infrastructure to build ships. In the second, the WPB took the position on the basis that 1941 machinery allocations to Productores de Artisela S.A. in Mexico City had already produced 1.5 million pounds of rayon per year, which was, by 1942, 44 percent of Latin America's production.[92] The United States was telling Mexico how it could spend its money. Some Mexican officials resented this situation; however, rather than stopping exports, the Avila Camacho administration urged the United States to find mechanisms by which the long-term goal of industrialization could be accelerated.

The Mexican-American Commission for Economic Cooperation formed subcommittees in six areas (agricultural development, transportation, industry, public works, tourism, and fisheries) and initially approved sixteen projects that would aid Mexico's goal of industrialization and also help the war effort. By the time of the final approval by President Roosevelt of the various projects, Salvador Ugarte, president of the Banco de Comercio S.A., had joined the Mexican delegation.[93] In each case, it was required that U.S. authorities allocate plants, equipment, and machinery to these projects.[94] U.S. staff members went to Mexico and were housed in nothing less than the Edificio Imperial in Mexico City.

These projects formed a major part of the benefits that "Mexico" received for its wartime cooperation. If one examines these projects, not from a perspective of the industry but with an eye to the politics of favoritism, an interesting pattern emerges. Overwhelmingly, foreign firms and well-connected Mexican corporations reaped the harvest of wartime spending. A pattern of crony capitalism became a prominent characteristic of the war effort.

BANAMEX proposed an alkaline salt recovery and soil reclamation plant at Lake Texcoco. The Mexican government's plan was to drain twenty thousand hectares of alkali land in the Valley of Mexico, use the salts, and return the land to agriculture. The centrifugal pumps and their corresponding power plants were quite expensive (2.6 million dollars). The firm Productos Químicos de San Cristóbal, chartered and financed by

BANAMEX, would run the project. The U.S. authorities were initially cool in their support of this undertaking, not being able to see any wartime purpose to it; however, the close links between the Legorreta family and the government saved the project.

The Monterrey Group and its U.S. partners did well from the wartime cooperation. The steel industry would be developed by an ARMCO International expansion project, supported by Nacional Financiera, for Altos Hornos de México S.A. A new blast furnace and spare parts were allocated for the Compañía Fundidora de Fierro y Acero de Monterrey S.A., and the development of coking coal by the Monterrey Group's subsidiary, Carbonífera Unidad de Palau S.A. Support was planned for: the casting projects of Hierro Fundido de México, a new enterprise, and Hierro Maleable de México, the expansion of an existing enterprise; a Bessemer converter plant for Hojalata y Lámina S.A., to be used to produce tinplate and other light-gauge metals; a project for an industrial machine shop by Fábrica de Máquinas S.A.; and smaller projects to aid knife and machete manufacturers, the Mendoza Machine Gun Company, hardware and motor manufacturers, specialized forgings, and consumers' durables. Other key areas also received special treatment.

Chemicals, sugar, and alcohol required additional equipment worth about 4 million dollars per year to increase output since all exportable surplus was sold by the Unión Nacional de Productores de Azúcar to the Defense Supplies Corporation. Another ten proposals in the areas of textiles, electricity, rubber, and cement were submitted. A fine cotton yarn mill for full-fashion hosiery in Guadalajara was seen as a substitute for silk and lost English yarns; the 600,000-dollar proposal was from Jesús Rivero Quijano. Since the war obviously interrupted the production of fine yarns, the committee supported the project.

Paper imports for newsprint had been supplied by Sweden before the war; however, since the outbreak of hostilities they came from Canada and Texas. Mexico was importing about forty thousand tons per year at a cost of about 10 million pesos. To produce this bleached paper required Fourdrinier machines; the raw materials needed were primarily wood pulp and sodium sulphite. Politically the manufacture of newsprint was highly sensitive. Thus, a plan emerged to use wood from the valleys of Toluca, Ixtlahuaca, and Zitácuaro, which were near Mexico City, to make paper. The government established the Compañía Productora e Importadora de Papel S.A.—the predecessor of PIPSA—and financed it through NAFISA to move into the paper industry by building a plant costing about 3.5 million dollars. This was a wartime measure that was to have a profound impact on the government's ability to control the media to the present day. Kraft paper, corrugated paper, and packing drums had formerly been imported by Cartón Titan S.A. The war's interruption of the flow of that material resulted in a proposal for Fibro-Tambor S.A. and the Monterrey Group to build a cellulose

manufacturing plant to make those products as well as air mail and cigarette paper.

Aarón Sáenz, in addition to being a PRM caudillo and a close collaborator of the Monterrey Group, was head of the Banco Internacional and
director of the Sugar Producers' Association. He also found time to head
the Asociación Mexicana de Turismo, a post that Miguel Alemán would
hold for many years after the end of his presidency in 1952.[95] Influential
figures such as Sáenz were able to place pet projects on the Mexican list.
Many of the early tourist promotion investments date from this time.

There was an ironic battle between the Mexican government and the
U.S. Federal Power Commission over exporting natural gas to Monterrey
from Texas, since, according to the knowledge of Mexican resources of the
day, the region was thought to be energy-poor. Carlos Prieto, president of
the Compañía Fundidora de Fierro y Acero de Monterrey, and Evaristo
Araiza, the general manager, had pressed hard for that energy to be sent via
the newly opened Reynosa pipeline. Not until the end of the war did Mexico
achieve that goal of importing U.S. natural gas.[96]

Many of the most significant projects of wartime cooperation were to
be run by U.S. firms operating in Mexico. Examples included the ASARCO
proposal to recover three hundred thousand tons of guano on a series of
small islands from the coast of Baja California in the Gulf of California as
far south as Acapulco. That project required shipping, radio equipment, steel
cables, copper, and railroad cars. About six thousand tons of the guano, or
ammonium sulphate, were used annually in Mexico—half of it was produced in that country by the Compañía Carbonífera de Sabinas S.A., a subsidiary of ASARCO, and the other half had been imported from Germany.
The fertilizer was appropriate for sugarcane, and therefore the project was
justified on the grounds that the United States was buying alcohol for the
war effort. The firm also proposed to build two plants: one of twenty tons in
Mexico City; and a slightly smaller facility in Aguascalientes, at a cost of
100,000 dollars. And the Celanese Corporation of America, through its subsidiary Celanese Mexicana, proposed a 2,750,000-dollar project to produce
acetate yarn, which implied the allocation of large amounts of iron, steel,
stainless steel, and copper from war production.

A number of plans were intended to improve Mexico's wartime infrastructure. In line with its role as an agricultural producer for the war effort,
4.6 million dollars' worth of farm machinery were allotted. Most important, the plan called for the wartime support of irrigation to bring two million acres of new land into production in the Pacific Northwest by 1946,
although the Mexican government wanted three million new acres. Irrigation equipment alone was proposed for 4.1 million dollars to support that
effort. Public works projects were also proposed: 8 million dollars were
allocated for equipment for seven power stations around the country, and
there was a plan for a second unit in the Ixtapantongo plant in the Federal

District, as well as for projects in Torreón, Veracruz, Jalisco, and Nuevo León. These facilities were located in states that were targeted for tourism development and were either under construction or soon to be initiated. Another 50 million dollars were projected for long-term electrification.

Mexico City still suffered from inadequate drainage, as had been the case since the Spanish destroyed the Aztec drainage system in a fit of religious excess during the Conquest. The Valley of Mexico was drained of rainfall and sewage by the Gran Canal del Desagüe, which extended some forty-seven kilometers until it entered a tunnel at the town of Tequixquiac. That tunnel, ten kilometers in length, had been constructed in 1900, the top part with bricks and the bottom carved out of quarry rock. The action of acids and gases had caused deterioration of the covering material to the point where a collapse was a possibility. That would be catastrophic since Mexico City is located in a basin. Photographs from the *porfiriato*, which showed the annual floods up to the second story in the Zócalo area, served as a reminder of the danger of a collapse in the Tequixquiac Tunnel.

In 1939 a new tunnel was started, planned to be 11.3 kilometers long and parallel to the existing one. However, the new location was so close to Lake Zumpango that three of the ten shafts were already flooded. Modern pumping equipment, hoists, and winches, therefore, became extremely important for the Maya Construction Company, the contractor of the project. The Mexican Light and Power Company had run two new power lines from its Nonoalco Substation in Mexico City to the site. In addition, equipment was desperately needed for repair work on the Gran Canal del Desagüe and for additional storage dams to contain the effluence.[97] This project was included in the Mexican list.

Wartime cooperation allowed long-standing issues to be addressed: a 1933 treaty between the two countries over what was called the "rectification" of the Río Bravo/Río Grande River and another plan to control the Santa Catarina River at Monterrey. Flood control projects emerged for the San Francisco River in Puebla, in Nogales, Veracruz, and along the Suchiate River dividing Mexico from Guatemala. Even ventures supporting tourism were suggested, although it was realized that tourist development would have to wait until after the war, and powerful politicians were already attracted to the area.[98] In short, this was a period of extraordinary economic cooperation between the two countries; there was scarcely an area of industrial activity that was not touched by the U.S. commitment to support the industrialization of Mexico. Having said that, it is important to recognize that some projects were special.

Pineapple was a fruit in high demand, the supply of which had been cut dramatically by the diversion of wartime shipping. However, it was scarcely a strategic product. Still, in order to prepare the Mexican pineapples for export, tin sheets were allocated in which to pack them, and after the war a Point Four program continued the effort. The fact that the technical aid

program centered on plantations in Veracruz that were owned by Miguel Alemán expedited its implementation.

The idea of shipping underutilized U.S. factories to Mexico attracted a lot of attention; however, the approach was proceeding slower than had been expected. The Mexican media were starting to complain, so a quid pro quo emerged in which Messersmith agreed with Avila Camacho on several plans that would have top priority. The projects were quite different from those recommended by the technical experts on the various subcommittees working for the U.S.-Mexican Committee on Economic Cooperation. Vested interests established the highest priorities.

A number of specific projects were deemed to be of importance to the war effort. Both governments took the projects seriously, and an integration of efforts emerged that would last long after the fear of war had passed. It was the United States that was courting Mexico. When Foreign Minister Ezequiel Padilla and Assistant Secretary of the Economy Ramón Beteta visited Washington in April 1942, they were given preferential treatment. The striking nature of that welcome contrasts notably to the numerous internal government reports that had tagged Beteta as a dangerous radical.

While in Washington in 1942, Beteta urged the economic warfare authorities to approve the plans for industrial development at Atenquique, near the Federal District. The project called for a hydroelectric plant, powered by two hydraulic turbo-generators, and a chemical pulp mill for manufacturing paper products. The State Department was reluctant to approve it because of the industrial equipment that would have to be shipped to Mexico. Secretary Hull thought that the progress that had already been made on the steel mill at Altos Hornos should be enough to satisfy the Mexicans. In addition, the chartering of all nine Mexican tankers, the progress of the railroad mission, and the maintenance of the petroleum industry, including the 100-octane refining plant, were proceeding on schedule. Hull further noted that the United States was supplying highway-building equipment according to the assessment of priorities by the Joint Mexican-United States Defense Commission. Therefore, U.S. planners gave the Atenquique undertaking a low priority, although they agreed that it would be a useful peacetime project. Beteta's argument was that it was necessary "for political reasons." Hull objected that it was a private Mexican project rather than a government one, that enough power plants were already being allocated for Mexico City, and that the operation had no military importance.[99] Messersmith responded by noting that power shortages were restricting mining exports; however, he counseled delay in making the decision.[100] In a more candid letter to Laurence Duggan, the U.S. ambassador noted that, in addition to the president's general interest in industrial development, several important people close to the latter were interested in the venture, including the Compañía Financiera Industrial y de Comercio Exterior and the banker, Espinosa de los Monteros, in particular.[101] Eventually, the WPB cut

the size of the Atenquique project in half and eliminated chlorine and soda production. In spite of Interior Secretary Ickes's open support of the high-octane plant, the State Department opposed it.

An entrepreneur named Sullivan offered Mexico eight cents per gallon above the BEW price for alcohol, so pressure on the U.S. price for sugar was strong. Department officials claimed that the United States was buying the alcohol as a "sop to Mexico and Cuba." However, the USDA, the OPA, and the BEW all had different views of the prospective sale of Mexican sugar to Pepsi-Cola.[102] The technical aspects of quality, source of supply, and terms of the purchase all intermingled with attempts by speculators to corner supplies. The sugar matter was, as ever, complicated. Pepsi-Cola wanted to purchase from twenty thousand to fifty thousand tons of sugar for the next few years, an announcement that enabled Mexico to plan for extra production. In 1941, Mexico had spent 8 million pesos rehabilitating the sugar industry and had turned the situation around; from a deficit of sixty thousand tons in 1940 it had an exportable surplus of twenty-five thousand tons in 1941. The agreement to purchase several million gallons of Mexican industrial alcohol meant that, in effect, the Pepsi-Cola Company purchased virtually all of Mexico's exportable surplus in the form of sugar syrup. That great corporation was able to purchase sugar through the price quotas more cheaply than the market price.

As always, politics entered into the picture. As Duggan put it when discussing the export of Mack trucks into Mexico, "A relative of the President by the name of O'Farrill was mentioned in connection with the truck situation."[103] In fact, the United States had allocated 1,581 light trucks to all of Latin America, of which 287 went to Mexico in the first quarter of 1942. In April, Mexico received 11 percent of the Latin American allocation of medium trucks. However, those proposals were not approved by the WPB. Similarly, a proposal for 573 heavy trucks was rejected. Rómulo O'Farrill's request for 54 Mack trucks on the border plus an additional 200 new trucks was also rejected.[104] Later, other requests were approved.

By July the Atenquique industrial project had been pending for three months. The problem was that it implied the diversion of considerable quantities of copper, zinc, steel, nickel, and electrical equipment from the war effort. The chief of the Power Branch of the WPB said that unless the political reasons for moving forward with the project were compelling, it could not proceed. As originally presented on January 19, 1942, the plan consisted of a small hydroelectric plant, a pulp and paper mill, a caustic soda plant, and a chlorine plant, the total cost of which was about 1.7 million dollars.

Enrique Anisz, promoter of the enterprise, was told informally in March that the amounts of material required for the project were excessive, so he presented a revised estimate of only 1.2 million dollars. Unfortunately 3,218 tons of steel were still needed for the project; thus, the WPB was still against

it. Sumner Welles then addressed a letter to Donald Nelson indicating that the project was a high political priority; the letter was shown to the head of the Power Branch, who stated that Welles's support was still not explicit enough to override the normal wartime criteria.

After discussions with Duggan in May, it was decided that the Atenquique project would go ahead "in the event that something happened to eliminate the ARMCO steel mill, now known as 'Altos Hornos de Mexico,' " since that mill had been experiencing great difficulties. Meanwhile, on June 8, the U.S. embassy presented a new plan aimed at trying to help the project's chances by reducing the amount of imported and regulated material required by eliminating the caustic soda and chlorine plants and by installing only one of the two hydroelectric turbo-generators originally suggested. That proposal reduced the import requirements to 900,000 dollars. Given the estimate that Altos Hornos could be completed by an expenditure of only 600,000 dollars, the case for Atenquique seemed weak, and indeed that was the technical recommendation of Henry E. Allen in July.[105]

## The Top Political Priority: Valsequillo

At the very top of the Avila Camacho administration's list was the Valsequillo project, to build a dam across the Atoyac River at the Balcón del Diablo canyon. The water would then be sent through a tunnel to irrigation projects in Puebla, with the hope of eventually irrigating one hundred thousand acres. The president, the foreign minister, the minister of agriculture, and the secretary of the treasury all had "continuously shown their deepest interest in the progress and the uninterrupted construction of the Valsequillo dam."[106] Samuel R. Rosoff's construction company, Constructora Rosoff S.A., was building the project at a cost of about 45 million pesos, and the close relationship between Alemán and Rosoff played a role. Not wanting Secretary Hull to miss the point, Lockett and Messersmith stressed that "it cannot be too strongly emphasized . . . that . . . the Mexican government are *vitally interested, both politically and economically,* in seeing the construction work on the Valsequillo tunnel continue without interruption. These officials are the ones that cooperated so very closely with Ambassador Messersmith and our Government during the very darkest days of the present war and, in fact, by fomenting and enlarging the economic and political support of the United States, they assumed a great responsibility by taking measures in collaboration with us which were far in advance of the thinking of the great mass of the Mexican public."[107]

The Valsequillo project promised to irrigate some one hundred thousand acres in the valley of Puebla, including the estates of top politicians, especially the president's. Something of the priority that it received may be

seen from the fact that the United States sent John A. Savage, chief of the Office of Projects of the U.S. Bureau of Reclamation, to oversee the technical problems encountered in building the Mirador Tunnel, even at the height of World War II.[108]

Here was a classic case where the wartime cooperation shifted priorities in several ways. By increasing the production of corn and wheat, planners hoped to help offset the country's deficit of two hundred thousand tons of corn in the second half of 1944; at the same time the Valsequillo project would create a resource to stimulate regional development in Puebla and also irrigate the lands of generals and politicians. Thus, the rating of the Valsequillo plan was raised from nonessential to essential for the war effort, and Rosoff was able to import irrigation and heavy construction equipment. But however helpful the project would be for major landowners in the state of Puebla, the cost of wartime cooperation with the United States would fall more heavily on other Mexicans.

# Notes

1. Dean Acheson spoke to the nation on NBC radio on November 21, 1941, and Adolf Berle was on NBC on November 28, preparing the country for war.

2. George Messersmith to Laurence Duggan, March 11, 1942, USNA/RG 59, 812.50/263.

3. Stiller, *George S. Messersmith*, 70–95. Stiller concludes that relatively few of Ambassador Messersmith's long memoranda actually reached the president.

4. Messersmith claimed that if it were left to Henry Wallace and the BEW, the staff would have grown to 2,000 or 3,000. GSM Papers, Memoirs, vol II, no. 11.

5. State Department economic planner Laurence Duggan once commented that Messersmith was such a keen correspondent that a note for him was a small pamphlet. "If he were encouraged to write notes to be passed on to the President we would probably receive one in every mail." Duggan to Raynor, October 16, 1943, USNA/RG 59, 812.5018/72A.

6. Franklin D. Roosevelt to Messersmith, November 26, 1942, GSM Papers.

7. Roosevelt to Justice Frank Murphy, November 26, 1941, Roosevelt Library, PPF 1662.

8. Messersmith rather arrogantly lectured Harry Truman in their first meeting after FDR's death. Truman, thereafter, dropped FDR's idea of naming Messersmith as the chief administrator of conquered Europe. GSM Papers, Memoirs, vol. II, no. 11.

9. Messersmith to Adolf Berle, October 10, 1945, GSM Papers.

10. Board of Economic Warfare, *Confidential Report on the Mexican Economy*, 7.

11. Allan Dawson to Duggan, June 10, 1941, USNA/RG 59, 812.6511/40.5.

12. Stabilization agreement, August 6, 1941, USNA/RG 59, 812.5151/315.

13. "Strictly Confidential Report on the Mexican Mining Industry," USNA/RG 59, 812.00/12-2944.

14. Messersmith to Duggan, June 30, 1944, USNA/RG 59, 812.5045/6-3044.

15. C. H. Bateman to the Foreign Office, April 30, 1942, PRO, FO/371, 30582.

16. Messersmith to Joseph F. McGurk, memorandum of conversation with J. R. Woodul, manager of ASARCO in Mexico, July 27, 1944, USNA/RG 59, 812.5045/7-2744.

17. Thorold to secretary of state, May 22, 1941, USNA/RG 59, 812.61326/8-1444.

18. Unpublished annex to the published report to FDR from the U.S.-Mexican Commission for Economic Cooperation, July 12, 1943, USNA/RG 59, 812.50/402.

19. Report on Mexican agriculture from the USDA to the State Department, May 6, 1942, USNA/RG 59, 812.61/141.

20. Walton to Duggan, "Chia seed importation from Mexico," July 2, 1937, USNA/RG 59, 812.61/83.

21. Memorandum, May 6, 1942, USNA/RG 59, 812.61/138.

22. H. W. Parisius to Courtney C. Brown, June 12, 1944, USNA/RG 59, 812.60/6-2144.

23. "Complementary Crops—Mexico," January 24, 1941, USNA/RG 59, 812.61/115.

24. Lauchlin Currie to Gathings, July 14, 1944, USNA/RG 59, 812.61322/10-244.

25. Hull to Paul H. Maloney, March 27, 1944, USNA/RG 59, 812.5018/123B.

26. Commission for Economic Cooperation to Roosevelt, July 12, 1943, USNA/RG 59, 812.50/402.

27. GSM Papers, Memoirs, vol. II, no. 15.

28. Board of Economic Warfare, *The Mexican Economy*, 9.

29. Report from the Mexican naval attaché in Washington, July 29, 1940, SRE, 39-10-2 (IV).

30. "Cooperación entre México y los EEUU en Defensa del Hemisferio," July 19, 1940, SRE, 39-10-2 (IV).

31. Alfred Wilkinson Johnson to Hull, August 12, 1943, USNA/RG 59, 812.50/399.

32. One U.S. diplomat commented that "the introduction of civilian military training has perhaps done more to arouse patriotic sentiments towards the war effort than any other single measure or event." "Review of the Mexican Political Situation," September 25, 1942, USNA/RG 59, 812.00/32056.

33. U.S. embassy to SRE, December 26, 1944, SRE, III-1707-3.

34. Messersmith thought that the number was "between 300 and 400 generals." GSM Papers, Memoirs, vol. IV, no. 15.

35. Ibid.

36. As he put it, "a good part of the population is still apathetic with regard to the war." Messersmith to Hull, May 6, 1942, GSM Papers.

37. Messersmith to Duggan, February 17, 1944, GSM Papers.

38. Messersmith to Roosevelt, January 8, 1945, USNA/RG 59, 812.002/1-1845.

39. Messersmith to Duggan, March 9, 1944, GSM Papers.

40. *El Nacional,* November 19, 1945.

41. Messersmith to Roosevelt, January 8, 1945, USNA/RG 59, 812.002/1-1854.

42. GSM Papers, Memoirs, vol. III, no. 18.

43. Bateman to the Foreign Office, September 28, 1942, PRO, FO/371, 30571.

44. Francisco Castillo Nájera to Ezequiel Padilla, December 25, 1942, SRE, 39-10-27.

45. *Diario Oficial,* November 23, 1942.

46. Zorilla, *Historia de las relaciones,* 2:488.

47. Castillo Nájera to Padilla, December 30, 1942, SRE, 39-10-27.

48. The petitions from Mexican soldiers to consulate officials may be found in SRE, III-777-1, III-778-1, and III-779-1 to 6.

49. Many such petitions can be found in SRE, III-901-6. The United Kingdom's propaganda group even issued press releases featuring Mexicans joining the Allied war effort. SRE, III-905-3.

50. *Hoy*, November 7, 1942.

51. Messersmith to John Willard Carrigan, July 10, 1945, USNA/RG 59, 812.61/193.

52. Ibid.

53. *Excélsior*, July 12, 1945.

54. Zorilla, *Historia de las relaciones*, 2:492.

55. Acuña, *Occupied America*, 254–63.

56. USNA/RG 59, 812.00B/4-1646.

57. Eduardo Villaseñor to Avila Camacho, June 13, 1941, AGN, RP/MAC, 606.3/8.

58. *Excélsior*, March 30, 1940.

59. Ibid., September 13, 1942.

60. Messersmith to Nelson Rockefeller, April 27, 1945, USNA/RG 59, 812.00/4-2745.

61. Ibid.

62. Rout and Bratzel, *The Shadow War,* 58–96.

63. Ibid.; Messersmith to secretary of state, February 14, 1944, USNA/RG 59, 812.50/536.

64. Economic Report, July 14, 1946, USNA/RG 59, 812.50/7-2446.

65. Messersmith to Hull, July 9, 1943, USNA/RG 59, 812.51/2691.

66. Spruille Braden to Berle, January 13, 1941, Columbia University Manuscript Collection, Braden Manuscripts.

67. Hoover to Berle, February 23, 1942, USNA/RG 59, 812.50/253.

68. Ibid.

69. Hull to director of the Board of Economic Warfare, October 12, 1942, USNA/RG 59, 812.50/309A.

70. *El Nacional*, September 1, 1942.

71. Hull to Roosevelt, May 15, 1943, USNA/RG 59, 812.61/193.

72. Duggan to Sumner Welles, May 17, 1943, USNA/RG 59, 812.50/328.

73. "Biographies of the Mexican Members of the U.S.-Mexican Committee of Wartime Co-operation," May 18, 1943, USNA/RG 59, 812.50/343.

74. Edward S. Maney to secretary of state, April 5, 1943, USNA/RG 59, 812.50/315.

75. *Excélsior*, *Novedades*, *La Prensa,* and *El Popular*, July 19, 1943.

76. "Report on Press Reaction on the Report of the Joint U.S.-Mexican Economic Commission," July 20, 1943, USNA/RG 59, 812.50/3658.

77 Hull to Crowley, September 3, 1943, USNA/RG 59, 812.50/397A.

78. *El Nacional*, September 21, 1943.

79. The forms have been preserved and can be found in USNA/RG 59, 812.50/416.

80. Thomas Lockett to secretary of state, "Mexican-American Industrial Commission," September 24, 1943, USNA/RG 59, 812.50/406.

81. Messersmith to secretary of state, April 14, 1943, USNA/RG 59, 812.51/2678.

82. Messersmith to Philip W. Bonsal, March 9, 1943, USNA/RG 59, 812.60/3-943.

83. Bray to secretary of state, July 15, 1944, USNA/RG 59, 812.50/7-1544.

84. State Department to the War Production Board, October 21, 1944, USNA/RG 59, 812.50/8-2244.

85. CFE's power application of September 11, 1944, USNA/RG 59, 812.50/9-1144.

86. McCartney, *The Bechtel Story*, 119–21.

87. Department of State memorandum, December 14, 1944, USNA/RG 59, 812.50/9-1144.

88. Memorandum from the Office of Economic Warfare to U.S. embassy in Mexico City, October 9, 1943, USNA/RG 59, 812.50/418A.

89. Effland to Emilio Collado, October 21, 1943, USNA/RG 59, 812.50/419-3/6.

90. Henry E. Allen to Collado, Duggan, and Acheson, May 2, 1942, USNA/RG 59, 812.50/287.

91. Memorandum of conversation between Castillo Nájera, Eduardo Suárez, Antonio Espinosa de los Monteros, and Welles, October 19, 1942, USNA/RG 59, 812.50/308.

92. Ibid.

93. Record of the Third Meeting of the Mexican-American Industrial Commission, October 25, 1943, USNA/RG 59, 812.50/423.

94. Lockett to secretary of state, July 13, 1943, USNA/RG 59, 812.50/347.

95. Report of the Mexican-American Commission for Economic Cooperation, May 21 to June 3, 1943, ibid.

96. Espinosa de los Monteros to J. Jesús González Gallo, July 2, 1946, AGN, RP/MAC, 527/180.

97. Report on Tequixquiac Tunnel, October 23, 1943, USNA/RG 59, 812.50/422 .

98. Annex of report to FDR from the Mexican-American Commission for Economic Cooperation, July 12, 1943, USNA/RG 59, 812.50/402.

99. Hull to Messersmith, July 17, 1942, USNA/RG 59, 812.50/277A.

100. Messersmith to Hull, August 8, 1942, USNA/RG 59, 812.50/281.

101. Messersmith to Duggan, August 10, 1942, ibid.

102. W. N. Walmsey to Duggan, June 26, 1942, USNA/RG 59, 812.50/285.

103. Duggan to George E. Winters, June 24, 1942, USNA/RG 59, 812.50/284. After the war the O'Farrills became a major business family in Mexico, operating in motor vehicle distributing, hotels, and the media.

104. Allen to Winters, June 26, 1942, USNA/RG 59, 812.50/285.

105. Allen to Winters and Duggan, July 1, 1942, ibid.

106. Lockett to secretary of state, June 9, 1944, USNA/RG 59, 812.6113/199.

107. Ibid. (emphasis mine).

108. Messersmith to the State Department, June 29, 1942, USNA/RG 59, 812.61A/4.

# 5

# The Impact of War

> Rapid rises in living costs have created actual hunger
> in the lower wage brackets, and hunger sometimes
> entails political implications.
> —*Harold D. Finley, first secretary of the U.S. embassy,*
> *Mexico City, 1943*

To the generation engaged in the horrors of war, the importance
of the battle seemed self-evident. Victory was held out as being of inesti-
mable value, and defeat was to be avoided at all costs. Leaders gained a
sense of purpose in roles that would otherwise be denied them, and no sacrifice was too great. As countless families contributed loved ones to the
projects of war, the pain of personal sacrifice merged inexorably with the
justification for the war. So it was reasonable for the generation that had
experienced the Great War to be concerned primarily with the course of the
battle and the causes of conflict. Yet with the passing of years the results
seem less certain, and the unexpected side effects seem to loom large.[1]

Even though Mexico was only marginally involved in the military aspects of World War II, that country tied a significant share of its economic
output to the war effort. Some of the resulting changes were fairly obvious.
An impressive increase in production took place as demand, for once,
outran supply—a highly unusual phenomenon in the West in the twentieth
century, Jean-Baptiste Say's law (supply creates its own demand) and
supply-siders notwithstanding. The control over production in the United
States during that period meant that Mexico was not paid in the normal way
for its raw materials and goods. Indeed, the very use of the nation-state as
the central analytical category is problematical, since much of the output
that was noted as Mexican was, in fact, in the hands of U.S. corporations,
acquired through intracompany purchases and intended for the war effort
anyway.

Innovative forms of payment emerged, given the central reality that
Mexico could only purchase products from the United States with the approval and support of the various wartime regulatory agencies. In addition,
the items for which approval was forthcoming were intended to augment
the war production effort. Large corporations—frequently American—entered into a complex pattern of bargaining. The corporation first decided

upon the imports it required; it then approached the Mexican government to have its purchases included in the latter's official purchase order. The Mexican list went to the U.S. embassy for coordination and approval, and it was then forwarded to the appropriate regulatory agency in the United States. At each stage, perceptions of wartime needs were supposed to have served as the criteria for the acceptance or rejection of a request for purchase.

The complex authorization process by which Mexico made purchases during the war led to several important consequences. The high demand was obviously a great stimulus to the country's production; however, it also placed great strain upon a relatively static productive system. At the same time that great profits were generated on the Mexican side (profits that could not be freely spent overseas), the war boom also inadvertently raised fundamental questions about the relationship between the subsistence and the export sectors, as well as about the prospects for postwar production. In short, a great deal of economic action was generated and financed by the war effort. However, it was not all a happy land of busy multipliers at work. Problems associated with allocation meant that production in areas linked to the war effort often hurt traditional regions, classes, and sectors. Areas that were not associated with wartime production tended to be sacrificed for other sectors judged by the war planners to have been more important.

Wartime production was anything but neutral. Income inequalities have always existed in Mexico, but they increased and changed markedly during the war boom. Perhaps even more important was the fact that nonrenewable resources were allotted in ways that proved to be enduring. Powerful firms established themselves, as had been the case in other countries as the rise of monopoly capital accompanied the Second Industrial Revolution, but they were possibly even more dependent upon political favors in Mexico than elsewhere. Yet before one can go very far in examining the impact of the war upon Mexico, it is necessary to reflect upon the kind of evidence and assumptions that most comments on this topic have been based.

## A Note on Official Statistics

Most students of Mexican development have turned to the government's statistical data to try to understand that period. Yet several problems emerge from the official statistics of the era. It is unclear how valid the data were for the period, that is to say, the degree to which figures actually measure that which they purport to measure, because categories and techniques of reporting frequently were fairly arbitrary and unclear. Moreover, there are two additional areas that create serious problems for the historian of Mexico in the 1940s.

Statistical methodology of the period was not yet clearly established in the 1940s. The U.S. national income accounting system was only beginning

to be implemented in Mexico. In Mexican statistics the categories of reporting changed, often from year to year. That, of course, magnifies a fundamental problem of historical statistics by making it difficult to obtain complete and comparable data so that one can make comparisons over time. After working on the data from Mexico in the 1940s, one has the feeling that the authorities in charge of statistical reporting must have achieved job satisfaction by means of constant methodological innovations.

While constantly changing statistical categories are frustrating, it should be noted that these changes also generate somewhat unusual opportunities. National income statistics for the period were not yet subject to such a narrow line of thought as would be the case after the U.S. method of defining progress was accepted (see Chapter 1). There were categories of reporting during the period that offer insights that were subsequently lost, such as foreign ownership of land, resources, and factories. While trying to avoid some of the obvious problems of changing categories of reporting, this analysis also endeavors to take advantage of the opportunities offered by what are—by today's standards—sometimes imaginative national income accounting procedures.

A second problem area in evaluating the impact of the war upon Mexico is that the categories of reporting, and subsequent analysis, are frequently so broad and so poorly related to the society of the day that one wonders what, if anything, the data of the period were measuring. More profoundly, there is great naiveté in assuming that even the best historical statistics can create an adequate level of understanding of complex phenomena. One must use official data critically in conjunction with other evidence.

Delving into the admittedly sparse historical literature on the economy of the period, one finds that different authorities render strikingly contrasting judgments even on the most seemingly verifiable questions of fact. Traditional views, most of which are overall assessments of Mexico's economic life, treat the 1940s as a period in which the essential preconditions were established for rapid industrialization. As World War II ended, Mexico City's Office of Economic Barometers issued an analysis of the impact of that war. Among the more important changes noted were a fundamental transformation of the structure of foreign trade, including a relative shift away from mining and metallurgical exports toward animal, vegetable, and manufactured exports, and a reduction in imports accompanied by a strengthening of the national currency. Capital inflows were accompanied by a repatriation of Mexican capital from the United States (to avoid wartime regulations). Increased wartime economic activity caused rises in the general price level, the nominal wage level, and production; however, real wages fell for most Mexican workers. In the early years of the war Mexico was caught in an unprecedented situation that generated forced savings and rapid capital accumulation, as a result of the increased demand generated by the war effort and the redistributive effect of a wage freeze in the face of rapid

price advances. Toward the end of the war, imports increased in proportion to exports, although it was only by late 1944 that mineral exports dropped.[2]

The question of living standards for the vast majority of Mexicans requires exploration. Suffice it to say that official data and the authorities who have examined the matter disagree. Governmental data have been traditionally viewed as conceding that real wages fell for the average Mexican. Some authors, however, argue the opposite case. James Wilkie, for instance, in his prize-winning volume, devised a "poverty index" and concluded that Mexican workers actually saw their living standards increase during the war.[3]

Some students of contemporary Mexico have looked at this period with a Rostow-like view, identifying preconditions that would eventually lead to the rapid industrial push after World War II. However, it has been treated quite differently by economists such as Clark Reynolds and Leopoldo Solís. Reynolds sees the period of the war as a major stage in the growth of industrial progress, while Solís perceives it as a period of relatively slow industrial development by contrast to that of the postwar boom.[4]

It is not always possible to transport the most seemingly obvious contemporary categories of national income accounting to Mexico without generating considerable misunderstanding. Part of the reason behind the striking discrepancies that exist on matters such as the standard of living during the war reflects problems with the data. However, more serious problems emerge

**Figure 1.  Value of Agricultural Production (1929=100)**

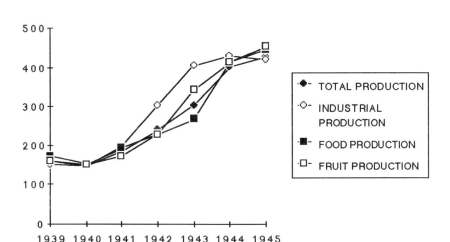

from the attempt to use categories that may seem clear to us today but, upon closer examination, are inappropriate to the Mexican reality of the 1940s.

## Agriculture and the War

Agriculture may seem to be a clear-enough category of analysis, and it is tempting to use governmental figures without serious doubt or reflection. Total figures on agricultural output have usually served as the basis for comments on rural progress during the war years, and toward this end the government released two sets of data on agriculture, one a report on the value of agricultural production (see Figure 1) and the other on its volume (see Figure 2).[5]

These price data give the reader the impression that agricultural production was booming and that there was prosperity throughout the Mexican countryside, at least by the standards of the day. It is also tempting to base a positive assessment of rural conditions on these figures, yet nothing could be further from the truth. If one looks at the actual amounts produced, a somewhat different picture emerges.

Figure 2. Volume of Agricultural Production (1929=100)

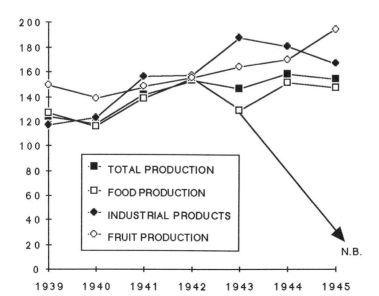

It is apparent that the physical output of agricultural products shows a different pattern from the price figures. The overall average for agricultural production reflects a significant increase across the years of World War II; however, this is an extreme case in which averages hide more than they reveal. The reader will notice that production fell dramatically in 1943, while production of what the government called industrial commodities increased markedly. There is a fascinating story behind these charts, one that raw data or economic indicators alone would never allow the student of Mexican history to penetrate. Indeed, these simple graphs thrust us into the heart of the wartime cooperation between the two countries because the United States had developed a clear idea as to what it wanted from Mexico during the war.

The story of Mexican agriculture during World War II might be said to have started with the formal inauguration of Manuel Avila Camacho in December 1940. Franklin Roosevelt had sent Henry Wallace, the vice president, as his personal representative to the ceremony. Given Wallace's origins in Iowa and his long involvement in rural issues (his family published the newspaper *Wallace's Farmer* in Des Moines), it was natural that discussions turned to rural matters with the new Mexican president and Marte Gómez, his minister of agriculture. Platitudes about agricultural cooperation appear to have been exchanged, and there was a general expression of the intention to share technical information.

Early in 1941 the U.S. Department of Agriculture (USDA) sent two agents to Mexico to study the possibility of that country's producing crops that would be complementary to its agricultural effort. The mission did not amount to much at the time, for at that stage the primary U.S. interest south of the border was in the area of medicine and nonfood products. In fact, it is not clear that the United States knew exactly what it wanted from Mexico's agriculture before Pearl Harbor. However, that situation soon changed when, later in 1941, the Rockefeller Foundation sent three experts to examine Mexican agriculture. It was more of a site survey than the initiation of a cooperative program, especially since the United States did not send a copy of this survey (known as the Stakman report) to the Ministry of Agriculture until 1943; and, even then, the USDA's version of the report had to be rewritten "to eliminate many derogatory remarks before it could be submitted to the Mexican Government."[6] Nevertheless, the possibility of integrating Mexican agriculture into the Allied war production had been raised.

The 1942 Suárez-Bateman Agreement was the central wartime economic pact between the two countries; although it dealt primarily with mineral production, it also established a broad pattern of U.S.-Mexican economic cooperation for other sectors as well. On August 13, 1942, the Export-Import Bank announced a 6-million-dollar loan for the steel mill at Monclova, Coahuila. There had been an earlier agreement for an expenditure of 30 million dollars for roads in Mexico and, as the war began, the

War Department was eager for the program to be accelerated. Some commentators began to view these policies as a change in the U.S. position, one that favored Mexico's industrialization push. Friends of the New Deal heralded this change in policy as a major innovation, and Ambassador Josephus Daniels made much of the new importance attributed to Mexico. Numerous other programs followed the Suárez-Bateman pact. The British legation called the Export-Import Bank's 1942 announcements part of a policy "aimed at the establishment of autarky in the American hemisphere."[7]

Cooperation in agriculture also emerged as an important aspect of this spirit of wartime collaboration. On February 19, 1943, the Rockefeller Foundation came to an important agreement with the Mexican government for a program to work on the improvement of varieties of corn, as well as efforts against wheat rusts and disease and soil control. In addition to initiating work that eventually led to the Green Revolution (the intensive use of hybrid seeds, fertilizer, and water), the immediate efforts were aimed at increasing agricultural output. Thus, Mexico gained technical assistance from the United States and moved toward agricultural specialization that would be helpful for the pursuit of World War II.

Since the 1942 planting and crop projections were high, a somewhat false sense of security existed. No conflict between domestic Mexican needs and wartime production seemed evident. As late as April 1942 the agricultural attaché in the U.S. embassy foresaw no problems in Mexican crop yields. He anticipated only a shortfall in lard and wheat, which was normal, or perhaps a bit more pronounced now due to the reduced land available for wheat production as a result of the war effort. In the main, however, self-sufficiency in agriculture was projected for the following season.[8]

Mexico entered into a rapid and significant reorganization of its agriculture to support the war effort. The U.S. embassy's agricultural attaché, David L. Crawford, worked closely with the Ministry of Agriculture, and together they proposed the creation of a plan that would rapidly increase Mexico's production of edible oils, useful fibers, timber, and other items of agriculture for the war cause. Their idea was for Mexico to specialize primarily in the production of edible oils, a need that producers had not met in the United States. Specifically, they proposed to increase the production of oils that were not traditionally used in Mexico, so that the population would not be tempted to consume them; hence, all of the additional production would go directly toward the war effort.[9] All of these proposals were developed at high and remote levels of governmental planning; however, they represented major changes for rural producers. The planners envisioned the need for the Ministry of Agriculture to organize, supervise, and negotiate these innovations with Mexican agricultural producers. In retrospect, it is remarkable how quickly they moved on the plan.

Even as the reorientation of Mexico's agriculture took place in 1943, danger signs began to appear. In July the U.S. embassy first signaled

concern to the war production and planning authorities over the possibility that the diversion of resources from subsistence agriculture to war production might create serious food shortages. Still, Ambassador George Messersmith recommended only the creation of a committee to study the problem of coordinating wartime agricultural production.[10] By October, Nelson Rockefeller, as coordinator of the Office of Inter-American Affairs, argued that the food problem was becoming more serious, and he suggested the creation of a more urgent program, one that the ambassador only coolly supported. Resentment was felt within the State Department over the encroachments by young Rockefeller into the foreign policy area. As a result, the Rockefeller proposal for a matching funds project was never presented to the Mexican government. Instead, on December 8, 1943, Ambassador Messersmith announced an agreement with that government to form a Mexican-American Commission on Agriculture to foster long-term cooperation between the two countries. That agreement was long on generalities and platitudes, or good intentions, if one prefers; however, its real importance was found in a corollary called an "Overall Agreement on Oil Seeds," which was negotiated and implemented in 1943 but only signed in Mexico City on February 15, 1944. The general thrust of the agreement was that Mexico should increase oil and seed production and guarantee the U.S. exports above the domestic (Mexican) requirements. In return the United States would send more than one thousand tractors and other items of farm machinery to Mexico. It was stressed that all U.S. experts, equipment, and technical assistance would be controlled closely by the Ministry of Agriculture in Mexico City.

U.S. technicians sent to monitor Mexican agriculture found the task far more difficult than they had anticipated. Projections were easier to make than to verify. As one of these technicians put it, there were many "fluid factors" in the equation, each of which made predictions difficult. In 1943, for example, 70,000 Mexican agricultural workers legally went to the United States to take the place of field hands who were being used in the war effort, and the figure was scheduled to increase to 115,000 the following year. As hard as it may be to imagine today, rural Mexico actually faced a labor shortage in 1943–1945 as illegal immigrants followed the legal braceros to find better-paying jobs in the war industries and in the cities.[11] The Mexican government supported this reorientation of agricultural production in ways that earned the respect of the U.S. agricultural specialists. These technicians had a high opinion of the competency of their Mexican counterparts in the Ministry of Agriculture on the eve of the food crisis.[12] In total, seven hundred thousand hectares went out of corn production between 1942 and 1943.[13]

No one had anticipated that nature and war would combine to create an alarming scarcity of corn by early 1944. Yet food shortages had become so critical and so generally known that by 1944 the Ministry of Agriculture

issued a general summary on the situation: the year 1943 had been the worst for Mexican agriculture in the twentieth century. The cumulative impact of late and then torrential rains, cyclones, droughts, frosts, and even a plague of locusts in Yucatán combined to push yields below even the levels recorded during the violent years of the Mexican Revolution.[14]

The food situation was disastrous. Only 3,048,317 hectares had been planted in corn in 1943, and, at an average yield of only 528 kilos per hectare, a total of 1,775,200 tons was produced. Less corn land had been planted only in 1925, 1929, 1930, and 1934–1937, and yields had been lower only in seven years: 1929–30, 1934–35, 1937–38, and 1940. Thus, 1943 combined reduced planting with low yields to make it the worst harvest in many years.[15] The problems of natural adversity were augmented by the diversion of production from subsistence agriculture to the production of cash crops. Moreover, the benefits of specialization were rendered useless. The war made it virtually impossible for Mexico to import staples in order to make up for a serious shortage. During the food crisis in 1943 it was able to purchase only eighteen thousand tons of corn (0.76 percent of its national production). The minister of agriculture announced that the country wanted to import up to two hundred thousand tons of corn in 1944 to supplement the bad harvests. That latter figure was twice the historic high level of corn importation of 1926.

Once it became clear that there was an acute scarcity of food and that it would be difficult to purchase supplementary grain abroad (and that even if one found a place to buy food, the wartime restrictions on shipping made it virtually impossible to transport the much-needed food to Mexico), the Ministry of Agriculture reacted strongly. On September 21, 1943, it issued a decree identifying corn-growing regions and forbidding the sowing of crops other than corn. Thus, before September 1943 these farmers were urged to diversify into crops for the war effort, but after that month farmers faced the confiscation of their crops if they grew anything other than corn! To rural Mexicans it seemed to be a muddle. On top of all this an outbreak of hoof-and-mouth disease in livestock soon followed and pitted government slaughter teams (including USDA agents) against peasants.

Early corn production was monitored closely in Nayarit, Sinaloa, Nuevo León, San Luis Potosí, Tamaulipas, Veracruz, Colima, and the coast of Jalisco in the hope that the first harvests (before the October harvests in the central highlands) could supplement the poor 1943 crop. More than seven hundred new tractors were thrown into this battle for food production by the government, and tractor stations were formed to use equipment more efficiently. These tractors were allocated by the war planners, even in the face of wartime exigencies.

Finally, the Ministry of Agriculture mobilized credit for additional corn production through the Banco Nacional de Crédito Ejidal and the Banco Nacional de Crédito Agricola. In a remarkably candid statement, Gómez

admitted that there had been numerous planning errors. The popular concern with the emerging food crisis was such that monthly production and consumption figures were prominently reported in the press, and the government reassured the population that if nature was even moderately kind in 1944, the country should be out of trouble by 1945. The production goal for the 1944 harvest was to plant 3,797,000 hectares in corn, a massive increase for a single year.[16]

Mexico's bad harvest of 1943 reverberated considerably beyond the nation's borders, and the political aspects were fairly intricate. Ambassador Messersmith became the central figure in this food crisis, as he realized that Rockefeller's earlier proposal to respond to it had merit. Originally he had opposed the plan, primarily out of his feeling of ambivalence over this powerful young man's intrusion into the State Department's preserve. Messersmith admitted that the food shortage had been brought about "by the diversion of corn lands to oil seeds and other more profitable crops" for the war effort. Since Rockefeller's office had seemed quite alarmist in the early stages of the crisis—estimating at one point that Mexico was producing only one sixtieth of the country's necessary corn—something had to be done.

Messersmith suggested the importation of corn from Argentina, the expansion of the program of technical assistance to increase output, the export of farm machinery from the United States, and, in the last instance, the export of food to keep Mexico's agriculture tied to the war effort.[17] The ambassador began to take the problem more seriously at this stage. However, he did not entertain the possibility of reversing the diversion of agricultural output back to food for domestic consumption. War took precedence over hunger.

The problem was that each U.S. government agency was acting without reference to the overall situation. Messersmith noted that there already was considerable disillusionment in Mexico over Avila Camacho's policy of cooperating with the war effort. This, of course, had the potential of threatening not only agricultural production for war but also that of strategic minerals. The problem of war production interrupting normal patterns of rural output was compounded by the difficulties in trying to transport anything to Mexico, since shipping was so tightly allocated according to the military effort. Messersmith therefore called for the formation of a top-level committee of representatives from the State Department, the Board of Economic Warfare, the War Food Administration (which could speak for the Commodity Credit Corporation), the USDA, and the Combined Food Board (CFB). His idea at this stage was that informed representatives of these agencies should go to Mexico to plan with ministry officials further international cooperation in war production.

Messersmith painted a picture of a Mexican government prepared to cooperate with the United States but unclear as to what was required, an

image to which he himself subscribed. The ambassador was convinced of the wisdom of the U.S. policy of not buying food from Mexico, for fear of a political backlash if its citizens could attribute food shortages to the war effort; however, he noted that private U.S. merchants were still making purchases of food in Mexico. As he saw it, that country should solve the problem by means of a system of export licensing. But, by July 1943, the problem seemed less than urgent. There still was time to appoint a committee.[18]

Food shortages became more acute in 1944, and eventually Mexican officials turned to Messersmith to intervene with the various war planning agencies to obtain the food to feed the population. Marte Gómez told Messersmith on May 4, 1944, that he feared shortages, especially in corn. He urged the ambassador to bring this situation to the attention of Secretary of Agriculture Claude Wickard.

By May, Messersmith was willing to recommend that grain be imported from Argentina, "much as none of us likes that solution." (Argentina was neutral during the war, and that infuriated U.S. officials.) The need to avoid grain shortages was politically sensitive because the Mexican Left had been primarily focusing its attention on the war as part of the battle against fascism; if the Left shifted its attention to the cost of living, much less food shortages caused by cooperation with the United States, it had the power to break apart the coalition in support of President Avila Camacho's policy of cooperation in the war effort. Ambassador Messersmith was eager to avoid that possibility, since the Left had been more favorable to the policy than much of the old Right.

In an accompanying letter to Wickard, Messersmith reminded the secretary that they were living through precarious times. He called the situation "intolerable" for the workers, since the price of basic necessities had gone up enormously and wage increases were not matched by adequate price controls. Messersmith believed that whereas there had been some speculation—the most popular explanation of shortages in Mexico—the real problem was that food production had been cut to make room for war production. The consequence was an inadequate supply of staples and rapid price increases.

Many U.S. agencies that oversaw the allocation of corn to Mexico looked upon that country's claim on U.S. food with a very intolerant eye. Time and again, Washington officials who were unfamiliar with Mexico's role in the war effort took the attitude that, during the period of emergency, the country ought to be able to feed itself. Attitudes formed upon highly racist assumptions about supposed Mexican incompetence were frequently at the heart of these assertions. Messersmith made a considerable and sustained effort to convince Secretaries Cordell Hull and Wickard that this was not the way to look at this situation. He constantly argued that it was necessary to supply corn to Mexico to make up for that which had been lost to the

country as a result of its cooperation in the war effort. Chaos would follow food shortages and this, in turn, would threaten the supply of all products coming out of Mexico. Due to the strategic position of the railroad workers' union, especially at the vital rail junction at San Luis Potosí, the Mexican Left could stop railroad shipments to the United States; even slight labor pressure on such a highly overburdened transportation system could have an immediate and magnified effect. There was also a problem with the "Argentinian solution." Even if Mexico could buy food in Argentina, the latter's shippers would not carry grain to Mexico; they could earn more on other runs, given the reduced cargos on the return trip. At least after Claude and Louise Wickard visited Mexico City, and stayed with the Messersmiths, the United States became more sympathetic to the country's food plight.[19]

Each suggestion for wartime cooperation carried with it risks and counterpressures, which complicated the matter. Messersmith's logic argued for increasing Mexican agribusiness, usually through subsidizing a project that favored someone close to the governing coalition. Certainly the war seemed to justify such an effort. Yet other voices in high circles pondered the long-term implications of this policy. State Department planner Laurence Duggan, for example, noted that by 1943 there were thirty-five projects in the Office of Economic Warfare aimed at increasing Mexican agricultural output of fats and oils for the purpose of war production. Duggan noted that six of these projects alone covered 310,000 acres in the lower Río Grande Valley. He cautioned that the postwar implications of this competition should be studied.[20] Duggan was raising long-term questions about postwar competition from Mexican producers. His position did not prevail, although many on the left in Mexico thought that this line of analysis was at the heart of its policy, and that the United States did not want the country to emerge as an industrial competitor.

Ambassador Messersmith became a sort of proconsul for food, upon whose effort the Mexican population depended far more than most of them realized. Normally, the country had been self-sufficient in corn production, and in food more generally. By September 1943 the estimates were that between sixty-five thousand and seventy thousand tons of corn would have to be imported by the end of the year. A year later those estimates would triple. In a number of states, governors were threatening to prohibit the export of corn, and the governor of Durango had just seized railroad cars loaded with corn for the Federal District in order to avert hunger in his own state.[21]

At several points Messersmith pulled out all the stops at the highest level of government in order to achieve his aims. He wrote to the extraordinarily powerful dollar-a-year-man Will Clayton, asking him to use his enormous influence on recalcitrant government officials in the various war control boards and regulatory agencies to get allocations of corn, lard, and sugar for Mexico to make up for the shortages. Messersmith presented

Clayton with a list of officials who needed to be convinced. He suggested that Clayton take them to the prestigous Metropolitan Club in Washington (he even specified the dates) in order to bring them around. The ambassador was using a big gun indeed, because, in addition to being an undersecretary of state, Clayton owned the world's largest cotton brokerage, Anderson, Clayton, and Company. Messersmith's ability to tap this man who operated at the zenith of both the public and private sectors of international agribusiness in order to support Mexico's claim for food allocations during the war is impressive, and it also serves as an indicator of the importance given to the problem.[22]

The Allies went to considerable lengths to solve Mexico's food shortages. At one point the problem even became global. Mexico had purchased grain in Canada. The grain was stored in the Toronto area and was desperately needed in Mexico. However, it proved impossible to allocate extra railroad cars to carry the grain across the United States, given the other wartime claims on transportation. The problem was aggravated by the difficulties in shipping grain on a southwest course across the country, as this ran against the normal patterns of transportation. Some alert functionary came up with the idea of a long-range swap: Mexico's grain in Canada could be turned over to the United States for use in the upper midwest in return for Allied grain, which could be more easily delivered into Mexico. Distances proved to be less important than availability of shipping. So the Allies actually mobilized a large grain order in Adelaide, Australia, purchased from the Australian Wheat Board, and found that it was easier to divert return ships from Australia to the west coast of Mexico (in exchange for Mexico's grain that was blocked in Canada) than it was to find transportation across the United States.[23] The Australian wheat was important in averting famine at a difficult time. There were moments, however, when it was a close call. In Yucatán, for example, the corn reserves were down to a few days in 1944.[24]

The food shortages were so acute that the Avila Camacho government responded by forming an agency called Nacional Distribuidora y Reguladora S.A. (ND&R). This response to the fear of famine in a poor country drew upon at least two quite different traditions. There was a centuries-long tradition of governmental intervention to prevent famine. Mexico's colonial *alhóndigas* (public granaries) provided one model of famine relief; a second approach saw U.S. diplomats urging the Mexicans to follow the U.S. lead in wartime planning and to create Mexican versions of the War Food Administration, the Combined Food Board, and other wartime agencies.

Within Mexico the most popular explanation of the wartime food crisis was that middlemen had been taking advantage of shortages to hoard supplies of food in order to raise prices. Nacional Distribuidora y Reguladora S.A. was set up to fight the reality, or at least the appearance, of that situation. The public was not aware until 1944 of the degree to which normal

output patterns had been diverted to war production, so there may well have been an overestimation of the degree of speculation, although it would be very difficult to measure the relative importance of speculation and falling production in the food shortages equation.

Even after the end of hostilities, Mexico was dependent upon war planners for foodstuffs, and the problem immediately after the war became much more galling. In early 1945, for example, the country received a tentative lard allotment of twenty million pounds. When the USDA learned that Mexico also was buying lard from Argentina, the agency reduced the 1945–46 lard and sugar quotas. To justify this action, the USDA studied patterns of Mexican lard consumption and asserted that per capita, it had increased from fifteen pounds before the war to eighteen pounds in 1945. During the same period, U.S. consumption had decreased from forty-four to thirty-seven pounds.

Similarly, in terms of sugar requirements, the USDA began to compare Mexico with the war-torn countries of Europe in order to determine post-war sugar quotas. They found that Mexico had increased per capita sugar consumption from an average of forty-two pounds (1934–1938) to nearly sixty pounds in 1945. (The comparable figures in Europe in 1945 were Italy, ten pounds; France, thirty-four pounds; and the United Kingdom, seventy-two pounds.) Mexico, therefore, found that it was in an entirely new category. Far from being a valuable ally who had contributed significantly on the economic side of the war effort, Mexico now found that national requirements were thrown into a global cauldron of calculations in which the U.S. military's desire to avert shortages in its conquered territories was judged against Mexico's domestic needs, much to that country's disadvantage.[25] In a secret telegram dated March 18, 1946, the issue of food exports to Mexico was raised at a meeting of the Combined Foods Board. Mexico was given a lower priority rating for food exports. On the Mexican desk in the State Department, J. Bernard Gibbs opposed the idea on the grounds that Mexico was still expected to supply the United States with preferential exports of hard fibers, coffee, chicle, lumber, edible oils, and minerals before other customers. In addition, it was still in the U.S. interest to import workers under the bracero program. There seemed to be an inconsistency. Other issues quickly intervened in the calculation of priorities.

At the same time that imports from the United States were rationed, Mexico was told not to use increased tariffs to prevent goods from flowing beyond its borders. The reduction of the country's quota in fats and lard was intended to mold broader trade policies; in Gibbs's view this innovation "stem[s] from a desire of the allocation authorities to chastise Mexico for what they consider a serious unwarranted action."[26] Even at this time Washington officials were still trying to use food quotas to open the door for the sale of U.S. industrial products to their neighbor; the war planners

also tried to block the sale of fats from Argentina to Mexico, a scheme designed to make up for their own reductions to the Mexican quotas. The CFB was on an ambitious track. It was also committed to preventing Mexican entrepreneurs from making private purchases in the United States from private sources. Even Nacional Distribuidora y Reguladora S.A. was prevented from making private deals in the United States.

There was certainly room for some competition; the U.S. embassy in Mexico City—particularly sensitive to the charges that wartime cooperation was causing the food shortages—discovered that the CFB was tolerating an additional 20 percent commission on its Mexican exports. The U.S. firms that received the export quotas charged a commission of 10 percent (5 percent as a finder's fee that went to the agent who made the sale, and 5 percent as a consignor's fee that went to the firm that supplied the commodity). On the Mexican side another 10 percent went to the importer for concluding the transaction, in addition to the normal profits that were earned in the two countries. The CFB would not allow Nacional Distribuidora y Reguladora S.A. to buy directly from U.S. producers in order to reduce the additional markup of 20 percent.[27] No parallel arrangement existed for the export of Mexican minerals during the war.

Such revelations were ill received south of the border, since many people were already operating close to the margin. Both Dr. Francisco P. Miranda, director of Mexico's National Institute of Nutrition, and the United Nations' Food and Agricultural Organization estimated that food consumption fell during the war. (Miranda later became one of the first nutrition specialists to work with the UN Food and Agricultural Organization.) Any reduction was serious since nearly half of the calories and protein consumed per person came from corn, while the average consumption of animal protein averaged only thirty grams per day. In short, the corn shortage mattered. The fact that corn in the United States was largely used for animal food, while in Mexico it was the popular equivalent of bread, added a certain passion to the issue. Certainly the U.S. embassy's reports on the wartime nutritional situation treated the problem seriously; as one report of a U.S. food expert stated, "Millions of Mexican people have the appearance both in stature and in the ability to work of being undernourished and despite the generally mild climate and the relative abundance of some native foods, there are many cases of individuals having died as a result of nutritional deficiency." The embassy opposed the CFB plan to reduce the Mexican export quotas until it adopted the tariff and trade policies of which the board approved, and it even worried that this malnutrition would compromise the bracero program.[28]

Near panic ensued on March 30, 1946, when the Mexico City press carried a report that wheat was being embargoed to Mexico as political punishment for following trade policies of which the United States disapproved. When the U.S. agricultural attaché called upon the administrators of Nacional

Distribuidora y Reguladora S.A. to identify the source of the report, he was told that it was based on statements from the Ullman Grain Company and the Continental Grain Company in response to War Food Order No. 144, which had been recently issued. Since the controversial grain had been pre-paid, and since mills in Puebla had actually closed for lack of wheat, the threat of a food blockade made the situation tense.

Mexican officials feared that the grain companies were trying to break the contracts that had been negotiated under wartime controls in order to take advantage of shortages. The mere suggestion that the secret telegram (No. 264, still not released) was an attempt to force Mexico to pursue par-ticular tariff policies, upon the pain of starvation, was too much. Under the glare of publicity the CFB issued further instructions releasing 21,488 tons of wheat for April distribution. Gibbs learned, however, that only 13,600 tons were really going to be released. Mexican officials vigorously pressed for the entire 200,000 metric tons of wheat owed to Nacional Distribuidora y Reguladora S.A. in the United States. The agricultural attaché, obviously in sympathy with the Mexican position, called the attempt to use food pressure to affect policy a "high handed action on the part of a friendly government."[29]

Several conclusions can be drawn from the story of agricultural dislo-cation during the war. Certainly the dependency that a country suffers vis-à-vis another country is increased if it becomes impossible to feed its population. Orthodox economic arguments about comparative advantage pale rapidly as the food runs out. Mexico entered the war in an advanta-geous bargaining position as the Allies wanted its agricultural and mineral contributions to the war effort; however, by the end of the war that country's interests were being juxtaposed to those of conquered nations, and coming in a poor second at that. Problems of dependency also were reflected in the fact that unequal business relationships existed on the two sides. War plan-ners were quick to prevent the kinds of extra charges that were applied to Mexico's purchase of agricultural commodities from being applied to U.S. mineral imports.[30]

From a methodological point of view it is absolutely clear that overall output data can hide fundamental truths. Increases in total agricultural pro-duction and price levels, in fact, disguised near-starvation in Mexico dur-ing the war. Thus, a poverty index that shows improvement in the face of food shortages must be found wanting. At the very minimum, rather than trying to copy the U.S. national income accounting categories, analysts might try to devise statistical categories that are more closely related to the Mexi-can reality of the day. In the case of agriculture it is clear that the subsis-tence sector should be separated from the agribusiness sector. One of the long-term problems with Mexican agrarian reform is that the subsistence sector is averaged together with the agribusiness sector, and governmental policies are constantly aimed at the latter rather than the former; there can

be no alleviation of rural unemployment and, concomitantly, urban crowding until that pattern is reversed.

## A Sectoral Analysis of Wartime Production

Overall data on the performance of the Mexican economy showed rapid progress during the war years. A recent estimate of the GNP showed an increase from 6.4 billion pesos in 1939 to 19.7 billion pesos in 1945.[31] The Mexican government's Barometer of Commerce showed an increase (1939=100) from 100 to 137 in real terms in those years. However, the argument here is that aggregate data alone can be quite misleading. The following analysis is an attempt to produce a reorganization of the governmental data for the war years to show more accurately some of the main productive divisions in the period. The national income accounting data have been organized around subsistence agriculture, agribusiness, mining and metallurgical production, manufacturing, infrastructure, services, and governmental expenditures. Finally, there is an attempt to examine the standard of living of the population and the general rate of capital accumulation, two factors that are often assumed (erroneously) to be antithetical.

Agriculture formed the basis of life for the vast majority of the twenty million Mexicans who were alive in 1940. Some 65 percent of those economically active were in the agricultural labor force, yet researchers have frequently generated confusion by using the category of agriculture in an overarching way. Peasant-based subsistence agriculture had very little in common with capital-intensive specialized production for the war effort. Policies that favored one sector often hurt the other branch of rural life.

In the subsistence sector, crops may be disaggregated into the production of rice, oats, corn, wheat, and beans. There were, of course, other minor fruit and vegetable products; however, they were of decidedly smaller magnitude so they have been eliminated from this calculation. Certainly, these crops provided the basis of the popular diet. Production during this period is shown in Figure 3. At first glance the poor production records of 1939 and 1943 appear to reflect the cyclical nature of agriculture. However, the crisis of 1943–44 was unlike earlier downturns because the war planning effort by the Allies made it virtually impossible to make up for a bad year with purchases abroad. The recovery of the 1944 crop, which was primarily felt in 1945, was only made possible by the reestablishment of zones of traditional agriculture.

By contrast, the record of production of the agribusiness sector—sesame, cotton, henequen, and cotton seeds—during the war years was quite different (see Figure 4). The output of crops for the war effort boomed at the same time that the production of staples stagnated or declined. Only the return to traditional production in 1944–45 and then the decline of demand

**Figure 3.  Subsistence Sector**

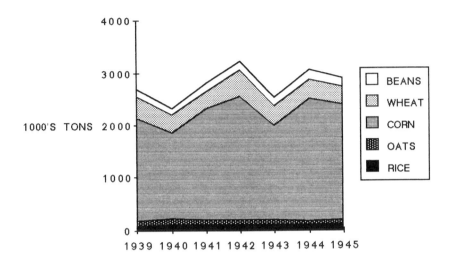

**Figure 4.  Agribusiness Sector**

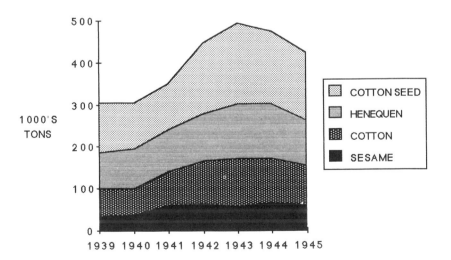

as the war wound down brought the boom to an end. The inflationary impact of the emphasis on edible oil and fiber production was clear to observers at the time.

Simple production data showing a decline in subsistence agriculture at the same time that agribusiness boomed do not necessarily demonstrate that the one phenomenon caused the other. However, when the food crisis is taken in conjunction with the large shift of land out of corn production, a case emerges to suggest that the growth in agribusiness took place at the expense of the subsistence sector. Although the data make it virtually impossible to distinguish between corn produced in the numerous minifundia in contrast to the capital-intensive sector, there was ample concern by wartime planners that the public would view the food crisis as being caused by agribusiness production. The admission on the part of Messersmith that such was the case, the strain on the transportation system caused by war exports, the impossibility of importing corn, and the shady history of the ND&R all strengthen the case for viewing the boom in agribusiness as having taken place largely at the expense of the subsistence sector.

The mining sector experienced a war boom as well. High strategic priority was attached to Mexico's nonferrous mineral wealth. It was not only the quantity of this mineral wealth that interested the Allies but also the security of having key resources located safely next to the United States; not having to rely upon dangerous maritime transportation made these resources important to the war planners. The fact that most of Mexico's mineral wealth was already in the hands of the Guggenheim firm, ASARCO, only made it easier to integrate these minerals into the Allied planning system.

The United States used its silver purchases as a powerful lever in trying to influence Mexico's policies. The first act of retaliation after that country's nationalization of its petroleum industry in 1938 had been the curtailment of silver purchases, a move compatible with the interests of the silver lobby in the U.S. Congress. Even after the rapprochement of 1941–42, Mexico's silver production declined from 2,300,000 kilograms in 1939 to 1,900,000 in 1945. Its delegation to the Bretton Woods Conference expressed the forlorn hope of getting silver reinstated as an international monetary standard. Similarly, gold production fell from 26,200 kilograms in 1939 to 15,500 in 1945. Wartime planning deemphasized the importance of precious metals.

When one turns to nonprecious metals, the impact of wartime production becomes more apparent (see Figure 5). Except for copper, the rapid increase in production of the other major metals—lead, iron, and zinc—is striking. A reduced purchase of Mexican minerals in the wake of the expropriation of petroleum lasted until the wartime pacts that centered around the Suárez-Bateman Agreement, which signaled a surge in mineral production that abated only after the U.S. stockpiles became a problem as the war

**Figure 5.  Major Metals**

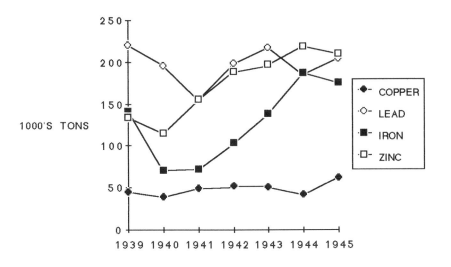

**Figure 6.  Strategic Minerals**

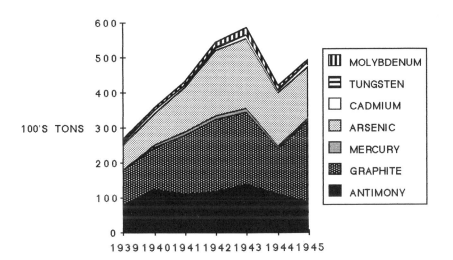

ended. The war boom of 1942–1945 placed great pressure not only on the mines and refineries but also on the transportation system. While not so dramatic in tonnage, there were other minerals that were equally important for their value in producing war matériel. The significance of these strategic minerals—antimony, graphite, mercury, arsenic, cadmium, tungsten, and molybdenum (used primarily to harden steel for armaments)—was based on the difficulty of finding economic substitutes for their uses (see Figure 6).

The rapid increase in production also applied to these strategic minerals. With the exception of precious metals, which did not show growth, there was scarcely a mineral produced in Mexico that did not at least double in output between 1939 and 1940, and 1942 and 1944. However, refining and smelting figures did not show so rapid an increase. The multiplier effect was exported.

Manufacturing is another of those traditional categories that are so broad that many disparate items and different techniques of production are included in aggregate figures. An overall index of the output of the industries of transformation is shown in Figure 7. Again, an initial image of prosperity emerges; however, it is difficult to escape the conclusion that while actual production increased only a little, it was the wartime inflation that created the greater part of the boom, and this had serious implications for the manufacturing sector after the war.

An analysis of the sectoral output of Mexican manufacturing shows the patterns found in Figure 8 (the curious juxtapositions of industries were those of the Mexican government). The older areas of industrial production—textiles, soap and shoes, etc.— performed poorly. Textiles were relatively flat, and the output of soap and shoes actually declined during the war. The most rapid boom was in beer and tobacco, a fact that may simply reflect the consumers' allocation of a larger amount of discretionary income, as well as changes from the products of cottage industry (pulque and mezcal) to the products of industry (beer and tequila). Nevertheless, it was a fairly odd leading edge of industrial development, especially during a war boom.

In terms of Mexico's great goal of industrialization, the most important area was labeled by the government as diverse production; it consisted of iron, steel, paper, cement, and the glass industries. An index that increased this rapidly in the course of six years represented an impressive achievement. The government could look at these figures and be assured that its development plan had been on course. If Mexico emerged from the war with an industrial capacity in basic industries where formerly there was no such thing, then it appeared to be a job well done. A strong case could be made that the nation's leaders had made the most of the economic windfall created by the war. Certainly, government spokesmen argued that line, and labor also saw it as an accomplishment.

**Figure 7. Industries of Transformation (1929=100)**

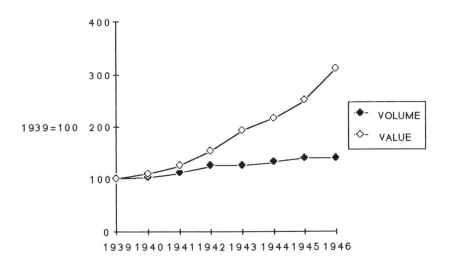

**Figure 8. Volume of Industrial Production (1929=100)**

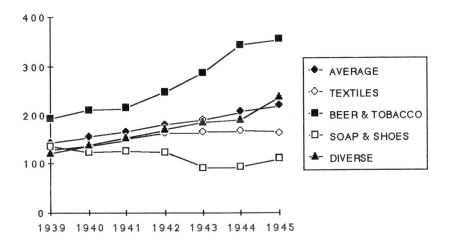

However, the item referred to as diverse production combined too wide a variety of industries, and also a number of different kinds of production. In addition to gigantic foreign firms there were great factories, such as the steel mills, that had close associations with North American capital; but there also was a large number of national enterprises, most of which were in the area of light industry. Beyond that, a proliferation of undercapitalized artisan shops often produced with great ingenuity and, frequently, under appalling working conditions. An analysis that lumps these disparate areas together is probably combining too many different kinds of activity. Ideally, it would be very useful to be able to disaggregate production in heavy industry from that in light manufacturing and artisan activities. However, the categories of reporting make this difficult.[32]

In spite of the difficulties in obtaining a sufficiently long run of data to make a constant comparison over the war years, several additional observations seem to flow from the census. There were some areas that experienced a wartime boom, which did not necessarily produce spin-offs for industry. Edible oils were a wartime priority, as we have seen; however, the production of vegetable oils processed in Mexico actually declined from forty-seven thousand to thirty-eight thousand tons between 1939 and 1945. In this case Mexican agriculture was seriously dislocated in order to increase the production of edible oils, but those oils were shipped to the United States for processing and did not lead to increased production.

Another characteristic of the period was a rapid decrease in the number of firms in most industries. This phenomenon had been occurring during the 1930s and was continued into the war years. The process of increased concentration was probably inevitable, given the increasing capital requirements of such heavy industries as steel, chemicals, and electricity; however, the war seems to have hastened that process. There was scarcely a branch of industry where this was not the pattern.

Investments in the country's infrastructure were striking. The number of hectares under irrigation increased from 126,000 to 816,000 from 1939 to 1945, and electricity generation increased from 2,500,000 to 3,100,000 kilowatt hours in the same period. Telegraph correspondence nearly doubled between these years, and mail increased at a similar rate. Although the telephone system was still in its infancy, there were 166,000 subscribers in the Mexican Republic by the end of the war.

The size of the railway grid was stable during the period; however, the annual cargo transported increased from 15,300,000 tons in 1939 to a high of 21,300,000 in 1943. The composition of the cargo also shifted as the movement of grain decreased and minerals increased, thus causing further wear on the rail system. The number of passengers using the system also grew to 35 million per year over the course of the war. Greater use during the war years placed so much strain on the railroad network that the United States sent a railroad mission to Mexico to help overcome transportation

bottlenecks during the war (as described in Chapter 4). In this area, unlike in the other areas of infrastructure, the war left the railroad relatively run down as hostilities ground to a halt; that was a problem the country never entirely overcame. By contrast the government claimed to have increased the number of kilometers of roads constructed from nine thousand to seventeen thousand per year between 1939 and 1945. So a picture emerges of the railroad network suffering considerable wear while roads began to be more important, although the road network was also in its infancy.

From the point of view of capital accumulation, the country seemed to advance. An index of resources in the banking system showed an increase from 100 in 1939 to 189 in 1945. Depositors' investments in banks rose from 48 million pesos in 1939 to 451 million pesos in 1945. A tenfold increase in capital invested through the banking system had to be a more general indication of a rapid growth in real capital accumulation. By either measure, capital accumulation was running considerably ahead of the rate of inflation.

## The Distribution of Gain

Certainly, inflation was severe in Mexico during the war years. The government's official wholesale price index (1929=100) shows price increases from 122 in 1939 to 244 in 1945. (Comparable figures for the United States in those years are 81 to 111.) Indeed, the severity of inflation was at the heart of the problem of *carestía*, as poverty was called in Mexico during those years. There was a wartime tripartite pact among labor, business, and government aimed at holding wages and prices in line so as not to damage war production. In that context, the high rate of inflation in a period of frozen wages produced a volatile political environment. In spite of the tripartite pact, there were many work stoppages.

The government's own statistical data revealed a picture of falling real wages at the time, and this precipitated even more popular action to remedy the decline in real wages. The Banco de México released a cost-of-living index that showed prices increasing more rapidly than the government's figures; prices by that reckoning went from 178 in 1939 to 434 in 1945 (1929=100). There is even more compelling evidence to suggest that the normal figures cited from the *Anuario Estadístico* understate the degree of privation of the period.

In the records of the Department of State there is a copy of a private cost-of-living index, prepared for President Alemán's eyes alone, of the true cost of living in Mexico. This index was compiled by the Ministry of Labor. The U.S. embassy's councilor for Economic Affairs, Elmer H. Bourgerie, obtained a copy of the document and forwarded it to Washington. Confidentially, he described the price index as "the only objective picture on real

wages developed by the Department [Ministry] of Labor" and urged that it should be treated with care and hidden from public view. He thought that even this cost-of-living index had a downward bias, since it was based solely upon the price of regulated goods in Mexico City and excluded manufactured goods because they were not subject to price controls. Nevertheless, the figures were dramatic enough, especially when we recall that only a quarter of the industrialized workers enjoyed the full benefits of formal pay increases. (The average earnings figures were notoriously overestimated, reflecting governmental decrees more than the reality of paid wages.)

Alemán's private index showed that the deterioration in real wages was stunning in that the fall was twice as bad as the publicly released figures had revealed. Average wages had increased from 100 in 1939 to 316 in 1950; however, the cost of living for the working class in Mexico City rose to 356 over the same period. The deterioration of real wages from 100 (in 1939) fell to a low of 82.1 in 1947. By 1953 the real wage index was only 96.6, that is to say, still below the level of 1939.[33]

Even Alemán's secret index may have understated the fall of real wages. Jeffrey Bortz is the most recent scholar to have examined industrial wages in Mexico City. Comparing real wages over time, he devised an index of real wages in the Federal District in which 1938=100. Wages fell to a low of 46.4 in 1947, and recovery was only marginal after that. Not until 1971 did the purchasing power of real wages regain the 1938 level.[34] By either index, the wartime pattern of capital accumulation via falling real wage rates set a pattern for some time to come.

Based upon the level at which wages were frozen on September 21, 1943, the CTM had estimated that the minimum livable wage for a family with three children was 6.90 pesos; since the minimum wage was only 3 pesos, and only the most favored workers received the minimum wage, the situation was desperate. In light of the suppressed cost-of-living data, it would appear that the CTM's figures were broadly accurate.

There is also an interesting indirect corroboration of this picture from other sources. In 1950 the U.S.-Mexican Mixed Commission, studying Mexico's industrialization, called the country "over-industrialized." By this curious expression they meant that effective demand (cash in the hands of consumers) was so acutely limited to upper-income groups that no further industrialization based upon popular consumption was possible. The National Chamber of Manufacturing Industries' monthly journal called for a strengthening of effective demand by placing more money in the hands of those with the highest marginal propensity to consume, to put it in the new Keynesian language.[35] That was a position held by the people in the national industrialist group. Their perspective drew upon certain traditions of underconsumption analysis by arguing that if, in fact, the working people could not consume the products of industry, it would be hard to sell those products.[36] A number of industrialists in this group were willing to make

political alliances with the left, and they certainly opposed falling real wages for the working class; their views were not to prevail.

In 1947 the Ministry of Economics published cost-of-living figures without a wage deflation index. Moreover, the government turned to a technique of reporting in which the changes in real wages were noted only within each year, so that January=100. This diminished the data's impact on the public quite dramatically, although the deterioration of the standard of living for the Mexican working class could hardly be kept secret.[37]

In short, the best quantitative data support the view of Ambassador Messersmith, writing to Secretary Wickard in 1944: "I have not been so pessimistic with regard to the outlook here at any time since I came to Mexico as I am now. The cost of living has gone up tremendously. We are living really on a social volcano here now. The situation of the workers is intolerable, for everything they eat has gone up enormously and wage increases do not seem to help for the price controls have been inadequate."[38]

Surprisingly, unemployment appears not to have been a problem in the period, certainly not by today's standards. The government reported unemployment data only for the early years of the war; the figures from the *Anuario Estadístico* showed monthly average unemployment figures falling from 198,593 in 1939 to 180,583 in 1941. Even though the *Anuario Estadístico* stopped reporting unemployment figures in 1942, the magnitudes are extremely low for a country of 20,000,000 people. (That is merely 3.17 percent, based upon an economically active population of 5,800,000 in 1940.) We may assume that unemployment in the rural sector was underreported; however, the very concept of unemployment does not rest very well with a peasant economy in which the village community still has some claim over the use of the land. It may also be true that the much smaller scale of production created more jobs. Still, the more common complaint during the period was that the war effort was siphoning off workers to the United States and, for the sectors involved in war production, was creating a labor shortage in Mexico.

Thus, a complex picture emerges of a boom in which those segments of the community associated with wartime production prospered. Capital accumulated rapidly in the hands of the strongest members of society. Falling real wages, reinforced by the tripartite pact with labor in the name of the war effort, erased much of the income improvement registered by the working class in the Cárdenas era. It is clear that the urban working class and the rural producers who were involved largely in subsistence agriculture benefited least from the wartime boom in Mexico. This much is clear from the statistical record of the period.

Contemporaneous accounts of wartime Mexico remind us that the impact of the war was quite uneven. Some regions were affected to a particularly substantial degree. The 1942 submarine war in the Caribbean acutely disrupted shipping along the Gulf Coast of Mexico. Travelers reported that

normally busy ports appeared quiet as business subsided there. Luis Morones of the CROM complained to the president that the war had hit the maritime trade hard on both coasts. Even on the West Coast, from Enseñada to Salina Cruz, his affiliates—stevedores, laborers, sailors, and launch drivers—were out of work. Many had formed together into fishing cooperatives to survive the adverse times.[39] Morones even wrote unsuccessfully to General Heriberto Jara, the minister of the navy, to ask that his workers be hired by the Mexican Navy for the duration of the war.[40] Similar petitions for relief from the dislocation of the war came from many quarters.

Overloaded railroads hit particular communities with bottlenecks and shortages. The railroad yards in Monterrey, San Luis Potosí, and other sensitive junctions were clogged while other centers were desperate for rolling stock. By the end of the war the United States sent railroad cars into Mexico only on a one-to-one basis when they were returned, so great was the disruption to the rail system caused by the war. Problems of rationing in various regions, sectors, and industries weighed heavily during the period. Fidel Velázquez, of the CTM, petitioned the president complaining about the adverse economic impact of the CFE's decision to reduce the voltage and the hours available to consumers of electricity.[41] In addition to the rationing of electricity, there were also blackouts as Mexico City practiced for possible air raids. Workers joined in on Sunday drills as the militias of the Cárdenas period shifted their ground from the protection of the revolution to the defense of the fatherland. Some wartime austerity measures hit close to the individual. For example, discarding the center of the popular bread roll, the *bolillo*, as had formerly been the custom, was now prohibited.

Sometimes high officials attacked the symptoms of the problems that had accompanied the war effort; a secret memorandum reveals the effort made by Minister of the Interior Miguel Alemán to influence newspapers not to report the difficulties being caused by the war effort. In a meeting on June 16, 1944, Alemán confronted the most important newspaper editors in the Federal District. After admitting that conditions were "rapidly becoming chaotic," the minister blamed the food problems on inadequate production, inflation, and disorganization in the railroads. He admitted that "for the first time in twenty-five years the socialist supporters of the PRM are grumbling at the government because of its inertia and apparent inability to cope with the situation." Alemán promised that profiteering would be stopped but asked the editors to play down the severity of the problems in the interim.[42]

There were riots and disturbances protesting against the scarcity of commodities and their inflated prices. On July 20, 1944, a riot in Mexico City blocked the Zócalo for two hours. Organized by the Frente Nacional Proletario, it appeared to tap mass discontent over living conditions. Embarrassed by the degree of public support, *El Popular* blamed this uprising upon the organizational effort of the friends of the rival conservative news-

paper *El Universal* and former CTM employees who had become disenchanted. The CTM and the government said that the rioting was caused by the right-wing Sinarquistas.[43] These rather lame protestations by groups normally sympathetic to popular mobilizations revealed the strains in the prowar alliance.

Even the nineteenth-century and revolutionary phenomenon of highway robbery reappeared at the height of the crisis of austerity during World War II. Armed bandits stopped cars on major highways in order to relieve the occupants of their assets. The journalist Betty Kirk, covering Mexico for U.S. and British publications, saw the return of *gavillas* (gangs) as a sign of renewed rebellion and a return to the violent phase of the Mexican Revolution rather than a result of the pressures generated by the war. So disturbances, shortages, inflation, falling real wage rates, and the dislocation of sectors that produced items of basic needs all formed part of the negative side of the war boom.

Yet there were some things deeply woven into the class structure of the country that wartime pressures would not be allowed to change. An interesting problem emerged related to the conditions of labor of Mexican workers who were becoming caught up in the war effort. New Deal legislation required that the government in Washington purchase items only from firms that adhered to the Department of Labor's standards on child labor, health, safety, and housing. The degree to which U.S. rules regulating the labor process would apply to material purchased in Mexico became an issue. A test case emerged as the Metals Reserve Company made its first purchase of forty thousand tons of zinc concentrate in 1942–43. The zinc was coming from the ASARCO mine at Santa Eulalia, Chihuahua. Company officials were eager to make sure they would not have to improve the miners' working conditions in order to comply with U.S. law, so Ambassador Messersmith intervened by rewriting the labor clauses in the purchasing contracts, and—by means of heartfelt appeals to Mexican sovereignty—he made sure that U.S. labor standards would not apply, even to ASARCO.[44]

If the war was not going to be allowed to provide windfalls for the poor, it certainly did affect life at the other end of the scale. Changing textures of life accompanied the onslaught of profits and economic action. Even the landscape of Mexico City told a tale. As most Mexicans found their real wages deteriorating, evidence of opulence for the few grew before people's eyes. Suburbs such as Lomas and later the Pedregal became the most visible repositories of personal wealth, and the skyscrapers along the Paseo de la Reforma filled with revolutionary industrialists and bankers of the sort that Carlos Fuentes immortalized in *The Death of Artemio Cruz*.

A new life-style—from Acapulco to the *Zona Rosa*—came to set the meaning of modernity for many. Nightclubs proliferated, and even the American ambassador worried about the degree to which U.S. gangsters were influential at the new racetrack, the Hipódromo de las Américas, started

by a U.S. citizen named Ben Smith. Messersmith lamented the arrival of what he called "improper elements" from the United States. He singled out the owner of the Circos nightclub, A. C. Blumenthal; the engineer Sam Rosoff, who had the contract to build the Valsequillo irrigation project; and Bruno Pagliai, the Italian-American who ran the racetrack. The ambassador's problem was that all of these men were close to Minister of the Interior Miguel Alemán.[45]

In the shadow of the opulence of such establishments as the Bankers' Club, owned by Raúl Balleres, the wave of promoters and speculators placed many basic items beyond the reach of workers. For them, even the cost of tickets to the bullfights became prohibitive. One U.S. diplomat was particularly upset by the fact that "while the great masses of peasants and low-wage workers are finding it difficult to purchase the bare necessities of life, Mexico is being flooded with Hollywood actors and actresses, high pressure American salesmen and promoters and international financiers."[46]

Through it all a new individual meaning of development emerged, much closer to a nouveau-riche model of conspicuous consumption than to the radical populism of the prewar period. Even the Cantinflas films served as a general barometer of change as sympathy for the *pelado* (common man) gave way to enthusiasm for the war boom. Mario Moreno, head of a union of cinema workers, was inexorably drawn toward the official party. Inflation, shortages, and opulence in the midst of poverty became the hallmark of the day.

It was not just dissident and fringe opinion that had noticed that Mexico's war effort had its negative side for the country. After a little more than a year of fairly intense wartime cooperation, Eduardo Villaseñor, head of the Banco de México, delivered a speech at the Escuela Nacional de Economía. As the nation's chief banker he spoke with authority, and when he attacked a fundamental policy of the Avila Camacho government it was an event of some importance. Indeed, Villaseñor's speech of April 6, 1943, caused shock waves in both countries.

The speech was a resounding attack upon the president's policy of close cooperation with the United States. The central contention was that if Mexico had followed a policy of neutrality in the economic sphere during World War II, it could have withheld sales until the United States agreed to pay for the nation's minerals with industrial equipment, rather than with dollars that could not be used to purchase very much.[47] Villaseñor charged that Mexico's goal of industrialization was being retarded because it was difficult to import machinery. The speech was bound to attract massive attention because, in addition to Villaseñor's position, Minister of Finance Eduardo Suárez had just released figures showing that in barely a year of wartime cooperation, Mexico had accumulated 140 million dollars that could not be spent, and that figure was increasing at the rate of 20 million per month.

George Messersmith reacted immediately to the Villaseñor charge. He sent his chief economic officer, Thomas Lockett, to have a long meeting with Finance Minister Suárez in the immediate wake of the speech. As the two men spoke, according to the U.S. record of the conversation, Suárez stressed the inflationary impact of the growing dollar balances in Mexico. Lockett responded that the problem with Villaseñor's approach was that the United States would have to divert iron and steel from the war effort to Mexico's industrialization program if Villaseñor's policies were to be implemented. In the American's view, the solution for Mexico was to sell war bonds in order to soak up the excessive number of dollars. He also suggested that the country could combat inflation by raising taxes, paying the country's foreign debt, and regulating prices in order not to interrupt the war effort.

Villaseñor was not entirely isolated in his views, for Suárez also described his country's effort as a Lend-Lease program from Mexico to the United States. He thought that the country could not absorb so many dollars and that the answer to the problem of surplus dollars was for the United States to sell more industrial equipment to Mexico. It was an interesting point. From any normal business perspective, or from Mexico's national perspective, Villaseñor's case was impeccable; however, his country had followed the United States into war and the government was committed to that policy. Messersmith's contention—by chance he was the next speaker after Eduardo Villaseñor in the series of conferences at the Escuela Nacional de Economía—was that Villaseñor's position was invalid because the United States was also sacrificing in order to fight World War II.[48] It was not the strongest argument imaginable.

U.S. intelligence reported that Villaseñor was claiming that the president had approved his speech in advance, that Eduardo Suárez also knew and approved of the controversial speech, and that Foreign Minister Ezequiel Padilla opposed it; however, the U.S. diplomats doubted Villaseñor's assertion that the president supported the nationalistic position.[49] Villaseñor's threat to regulate U.S. capital, which was trying to buy into Mexican firms rather than building new industries, was an effective challenge to which Messersmith responded.

Messersmith met with President Avila Camacho and reported back to Secretary of State Hull: "The President last evening spoke to me very strongly about Villaseñor's speech and expressed his strong displeasure of it. He could not have spoken in stronger terms, and I know that he has told Suárez what he thinks of it and that he has told Suárez to tell Villaseñor."[50] The ambassador could scarcely contain his enthusiasm for Avila Camacho: "The President here is in my opinion perhaps the firmest and soundest friend, and the most powerful, that we have in the American Republics. . . . His whole policy is firmly based in the most complete collaboration with the United States for the present and for the future." Messersmith credited the

Mexican president and Foreign Minister Padilla with blocking the nationalistic policies of other members of the cabinet.

There was a curious epilogue to the Villaseñor affair. Ambassador Messersmith was hosting a dinner for W. L. Hemmingway, president of the Mercantile Commerce Bank and Trust Company of Saint Louis, who was head of the American Bankers' Association in 1943. Initially, he had excluded Villaseñor from the guest list as an indication of his displeasure over the April speech, but then he recanted and personally called him to invite him. Villaseñor responded by also inviting Ambassador Messersmith to a dinner in the new and luxurious Bankers' Club in the Banco de México. The following day *Novedades* reported the meeting on page one as evidence of cordial relations between the two men, despite Villaseñor's speech. Messersmith saw the dinner as a setup aimed at projecting the image that Villaseñor was now out of the president's "dog house."[51]

It would be fascinating to know, disclaimers notwithstanding, if Manuel Avila Camacho had authorized the Villaseñor speech in order to increase his bargaining power with the United States or whether he simply took advantage of the situation after the fact. In any case, Villaseñor's position did not prevail. There would be no challenge to wartime cooperation and the newly emerging approach to industrial development, even from the august offices of the Banco de México.

The U.S. ambassador felt, in the final analysis, that President Avila Camacho's policy of cooperation with the United States was saved by a profound ambivalence within the Cardenista camp. Nationalistic cabinet members were tempted to bargain for the best possible deal with the United States, to block wartime cooperation, and to emphasize the protection of the poor; however, they also wanted to defeat the Axis forces. These conflicting tendencies divided the Cardenistas and therefore aided the president.

In his private correspondence with Secretary of State Cordell Hull, Ambassador Messersmith stated a position quite distinct from that which he argued to the Mexican leaders. The United States opposed a revaluation of the Mexican peso as a response to the rapidly growing currency reserves because it was feared that revaluation would raise the cost of purchasing raw materials for the war effort. To the Mexicans, Messersmith argued against revaluation of the peso on the grounds that it would add to the cost of basic materials for the poor. This attitude contrasted strikingly with the U.S. position on extra charges associated with Mexico's purchase of agricultural commodities. There, the impact upon the poor was not a consideration.

The ambassador did realize that Mexico was not getting much for its part in supplying the Allies. So he argued that the United States should try to speed up shipments for Mexico and possibly divert material that was being blocked for shipping to South America. Clearly, Messersmith thought

that with the strong pro-U.S. position of Avila Camacho and Foreign Minister Padilla, the Villaseñor threat had been thwarted.[52]

That impression was confirmed when Finance Minister Suárez and the head of NAFISA, Espinosa de los Monteros, visited the United States for important negotiations with officials in the Roosevelt administration on October 12, 1943. Representatives of the State Department, the Treasury, the Office of Economic Warfare, and the War Production Board meeting with Minister Suárez were assured that Mexico would not revalue the peso in view of the Stabilization Agreement of November 1, 1941.[53] Since the U.S. plan for 1944 called for a further purchase of 84.3 million dollars' worth of raw materials in Mexico, that was good news indeed in Washington.

It was to the immediate problem of the trade imbalance that several programs of economic cooperation were directed. Committees of leading Mexican industrialists were created and charged with finding ways that their country could be rewarded for its wartime cooperation. The composition of those committees and the rewards they distributed were central to the postwar Mexican development program.

## Managing Boom amid Want

Wartime inflation first hit Mexico quite hard in 1942 and continued throughout the war. An index of eighteen basic foodstuffs increased by 59 percent in the next two years. In a poor country, which was experiencing a war boom, this price increase for basic agricultural commodities was life-threatening. The fact that the vast majority of the Mexican people felt little direct involvement in the war made the price increases in their daily bread taste bitter indeed. The wage pact with the CTM could scarcely be expected to survive this pressure. In addition, for a government that had enthusiastically joined the war effort—and which had just signed a reciprocal trade treaty with the United States, on December 23, 1942—the threat of famine was too much to ignore. The government had to do something.

Price controls were announced in Mexico on March 2, 1943. A consortium was created under the control of ND&R and included two agricultural banks and a trading company. ND&R was given the responsibility for conserving food stocks and for regulating market prices. Tapping an ancient mercantilistic tradition in Mexico, ND&R was also given control over export licenses in order to prevent the export of food for profit when the period of scarcity continued. Finally, ND&R was given the authority to coordinate all government and semigovernment purchasing of agricultural commodities.[54] It tried, with only moderate success, to become the sole agency in Mexico for the importation of food.

On May 21, 1943, ND&R did establish maximum prices on wheat, corn, beans, flour, salt, butter, sugar, and meat; however, merchants rigidly re-

sisted lowering prices. Three days later Francisco Javier Gaxiola, minister of the national economy, announced the first sanctions and set up a committee to watch for violations of the price regulations. In the view of the head of the British Legation, "The small fry among the speculators have been forced to toe the line, but a sterner policy will be needed to discourage the large racketeers, among whom may be counted Governors of States, generals, politicians, and labor leaders, whose habitual exploitation of their weaker brethren it will need more than decrees of the government to extricate."[55]

ND&R was headed by Nazario S. Ortíz Garza. Yet even by the end of the war, he had not managed to implement the presidential directive of October 28, 1941, ordering Ferrocarriles Nacionales de México to grant the highest priority to ND&R for transporting articles of basic need. On March 31, 1945, Ortíz Garza had to send an urgent telegram to J. Jesús González Gallo, the personal secretary to the president, in order to commandeer railroad cars at Toluca to ship wheat to Mexico City. He even went so far as to ask for the use of troops to force the National Railways to release the cars.[56]

There is ample archival proof of the ongoing bureaucratic battle between Ortíz Garza and Raúl Nevarez, head of the railroad, over ND&R's use of the nation's railway system. In one petition to the president, Ortíz Garza described the two men's relationship as "an open state of conflict." Similarly, Efraín Buenrostro, the head of PEMEX, also had to appeal to the president on a daily basis over the priorities for the use of the railroad cars for PEMEX against ND&R.[57] At times shortages of, and rivalries over, the use of railroad cars even threatened to waste precious crops. According to the version of events from Ortíz Garza, problems in the railroad allocation system threatened the 1945 rice crop in Sonora, Sinaloa, and Michoacán.[58]

Most observers at the time, and subsequently, have viewed the railroad crisis as either a problem whose origin was to be found in the overburdened nature of the railroad system or in managerial incompetence, especially since President Cárdenas had introduced worker administration to the railroads. Yet the problem of the railways was political, in large part. Not only did executive orders grant ND&R preferential use of the railroad system when transporting basic foodstuffs, they also granted a 50 percent discount on moving food. The Secretaría de Comunicaciones y Obras Públicas, which was headed by the president's colorful brother, Maximino Avila Camacho, had applied that discount to private merchants as well as to the commodities shipped by ND&R. These subsidies were highly controversial. The railroad workers' union (STFRM) objected profoundly to this state subsidy to the private sector, for the railroads lost money by shipping under these conditions. Indeed, according to the union's estimates the railroads were losing 6 million pesos per year as a result of Maximino's subsidies to private businessmen.[59]

The battle against *carestía* was, from a political point of view, to be the job of Minister Gaxiola. He blamed a wide variety of factors for the

problems but above all claimed that as minister of the national economy he was in charge of effects rather than causes. He did concede that meat shortages were a result of beef exports to the United States and even admitted that the quantity of fruits, vegetables, and grains into the Federal District fell by 100,000,000 kilograms between 1942 and 1943. However, his main explanation of the problem was to be found in poor agricultural production, the lack of electricity-generating capacity, problems in the team charged with the administration of the war rationing, and problems of transportation.[60]

Initially only the very poor felt the pinch acutely, but by 1943 even artisans and office workers were feeling the pressure. As a conservation measure aimed at protecting the country's forests, the poor had been given a year, starting in 1941, to get rid of their braziers and to replace them with oil stoves. A policy of restricting charcoal supplies, in the name of conservation, combined with the food shortages and the price increases to make matters worse by the height of the war. The magazine *Hoy* launched a campaign blaming Minister Gaxiola for the shortages and high prices and claiming that official corruption was at the core of the problem. Gaxiola was vulnerable to the charge, and it spread rapidly. His political base had been his close association with General and former President Abelardo Rodríguez. As his personal secretary, Gaxiola was the incarnation of the most hated segment of the official party, from the point of view of the Cardenistas. If anyone was in a position to use his official position, or at least to be seen to be thus using it to aid his *compadre*, it was Gaxiola. Some observers, including the British chargé d'affaires in Mexico, certainly believed that Gaxiola had personally profited from the wartime shortages. He called it an "open secret" that the very agency established to control shortages was led by men who were "cornering and selling to the black market at profits which vary in direct proportion to the artificially produced scarcities."[61]

Later in September the government extended price controls to some industrial products, but they too were ineffective if one is to judge by the comments of the day. Pressures continued to build, and Gaxiola remained a favorite target for those unhappy with the wartime inflation and scarcities. Eventually his close association with Abelardo Rodríguez became too much of a political liability. At the end of June 1944, Francisco Javier Gaxiola finally resigned, and it was difficult to find many who would take his side. His resignation was tendered without the usual reference to the standard and approved pretexts. Even the president's letter accepting his resignation was without any warmth.[62]

The problem with price controls is, of course, that rewards abound for those who break the rules. Merchants have an incentive to withhold supplies, farmers opt for production of items that are not controlled, black markets proliferate, and officials charged with administering the system too often find that their friends and relatives have made remarkable profits from

inside trading. As British Chargé d'Affaires Bateman observed, "I am skeptical of the results which the new measure will achieve. The more fingers in the pie, the greater, it seems to me, will be the opportunities for graft and food racketeering."[63]

The U.S. response to the food crisis was also based on this skeptical assessment of the likelihood of price controls working in Mexico. The very nature of food production and distribution in Mexico, based upon so many small producers, argued against the effectiveness of measures of control. Still the problem could not be ignored. As Messersmith explained: "It has got to be considered that of these 20 million people who live in Mexico, the overwhelming majority live in great poverty. Their buying capacity is low. Their standard of living is low. If the basic commodities which they consume, principally foodstuffs, go up, these people will be in a terrible way, and I see ourselves being made the goat."[64]

U.S. officials took the attitude that Mexico should replicate their solution to the problem by attacking the "problem" of excessive demand. They urged Mexico to sell war bonds. The government followed this advice and tried to sell them in order to soak up excess funds; however, it proved impossible to sell bonds in Mexico. The population lived too close to the margin to have the money to spend on war bonds, and the people did not feel much empathy for the war effort. NAFISA offered 50 million pesos' worth of bonds in August and September 1943; however, Espinosa de los Monteros confided that only 15 million of the issue had been subscribed; and indeed, in the same period, 20 million dollars had entered Mexico.[65]

The Ministry of Finance next considered limiting dividends to a fixed percentage, to require surplus profits to be invested in government bonds, to institute an excess profits tax, and to increase the top income tax rate to 45 percent on annual incomes in excess of 500,000 pesos. Planning to link these changes to the 1944 Revenue Law, the ministry inadvertently precipitated a storm of protest by the business community, for whom no amount of profit could ever be excessive. Salvador Ugarte, director general of the Banco de Comercio, was particularly prominent in arguing against the proposal limiting tax-free dividends to 2 percent and to the requirement that profits would have to be invested in government bonds.[66]

Retreating from the Ministry of Finance's proposal, the Mexican government tried another tack in 1944. On August 16, 1943, a new rule had required banks to leave one third of their deposits with the Banco de México. That reserve requirement was increased to 50 percent by March 1944. The attempt was initially a wartime measure to soak up money from within the banking system and thereby restrict credit and combat inflation. Eventually this device became a technique in Mexico by which the federal development agency, Nacional Financiera, channeled deposits into approved development projects in both the private and public sectors. So it happened that the provisions developed to fight wartime inflation grew into a major

technique by which the Mexican state financed the development projects for decades to come. It often happens in history that the important turning points come from the most unexpected origins.

A balance sheet of the impact of the war on Mexico shows a fairly clear picture. On the positive side, the most immediate impact of the war was almost certainly increased economic activity. Production rose in most areas: agriculture, mining, manufacturing, and especially in the export area. At the height of the war boom the increased exports created a forced savings which gave Mexico the ability to both make new investments and to retire a large part of its external public debt for the first time since independence.

From a political perspective, the war boom generated great leverage for the government. As in the *porfiriato*, there were simply more favors to spread around. The link between the issuing of contracts and the politics of the day was close indeed. Capital accumulation increased significantly, and the great national goal of industrialization came a bit closer to fruition. In addition, Mexico gained further access to industrial technology, a lack of which was widely believed to have been a problem for the country.

On the negative side, the war gave Mexican nationalism a terrible thrashing, and dependency increased notably. Specialization in agricultural production for the war effort, when combined with the floods, droughts, and freezes of 1943, created a crisis of austerity that precipitated a decline in living conditions for the vast majority of the Mexican population. A war-generated famine was on the horizon by the end of the conflict. Patterns of distribution that emerged during the agricultural crisis and the resultant crisis of *carestía* continued beyond the bad harvests and set a pattern for the coming years. The central role of diplomats "helping" Mexico avert that disaster markedly increased the influence of the United States in the development process south of the border.

Mexico's role as a producer of minerals and agricultural products provided a prime example of the kind of analysis that was being adopted by the United Nations' Economic Commission on Latin America and became known, after its founding director, as the Prebisch thesis. The belief that the terms of trade for primary products deteriorated in comparison with the products of industry seemed well based in the immediate postwar period. As the war ended, the movement of the terms of trade and postwar inflation combined to make Raúl Prebisch's prescription seem correct. The conditions were set to make reasonable planners think in terms of adopting a model of import substitution, rather than sticking with economic nationalism; and that tendency was reinforced in the marketplace by personal benefits to be enjoyed by close cooperation with foreign industrialists.

The highly regressive impact of the war boom on income distribution established a pattern that was to be the wave of the future. In a reversal of the redistributive patterns of the early Cárdenas years, the acceptance of a

kind of prosperity based upon mass contributions to the most privileged created a different kind of Mexican Revolution. A revolutionary elite grew in close association with government policies. War contracts, tax breaks, falling real wages, a regressive tax structure, and monetary favors involved the state in the process of capital accumulation, all within the terms of a dependent relationship with the United States.

The war created a period of broad agreement on the basic goal of using the wartime cooperation to pursue the national goal of industrial development. Public goals and private interests combined in the pursuit of this objective, and a measure of success was achieved. But in the process the meaning of success changed. Instead of having an increasing part of the nation's income distributed to those most in need, the lion's share went to the most privileged. Within a few years Miguel Alemán would make this explicit, and his justification of unequal income distribution would be virtually identical with that of classical economic liberalism, albeit with a much larger role for the state than the advocates of laissez-faire theory would accept.

For most Mexicans reality meant austerity and wage freezes in a period of inflation, in short, a declining standard of living. However, the combination of falling real wages and economic boom diminished sympathy for the poor. Illusions, of course, accompanied this process and helped people accept these fundamental changes. The success of a few Mexicans seemed to point the way to a modern life-style for others, and these winners knew how to flaunt their wealth. A newspaper chain added insult to injury as it launched an advertising campaign under the banner *"el sol sale para todos"* (the sun shines for all). That could be said to have been a great illusion of the day. Revolutionary rhetoric notwithstanding, the benefits of Mexico's participation in the war flowed to the privileged few and the costs rested on the many.

## Notes

1. An earlier version of this chapter appeared as Niblo, *The Impact of War.*

2. Data in this chapter come from the *Anuario Estadístico de la República Mexicana* for the year corresponding to the dates cited, unless otherwise indicated.

3. Wilkie, *The Mexican Revolution,* 236–37. Wilkie's calculations led him to conclude that the percentage of the population living under the poverty line fell from 46 to 39.4 percent between 1940 and 1950. His index of poverty fell from 100 in 1940 to 85.7 in 1950.

4. Reynolds, *The Mexican Economy,* 36–38; Solís, *La realidad económica mexicana,* 113.

5. Secretaría de Economía, *Desarrollo de la Economía Nacional,* 41, 92–93.

6. Joseph F. McGurk to Laurence Duggan, May 9, 1944, USNA/RG 59, 812.61/ 193.

7. *El Universal,* August 17, 1942; C. H. Bateman to the Foreign Office, August 18, 1942, PRO, FO/371, 30590 .

8. Ibid.

9. George Messersmith to Cordell Hull, July 2, 1943, USNA/RG 59, 812.61/156. This paralleled the Mexican *Plan de Movilización Agrícola de la República Mexicana,* published at the same time.

10. Ibid.

11. In March, Messersmith stated that the basic strategy was to sell cotton to Mexico and shift cotton lands into war production. Messersmith to Hull, March 11, 1943, USNA/RG 59, 812.61/147.

12. McGurk to Duggan, May 9, 1944, USNA/RG 59, 812.61/193.

13. *El Nacional,* January 28, 1944.

14. Ibid.

15. Later the government reported that the hectares sown in corn declined from 3,491,968 in 1941 to 3,082,732 in 1943. That estimate of a decline of 436,236 hectares from the *Anuario Estadístico de la República Mexicana* clashed with the earlier figure of 700,000 hectares published in *El Nacional.*

16. *El Nacional,* January 28, 1944. See also "Report on Corn Production," January 31, 1944, USNA/RG 59, 812.61/315.

17. Messersmith to the Department of State, October 27, 1943, USNA/RG 59, 812.61/171.

18. Messersmith to Hull, July 2, 1943, USNA/RG 59, 812.61/156 and an accompanying report entitled "Desirability of an Overall Program for Collaboration in the Agricultural Field."

19. Messersmith to McGurk, May 21, 1944, and Messersmith to Claude Wickard, May 21, 1944, USNA/RG 59, 812.60/31.

20. Duggan to McGurk and P. Bonsal, August 24, 1943, USNA/RG 59, 812.61/167.

21. Finley to secretary of state, September 23, 1943, USNA/RG 59, 812.00/32196.

22. Marchant to Edward G. Cale, September 20, 1945, USNA/RG 59, 812.6135/8.

23. The account of this long-range swap of wheat is contained in USNA/RG 59, 812.5018/95.

24. USNA/RG 59: 812.61315/11-545, 812.61315/2-1246, and 812.5018/74. There are scores of specific estimates of agricultural output for various crops in Mexico in the file 812.5018.

25. "Wartime Controls Affecting Mexico," September 20, 1945, USNA/RG 59, 812.6135/8-1445. See also USDA report, USNA/RG 59, 812.5018/116A. It is particularly interesting in that Secretary of State Edward Stettinius spells out the rules for food allocation in the face of postwar food shortages.

26. J. Bernard Gibbs to secretary of state, April 3, 1946, USNA/RG 59, 812.5018/4-346.

27. Ibid.

28. United Nations, *Second World Food Survey, 1952.*

29. Ibid.

30. Laurence Duggan was a major strategist for economic affairs within the State Department before he became disillusioned over the treatment of Latin America after the war. Ultimately he committed suicide while under attack from Senator Joseph McCarthy.

31. Reynolds, *The Mexican Economy,* 345.

32. A category such as "fundición y manufactura de artículos metálicos" cuts across quite different techniques of production and ultimately combines the output from a steel mill with that of an artisan's workshop.

33. Real wages stayed at this low level after the war; and even after prices stabilized from 1951 to 1954, the devaluation of 1954 wiped out nearly all of the gain in real wages from 1951 to 1954. Miguel Alemán's private cost-of-living index was prepared by the Mexican Ministry of Labor. A copy can be found in Elmer H. Bourgerie to secretary of state, August 30, 1954, USNA/RG 59, 812.061/8-3054.

34. Bortz, "Wages and Economic Crisis in Mexico," 45.

35. *Jornadas Industriales*, May–June 1954, 1.

36. Underconsumption analysis is probably the most heterogeneous tradition of Western economic thought. Frequently shared by people of quite different ideologies, it commands wide support beyond the circle of economists. For a modern analysis of this influential tradition see Bleaney, *Underconsumption Theories*. The economic nationalists of the day were studied and praised by Sanford A. Mosk in his *Industrial Revolution in Mexico*.

37. Secretaría de Economía, *Desarrollo de la Economía Nacional*, 58–61, 118–19.

38. Messersmith to Wickard, May 21, 1944, USNA/RG 59, 812.60/31.

39. Luis Morones to Manuel Avila Camacho, January 30, 1942, AGN, RP/MAC, 497/10.

40. Morones and James Barragán to Heriberto Jara, February 27, 1942, ibid.

41. Fidel Velázquez to Avila Camacho, May 2, 1941, AGN, RP/MAC, 523.4/2.

42. Secret report dealing with Miguel Alemán, July 15, 1944, PRO, FO/371, 38312.

43. *El Popular*, July 21, 1944. See AGN, RP/MAC, 545.3/17 for the petitions of those protesting their arrests and proclaiming their innocence of all charges.

44. Arthur Paul to Fineletter, January 11, 1943, USNA/RG 59, 812.504/2166 1/2. See also Morris S. Rosenthal to Otis E. Mulliken, April 24, 1943, USNA/RG 59, 812.504/2198.

45. Messersmith to Dean Acheson, January 12, 1946, USNA/RG 59, 812.00/1-1246.

46. William K. Ailshie to secretary of state, April 2, 1943, USNA/RG 59, 812.504/2196.

47. *Excélsior*, April 7, 1943.

48. Memorandum of conversation between Eduardo Suárez and Thomas Lockett, April 8, 1943, USNA/RG 59, 812.51/2691.

49. Memorandum of conversation between Lockett and Suárez, April 14, 1943, USNA/RG 59, 812.51/2678.

50. Messersmith to Hull, April 14, 1943, USNA/RG 59, 812.51/2692.

51. *Novedades*, June 11, 12, 1943. Also, Messersmith to Duggan, June 15, 1943, USNA/RG 59, 812.516/668.

52. Messersmith to Hull, April 14, 1943, USNA/RG 59, 812.51/2691.

53. McGurk to Messersmith, October 12, 1943, USNA/RG 59, 812.51/10-1943.

54. *Diario Oficial*, March 3, 1943.

55. C. H. Bateman to the Foreign Office, June 2, 1943, PRO, FO/371, 26087.

56. Nazario S. Ortíz Garza to J. Jesús González Gallo, March 31, 1945, AGN, RP/MAC, 545.22/160-1.

57. Ortíz Garza and Efraín Buenrostro to Avila Camacho, May 7, 1946, ibid.

58. Ortíz Garza to the president, April 20, 1945, ibid.

59. Ibarra, secretary general of STFRM, to Avila Camacho, March 9, 1942, ibid.

60. Gaxiola, *Memorias*, 297–99. See also Niblo, "Decoding Mexican Politics," 23–39.

61. *Hoy*, July 24, 1943. *Hoy*'s campaign reached a peak on July 31, 1943, when it published three articles attacking Gaxiola personally for being in league with the speculators. Bateman to Anthony Eden, August 9, 1943, PRO, FO/371, 33990.

62. Gaxiola published his memoirs in 1975 in which he proclaimed his complete innocence from all charges of wartime corruption. Gaxiola, *Memorias*, 303–7.

63. British Legation in Mexico to the Foreign Office, March 4, 1943, PRO, FO/371, 33990.

64. Messersmith to Hull, April 14, 1943, USNA/RG 59, 812.51/2691.

65. Messersmith to Hull, October 2, 1943, USNA/RG 59, 812.51/2678.

66. *Excélsior*, December 18, 1943.

# III POSTWAR STRATEGIES

# 6 Strategies of Industrialization

A deeply shared commitment to a rapid program of industrialization was fortified by the wartime cooperation between the United States and Mexico. With the political will in place, attention turned to matters of implementation. The shift was away from a strategy of national industrialization based on an underconsumptionist analysis that saw the poor as future customers of the products of Mexican industry, to an international strategy that linked Mexican efforts with powerful foreign partners and reduced the role of the poor to generating a surplus in which they would not share. A new role for the state also emerged. Eschewing the direct industrial initiatives under President Cárdenas, the presidents of the 1940s harnessed the resources of the state to the private sector in a frenzy of industrial activity that culminated under President Alemán.

One of the surprising side effects of the nationalization of petroleum in 1938 was to convince President Cárdenas to change his approach to industrial development by cutting back on direct involvement in state industrialization projects in favor of disguised state support for private sector projects. This helped to convince the United States and the business community that petroleum had been an isolated case, and not the beginning of a general program of nationalization of private assets in Mexico. The other important U.S. economic interests in Mexico (land and minerals) and the approach of war in Europe made the pressures for an accommodation with major segments of U.S. capital outweigh the desire for revenge. The first example of this change to the strategy of industrialization was in the planning of the Altos Hornos steel complex. In effect, the project was denationalized as capital, technical expertise, and management flowed from Alabama to Coahuila. Earlier Cardenista dreams of a purely national industry were set aside.

After it became clear, in the approach to the 1940 election, that considerable segments within the governing party wanted a respite from the pace of change under Cárdenas, the prospects of economic nationalism receded further. Manuel Avila Camacho reversed course quickly, taking the process far beyond the pragmatic retreat after the petroleum nationalization. While still his party's candidate before the 1940 election, Avila Camacho privately began to come to terms with the Monterrey Group, the most powerful

consortium of private industrialists in the country. This represented a leap to the right for a member of the revolutionary family.

The platform upon which Avila Camacho had campaigned tended to confuse people about the new president. The PRM had just unveiled a second Six-Year Plan that appeared to be an extension of Cardenismo; it was adopted in November 1939 and published the following January. Deeply committed to a rapid industrialization program, it still envisioned a governmental commitment to programs in which the state had joint participation with the workers in the control and administration of industrial enterprises. Campaign material called for the establishment of a government office to evaluate and coordinate all plans for industrialization. The proposed plan appeared to be the realization of the call for the industrialization of the country on the terms of the economic nationalists. And the fact that as many as twenty thousand CTM members belonged to the workers' militias made this vision of worker-controlled industries more formidable. A reading of public election pronouncements might have led one to view Avila Camacho as appearing to run for the presidency on a platform calling for the continuation of the the the radical nationalism of the Cárdenas years, including the workers' administration that already existed in railroads and petroleum.

The 1940 election program was, on at least one account, written by Vicente Lombardo Toledano. It promised to carry forward the participation of organized labor in the administration of industry, further collectivization of agriculture, and the nationalization of heavy industry. Yet it is interesting to note that, even during the campaign, the U.S. embassy thought that the acceptance of this plan was the price that General Avila Camacho had to pay in order to gain labor's support and the PRM's nomination. People who expected the candidate to make good on his electoral platform were in for a rude awakening.[1] Even observers in the U.S. and British embassies initially believed that Avila Camacho represented a continuation of Cardenismo. Conventional wisdom of the moment was tapped by the American consul in Mexicali who reported: "It appears at this time that all local substantial Mexicans who are holders of property and real assets are realizing that a regime under General Camacho [*sic*] would prove contrary to their personal interests and be largely devoted to the application of purely socialistic philosophy."[2]

Supporters of President Cárdenas's reforms felt that they had no place else to go, in the face of the right-wing threat of General Almazán in the 1940 campaign. Even *La Voz de México*, the organ of the PCM, called upon all workers to support Avila Camacho and the second Six-Year Plan and to oppose those who seemed to be their greatest enemies of the day: Emilio Portes Gil, caudillo of the CNC; Luis Montes de Oca, director of the Banco de México; Foreign Minister Eduardo Hay; Ezequiel Padilla and Gonzalo N. Santos of the PRM; and, of course, agents of Trotsky.[3]

Appearances were deceptive. We now know that the selection of 1940 was already associated with a conservative pullback that had started within the Cárdenas administration itself after the nationalization of the petroleum. Certainly the official candidate had no intention of carrying forward the policies of his predecessor. Attentive followers of the campaign noted that on December 19, 1939, in a press interview, the candidate began to distance himself from Article 3 of the constitution.[4] Josephus Daniels had it right, in writing to Secretary of State Cordell Hull: "Without any necessity for doing so, he [Manuel Avila Camacho] has indicated that he is conservative, and has practically informed the CTM, and its leader Lombardo Toledano, either to accept his position or leave it."[5]

Daniels had received reports of conversations between staff members and General Luis Bobadilla, who had been the candidate's chief of staff when Avila Camacho had been minister of defense. As early as March 6, 1939, he was told that "the General [Avila Camacho] is desirous of quieting down the present radical tendencies of labor, and states that Lombardo Toledano is agreeable to such a procedure, and that President Cárdenas has given his assent to this."[6]

This is especially revealing information because it shows that Cárdenas was considerably more moderate than many of the Cardenistas. That impression is also given by the willingness of President Cárdenas to tolerate men of the extreme right in key economic positions, especially Montes de Oca at the Banco de México, and his regular use of Luis and Agustín Legorreta of the Banco Nacional de México to formulate economic policy and evaluate the performance of the petroleum industry. In the end, radicals such as Lombardo Toledano of the CTM and Graciano Sánchez of the CNC used the negotiations leading to the 1940 election as a way to bargain for more seats in Congress for their factions or other immediate rewards, and they gave up earlier Cardenista plans for autonomous national industrial development; in historical perspective, their rewards were often illusory.

## 1940 and the Monterrey Group

Although it was not generally known at the time, the PRM candidate even began to forge alliances with the people who had been the most unyielding opponents of the major reforms associated with the Mexican Revolution. The powerful Monterrey Group was surprisingly influential in the events leading up to the election of 1940. The original founders—men such as Patricio Milmo (né Patrick Mullins), Isaac Garza, Francisco Sada, José Muguerza, and Valentín Rivero—had been followed by a second generation that had come of age after the revolution of 1910. Combining a deep opposition to the revolution with a close group affinity and an ambivalence

toward the United States, members including Luis Garza of the Fundidora steel mill, Roberto G. Sada (head of Vidriera glassworks), Luis G. Sada (Cervecería Cuauhtémoc), Joel Rocha (Salinas y Rocha department store), Manuel Barragán (initially of Topo Chico soda works, then Coca-Cola distributor, and finally the editor of *Excélsior* after 1928), Pablo Salas y López (Cementos Hidalgo), Arturo Padilla (Casa Calderón), and newcomer Emilio Azcárraga (owner of the Ford distributorship in Monterrey) came to occupy the most extreme position on the far right within the private sector.

The Monterrey Group had been through a long period of opposition and, for some members, even exile, since Bernardo Reyes had been forced out of the governorship in 1909. The members had tried to find a political replacement for Reyes for decades. For a while in the 1920s, Aarón Sáenz appeared to be their man. Indeed, he had been a front-runner for the candidacy for the presidency in 1929 when President Calles surprised the country and brought a virtual unknown, Pascual Ortíz Rubio, back from his ambassadorship in Brazil to be the official candidate of the PNR. Ultimately, Calles was confident that Sáenz would not join the Gonzalo Escobár rebellion. One recent historian of that political battle finally characterized Sáenz as too weak, opportunistic, and grasping to take a chance on joining Gonzalo Escobár.[7] Eventually, Sáenz made his peace with the official party—for which he gained state favors for his interests in the sugar and banking sectors—and the Monterrey Group lost its man at the center of the national political arena.

After the crisis following the assassination of Alvaro Obregón, in 1928, the Monterrey Group founded the Confederación Patronal de la República Mexicana (COPARMEX), and the bosses from Monterrey became drawn more into the politics of opposition. COPARMEX adopted a laissez-faire attitude opposing governmental action in the economic sphere, a highly unusual position in Mexico. It was, in large part, the economic independence of the brewers and steel makers from the government that enabled this organization to take an antistatist position. It is important to recognize that a fundamental difference between the Monterrey Group and the rest of Mexican industry was that the *norteños* (northerners) developed industry without much aid from the state, save in the broadest protectionist sense. The extreme laissez-faire position of the group made alliances, even with PRM conservatives, quite difficult.

Even leaders on the right of the PRM were seen to be radical by the standards the group adopted. Men such as Plutarco Elías Calles and Emilio Portes Gil became bitter enemies by taking an anticlerical position and by leading the battles to produce a labor code that would partially implement Article 123 in the years from 1929 to 1931. The Monterrey Group, through its front COPARMEX and using its new voice, *Excélsior*, adopted a position of absolute intransigence against the government's reforms along with the view that the state should not intervene in either its state elections or its

factories. The group was also unusual in that it adopted an extreme version of fundamental Catholicism, "*católico, romano y apostólico*," as the saying went. People working for the Monterrey employers had to follow a very conservative social line, given the dominant attitude that there was no private space beyond the employers' scrutiny. At times, divorce was enough to elicit dismissal. The anticlericalism of the *reforma* and the revolution was foreign to the bosses in Monterrey.

The other favorite son of the Monterrey Group as early as the 1920s had been General Juan Andreu Almazán, head of the Monterrey garrison of the army in 1926. Having come to an understanding with the main figures in the group during his posting in that city, he had gained a large number of favors for his Anáhuac Construction Company. For a while he seemed to represent a great opportunity to the organization in the 1940 election. Scarcely able to believe their good fortune, the leaders of the Monterrey Group also discovered a far more amenable figure in the person of the new candidate of the PRM, General Manuel Avila Camacho. For the first time since 1910, the patriarchs of Monterrey viewed the approach of an election with hope. This represented a major change. During the 1940 election the group hedged its bets by supporting both Avila Camacho and Almazán.

In 1935–36 an epic conflict took place between the Monterrey Group and the forces of President Cárdenas. Lombardo Toledano of the CTM had supported, or perhaps inspired, an attempt to organize the workers in the Garza-Sada factories into a progovernment union to replace the company union that the Monterrey Group used to dominate labor in its factories. The conflict focused on its glassworks, the Vidriera. Between November 1935 and July 1936 there were pitched battles, shoot-outs, lockouts, strikes, and high political maneuvering between the two sides. The height of conflict came on the night of July 29, 1936, when a progovernment rally clashed with a progroup rally; two CTM supporters were killed, and six hundred of the group's Acción Cívica members were arrested, including Joel Rocha and Virgilio Garza, Jr.[8]

The results were mixed. The federal government lost in its bid to bring the CTM into Monterrey. However, the Cárdenas administration was able to impose its candidate as governor. Having salvaged something in the political arena, the Cárdenas administration then gave up the battle to bring the Monterrey Group's economic activities into line with the rest of the country. In retrospect the battle seemed to be something of a turning point as the president began to pull back from the more radical experiments of the earlier years, except for the petroleum expropriation, which is best viewed as a special case.

As World War II broke out in Europe, Manuel Avila Camacho was in Monterrey. He appears to have courted the Monterrey Group, or possibly it was the other way around. To this point no one has turned up any record of the negotiations between General Avila Camacho and leaders of the group.

However, we do know that he was in the city four times in October 1939. On October 8 he was given an opulent luncheon by the Cervecería Cuauhtémoc. As world war loomed, the importance of an accommodation between the country's largest industrial group and the man who would be the wartime president could not have been underestimated.

This moment in October was the point at which Luis Javier Garrido argues that the existence of a candidate to the right of the official candidate had the effect of moderating the PRM in general and Avila Camacho specifically. Alexander Saragoza also thinks that, in these dealings, the group's support for the Acción Nacional further moderated positions taken by the PRM.[9] Ironically, U.S. officials still opposed the influence of the Monterrey Group, thinking that the *norteños* were soft on the Nazi threat.

From his earliest moments as the official candidate, Avila Camacho placed the Cardenista commitment to a rapid program of industrialization at the center of his agenda. Once in power, the new administration in Mexico City quickly presented a plan for major borrowing to the U.S. Treasury Department, in the hope of obtaining a favorable report for the Export-Import Bank and thus qualify for loans. The Avila Camacho project included plans for a dam at the Valle del Bravo and for two hydroelectric plants at Ixtapantongo. The plans for hydroelectric plants at Perote, Veracruz; the Chapala hydroelectric system in Jalisco; the Sistema del Chongos, covering parts of Chihuahua and the Laguna; and a new plant at Poza Rica were all presented to the U.S. government authorities at the beginning of the 1940 *sexeño*.[10]

Avila Camacho moved to mend his fences with the most profoundly counterrevolutionary forces in the private sector in Mexico and with foreign investors. That political reorientation was justified by the nation's broad commitment to the great goal of industrialization. Avila Camacho believed that, for the country to industrialize, it was necessary to court rather than to oppose the powerful industrialists, no matter how reactionary they were, and no matter what their nationality.

Early statements by the candidate gave some indication of his new orientation. In a postelection interview Avila Camacho signaled a more probusiness attitude by characterizing his government's orientation as favoring "ample guarantees to capital; help to the workers and peasants; development of industry; improvement of justice; better diplomatic and commercial relations with the rest of the countries in the world; democracy; absolute freedom of press and thought."[11] Or again, he stated to *La Prensa*, "It is necessary to create confidence in the investor; first in the Mexican investor, and then in the foreign investor."[12] One British diplomat quickly captured the new attitude: "The President has thrown out hints to capitalists and foreigners that he is prepared to cooperate with them."[13]

More than press statements, the composition of the first cabinet of a president often provides a gauge of the balance of forces, not necessarily in

the new administration but of the relative strengths of the internal factions that took place during the negotiations within the governing party at the time of the selection of the new candidate. Avila Camacho's cabinet contained men from virtually all parts of the PRM spectrum. It was not that the new president immediately excluded the center and left of the party; rather, he used the war and the great goal of industrialization to shift the entire party more toward a model of development based upon the creation of a favorable climate for private capital, foreign and domestic.

Since foreigners tended to control more capital, they loomed large in the government's strategy of industrialization. Once in power, President Avila Camacho moved in the new direction. By the end of his term, he was able to boast that, since January 1939, he had brought some 360 new industries representing 400 million pesos of new investment to Mexico.[14] The techniques he used were interesting.

The new administration quickly began to distance itself from the left wing of the party. Education has always been a highly symbolic battleground in revolutionary Mexico. Therefore, when Avila Camacho dismissed Luis Sánchez Pontón and replaced him with the right-wing Octavio Véjar Vásquez, it represented more than a purge of the education establishment; it was a clear and symbolic signal that policies were changing in a more conservative direction. And when he referred to President Cárdenas's support for the *ejido colectivo* as his "cardinal sin," he was also sending strong signals abroad.[15]

We have seen how cooperation in the Second World War forged links between the elite of the two countries in both the public and private sectors. Specifically, sixteen projects of industrial and infrastructure development received high priority during World War II, as a price for Mexico to continue shipping raw materials for the war effort. There was even a flirtation with industrial barter as a few factories were shipped south in another form of payment, and some of those projects favored the interests of the highest politicians in the country. However, Mexican leaders were looking for a more lasting motor force for industrialization.

Initially, they thought they had found a way forward with Axel Wenner Gren, a Swedish citizen who was thought by Allied diplomats to have had close economic links with the German regime. Wenner Gren promised to organize a group of investors and commit 500 million dollars to projects of industrialization. The president's brother, Maximino, became a business partner of Wenner Gren, and he tried mightily to convince the Mexican president to have Wenner Gren head the country's industrialization effort for the private sector; pursuant to that plan, it was necessary to remove him from the blacklist. President Avila Camacho, Interior Minister Alemán, and U.S. businessmen in Mexico, Ben Smith and Ed Flynn, all pressured U.S. authorities to take Wenner Gren off the blacklist. Ambassador George Messersmith reported that FDR was aware of the situation: "He [FDR] knew

that [Hermann] Goering in conversation with me in 1934 in Berlin had mentioned Wenner Gren as one of the very important businessmen and bankers who would be able to bring about a proper understanding of what the Nazi movement was really like in England and in France and in the United States and in Scandinavia."[16]

The group around Maximino and Wenner Gren was not successful in the attempt to change the blacklist. Neither did its grand plan for industrializing Mexico bear fruit, at least in the direct form envisioned at this stage. Yet there were several elements in this plan that were to be common denominators to the future projects of industrialization. In all of these projects the role of the supportive state was central. Not only did the government decide upon the priorities for imports, grant tax favors, underwrite borrowing, and provide assets, but at times it also provided the capital.

## Capital

The country's private bankers expected to make investment decisions in line with their traditional role as lenders of the community's savings. However, there was a problem from the viewpoint of those who wanted rapid industrialization. The long history of Hispanic mercantilism tended to work against industrial entrepreneurialism. There was a profound tendency, which could be traced back to Spain's precipitous decline into *la decadencia* from the seventeenth century, to punish producers and reward rentier landholders. An anti-industrial bias became a part of the Hispanic legacy, and in Mexico it was reinforced by the cycles of dictatorship and chaos that typified the early republic. As a result, it was common in the 1940s to hear the nascent industrialists complain about the country's bankers on the grounds that they favored relatively safe but sterile investments in urban property, estates, and specie rather than in projects of industrialization that carried a much higher multiplier effect.

The meeting of the Tenth Mexican National Convention of Bankers, held in Monterrey in April 1944, revealed the depth of tension relating to changes in the government's financial policies. Prominent among the government's participants were Minister of Finance Eduardo Suárez and Octavio Véjar Vásquez (who enjoyed a certain popularity in business circles as the former minister of education who had wanted an even more severe purge of leftists from within the Ministry of Education). In the private sector, key figures included Evaristo Araiza, director of the Compañía Fundidora de Fierro y Acero de Monterrey S.A. and a member of the U.S.-Mexican Commission; Luis G. Legorreta of BANAMEX; and Salvador Ugarte, president of the Banco de Comercio.

Notable among the discussions of the effect of the wartime boom on price levels, credit policies, and investment rules was an attack on the agrar-

ian reform program of the revolution. José F. Ortíz, of the Banco de la Laguna, recognized that private bankers could and would not support agrarian reform, especially in light of Supreme Court rulings denying private property holders protection against invasions from peasants demanding land for their ejidos. Felix Palavicini, one of the *constituyentes* of 1917, also asserted that the reformers had not meant to damage private property by means of the division of large estates in 1917. The bankers applauded energetically as José Lino Cortéz of the Banco de Michoacán attributed food shortages to the agrarian reform projects of the government. At that point, Eduardo Villaseñor, director of the Banco de México, spoke. He avoided the issue by limiting himself to technical banking considerations; by taking this tack, he refused to support the program. When Eduardo Suárez spoke, he also distanced himself from the land reform. He mentioned that some thirty-two million hectares of land had been distributed, and that this made him wonder how much more land could be distributed. He said that he favored some arrangement to protect private rural property. Thus, two of the top economic ministers in the Avila Camacho government failed to defend the tradition of land reform to the Mexican and U.S. bankers.[17]

Neither the country's top bankers nor the economic ministers wanted to concentrate capital in the countryside, at least in the collective ejido sector. The foreign bankers in attendance also agreed upon that fundamental tenet, and that policy would deprive the vast majority of agricultural producers access to sufficient capital, even in cases where normal business criteria were fulfilled. The point is that these attitudes in the banking sector were far more important than those in the growing agrarian bureaucracy. No matter how promising a rural enterprise would be, the bankers and finance ministers would starve it of capital. Without passing any law or even focusing public debate on the issue, they effectively rescinded the land reform program of the revolution, leaving only the hypertrophy of the agrarian bureaucracy. Within this context, corruption also came to play a systemic role in undermining the proposed changes, especially in the land reform banks, where the same private bankers who sat on the boards tolerated corrupt practices that they would not have allowed in their own financial institutions.

## Plans for Postwar Industrialization

The high strategy of industrialization was worked out at an international level. When Presidents Roosevelt and Avila Camacho met to put a seal on the wartime cooperation between the two countries, they faced, on the one hand, the unique problem that the United States wanted to import without exporting freely to Mexico; on the other hand, they also were forming a top-level strategy for future industrial development. They created the

Mexican-American Commission of Economic Cooperation in order to allocate scarce imports to projects of the highest priority. In order to implement their strategy, they brought together powerful entrepreneurs from the two nations. President Roosevelt first approached Eric A. Johnston, president of the U.S. Chamber of Commerce, to head the delegation. Johnston refused formal participation due to his political abhorrence of Harry Dexter White, Secretary Henry Morgenthau's assistant at the Treasury Department. In spite of Morgenthau's reputation, the commission took the position that their efforts to absorb surplus Mexican funds should be tied closely to the private sector in the United States. Johnston also was the chairman of the United States Inter-American Development Commission, an organization of the private sector. As "private citizens acting with full government approval," Johnston agreed with the members of the Mexican-American Commission of Economic Cooperation that the U.S. businessmen would "interest American firms in the establishment of new industries in Mexico preferably on a joint basis with Mexican interests."[18]

The president's brother, General Maximino Avila Camacho, also went abroad seeking business deals after 1940. He made contact with a number of highly placed U.S. entrepreneurs of varying reputations. No sooner was the new Mexican administration in place than Associated Press columnist Jack O'Brian broke the amazing news in the *Washington Post* that a group of twenty bankers and promoters was prepared to invest 100 million dollars in Mexico. As O'Brian reported, "the plan is believed to be contingent on action by Avila Camacho to protect profits against any attempt to continue the Mexican Revolution."[19]

The consortium that Maximino had put together was led by George Houston, former head of Baldwin Locomotive Works and now the senior partner in the Wall Street investment company, Houston and Jolles. William Gibbs McAdoo, former secretary of the treasury under President Woodrow Wilson, reportedly represented seventeen investors who would put 5 million dollars into the project. Former New York State Senator John A. Hastings and Frank Fageol, a bus and truck manufacturer, also were involved in the consortium, as was the California publisher with a famous name in Mexico, George Creel. "Carbon copies of the American proposal, now under study by the nine-day-old Camacho [*sic*] administration, were exhibited privately at the Hotel Reforma today, and it became evident that hardly an item of production or possible profit had been overlooked."[20] As another New York journalist reported it, the plan called for the twenty industrialists to "virtually take over" the wartime boom expansion of Mexico "lock, stock and barrel."[21]

By October 1943, Primo Villa Michel and the other well-connected Mexican commissioners were meeting with Eric Johnston and U.S. businessmen in Washington to plan the specific content of the cooperation between the two countries. Johnston, in turn, visited Mexico in November to

pursue these contacts.[22] The commission hired an engineering consulting firm, Ford, Bacon, and Davis, to do a series of studies of Mexican industry, which eventually came to some four hundred pages, part of which was published by the Banco de México in 1943; the section dealing with agricultural machinery was reviewed by Miguel Gleason Alvarez of the Colegio de México.

At times, the U.S. government sent technical specialists, such as Edward Flack, the deputy director of the Office of War Utilities, and Gerald Cruise, chief consulting engineer of the Industrial Products Division of the Office of Foreign Economic Administration, to assess the power situation in Mexico.[23] Clearly, the country was receiving high-level technical information from both the public and private sectors in the United States. It was an indication of how far the Mexican government had shifted its political position as well as its strategy of industrialization that it then strongly supported the 10,000-kilovolts-per-year electrical-generation expansion project for the Monterrey Group. The politics of wartime cooperation was enabling U.S. businessmen to regain ground lost since 1910. Mexicans close to the administration were eager for those links.

## The Armour Foundation and the Illinois Institute of Technology

Mexico's government contracted another major study of the country's industrial potential from the Armour Foundation of Chicago. The initiative had come from Secretary of Commerce Jesse Jones and Nelson Rockefeller, the coordinator of the Office of Inter-American Affairs, in 1941. The foundation had organized a tour of scientists and engineers around Latin America. Their instructions from the National Academy of Sciences were to prepare for Rockefeller "a report on the opportunities for cooperative industrial development between the United States and the other American Republics through the application of North American technical skills and production methods to Latin American raw materials."[24] Mexico emerged as a proving ground for the new techniques of influence, due to its position and resources during the war. As Director Vagtborg of the Armour Foundation put it in 1944, "The industrialization program of Mexico will be broader, deeper, and more immediate than any other Latin American country." In an arrangement with the Banco de México, the foundation was to study industrial proposals for Mexico to evaluate the proponents, and to act as the agent to employ the best available specialists for specific projects.

George H. Houston, a partner of Houston and Jolles, explained that, on the management side, his firm was playing the same role of broker for Mexican projects of industrialization as the Armour Foundation was playing on the scientific and technical side. And James Drumm, vice president of the

National City Bank of New York, picked up the other end of the Rockefeller interests and discussed the financial terms of industrial cooperation. In a classic Open Door statement he stressed the need of economic expansion to avoid domestic depression.

A conference was held at the Illinois Institute of Technology in Chicago from September 30 to October 6, 1945. Scarcely a typical academic conference, it was the dream of every academic entrepreneur. The culmination of years of well-funded study of a wide variety of industrial projects, it brought together powerful decision makers in business and government from both countries with relevant scientists and engineers. There were powerful U.S. industrialists, and the Mexican delegation was unprecedented. It consisted of thirty-six of the country's top bankers, industrialists, and government economic authorities. It would be virtually unheard of today for the chief executives of all the country's top banks, industries, and economic ministries to attend such an academic conference.[25]

The enthusiasm of the moment was captured in the evocation of industrial progress by Maurice Holland of the Armour Foundation when he cited a recent case of industrial development as characterizing the new international approach to science and technology: "The 2-billion-dollar atomic bomb which brought military Japan to her knees was a magnificent 'symphony' of international science. French, English, American, Italian, Danish—even German and Austrian—scientists played their part in the death dirge of Hiroshima."[26] Even greater experiences awaited Mexico as it joined in the march of "technology on the international front." Holland set the tone by saying that "we do not intend to play technological Santa Claus to the world!" Rather, there was a frank recognition that the U.S. industrialists would exchange technical expertise for participation in Mexican industrialization. This was a reality that was not widely appreciated in Mexico, beyond the higher echelons of the business community.

The Mexican delegation was enraptured by the prospects. Carlos Trouyet put it this way:

> The best compliment we can pay you is to say that we attended each and every one of your sessions. . . . We were greatly interested in everything we heard and saw. . . . Many of us have decided to send our children for a certain time to the United States to let them finish their education, because we have so great an admiration for what you have achieved. . . . I am in the investment banking business. My firm is absolutely sold on the idea that it is our duty to cooperate in the development of any new enterprises and new businesses for Mexico, an intermarriage, let us say, between American technique, American know-how, American experience, and Mexican desires for enhancing the future of their country.[27]

Trouyet reported that his firm had already been successful in bringing projects involving the Celanese Corporation, Westinghouse, the Marquette

Cement Company of Chicago, A. P. Green Fire Bricks Company, Abbott Laboratories, and the General American Transportation Company to Mexico. Eduardo Villaseñor said that he had had a dream that he had won the lottery, become a millionaire, and started a Mexican industrial research foundation, in the image of the Armour Foundation. It was a moment of euphoria as Mexican and American entrepreneurs planned for their future.

The Mexican president had also sent out many feelers within the U.S. business community. In 1943 he met with Arthur Lynch, deputy treasurer of the City of New York, and his business associate, Gregory Linder, who was based in Mexico City. Apparently the chief executive authorized Lynch to scout around for foreign firms that might be interested in coming to Mexico. Lynch reported back to Avila Camacho that one of his business interests, Watson-Flagg Engineering Company, would establish an office in the Federal District to provide equipment for three hydroelectric plants and the Lerma water supply system. Lynch seemed to have a fairly broad assignment to attract U.S. firms to Mexico.[28]

## The Plan for the Industrialization of the Federal District

At the beginning of February 1941 the government presented a plan for creating the Industrial Subdivision of Atzacoalcos to the Office of Planning of the DDF.[29] This plan provided for the centralization of industrialization in the Federal District. It took until June 1944 for Director of Public Works Guillermo Aguilar Alvarez and other planning officials to approve turning a large tract of land in the district—bounded on the north by the Río de los Remedios, on the east by the Ferrocarril Mexicano and the old Carretera de Pachuca, on the south by the Cerro de Guerrero, and on the west by the new Carretera de Laredo—over to the development corporation.

The land was vested in a corporation called Ciudad Industrial S.A. headed by Tomás Gurza. A great deal of planning was necessary to try to match industrial blocks to the proximity of the railways and highways, depending on the kind of production. Infrastructure had to be developed: highways, sewage, electricity. In one portentous report to the president, Gurza recognized that the proposal created a series of environmental problems; as he put it, "The most important railways enter Mexico City from the Northeast and the Northwest, and it is logical that industries be located near the railway terminals for passengers and cargo, but the dominant winds come from the Northeast and the Northwest and as they approach Mexico City they will bring *inconvenient gases and smoke that will bother the inhabitants.*"[30]

Gurza related that the decision had been taken, in spite of the problems associated with locating heavy industry upwind from the city, near the railroad lines. With a touching faith in technology, the planners decided to rely upon "modern industrial technical procedures in order to avoid injuries and annoyances to the inhabitants of the Federal District by industries to be located there." Ten prominent architects and engineers were invited to join in a competition to submit plans and designs for the industrial city.

A block of 50 hectares of the projected Ciudad Industrial had been granted to the inhabitants of the pueblo of Santiago Atzacoalco by a presidential decree on November 30, 1922. The land was now seized and the inhabitants were moved out, although the president conceded the residents a grant of 259 hectares elsewhere (unfortunately, the new grant was not implemented by the Ministry of Agriculture). The Supreme Court also ruled against an attempt by one Roberto Martínez to gain an *amparo* for those lands in 1942, only to have the previous owner emerge, also claiming ownership. Other lands in question, by the terms of their grants, had to be used for agriculture and could not be alienated. Therefore, executives of Ciudad Industrial had to appeal for presidential action to proceed with their plan to industrialize the Federal District.[31]

The centralization of industry under the firms located in the Federal District became a major part of the strategy of industrialization. Beyond this project to provide land and infrastructure for the new industries, there also was a reorganization of the formal structure of the chambers of industry in 1941, to which many organizations of businessmen outside of Mexico City objected. The issue, in their view, was the reorganization of the manufacturing industry around the district-based Cámara Nacional de Industrias de Transformación. In their view this reorganization placed industrial firms in the Federal District at considerable advantage over those in the rest of the country.[32]

The case of the provincial industrialists seemed strong; however, for reasons that relate to the cultural and historical predominance of the great city over the rest of the country and also to the corporativist urge within the governing party, they never stood a chance of having equal treatment. Favors would flow first to the industries located in the Federal District, and firms outside received second-class treatment. Only those in Monterrey were able successfully to go it alone, mostly because their products already had strong market positions and were not so dependent upon government favors. Industry would be concentrated in the district, because it was dangerous to be far away from the center of political decision making, and the population would grow exponentially since the decapitalization of the rural sector created an irresistible push off the land. Subsequent efforts at industrial decentralization always were forlorn, given the realities of this plan.

## Postwar Planning and the Postwar Settlement

During the war the Mexican-American Commission of Economic Cooperation had set out to build bridges between U.S. and Mexican entrepreneurs. Clearly recognizing that they wanted help from the two governments, successful entrepreneurs avoided the kind of blanket opposition to government intervention in the economy if it aided them. And Primo Villa Michel, Mexico's representative to the commission, took pride in reporting to the president's personal secretary that he had included private businessmen at every stage in the commission's planning of the distribution of wartime financial surpluses.[33]

In January 1944 the president announced that he was going to form a Comisión Nacional para el Estudio de los Problemas de México en la Posguerra (commission to study postwar problems). By mid-February the members of the commission were named; they were a mixed group, to say the least. Octavio Véjar Vásquez and four other figures were from the far right of the political spectrum. As Avila Camacho's first minister of education, Véjar Vásquez had led a purge of the leftists in the ministry. Wanting to go much further than the president, he had been forced out shortly after his appointment. Therefore, the naming of Véjar Vásquez to the head of the Comisión Nacional was provocative.

Victor Manuel Villaseñor (not to be confused with the banker Eduardo Villaseñor) first accepted an appointment to the commission; however, he soon became convinced that "the heterogeneous tendencies represented at that time made me doubt that the commission could carry out an efficient function from the perspective of the vast majority of the Mexican people."[34] Specifically, he also complained to the president that the Comisión Nacional had too deep links to the international business community and that its thirty-two members were merely acting as cover for the real decisions made by a core of five people. This inner circle was motivated by the desire to do their work out of sight of the general public.[35] Victor Manuel Villaseñor objected publicly to the formation of the commission before resigning.[36]

Luis Cabrera organized a series of conferences to publicize the industrialization program for the DDF. Filling the Palacio de las Bellas Artes in Mexico City in 1944, he reported on the work of the president's Comisión Nacional de Planeación para la Paz, which was to deal with problems of postwar development. Acutely aware that Mexico's role in the postwar world was going to change, and also conscious of the historical imbalance of power with the United States, he tried to keep up the country's spirits. Characterizing Mexico's history as having passed through three revolutions (the independence, which established the nation; the *reforma*, which freed the country from the Church; and the "revolution of equality," which he thought reestablished the sovereignty of the state over the national territory,

guaranteed land to peasants, and jobs for workers), Cabrera now saw the Atlantic Charter as guaranteeing the inviolability of the national territory and also the economic cooperation to achieve the industrialization that appeared to be the key to the future. The commission's endeavor was, by this time, a public relations effort to keep the country's spirits high as the important decisions shaping the postwar world approached.[37]

At virtually the same time another conference was organized by Nelson Rockefeller in association with the Inter-American Development Commission, for the entire Western Hemisphere. The final meetings of the Conferencia de Comisiones de Fomento Interamericano took place in New York in May 1944. Mexico's delegation was comprised of Eduardo Villaseñor of the Banco de México, Minister of the Economy Francisco Javier Gaxiola (referred to as Jorge in the official documents), and Salvador Ugarte of the Banco de Comercio. Implementing the recommendations of such groups as the Council on Foreign Relations, the National Planning Association, and the State Department, the Inter-American Development Commission pushed for private enterprise, free trade, a favorable investment climate, and the other elements in the U.S. program. For the Latin Americans, technical aid and loans from official agencies were clearly the reward for those who would combat economic nationalism.[38]

At times the older attitude still surfaced. In July 1944, President Avila Camacho announced the formation of the Comisión Federal de Fomento Industrial. The idea was to make up for the deficiencies of the private sector by organizing state enterprises to fill gaps in the productive system and to provide a central agency that would plan and organize the technical and economic development of the country.[39] In response, the Confederación de Cámaras Industriales (CCI) took issue with the government. These industrialists denied that there were deficiencies in the activity of the private sector, laying blame for shortfalls in production on the government itself for inadequate provision of infrastructure, most notably in petroleum distribution and electricity generation. Rather than start their own competing industries, the CCI argued that "the state should provide a part of the capital that could be represented in preferred stock, and if it were thought necessary, concede extensions and give subsidies to private industries."[40]

## Alemán's Plans for Industrialization

Following Avila Camacho, in the administration of Miguel Alemán the desire to attract foreign investment grew even stronger. The postwar boom in the United States provided a never-ending stream of products and techniques for Mexican entrepreneurs to import into their country. President Alemán put one of his closest friends and business partners, Francisco Buch de Parada, in charge of opening channels to U.S. business, and

together they made a canny selection. Donald Nelson had been the head of the War Production Board (WPB) in the United States during World War II. He was extremely well informed and well connected. He had organized the board so that it would push production for the war effort without offending vested interests in the various industries involved. By 1943, Nelson had staffed the WPB with some eight hundred dollar-a-year men who had looked after their industries' interests even as they had pushed the war effort.[41] Nelson's attitude was not so open to labor: Sidney Hillman of the CIO was pushed out and the Truman Committee's criticism of probusiness attitudes of the board was ignored.

President Alemán and Buch de Parada thus found an important ally by recruiting Donald Nelson to come to Mexico to organize a study of its industrialization program. Nelson urged the Mexicans not only to think of the official sources of capital such as the Export-Import Bank or the World Bank but also to think of private sources, a point that Undersecretary of State Will Clayton and Spruille Braden also had been pushing to the Mexicans. Guy Ray, one of the most important diplomats in the U.S. embassy, stressed the inadequate performance of the transport sector and also of PEMEX. The national petroleum company only produced 45 million barrels per day when it should have been able to produce 200 million barrels. These strategic planners also agreed that Mexico's standard of living could only be increased if production generated exports to cover the cost of imports and not by restricting the latter. Nelson was able to tell the Mexicans that if they moved in this direction, as they agreed, he "was going from the [State] Department to the White House, where he had an engagement with the President at noon."[42]

In spite of Ambassador Messersmith's early doubts about Miguel Alemán, it was clear that he would run a probusiness administration. When he was preparing to take power, Alemán approached the Confederación de Cámaras Nacionales de Comercio and asked it to help identify and invite "prominent businessmen from Detroit and New York" to make contact with the new administration. The Mexican Chamber of Commerce was happy to oblige.[43]

Once Miguel Alemán had been elected, he was wooed by U.S. officials. Immediately after his election, U.S. and Mexican officials began to negotiate the terms of their future relationship. The continuation of the wartime cooperation quickly shifted to loans for industrial projects. In the words of one U.S. diplomat, "For months administrative committees have burned the midnight oil and consumed great grosses of pencils working out projects which would stand the scrutiny of keen appraisers of Mexico's economic situation, both financial and economic."[44]

The Alemán administration approached the United States with a plan for ten major projects of public works and industrial development to be financed through the International Bank for Reconstruction and

Development and the Export-Import Bank. U.S. Treasury Secretary John W. Snyder went to Mexico in the first fortnight of December 1946, and he immediately entered into detailed discussions with Ramón Beteta, Torres Bodet, and other high officials of the new administration. At a meeting with Beteta on December 5, Mexico agreed to continue to meet its financial obligations, to come to a rapid agreement on the repayment of Lend-Lease loans, to maintain free movement of investment as well as the fixed exchange rate, and to submit possible projects to the U.S. embassy for evaluation. The Mexican account of the meeting mentioned a verbal offer and an agreement in principle by Secretary Snyder to undertake the financing of projects to last throughout the Alemán presidency. The question of foreign finance was pressing because, in the last eight months of the Avila Camacho administration, the gold and foreign exchange holdings of the Banco de México had decreased from 372 million to 256 million dollars.

The Alemán administration approached the United States for 1.7 billion pesos for the National Irrigation Commission for construction of the Alvaro Obregón Dam on the Yaqui River in Sonora, the El Márquez Dam in Tehuantepec, and the Falcón Dam on the Río Bravo. The plan was that these projects would irrigate 3,700,000 acres of new farmland. Another 119 million pesos would build hydroelectric plants. Mexico would match these funds with 1.5 billion pesos of its own, thereby bringing 1.5 million hectares of new land under cultivation. The U.S. engineer J. A. Savage, formerly with the Bureau of Reclamation, had served as the consulting engineer on these projects.

There was also an important political-legal change in the Alemán irrigation proposal. The old way of building irrigation systems was based upon a 1926 law that shifted the cost of irrigation projects to the landholders, thus increasing land taxes and water charges. President Alemán's approach stressed the role of the state in funding the projects, issuing the contracts, and underwriting the necessary loans. Thus, the cost of the projects was shifted away from the immediate beneficiary to the entire community. The administration argued that this would increase production and lead to a decrease in the cost of food for the consumer; in this way the entire community was supposed to benefit. Since the minister of hydraulic resources was understood to be a friend of the private landowners, the new law was a windfall to the private sector and another setback to the ejidos.

There was a plan for a Tennessee Valley Authority-style complex for the Northwest, consisting of a dam on the Fuerte River in Sinaloa, the completion of the Chihuahua-Pacific Railway, and port works in Topolobampo, Manzanillo, and Tampico. Further improvements of the Isthmus of Tehuantepec included a transisthmian highway, as well as port works at Salina Cruz and Puerto México. There also was a plan for an oil pipeline between Minatitlán and Salina Cruz.

Industrial projects included a gas pipeline between Poza Rica and Mexico City, which would—according to U.S. engineering firm E. Jolly Poe and Associates—capture natural gas that was being wasted. That project was particularly important to Mexican Light and Power for the generation of electricity in thermal plants for the capital. And there was a proposal, by the Chemical Construction Corporation, for a sulphate of ammonia plant. A fifty-one-oven coking plant for ASARCO was included as a Mexican project.

NAFISA had been running the Nueva Compañía de Chapala's Colimilla Dam since 1938, and there was a proposal to increase the generating capacity. In addition, seventeen enterprises in Monterrey—operating through Gas Industrial S.A.—wanted a gas pipeline from Reynosa to Monterrey to bring natural gas from the United States to that industrial city. At the time, it was not known that Mexico was rich in that resource. There also was a proposal to upgrade the textile industry.

The total cost of these projects initially amounted to 180 million dollars; it soon increased to 240 million dollars to be financed over twenty years at 4 percent interest. The U.S. diplomats immediately recognized that the overall figure would only be reached over many years.[45] The proposal reached President Truman's desk by mid-December, and it became tied into complex negotiations over loans to PEMEX; the project was then submitted to the Export-Import Bank on February 26, 1947, for 175 million dollars, in spite of the fact that the bank had indicated a willingness to loan only 50 million when President Alemán visited Washington.[46] Mexico was financing these projects through dollar loans, which Nacional Financiera would administer.

At the heart of the accommodation with Washington was Mexico's rapidly deteriorating international account. The country had been on a roller coaster ride in the international arena. The average accrued net increase in the Banco de México's reserves was about 9 million dollars per year. The reserves then jumped to an average of 46 million dollars between 1943 and 1946. This forced savings was a result of Mexico's contracts to sell a long list of products to the United States at fixed prices, in conjunction with the difficulty of purchasing during wartime rationing. As conditions returned to normal, Mexico's reserves fell by 85 million dollars in 1946 alone. Mexico also faced an outflow of about 20 million dollars per year in servicing its 447 million in international obligations.[47] The situation was not critical at the moment since the Banco de México held 262 million dollars in gold, silver, and foreign exchange by the end of 1946. Indeed, income tax receipts had increased by 600 percent during the course of World War II. However, it was easy to see the service requirements eating up the nation's reserves in the future.

To fulfill the Mexican desire for industrialization, loans for postwar development projects meant that Washington's rules must be followed. And

the U.S. embassy continued to play a key role in assessing the viability of projects for which borrowing from the IMF, the World Bank, the Export-Import Bank, or private banks was involved. Adolfo Orive Alba, the minister of hydraulic resources, cooperated intimately with Merwin L. Bohan (counselor for economic affairs), Lew B. Clark (commercial attaché), and Horace H. Braun (economic analyst) in evaluating all loan proposals.[48] Detailed embassy assessments of projects, which had begun as a wartime measure to help Mexican imports in finding their way through the new regulations governing war allocations, were continuing as normal procedure in the postwar period.

At the same time the new administration was following leads in the private sector. At the end of January 1947 there was a conference in the offices of Turner Construction Company in New York. Representatives of the largest civil engineering and construction companies in the United States were present, including Turner Construction; Spencer, White, and Prentis; Morrison, Knudsen, and Company (which had just built Boulder Dam and Grand Coulee Dam, and was constructing the Sanalona Dam in Sonora); and Raymond Concrete Pile Company. These firms had built many of the most important engineering projects during the war.[49]

## Alemán and Business

By the end of his term in office, Miguel Alemán was on very good terms with international business. *Fortune* magazine ran a series of articles by Charles Koons in 1948 on the Alemán industrialization program, a fact that greatly pleased Antonio Ruiz Galindo and the president.[50] Alemán had also developed close personal relationships with major corporate executives. Judging from the enthusiastic letters thanking him for his hospitality, President Alemán was finding Mexico's tourist attractions very helpful in developing close links with large international corporations.[51] Indeed, his hospitality was becoming legend. For example, in April and May 1952 the president entertained top executives from Anaconda Copper; Industrial Rayon Corporation; Monsanto Chemical Corporation; Chemical Bank and Trust Company of New York; B. F. Goodrich; the Bank of America; Sears, Roebuck; Mercantile Trust Company of Saint Louis; American Zinc, Lead, and Smelting Company; and *Nation's Business*.[52]

There is, therefore, little wonder that one finds in a secret report from a Wall Street bank the following assessment of the Mexican situation: "Mexico's long history of political instability acts as a deterrent to investment. But recent political experience is reassuring and there is reason for confidence that in an environment of economic expansion the fiscal, political and labor problems which were so pressing in the decade of the thirties are not likely to block the road to economic progress."[53]

Two administrations in Mexico had clearly departed from the radical nationalism of the Cárdenas years in favor of courting international capital on its own terms. Deciding that it was not likely to be able to go it alone, Presidents Avila Camacho and Alemán reverted to many aspects of the high strategy of the *porfiriato* and simply tried to please foreign capital. The economic action thus generated helped the two industrialists to placate their important domestic critics by giving them a share in the large number of industrial projects that entered Mexico after the war. This time around, however, they wanted a bit more from the foreign investors than a few seats on the board of directors.

Several institutions made provisions to become involved in this great national project at a technical level. The Armour Foundation and the Banco de México set up an investigative unit (Instituto Technológico de Investigaciones Industriales, the ITII) to support projects of industrialization. The Monterrey Institute of Technology developed close links with similar institutions in the United States (primarily the California Institute of Technology and the Massachusetts Institute of Technology), and the National University also committed resources to a new curriculum in industrial relations and management. Point Four resources (the main development initiative of the Truman administration) were also channeled through these mechanisms. Members of top private industrial corporations sat on the board of ITII. Point Four was especially interested in improving the skills of Mexican technicians in the U.S. corporate structure. Aid and embassy personnel channeled industrial projects through U.S. management and industrial engineering firms: Arthur D. Little; Ebasco Services; George Camp; Norris and Elliot Company; Armour Research Foundation; and the Southwest Research Institute of San Antonio. Major accounting firms brought U.S. accounting practices to Mexico, including: Price, Waterhouse, and Company; Deloitte, Plender, Haskins, and Sells; Arthur Anderson and Company; and Peat Marwick, Mitchell, and Company.[54]

## Point Four

By the end of the Truman and Alemán administrations, foreign aid at the highest technical level had become more important. More than the dollar amounts of aid involved, the Point Four program offered strategic technical assistance. Clearly, one form of expansion was to accomplish elsewhere what had been achieved in the metropolitan center. From the viewpoint of Mexican industrialists, access to new techniques was vital because the long border and the phenomenon of smuggling allowed U.S. products into Mexico.

Increasingly, Washington officials were looking at the superpower struggle, and at times they even discouraged Mexican officials who wanted

to increase the Point Four program too rapidly, arguing that it was Mexico's agriculture that was lagging behind. Citing the fact that, in 1952, the country was importing one half of its wheat and large quantities of corn, rice, and even garbanzos (a traditional export) from overseas, officials came to view the problem as essentially technical.[55]

Absolutely central to the Mexican strategy of industrialization was the desire to produce a wide variety, even a comprehensive section, of industrial goods. Even as the sales of industrial products began to clog in the early 1950s, Mexican industrial strategists in the private and the public sectors held to that view. As much as bankers and ministers might disagree over the limits of each other's prerogatives, they all thought that it was central to avoid the trap described by Raúl Prebisch of importing industrial products and exporting raw materials. Chase National Bank, in its *Latin American Business Highlights,* argued a fairly traditional orthodox (Ricardian) line on comparative advantage, arguing that Mexico should be emphasizing the export of raw materials.

José Crowley, president of CONCAMIN, likened the idea to the suggestion that Mexico should be a "colonial supplier of raw materials to the industrialized countries." The depth of opposition to such ideas formed an absolutely central core of belief to the economic decision makers in the private and public sectors. This was a great idea whose time had come, and this created a powerful alliance between the economic theory of the dominant decision makers and the vested interests of the prospective industrialists.[56]

In conclusion, the decade after the nationalization of petroleum had seen an amazing about-face in the nation's strategy of industrialization. A desire to promote national industrialization gave way to a policy of direct association with U.S. industrialists. One of the notable aspects of this phenomenon is that many of the key policymakers shifted their views from the radical nationalism of the 1930s through the wartime cooperation to the frenzy of industrialization after the war. In some cases, personal animosity to the United States was suppressed for the project of modernization and, in nearly all cases, anti-U.S. views were moderated. Here the case of Ramón Beteta comes to mind. Beteta, who had suffered racial abuse while a student at the University of Texas at Austin, was perhaps the most vociferous exponent of the nationalization of petroleum in 1938. By the 1940s he had shifted his economic nationalism into line with the war effort and the more moderate views of Eduardo Suárez. After the war the old radicalism was gone, and he welcomed the foreign investors back to Mexico again.

Of course, Mexico's system of presidential centralization plays a large part in this change. Opposing the president was out, and a figure such as Alejandro Carrillo—who opposed the great shift from his position in Congress—stands out in high relief. In the main, Sam Rayburn's dictum that one "goes along to get along" in politics is at least as true for Mexico as for

the United States. A more conservative government under Avila Camacho had given way to a virtual counterrevolution under President Alemán. Massive attacks on labor and on the peasant sector, the purge of the left in the educational sector and within the semigovernment mass organizations, and favorable treatment of business groups all combined to shift wealth and income from the poor to the rich. The fact that this could be done under the cover of revolutionary rhetoric was a testimony not only to the political skills of these leaders but also to the broadly shared consensus of the period.

In addition to political realism, a commitment to the pursuit of the war effort, and a profound desire to bring industrial modernity to Mexico, there were also enormous vested interests at stake. Mexico was poised after World War II on the brink of the exceptional period in the history of the twentieth century, the long postwar boom from about 1948 to 1973. Officials originally worried about the return of the Great Depression of the 1930s; however, we now know that this was a time when resources were allotted in ways that were lasting. Waves of innovation merged with opportunity that seemed unlimited. Adopting the correct strategy of industrialization and ingratiating oneself with the decision makers could provide dramatic results, a sort of development program at the personal level. The interplay between the strategy of industrialization and the personal vested interests of the players was always central to the process of economic growth in Mexico.

## Notes

1. James B. Stewart to secretary of state, March 8, 1939, USNA/RG 59, 812.00/30700.
2. Horatio Mooers to secretary of state, January 16, 1940, USNA/RG 59, 812.00/30918.
3. *La Voz de México*, February 2, 1940.
4. See Manuel Avila Camacho's interview in *Hoy*, December 19, 1939.
5. Josephus Daniels to Cordell Hull, February 2, 1940, USNA/RG 59, 812.00/30927.
6. Daniels to secretary of state, March 6, 1939, USNA/RG 59, 812.00/30704.
7. Saragoza, *The Monterrey Elite*, 287.
8. Ibid., 320–39.
9. Garrido, *El partido de la revolución institucionalizada*, 227; and Saragoza, *The Monterrey Elite*, 369.
10. Ezequiel Padilla to Francisco Castillo Nájera, July 31, 1941, SRE, III-2412-14.
11. *El Universal*, September 20, 1940.
12. *La Prensa*, September 19, 1940.
13. T. I. Rees to the Foreign Office, January 7, 1942, PRO, FO/30571.
14. Avila Camacho, February 1946, AGN, RP/MAC, 523/54.
15. Secret report of a conversation with the president from unnamed businessmen to the Foreign Office, March 3, 1941, PRO, FO/26067.

16. GSM Papers, Memoirs, vol. III, no. 13.

17. For accounts of the meeting see *El Porvenir* and *El Norte*, of Monterrey, April 18–20, 1944.

18. Nelson Rockefeller to Peter Collado, October 5, 1943, USNA/RG 59, 812.50/415.

19. *Washington Post*, December 11, 1940.

20. Ibid.

21. Robert Conway writing in *The Times Herald*, December 11, 1940.

22. Messersmith to P. Bonsal, October 21, 1943, USNA/RG 59, 812.50/427.

23. Report of the "Mission to Survey Power Requirements . . .," November 20, 1943, USNA/RG 59, 812.50/440.

24. Ibid., 128–29.

25. Some of the best-known figures were bankers: Luis Legorreta, BANAMEX; Luis Montes de Oca, Banco Internacional S.A. and former director of the Banco de México; Vigilio Garza, Crédito Industrial de Monterrey S.A.; William Richardson, National City Bank; Gonzalo Robles, Banco de México; Carlos Trouyet, investment banker; Salvador Ugarte, Banco de Comercio; Gustavo Velasco, Banco Internacional; and Eduardo Villaseñor, Banco de México. Among the top industrialists were: Sealtiel L. Alatriste, Cruz Azul S.A.; Tom Braniff, Braniff Airways; José Cruz y Célis, Confederación de Cámaras Industriales; Priciliano Miguel Elizondo, Compañía Fundidora de Fierro y Acero de Monterrey S.A.; Romulo Garza, Vidriería de Monterrey S.A.; Pablo Macedo, Sosa-Texcoca and many other industries; Antonio Ruiz Galindo, Distribuidora Mexicana S.A.; and Enrique Sarro, Altos Hornos S.A. In addition, the ministers of finance and the economy and the heads of the CFE and the faculty of sciences at UNAM were there.

26. Armour Foundation, *Proceedings of the Mexican-American Conference*, 127.

27. Ibid., 147.

28. Arthur Lynch to Avila Camacho, April 30, 1943, AGN, RP/MAC, 545.22/206.

29. *Diario Oficial,* February 4, 1941.

30. Tomás Gurza to Rogerio de la Seva, July 9, 1948, AGN, RP/MAV, 523/62 (emphasis mine).

31. Ibid.

32. Lázaro Martínez to Avila Camacho, December 3, 1941, AGN, RP/MAC, 545.2/7 contains numerous similar objections to the plan.

33. Primo Villa Michel to J. Jesús González Gallo, October 4, 1944, AGN, RP/MAC, 545.22/262.

34. Victor Manuel Villaseñor to Avila Camacho, June 14, 1944, AGN, RP/MAC, 433/310.

35. Villaseñor to Véjar Vásquez, March 14, 1944, ibid.

36. *Excélsior*, May 7, 1944.

37. Luis Cabrera to Avila Camacho, June 27, 1944, AGN, RP/MAC, 443/310.

38. Inter-American Development Commission, *Comisiones de Fomento Interamericano*, 8–23.

39. *Diario Oficial,* July 1, 1944.

40. José Cruz y Célis to Avila Camacho, September 14, 1944, AGN, RP/MAC, 545.22/262.

41. Brody, "The New Deal and World War II," in Braeman, *The New Deal*, 289.

42. Memorandum of conversation: Donald Nelson, Francisco Buch de Parada, Guy Ray, and William G. MacLean, April 29, 1947, USNA/RG 59, 812.50/4-2947.

43. AGN, RP/MAV, 523.5.

44. Lew B. Clark to secretary of state, May 9, 1947, USNA/RG 59, 812.50/5-947.

45. Walter Thurston to secretary of state, December 18, 1946, USNA/RG 59, 812.51/12-1846.

46. Foreign Office Note, December 18, 1946, and D. R. Bell to Braun, July 14, 1947, Truman Library, PSF, 130.

47. Banco de México, *Transaciones Internacionals de México*; n.a., *Seis Años de Actualidad Nacional.*

48. Merwin L. Bohan to secretary of state, AGN, RP/MAV, 606.3/247.

49. Eduardo Hidalgo to Miguel Alemán, March 7, 1947, AGN, RP/MAV, 451/(32)/3273.

50. AGN, RP/MAV, 704/170.

51. Letters from R. S. Kersh, Westinghouse; Donald P. Gilles, Republic Steel Corporation; and William R. Kuhuns, editor of *Banking*, the journal of the American Bankers' Association, AGN, RP/MAV, 002/6072.

52. Ibid.

53. Murray Shields to Alemán, February 16, 1951, AGN, RP/MAV, 294/20676.

54. Francis White to Edward G. Cale, June 23, 1953, USNA/RG 59, 812.00-TA/6-1253.

55. "Industrial Development Program in Mexico," June 2, 1952, USNA/RG 59, 812.19/6-252.

56. "Activities of the National Chamber of Manufacturing Industries," June 26, 1953, USNA/RG 59, 812.19/6-2653.

# 7 Battles over Foreign Investment

Mexico's great goal of industrialization seemed within reach as the bonanza of wartime sales brought unprecedented amounts of capital and a plethora of new industrial products into the country. Popular enthusiasm for the industrialization project of the 1940s is still striking. When a new Sears, Roebuck store opened in Mexico City in February 1947, an estimated fifteen thousand to eighteen thousand people visited it in the first three days and another ten thousand to twelve thousand were turned away daily, according to the manager. Some fifty guards were required to handle the crowds. According to the account of events from the U.S. embassy, which quoted an official of the company: "Happily, casualties were normal, no more than occurred in any other large Sears store during the last Christmas rush for nylons."[1]

Popular demand created an environment that made foreign investors more welcome in the eyes of many consumers who yearned for the industrial products that would make their lives easier. This desire for industrial products also converged with the interests of those Mexican industrialists who found that acting as an intermediary for foreign investors was a shortcut to profit.

The political alliance between segments of the governing party and industrialists in favor of national industrial development clashed with U.S. political and business leaders who wanted back into Mexico. The major battlefield between the economic nationalists and the foreign investors related to the rules governing foreign investment. Since industrialists and political leaders required capital, if they hoped to proceed beyond the early wish lists in which earlier planners simply enumerated the kinds of industries they wanted, the rules governing capital were on center stage.

## Inadequacy of National Capital

There had been several attempts to base an industrialization program upon self-contained efforts. Slightly reminiscent of the attempt before the *porfiriato* to finance railroads by the sale of lottery tickets, the early plans to finance the great industrialization program out of Mexican resources proved to be inadequate. For a while, it appeared that the

problem of scarce capital might disappear. During the early years of World War II, funds did pile up in the financial institutions at unprecedented rates; however, it was difficult to convert those resources into capital investments due to wartime restrictions. Soon after the end of hostilities, a combination of inflation and rapidly increasing imports eroded wartime reserves. The terms of trade quickly shifted against Mexico.

As reserves diminished, thoughts once again turned to raising capital to finance investment projects. Domestic sources were quickly tapped. In April 1947 the government produced an attractive advertising campaign aimed at helping the Banco de México sell its bonds to the public, offering them to the investor at 6 percent and using the funds to finance industrialization projects.[2] Not many investors reacted favorably to the plan. Interest rates of 6 percent seemed high by U.S. standards of the day; however, in Mexico, investors were able to earn between 12 and 18 percent. There was the phenomenon of twelve-hour loans through the Banco de Pequeño Comercio for which 0.5 percent was charged for the day's interest! Apparently many small shopkeepers borrowed on a daily basis to finance their operations even though on an annual basis that would mean they were paying—if they operated six days per week—an annual rate of 156 percent for their operating capital.[3] And the *agiotistas* (moneylenders) charged considerably higher rates.

**Imports and Exports per Capita**

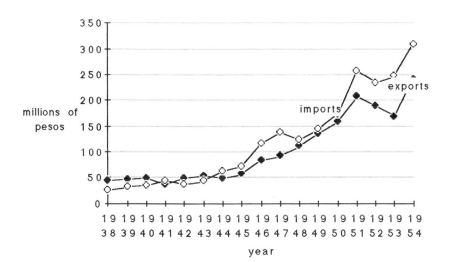

year

A fundamental problem blocking industrialization, therefore, was the high interest rate. Investors simply placed their funds in real estate and other traditional areas, such as short-term money lending. By contrast, in periods of rapid industrial development in such countries as England, the United States, and Japan, interest rates have tended to be very low, thus forcing investors to move into productive new fields rather than clip coupons.[4]

Scarce capital caused some serious bottlenecks. The centrality of electricity-generating capacity to an industrialization push is obvious. Yet the Compañía de Luz y Fuerza responded to the pressures on electrical generation by suspending service for several hours each day, by cutting the current to public offices, by reducing the voltage, and other stop-gap measures. In July 1947 the Mexican Light and Power Company restricted power supplies by 40 percent for Mexico City as well as for the states of México, Hidalgo, Morelos, and Puebla. Droughts in 1947 had affected the rainfall in the Necaxa and Lerma river watersheds. The CFE had not yet completed the Valle del Bravo Dam or the second Ixtapantongo generating unit. Those restrictive measures created an angry response, especially in the face of rate increases. The power companies argued that their profits were low, a proposition that was widely doubted.

A cooperative factory, Fábrica de Fibras Duras Atlas in San Luis Potosí, described the kind of damage that electricity shortages could cause. During 1946 the factory was without any electricity for one hundred days, and even after that figure dropped to twenty-three days in 1947, on most days they only had electricity for three hours. This obviously had the most severe impact on their productivity and condemned them to export more raw materials than finished products.[5]

Deputy Rafael Cárdenas R. headed a congressional committee that looked into the problem of inadequate electricity generation. He stressed the unwillingness of the private sector to invest in increasing generating capacity and called for a 50 to 60 percent surtax, since the budget had no funds for such an investment. Isidro Fabela, drafting a response for the government, stressed the lack of rains and the theft of electricity by individuals who threw wires across power lines, thus diverting electricity to their own use. However, that level of response scarcely promised an increase in electricity generation.[6]

The availability of Export-Import Bank money, after the settlement with the United States in 1941–42, seemed like a marvelous solution to the problem of power scarcity. When, after the war, the U.S. Navy leased a railroad train with a massive power generator to Mexico, it appeared to be a great example of how wartime cooperation was solving central problems. (The power train had been built as a precaution during the war in case enemy action interrupted power generation.) To some Mexicans, the return of foreign investment promised to solve even more intractable problems. The inadequacy of national capital was clear. By contrast, the glitter of industrial

products constantly making their way south made the deficiencies of national industry altogether too apparent.

## Reassuring Foreign Capital

Even at the height of the radical nationalism of the Cárdenas era, there were powerful political voices that wanted to attract foreign resources rather than to expropriate, regulate, or dominate foreign capital. Former President Abelardo Rodríguez, who was a figure on the right of the governing party, and Governor Maximino Avila Camacho of Puebla forged political alliances between the new revolutionary coalition and foreign business. The governor of Veracruz, Jorge Cerdán, anticipated national measures to protect and favor foreign capital, even before the federal governments of the postwar era. On December 12, 1940, he passed a reduction of between 99 and 50 percent on land taxes that would affect commerce and industry; that was followed, on the first day of 1941, by a law exempting for five years the developers of new hotels, homes, and local businesses from 95 percent of the state and local taxes. A 90 percent reduction in state taxes was applied to cinemas, theaters, and sporting complexes. The governor was quite proud of these innovations and knew that they would please the new president of Mexico.[7] The changes were widely copied in other states.

In the Cardenista period, conservative bankers such as Luis Montes de Oca and Luis Legorreta reassured foreign investors; and, under Avila Camacho, immediate problems of wartime cooperation brought many foreign firms into the picture. As the war ended, disagreements between government ministries that had a role in the regulation of foreign investment were addressed by Alemán. By creating a mixed intersecretarial commission in 1947, consisting of the ministries of finance, foreign relations, interior, agriculture, and economy, President Alemán was trying to streamline the entire business of investment.[8]

The Mexican government was convinced that benefits would flow to the community by once again attracting foreign capital. Increasingly, as the 1940s proceeded, state and federal governments moved to reassure capital that the era of nationalization was past. What remained to be clarified were the terms on which foreign capital would reenter Mexico. Apart from guaranteeing the right to private property for foreign capitalists who obeyed Mexican law, there was a series of issues that had to be defined.

## Public Sector versus Private Sector

There was never much of a tradition of laissez-faire in Mexico. Perhaps the mercantilist traditions of the Spanish empire made the notion

of government noninterference in the economic life of the country foreign to its experience, although there were some vestiges of a laissez-faire position in such groups as Confederación de Cámaras Industriales de la Ciudad de México and a few businessmen cloaked their hostility to the revolutionary tradition in laissez-faire terminology. Yet even the more conservative governments of the 1940s opposed this tradition. In a talk to the Confederación in 1944, President Avila Camacho attacked the laissez-faire position directly by stating that government initiative was vital in areas where private efforts were inadequate. He cited the Altos Hornos project and the chemical industry specifically, and dismissed as reactionary the laissez-faire position supported by the organization.[9]

It was far more common to find representatives of business doing battle against the mercantilistic practices of the past. In 1949, for example, the Confederación de Cámaras Industriales was still waging a battle against export taxes.[10] At times the older capitalist groups expressed hostility to the government's involvement in the industrialization process, as the Confederación de Cámeras Industriales de los Estados Unidos Mexicanos did on September 14, 1944, when they opposed the formation of a Comisión Federal de Fomento Industrial. Avila Camacho answered them quite candidly. Rejecting the laissez-faire attitude of the conference of the Comisiones de Fomento Interamericano that had just taken place in New York, he reminded the captains of industry that the active participation of the state and the revolutionary tradition were written into the laws of the land. Moreover, the president noted that, whereas he desired "to only intervene in economic matters to the minimum necessary degree," there would be no chemical, cement, or electrical industry and a very inadequate steel industry if the government had not taken a hand in protecting and supporting those industrial developments. Since there were so many areas in which "private initiative has been inadequate," it was necessary for the state to act.[11] There was no way that industrialists were going to bring the precepts of the Manchester School to Mexico.

Even when differences between the private bankers and the government appeared, as at the 1951 Bankers' Association Conference in Guadalajara, debates over laissez-faire economics frequently related to other issues. Aníbal de Iturbide of the Banco de Comercio clashed openly with Ramón Beteta; however, upon close examination of the record of the debate, it is fairly clear that at issue was who should make the investment decisions— the government or the private bankers. Beteta represented a current of opinion that viewed the private bankers as being too likely to stay with reliable, but economically sterile, investments in real estate rather than in industry, which he viewed as having higher multiplier and accelerator potential. Iturbide challenged the government's right to set the rules and make investment decisions; however, in practice even the private bankers were eager to receive favors from the government in terms of tax breaks and

advantageous accounting rulings. Beteta's central political argument was that by implementing "moderate controls, [he] has in fact prevented the ultimate development of collectivism." His central economic argument was that development could not take place with 10 to 12 percent interest, the rates currently being charged by the private bankers; therefore, the state had to act to make investment funds available at lower rates.[12] By the time of the next bankers' conference in Chihuahua the positions were much less adversarial. Luis Latapi, director of the Banco de Crédito Minero, limited his keynote address to a technical discussion of banking and tax rules and the accomplishments of the private banking sector that year. An accommodation had been reached.[13]

The high point of the government's challenge to the bankers' prerogatives emerged at the Acapulco convention in 1953. José Crowley, president of CONCAMIN, reacted vigorously to the government's proposed Ley de Atribuciones del Ejecutivo Federal en Materia Económica. This law proposed that the president take whatever steps he felt necessary in the area of price controls or protection. By the time of Antonio Carrillo Flores's talk to the bankers on April 26, 1954, he avoided an open quarrel over fundamental issues of decision making. The range of disagreement over the central rules of the Mexican system had been diminished.[14]

Having reassured foreign and domestic capital, and recognizing that very few had any interest in excluding the state from the process of industrial development, the battle shifted to another eternal theoretical debate: economic nationalism versus foreign penetration. This is an area where theoretical arguments overlap with vested interests. At one level the issues were already well worked out. In the English-speaking world, proponents of free trade could easily trace their roots back to Adam Smith and David Ricardo; and within the Spanish tradition, there were proponents of that view who even antedated Adam Smith, from Bernardo Ward to Gaspar Melchor Jovellanos.

## The Economic Nationalists

The Cámara Nacional de Industrias de Transformación held a view different from that of the more established business groups. Formed to oppose the Cámera Nacional de Industria and the Cámera Nacional de Comercio in 1942 with 2,135 individual industrialists—the vast majority of whom owned small concerns—their membership had grown to 5,080 by 1945. Having no sympathy for the laissez-faire position, they also disliked the class-warfare attitude of the Cámaras de Comercio and the Centros Patronales, which were eternally opposed to all workers' demands. The new industrialists based their attitude toward labor on the underconsumptionist

view that workers would have to earn more if industrialists were going to be able to sell their products; moreover, they were also eager to have the government fund, protect, and support their struggling industries. They also saw political advantages in coming to terms with the CTM. Labor leaders such as Vicente Lombardo Toledano could scarcely contain their amazement: "It was a great surprise to us—the CTM, the majority of industrial unions, the Confederation of Latin American Workers, and other important labor groups—that these [industrialists] publicly backed our position in the press."[15]

Antonio Ruiz Galindo, among many economic nationalists of the day, put the classical case for protectionism to the president in February 1945. Infant industries required protection, as argued by Alexander Hamilton in the United States, since they had neither the technicians, machines, nor capital that existed overseas. As a result, a low volume of production led to high prices that made Mexican products of industry expensive. Dependence upon foreign imports to run the factories made the situation worse. Since the role of industry was, he argued, to raise the standard of living of the people, it must be protected for ten years or more while skill levels and transportation networks improved. Ruiz Galindo added the underconsumptionist element as he concluded: "The existence of national industry is a matter of national progress; ultimately, questions of our independence and nationality are based upon our own industrial production and consumption."[16]

This community of interests between labor and the new industrialists made for a potent political alliance between workers, peasants, and the national business sector. Moreover, the widely shared goal of industrial progress cemented the coalition around an easily identifiable issue that commanded nearly universal support. Its attitude toward foreign investment, however, was delicate. In one presentation to the president, in 1946, José R. Colín recognized that "Mexican capitalists lack the audacity that is required for this kind of [industrial] enterprise." Short-term mortgages, real estate, and construction of homes all seemed safer to Mexican investors than industrial projects. Colín represented these groups as the new breed of industrialists who were willing to tackle difficult fields. They had the vision, the cooperation of the workers, and the natural resources to proceed. They required "stimulation by the state and support from the people." Since the capital was scarce they partially backed the government's decision to open the country to foreign investment. But this was the critical point: "We Mexican industrialists want foreign capital to be nationalized and to really become ours, the same as the industries that it stimulates; thus all industrial activities that are established in the Republic will enjoy the same rights and obligations."[17]

This kind of statement contained a number of elements, all of which were not compatible. The idea that capital should become nationalized

certainly conflicted with the U.S. goal of the free movement of capital. The demand that foreign capital would operate under the same rules as national capital was not negotiable; indeed, the Mexican Revolution had achieved that legal reality. However, the meaning of capital becoming "really ours" was less clear. Part of that meaning, in Colín's view, was that capital "does not want to progress at the expense of the misery of the people."[18] The mobilization of all possible capital by the state for industrial projects, the suppression of most imports to favor domestic production, and the total exclusion of luxury imports were required. Tariff and price controls created a system to allow workers to purchase articles of prime necessity at wholesale prices, and subsidies for raw material production would hold down prices on essential goods. The trade agreements with the United States were denounced. Above it all, a National Economic Council should coordinate the industrial push.

A case under discussion made the issues clear. The price of cotton became controversial after the postwar devaluation. By 1949, José de la Mora, president of the Atoyoc textile group (whose factories included Fábricas de Hilados y Tejidos San José de Mayorazgo, San Juan de Amandi, and the Fábrica de Casados, all in Puebla), was the largest textile producer in the country. After the devaluation, the price of cotton increased, notably forcing the Atoyoc mills to close "for lack of funds to buy cotton and meet financial obligations." The firm off-loaded the crisis onto its workers by precipitating a strike, claiming that "we find it painful to create economic conflict by closing our factories temporarily while we solve this problem." De la Mora reported to the president as he asked the government to stop the export of raw cotton on the grounds that their factories benefited Mexico. Instead of simply exporting raw cotton, they paid wages, made other expenditures, used transportation, and generated wealth. De la Mora accused the cotton brokers, principally Anderson, Clayton, and Company, with speculation in the cotton market.[19] This was a clear case where national capitalists blamed the cotton giant for their problems.

In retrospect, several arguments made by the economic nationalists loom large. They wanted to focus on domestic consumption, and they thought that industries should be avoided if they rested primarily on the export of irreplaceable natural resources. Similarly, industries that were based on low wage scales should be shunted, and they talked about creating an "index of the absorption of labor" as a criterion by which projects should be judged, subsidized, and financed. They reasoned that if industrialization did not create opportunity for Mexican workers, then there was no real gain for the country and no new markets for industrialists to supply. As it turned out, these fundamental points—which still relate to contemporary problems of unemployment and contamination—were ignored by decision makers in the 1940s.[20]

## Labor and the Economic Nationalists

There was a considerable degree of harmony between the economic nationalists and the CTM. As socialists, leaders such as Lombardo Toledano followed a fairly orthodox analysis, arguing that since Mexico was not ready for socialism, and since fascism was the most terrible threat of the day, progressive people should join in a grand coalition supporting the Allies in World War II. This was also compatible with a belief that at the top of Mexico's list was the need to industrialize. There were to be no challenges to the regime of private property, and even foreign investment would be welcome in the country, as long as it followed Mexican law. As Lombardo Toledano said at a banquet commemorating the first anniversary of the Pacto Obrero-Industrial at the Casino Militar in Mexico City, before the president and top industrialists: "The new type of industrialists think like workers, not just of themselves, but of the entire Mexican fatherland." Unions, he explained, were no longer "the old leagues of resistance against capital" but rather organizations that would collaborate with the new industrialists.[21]

The convergence between the goal of industrialization and the patriotic war effort created a powerful political force. It enabled Lombardo Toledano to boast of the wartime gains to productivity in highly selective terms that ignored the extreme hardship (*carestía*) during World War II. "The volume of economic production in each and every area has increased considerably; and ultimately, the flowering of this effort has begun to develop a national industry that truly deserves that name."[22] The fundamental agreement between most segments of the labor movement, the government, and a significant group of industrialists created a powerful political force. In 1945, Antonio Ruiz Galindo was warning the president that the United States was likely to use its unique position as the war ended to press for free trade, a pressure that he thought Mexico would have to resist for ten years.[23]

On the surface, the combination seemed formidable. It did not seem possible that the economic nationalists could lose; yet they did.[24] Within a few years Ruiz Galindo had abandoned the economic nationalist position and was working actively on the other side of the issue, and those who sustained the nationalists' position were excluded from the circles of power. It is useful to understand how that happened.

## Opponents of the Economic Nationalists

Many factors led the Avila Camacho and Alemán administrations to turn away from the economic nationalists, of which U.S. opposition was central. As George Messersmith explained, "[José Domingo] Lavín represents a certain tendency in Mexico which is very vocal and very vociferous.

I think that we have given them some hard knocks recently but they are not going to be knocked down easily."[25] In this battle U.S. diplomats counted on the support of top bankers, who favored monetary conservatives: "Our mutual friend, Mr. Montes de Oca, is, I think, about the soundest and ablest banker in Mexico."[26]

The group within Mexico most closely associated with the battle against the economic nationalists was the Frente Patronal. Its leaders wanted few or no restrictions on imports into Mexico and certainly no price, production, or distribution controls. Rather than having a politically directed industrialization program, they wanted maximum funds left within the banking system and the investment decisions left to the bankers. The only agrarian policy they favored was protection of property rights, and they wanted labor laws modified to curb union power, to freeze wages, and to curtail the right to strike. At the extreme, they wanted the state out of the development effort, the government's overdraft eliminated (to curb inflation), and no limits on decision making by the private sector.

After the war there was, in U.S. government and business circles, an increasingly prevalent view that Mexico could be trusted. Although revolutionary rhetoric still abounded in the country, and in spite of the losses suffered by investors in the past, a new view emerged of the governing party. As a CIA analysis put it in one of its National Intelligence Estimates, "Only in Mexico is the existing political machine strong enough to permit a reasonably confident estimate that it would be proof against overthrow by demagogic opposition."[27]

There were those who were still worried by the outburst of radical rhetoric and the occasional nationalization of a particular industry (usually a natural monopoly); however, in the main, U.S. officials came to understand that policies were moving in their direction. Support for Mexico's goal of industrialization was central to wartime cooperation, and officials in Washington gained a great deal of leverage as they administered wartime regulations. After the war, loans from the IMF, the World Bank, and U.S. investment kept economic diplomats deeply involved in the development process. As one diplomat of the era put it in a communication with the president, "We encourage the industrialization of Mexico but only along sound economic lines hoping to avoid the establishment of unsound industries which would require exaggerated protection."[28] The key to understanding the relationship between the two countries lies in the definition of the term "sound."

The United States had changed its position on protectionism under President Roosevelt. The New Deal had moved over the years to dismantle the protectionism of the Smoot-Hawley tariff. Embarrassed silence at Montevideo in 1933 had given way to the use of reciprocal trade agreements to increase trade. At the Chapultepec Conference in 1945, the United States was committed to the view that a renewal of the Great Depression of the 1930s could only be avoided by free-trade policies.

Roosevelt's diplomats opposed economic nationalism in all of its forms: high tariffs, state trading companies, export restrictions, differential exchange rates, and the regulation of capital. Calls for a Latin American customs union were intolerable. From Chapultepec in 1945 to Havana in 1947 the United States argued that only free trade could prevent another depression. George Messersmith spelled it out to Cordell Hull: "In other words at the end of the last war we entered into the 'assembling' stage for certain products abroad; at the end of this war we shall have to actually begin manufacturing certain articles abroad. We can do this through branch American companies of the parent plant at home, using the same methods and techniques that we use at home and selling our goods under the same trade marks, but having the advantage of cheaper or more easily available raw materials, and particularly of labor cheaper than our own."[29]

The government saw its role as monitoring projects for which private capital was either not forthcoming or only partially forthcoming in order to ensure that Mexico's push for industrialization would not lead to protectionism. U.S. diplomats viewed the economic nationalists as the real enemy. Their program was "enough to chill the marrow in the bones of anyone interested in furthering the commercial policy principles of the United States."[30]

Some organizations of the private sector in the United States were interested in avoiding conflict with the government. Unlike the National Association of Manufacturers (NAM), which followed an accountant's model and viewed the government as an expense and therefore as an enemy, the Council on Foreign Relations had been formed as a high-level policy board uniting top businessmen, policymakers, and suitable academics. The CFR had planning groups working on postwar strategy from even the early stages of World War II. Their influence was clear on the (second) charter of the Export-Import Bank in 1934, and they anticipated the strategy of using loans, and later aid, to support U.S. exports.

The Mexican president was in close contact with the CFR and another organization of the U.S. business elite, the National Planning Association (NPA). Headed by Charles E. Wilson, president of General Motors Corporation, the group included high officials in the corporate sector, finance, publishing, and even certain unions. The NPA stressed the need to finance exports and to work on the problem of the imbalance of the gold supply among nations in order to keep trade and investment flowing. These corporate leaders argued, "It is hard to conceive of the continuation of development programs without public loan agencies aided by survey committees or development agencies in every area." Mexico was singled out as one of the countries in which officials had "taken the initiative in formulating national objectives for investment and in devising methods for administering projects." Most interestingly, the NPA considered with which specific groups in Latin America U.S. investors should associate. In the thinking of the

NPA, old reactionaries tended to be contrasted to the new industrial mod-
ernizers.[31] These business strategists understood that to coordinate their efforts with government policies was essential to future success.

A company that was at the cutting edge of the new links between business and government was the agribusiness giant Anderson, Clayton, and
Company. The Houston-based brokerage dominated the world's cotton business and was expanding rapidly into the production of edible oils. Will
Clayton had flirted with older anti-New Deal business groups in the 1930s
like the NAM. However, he quickly changed his politics as he saw how
helpful recent reforms could be. In one particularly valuable account, Anderson, Clayton, and Company profits, in the first half of 1941, consisted of
1 million dollars earned from its domestic activities, 1.5 million dollars
collected from U.S. domestic agricultural subsidies, and 1.3 million dollars
from its Latin American operations.[32] This valuable information shows how
profitable the new kind of cooperation between business and government
could be.

## After Wartime Cooperation

The use of loans to mold Mexican policies was far more effective than force. This is certainly reflected in the documentary record of the
period. The expansion of the highway program was seen as being intimately
linked to the export trade, and not merely to a romantic vision of linking the
Americas together from the North Pole to south of Patagonia. As the U.S.
ambassador put it as the postwar loans were being negotiated for the construction of the Mexican highway network, "American export trade will be
benefited in many ways by the augmentation of these communications facilities between the two countries, in addition to the direct benefit deriving
from the sale of additional road construction machinery, filling station equipment, et cetera. Additional sales to Mexico of automobiles, trucks, parts
and accessories are only some of the items which are bound eventually to
enter in larger volume by reason of the additional mileage added to the
highway system."[33]

In 1945 the Export-Import Bank was involved in loan negotiations to
enable the ITT subsidiary in Mexico, MEXTELCO, to buy out the parallel
Ericsson system. Henry Wallace recorded that he and Ambassador
Messersmith opposed the Treasury Department's Norman Ness, on the
grounds that "it was obvious that the State Department was very keen about
the deal and [Emilio] Collado said Messersmith very much wanted to have
the matter approved by the EXIMBANK for the sake of strengthening his
hand when he returned to Mexico City."[34]

Expansion into the airline industry also showed how closely transportation and communications were linked to the reentry of U.S. corporations

into Mexico. When war broke out, the Pentagon placed importance on having access to Mexican airfields. President Cárdenas had, however, placed significant restrictions on the access of U.S. military personnel to Mexico for reasons relating to national sovereignty, so the army entered into a secret agreement with Pan American Airways to accomplish this purpose. The problem came after the war, when the airline took the position that the improvements and construction done in Mexico were their property. Moreover, Pan Am officials denied Braniff and even the Compañía Mexicana de Aviación access to the new facilities. Ambassador Messersmith was concerned to block Pan Am on this, since he thought that such action was inviting nationalization of the landing facilities and possibly even the airlines. Clearly, the war effort gave Pan Am a significant advantage over its competitors, an advantage that lasted for years after the end of hostilities.[35]

The end of the war meant that price and production regulations were to be wound down. Unanimity in the business community was matched by near unanimity in the government sector, which favored a quick return to the marketplace. Officials faced the two perennial problems of protectionism and—within a context of dollar shortages—stimulating demand for products of U.S. industry. Protectionism was opposed by the economic diplomats; however, U.S. strength was so one-sided that the country scarcely had any trading partners left. The dominant view in the United States was that protectionism reduced exports and therefore contributed to the gravity of the Great Depression of the 1930s. Since Europe was unable to import due to dollar shortages, U.S. economic strength again threatened its own exports. *Business Week* described the attempt by countries around the globe to restrict imports of luxury goods to solve the problem.[36] Britain led the way with an initiative by Chancellor of the Exchequer Hugh Dalton in attempting to reduce its imports by between 80 million and 100 million dollars. Sweden, the Netherlands, Argentina, Chile, Peru, and Mexico were all following this approach.

Since 1944, Mexico had been trying to limit its imports by means of a permit system that, at least in theory, was supposed to channel its foreign exchange toward items essential for its industrial development. As wartime surpluses quickly dried up—as a result of imports and inflation—Mexico tried several times in 1945–46 to urge a revision of the trade agreement with the United States. The growing dollar shortage meant that the Truman administration could not adopt an absolute line against all tariffs, however much it preferred that position. It drew its first line of battle against quotas as being even more reprehensible than tariffs. Clair Wilcox, director of the Office of International Trade Policy in the State Department, expressed a view that was central to U.S. economic diplomacy of the period. Speaking before the Export Managers' Club of New York, he made the point that tariffs could be overcome by market forces, whereas "quotas are fixed, not

by private traders but by public officials. . . . This is regimentation at its worst. And this is the direction in which much of the world is headed at the present time."[37] In his view, this tendency had to be opposed since regulations beget further retaliation and thus create the kind of downward trade cycle that had characterized the Great Depression.

Ambassador Messersmith was able to convince President Avila Camacho to suspend the practice of using Treasury circulars as a gambit to limit luxury imports in 1946. He managed to obtain an agreement that the Mexicans would give U.S. officials two weeks' notice before discussing any specific changes to tariffs: "If we take the attitude that we cannot agree to any tariff increases, it will be an utterly unreasonable attitude for there are some increases which, in our opinion here, are necessary to protect some sound industries which have developed here and which will go by the boards if they do not have a measure or a greater measure of protection. On the other hand the Mexicans must be reasonable because they must not ask for protection for unsound industries because this would merely be to create problems in their own economy."[38]

Trade was to be furthered by aid. At the beginning of the Alemán administration there was a plan to seek development loans through the World Bank and the Export-Import Bank. The total cost of these projects amounted to 180 million dollars, to be loaned over twenty years at 4 percent interest. The U.S. diplomats immediately recognized that they would supervise these funds over many years. As the negotiations proceeded with Ambassador Thurston, Finance Minister Beteta tried to increase Mexico's bargaining power by linking the question of the exchange rate and exchange controls to the loan. Beteta suggested that the drain on the Banco de México's reserves was so rapid, especially for "expensive luxury goods" such as automobiles, consumers' durables, and furs, that his country would have to look at exchange controls. Thurston leaped to the attack: "I stated that in my opinion the new Mexican regime had gotten off to a brilliant start." He complimented President Alemán on his inauguration speech and his new policies toward labor and capital. However, in the ambassador's view, the threat of exchange controls to preserve foreign exchange for industrial investment, rather than opulent consumption, was intolerable. "I stated that I would venture to urge that the greatest care be taken not to nullify the good start and that if the slightest doubt existed as to the propriety or the advisability of any such action as that which he mentioned, my advice would be to abandon the projected action instantly."[39] The point was not lost on Beteta. According to the U.S. account, "Licenciado Beteta stated that my remarks were approximately what he had expected, that they had clarified his own thinking, and that he would abandon completely the idea of tampering with the tariff or Trade Agreement."[40]

In 1947, Mexico moved to try to arrest the deterioration of its international account, and U.S. diplomats monitored the moves closely.[41] Sixteen

changes were announced, of which six dealt with motor vehicles. Since 1946, Mexico had spent 300 million pesos on motor vehicles, of which two thirds were taken up in trucks and buses. Only half of the remaining number consisted of luxury automobiles, and those purchasing them were not about to be thwarted by substantial rate increases. Still, rates had not been increased for "ten or fifteen years" in most areas.

This postwar deterioration contrasted sharply to the dramatic increase in Mexico's gold and foreign exchange resources from 51 million dollars in January 1942 to 372 million dollars by February 1946. This improvement had been due to a favorable balance of trade, increasing tourist expenditures, foreign investment, refugee capital, remittances from braceros and tract laborers, Lend-Lease expenditures, U.S. government procurement programs, expenditures of the Office of Inter-American Affairs, production of specie, and Export-Import Bank loans and RFC credits.[42] The Avila Camacho administration between 1941 and 1946 had expended 2,573 million pesos in public works. Some of the main areas were 796 million in highway construction, 626 million in irrigation, 260 million in power projects, and 168 million in railroad construction. By contrast, private construction invested 3,000 million pesos in the Avila Camacho period.

All of the factors that had led to the wartime increase of reserves, however, were ephemeral. As the war ended, pressures on the country's reserves stepped up. Postwar inflation eroded the value of the wartime reserves, and by the middle of 1947 they were down to 200 million dollars. Given the fact that Mexico had to maintain reserves against the nation's currency of 140 million dollars under IMF requirements, it was getting close. A reduction in reserve requirements was not possible; even if it were implemented, it would be counterproductive in that it would lead to a run on the peso. Mexico's original contribution to the IMF also placed pressure on the peso, although the U.S. Treasury had opened up a 50-million-dollar stabilization fund.[43]

## Mexican Proponents of Protectionism

On January 8, 1947, at the Consejo Superior Ejecutivo de Comercio Exterior, officials decided that their country should participate in the World Trade Conference, and the Mexican delegates were instructed to keep the resolutions adopted at Chapultepec in mind. Armando Amador, of the Ministry of Foreign Relations, as the secretary of the commission, was to receive submissions. At the same time, buried in a new Ley de Ingresos was a provision for the president to have the power to modify export and import duties "in the terms which the Tariff Commission may propose."[44] In the United States, the *New York Herald Tribune* put out a special section dealing with Mexico. It carried a prominent statement from President Alemán calling for industrial development; however, the newspaper contrasted this

with Mexican moves toward higher tariffs and the modification of the trade agreements between the two countries.[45]

In his State of the Union message in January, President Harry Truman called for tariff reductions in general. José R. Colín linked the two countries and charged the United States with being opportunistic and trying to limit Mexico's industrial growth. He claimed that his country had the same right to protect infant industries as the United States had done in its earlier stages of industrial development. *Novedades* supported Colín in this position—a position that U.S. economic diplomats hated. In an interesting analysis, aimed as much at helping diplomats handle the obvious justice of the comparison, Merwin Bohan admitted that the tradition of Alexander Hamilton was very similar to the position that Colín and the other economic nationalists were arguing. However, in his view the size of their market meant that U.S. manufacturers were faced with internal competition, whereas in Mexico a single producer, or even a small group of investors, meant that the industrial producer could take refuge behind tariff walls and gouge the public. The new tariff wall, as erected in July 1945, protected Altos Hornos, for example. According to Bohan's figures, U.S. cold-rolled sheet steel, after paying a 10-cents-per-kilo duty, could still be sold in Mexico City for 52 cents, whereas Altos Hornos charged between 95 cents and $1.25. Favored by tariffs and import controls, Altos Hornos simply enjoyed a protected market. The problem was compounded since political reasons were behind the poor location of Altos Hornos, thus making transportation of virtually all the components that went into steel making more expensive. Of course, Bohan's conclusion was to lower tariffs, a position that merged remarkably with the interests of U.S. steel makers.[46]

In practice, officials did not return to a laissez-faire world of the orthodox liberal economists. The State Department found that in order to make its case credible against protectionism, it was important to have bait with which to deal with the Mexicans. The Department of Commerce—known as "Hoover's Folly"—began to work with the State Department in a corporativist project of negotiating market spheres. The Department of Commerce went into negotiations with the country's steel industry to allocate its production between domestic and foreign customers, to oversee direct sales to customers, and to regulate agents' commissions and resellers' markups. This was clearly seen as a way of combating the desire of industrializing countries to protect their infant industries.[47]

When the First National Congress of the Cámara Nacional de Industrias de Transformación opened on April 21, 1947, it was a battleground. With the president as well as foreign diplomats present, General Joaquín de la Peña set the issue squarely. Claiming that Mexico's postwar economic downturn stemmed directly from provisions of the Chapultepec agreement and the trade agreement with the United States, he urged the president to pro-

tect domestic industry. That agreement, in his view, was damaging industries that had grown during the war and that now had to face international competition from the giant U.S. corporations. "Not to remedy this situation means a death sentence for Mexican industry," he stated. This represents not only protectionism, but also a "system of legal and economic defenses . . . against establishment of subsidiaries of powerful foreign enterprises which sap, absorb or replace domestic factories." In response to General de la Peña, the undersecretary of the Ministry of the National Economy, Manuel Germán Parra, who was replacing Ruiz Galindo, asserted that many of his country's industries were "a hundred years behind" and that their owners demonstrated little interest in modernizing, a point not calculated to please the members attending the conference.[48]

At the Thirteenth Annual Bankers' Convention in Acapulco in April 1947, Ramón Beteta still held to his call for limits on the imports of articles of opulent consumption, again a position not calculated to please either the United States or the majority of the bankers in his audience. Beteta, the former Cardenista who rapidly came to terms with the Avila Camacho-Alemán adjustments, still tried at times to maintain a degree of economic nationalism. Speaking at the convention of the American Investment Bankers in Monterrey, on April 10, 1947, he stated that Mexico entered this age of new prosperity committed to self-sufficiency in production of foodstuffs and industrialization, at least to the point where raw materials that were formerly exported could be transformed in the country. He did see a role for foreign investment: "I am convinced that if foreign capital comes to Mexico and aids in accelerating the industrialization process, it will benefit the country greatly. I know that as long as it complies with the laws, it will have nothing to fear. . . . In brief, foreign capital should not expect any special privileges in Mexico; nor should it fear discrimination."[49]

Another economic nationalist of the early 1940s, Antonio Ruiz Galindo, soon to become Miguel Alemán's minister of the national economy, tried to maintain a differentiation between industries that merely assembled products that were manufactured overseas, such as automobiles, and items that were truly made in Mexico. As the director general of Distribuidora Mexicana S.A. he reassured the president that his firm, in the manufacture of refrigerators, would not be merely assembling foreign parts.

U.S. diplomats tried to exploit this weakness in the nationalists' case. One diplomat marveled that in Mexico City frozen chickens imported from north of the border were six pesos cheaper than locally produced chickens, or that rehydrated Sello Azul milk from the United States undercut domestic milk. U.S. diplomats at this time had no trouble with the idea that Mexico should become self-sufficient in foodstuffs. Indeed, given the association between wartime cooperation, war shortages, and high prices they welcomed an increase in Mexican agricultural production. (It is useful to keep in mind

that there was a food shortage internationally during this period. The U.S. food surpluses had not yet developed.)

Beteta's appeal was to the international investment bankers. He thought that by offering a 6 percent coupon on government bonds, he could lure foreign capital and get around the problem of high-cost industrial production. That was attractive; as the U.S. commercial attaché in Mexico City put it, "How they would love to believe such a statement [that investment in Mexico was safe], for these, remember, were investment bankers. They probably haven't had a decent domestic offering on their shelves in years that carried anything better than 3 or 3.5 percent interest, and here is a gilt-edged engraving all decked out in (presumably) a 6 percent coupon and other attractive features."[50]

Additional funds did not convert into additional production, however, and conditions continued to deteriorate. When the trade figures for May 1947 were released, the ratio of imports to exports continued to grow, thus taking the deficit for the first five months to 545 million pesos. In the first week of July the Banco de México lost more than 1 million dollars daily in foreign exchange, and the bank began to ask depositors why they were withdrawing their funds; acute observers viewed that as an early warning of devaluation. In the first half of the year, imports were 1,744,000 pesos and exports were only 1,087,000 pesos, with a deficit of 657,000,000 pesos, or nearly 135,000,000 dollars.

On July 11 the government responded to the deterioration by suspending the importation of products falling under 128 "fractions" of the import tariff and by increasing the duties dramatically on another thirty categories. These bold changes included automobiles, refrigerators, and electrical products. Reaction was immediate. One refrigerator distributor claimed that he could not get into his own store on the Saturday after the decree. Another electrical dealer reported that his daily sales of 2,500 pesos jumped to 18,000 per day. In a pattern that would be repeated in future economic crises, merchants cashed in on existing stocks by immediately raising prices, and those with high inventories found a great windfall as they sold the products purchased at old prices now at the new ones.[51]

Proponents of protectionism then turned to indirect devices: the Treasury decree of April 15, 1944, which enabled the Ministries of the Treasury and National Economy to restrict imports by issuing custom house circulars; Article 28 of the constitution and the Law of Monopolies, which also gave the government very wide powers; and a further suspension of imports in August.[52] Overseas, the New York financial press interpreted these developments as evidence that Mexico was about to adopt exchange controls.[53] The restrictions did have an immediate effect in certain areas. However, some saw these events as part of the bargaining process between the two countries.[54]

## The Havana Conference

By the end of 1947, as the Havana Conference approached, the battle heated up. The combination of the end of the war boom, the rapid adverse turn of the trade balances, the halting attempts to protect the Banco de México's reserves, and U.S. pressure in favor of free trade through the inter-American system all generated political momentum in favor of protecting Mexican industry. The country saw the unusual spectacle of CONCAMIN, CONCANACO, and their archival, the CCI, all join the Cámara Nacional de Industrias de Transformación in arguing for protection. Rhetoric became impassioned as public demonstrations broke out in the streets of Mexico City. Finance Minister Ramón Beteta, on October 21, 1947, spoke out against protectionist pressures in favor of a U.S.-Mexican trade agreement, in a forlorn attempt to reverse the growing concern. U.S. diplomat Merwin Bohan described the storm of protest from the Chambers and in the Mexican press: "Both the Trade Agreement and Finance Minister Beteta's pronouncements of October 21 were also brought under the guns of ignorance, prejudice, and nationalism."[55]

Reports circulated of emergency meetings among the industrialists of Monterrey to consider the rumors that all tariff barriers would be eliminated by the revised trade agreement between the two countries. Moreover, many feared that the much-discussed Clayton Plan, which meant the elimination of all trade barriers, would be implemented at Havana. As the industrialists expressed it in their petition, "If in the coming Havana Conference the Clayton plan triumphs and free trade becomes the inflexible standard of international commerce, all of our desires and hopes for economic development and industrial growth will be frustrated and Mexico will be chained forever to a semi-colonial economy." Bohan responded, "Forgive us if we mutter 'Baloney.' "[56]

Surprisingly, the CTM took a less nationalistic position in the face of the Clayton Plan than the employers. The country's primary labor organization agreed that Mexico should struggle against tariffs and it also stated its support of foreign investment, if that investment was tied to the "authentic progress of Mexico." The CTM meant that foreign investment should be regulated only to prevent "the exhaustion of national resources, the displacement of national capital, or control of certain resources which might serve as a blind for political or economic control by international monopolies." As one surprised U.S. diplomat put it in reaction to the CTM's position, "Even Mr. Clayton could hardly have asked for more."[57]

The pressure for protection increased, and the government responded with the new tariff on November 13, 1947. It was a combination of a specific and ad valorem system that increased tariffs from 15 to 100 percent. The announcement meant the restoration of tariffs that had been cut during

the war, and the increase was to be on the basis of real price levels.[58] General de la Peña, the new president of the Cámara Nacional de Industrias de Transformación, and the group's former president, José Domingo Lavín, were pleased.

## The U.S.-Mexican Trade Agreement of December 12, 1947

The agreement, announced simultaneously by the two countries, immediately restored tariffs to the 1942 level. U.S. diplomats accepted the inevitability of some Mexican reduction of trade so they decided to mold rather than resist the pressure. Total opposition was ruled out: "It [unwillingness to agree to higher protection] would have lost for the United States the opportunity to check the amount by which the Mexicans would have increased the rates on Schedule I items and to obtain compensation for such increases by further bargaining."[59] Washington officials viewed these changes as necessary to correct the imbalances in trade between the two countries. The agreement represented a rejection of quotas or specific trade prohibitions, a fact that U.S. diplomats noted with relief.

The International Trade Organization meeting at Havana at the end of the year was the moment when Will Clayton, speaking for the United States, made the strongest case for free trade. The Latin Americans were divided, but cool. The Argentinean delegates confided to their Mexican colleagues that they had come to oppose the Clayton Plan. When Beteta arrived at Havana, he was immediately confronted by Clayton, who expressed opposition to tariffs, quotas, and the regulation of capital. Clayton's position was tricky since the United States was still administering a worldwide system of export quotas, which he assured Beteta would end soon. The Mexican representative in return argued that the commitment to industrialization was central. They eventually agreed that Mexico should protect its industries by means of tariffs and not by quota restrictions on imports. Beteta moderated his view of his country's right to raise tariffs and regulate capital as he recommended to the president that Mexico drop the import restrictions that Clayton so opposed, lest they "irritate" the United States. Aware that this would displease the Cámara de Transformación, Beteta told his president that this was the best that Mexico could get.[60] Beteta was, by this point, gaining favor in the eyes of the foreign business community that dealt with Mexico. When Beteta addressed the National Foreign Trade Council, on his way to Havana, Gale F. Johnston, president of the Mercantile Bank and Trust of Saint Louis, cabled President Alemán that Beteta's "thoughts brought forth a tremendous ovation."[61]

## Mexico's New Deal for Foreign Investment

At the end of 1947 one embassy official summarized the importance of Mexican trade to the United States: "We do not need Mexico's trade today. We can get along without shipping a single motor car or refrigerator or radio to this country. It may hurt individual American businessmen abroad but it means nothing to foreign trade in general, [but] . . . the day will come when the shipment of those products to Mexico will have a direct relation to employment in the United States. Our greatest duty . . . is . . . to keep the market 'sweet' for the future, to help maintain Mexican purchasing power against the day when Mexican trade will be needed to lubricate the wheels of American industry."[62]

Mexico's strategic importance was fading and the country was becoming something of a sideshow for the Cold War. In this context, the rules governing the ability of foreign businesses to invest in Mexico became the most important issue. Without question, the Cárdenas period had been a great trial for foreign capital in the country. The techniques of what we might call the old capitalism, best illustrated by the petroleum companies, had led to disaster. Taking a position of absolute intransigence served the major foreign firms poorly. Moreover, it gave economic nationalists a clear target upon which to focus.

By contrast, Anderson, Clayton, and Company took a different approach and had a remarkably profitable business. Forty years of high profits were marred only in 1939 by a slight downturn. In spite of three antitrust actions in the United States, the firm had emerged with ever larger shares of the world market. By World War II it traded in all cotton-exporting countries, including areas under Axis domination. It was one of the first multinational agribusiness corporations, and half of its profits came from its overseas operations.[63]

A moment of crisis for A.C.&Co. came in 1936–37 when President Cárdenas expropriated cotton-growing lands in the Laguna area and in Baja California.[64] In 1937 he held a meeting with Clayton in which he reassured Clayton that Mexico continued to welcome A.C.&Co. Indeed, from 1937 on, A.C.&Co. continued to increase its operations in Mexico so that by 1941 the company's cotton loans amounted to 21 million pesos, of which 11 million went to the Banco Ejidal. Company representatives were scrupulous in honoring Mexican sovereignty. As the company director, Lamar Flemming, put it in 1942, "We particularly wish to affirm to you, Mr. President, our desire that our Mexican companies be considered, at all times, as Mexican entities owing the same loyalties and obligations to Mexico, as the other Mexican organizations and our intent always to operate in this country in that spirit."[65] President Avila Camacho was so moved by Flemming's reassurances that he made public statements to the press praising A.C.&Co. as a

model enterprise, a development for which Flemming apologized profusely to Clayton in their private correspondence. The Clayton interests had learned that publicity served them ill in Mexico.

As the most important intermediary and cotton processor in the country, A.C.&Co. played an important role within the agrarian bureaucracy. It had its friends and enemies. Luis Montes de Oca, former head of the Banco de México, was close to the company as was Eduardo Suárez, the minister of the national economy, whom they called "a wonder." The company's attorney advised its executives at the time of the 1942 meeting with the president to be, in effect, hostile: "Our old lawyer Mr. Jorge Vera Estañol, like Montes de Oca, thought we ought to see the President under any or no auspices, and had a questionnaire for us to hand him like Johnny Crooker cross-questioning a government tax witness. Of course he [Vera Estañol] is pretty reactionary."[66]

Instead, company officials (Lamar Flemming and Joe Sharp, head of the Mexico City office) had lunch with Marte Gómez, the minister of agriculture, and discussed a 10-million-peso loan to the Banco Ejidal. George Messersmith was pleased with their approach. The problem that Joe Sharp saw as endangering A.C.&Co.'s interests was CEIMSA, the government agency that entered commodity trading from time to time. Sharp feared that CEIMSA represented a government attempt to eliminate the middlemen and bring cotton directly from the field to the mill. (The principal middlemen in cotton at the time were A.C.&Co., Pepe de la Mora, and foreign traders Woodward and King.) A combination of pressure from the firm's political friends, the reassurances of loyalty to the president, loans to the Banco Ejidal, and the promise of additional investments in the industry saved the day for the middlemen.

Company officials also were pleased when Marte Gómez shifted Director Adame out of the Banco Ejidal to a position as subdirector of the Ministry of Agriculture under his schoolmate Fernando Foglio Miramontes, since Adame was a more radical figure, in the Cardenista mold. Since the company executives understood that the president was moving toward private agriculture, they stood ready to lend funds as soon as the right of *ejidatarios* was superseded by private landholdings that could be mortgaged.[67]

It is useful, however, to realize that A.C.&Co. was investing funds in Mexico that had been generated in that country. The purchase of the Chávez mill in the Laguna, for example, was attractive to the firm due to the difficulties of obtaining machinery during wartime. However, as Lamar Flemming put it in a letter to Clayton, "I have not let myself think in terms of sending capital abroad for expansion, but rather in terms of re-employment of foreign profits and depreciation allowances."[68]

Flemming was still worrying about what he called the "combined Indian and European philosophy of communism." A.C.&Co. executives were

wary of the tradition of radical nationalism and, more specifically, the provisions of the labor law against running their mills for a third shift. This led Flemming to observe that "the way I size it up is they [the Mexicans] do not want their Country to be a white man's Country, which is what we would like to make of it."[69] Anderson, Clayton, and Company had survived Cardenismo, and other firms learned from their new techniques to foster the reintroduction of foreign capital. It was able to go it alone in the cotton business; however, partnership deals between U.S. and Mexican firms, combining efforts from the private and public sectors, became the new norm.

Altos Hornos also provides an interesting case study of the new approach to foreign investment. The board of directors brought together people from quite different backgrounds. Some directors came from old families that were prominent in the *porfiriato*: Pablo Díaz and Pablo Macedo. Revolutionaries included Abelardo Rodríguez and Antonio Espinosa de los Monteros. French capital was well represented by Julio Lacaud, Antonio Signoret, Emile Goldschmidt, and Carlos Trouyet. U.S. interests were represented by Morton S. Leishman, Earl Emerson, Robert Bobay, Harold Pape, and John Malloy. Even the training of the staff of Altos Hornos took place at the United States Pipe and Foundry Company in Birmingham, Alabama.[70]

The advantages of the arrangement were clear. From the viewpoint of foreign investors, the presence of figures of the revolution provided enormous political protection. The government could call the factory a Mexican enterprise and justify the foreign participation on the grounds of attracting outside capital and expertise. Even labor in the factory was primarily concerned that the government might be building excessive steel-making capacity, since the Fundidora in Monterrey was being expanded at the same time that Bethlehem Steel Export Corporation, Jones and Laughlin, and Republic Steel Corporation were dumping steel in Mexico.[71]

At other times, however, the creation of national industries to replace imports was largely cosmetic. When the Gillette Company opened a factory in Mexico, capable of producing fifty million razor blades per year in 1949, it imported Swedish steel for the blades and the special lacquer coating from the United States. Only the paper wrappers were produced in Mexico.[72] On a larger scale, automobile assembly, which only reached 15,900 units in 1949, showed the same pattern.

It was clear at the time that not all industrial projects in the private sector pursued this new game plan, especially in Monterrey. There, the more autonomous industrialists were quite capable of trying to force out their U.S. partners. In the case of Cristales Mexicanos S.A., the Corning Glass Works of New York was a minority stockholder, holding 35 percent of the shares as late as 1952. A young member of the Garza Domínguez family, Humberto Garza Domínguez, managed to concentrate the remaining family stock in his control and tried to force Corning to sell out at a loss.[73] This

kind of maneuver probably explains why U.S. officials were cool to the Monterrey industrialists, preferring the government's new approach.

## Implement the New Approach: The Professionals Law

There was an issue that was acutely disputed immediately after World War II. Would foreign professionals, principally lawyers, be allowed to practice in Mexico? A new law governing the practice of professions was promulgated,[74] and the fines and penalties for failure to comply were subsequently defined.[75] These innovations defined professionals broadly to include, among others, lawyers, doctors, dentists, accountants, nurses, midwives, economists, and teachers. It was necessary to register with the Dirección General de Profesiones, a subsidiary of the Ministry of Education, in order to practice one's profession in the country. In turn a Mexican degree and citizenship, whether by birth or naturalization, were required for registration. Existing foreign professionals could register as *inmigrados*, or *inmigrantes*, although when their documents expired there would be no continuing right to work. The purpose was to give the Mexican government the power to regulate foreign professionals. Washington officials cared about the rules governing these persons because they played a central role in the reentry of U.S. firms to Mexico.

The experience of the U.S. soft drink manufacturer, Dr. Pepper Company, provides a case in point. Mexico was a natural target of expansion for soft drink makers because the syrup could be sold to local bottlers, who in turn sold drinks at cheap prices to the population. The Dr. Pepper Company wanted to organize a subsidiary that would be owned outright by the parent firm, but it was having trouble with this format. It consulted Dr. Julius Klein of the investment banking house of Klein and Saks. Klein wrote to Merwin L. Bohan, the head of the U.S. embassy's economic unit in Mexico City in 1947.

Bohan explained to Klein that the Mexican law of July 7, 1944, granted the Foreign Ministry the authority to pass on applications of U.S. corporations to charter in Mexico. As Bohan put it, "The policy of the Foreign Office has been quite liberal to date." However, it insisted that 51 percent of the capital be held by Mexican citizens. Bohan knew the answer to their problem: "Why not have Dr. Pepper in the United States form a separate and wholly owned corporation for the sole purpose of handling the export business? This is by no means a devious procedure. It was recognized as a necessity by the Senate Finance Committee in its hearings on the revenue act of 1942, Sections 15 (b) and 109, the United States Internal Revenue Code. This provides for certain tax exemptions to United States corporations, the so-called Western Hemisphere Trade Corporation. Such a corpo-

ration could open a branch in Mexico."[76] Indeed, Bohan suggested that he contact Jess N. Dalton, "an American practicing law in Mexico," who had actually published a detailed model of the way that foreign firms could get around the Mexican law.[77] Filing the appropriate forms from the Department of Commerce and the office of the Mexican ambassador in Washington, establishing the proper boards of directors including Mexican citizens, and following the Mexican requirements on paperwork thus entitled a U.S. firm to find a way to circumvent the 51 percent requirement.

Jess Dalton, who boasted of descent from the Dalton Brothers in Missouri, went even further. He became one of a very small number of U.S. citizens who took up Mexican citizenship. (The vast majority of foreigners working in Mexico are only allowed to have the status of *visitantes* or *inmigrantes*.) By converting his citizenship, Dalton was in a position, through his law firm of Goodrich and Dalton, to participate on the boards of many U.S. corporations that came to Mexico after World War II.[78]

## The 51 Percent Law

A famous decree, cited by many as the high-water mark of economic nationalism, was promulgated on June 29, 1944, under the emergency war powers of the period.[79] The Ministry of Foreign Relations was given the power to reject the legal charters of any firm engaged in a wide range of activities (industry, agriculture, livestock, forestry, real estate, and the like). Since the emergency war-powers act lapsed automatically with the end of hostilities in 1945, a decree of September 28 provided for a continuation, and by December 28, 1945, a law to that effect was passed, although the minister of foreign relations interpreted the situation as still provisional. The Supreme Court also applied the right of injunction, or *amparo*, to specific cases. As U.S. economic diplomats pursued the effective meaning of the provisions, they concluded that "it seems reasonable to infer [from the delay in implementing the 1946 law] that the project has been either withdrawn or indefinitely postponed at the request of the executive branch of the government. Ever since Lic. Alemán's election was assured . . . one of the principal objectives of his administration would be to attract foreign capital to invest in Mexico's industrialization program. The inhibitive character of the project, as presented to and passed by the Chamber of Deputies, upon foreign capital investment in Mexico is obvious."[80]

In 1947 the Supreme Court appeared to have invalidated the decree; however, the Foreign Ministry considered it still in effect. In April 1945, Foreign Minister Ezequiel Padilla had issued a departmental directive indicating the areas to which the decree would apply: radio broadcasting, motion pictures, domestic air and urban transportation, publishing, and fishing. Padilla, in his own handwriting, added soft drink bottling.[81]

At the same time, Mexico, according to Secretary of the Treasury John Snyder, was requesting loans of 193 million dollars from the IBRD and 150 million dollars from the Export-Import Bank.[82] The New York press called for care to make certain that U.S. private business was not being adversely affected in Mexico, to which *El Nacional* simply answered that negotiations were continuing.[83] U.S. diplomats took the attitude that the less said of linking loans with the condition of foreign capital in Mexico, the better. As the top U.S. economic diplomat in Mexico put it, "It is extremely fortunate that the EXIMBANK is run by a group of men who, while sincerely believing in the need for and possibilities resulting from financial cooperation, are thoroughly aware that credit is like water—the right amount will make economies and goodwill flourish; too little or an excessive amount will damage not only economies, but also goodwill."[84]

U.S. diplomats worked to convince investors that, appearances notwithstanding, the 51 percent law did not mean that outsiders could only own 49 percent of an enterprise in Mexico. In spite of a long list of areas that could be covered, an Inter-Secretarial Commission was established to rule on specific cases. An early test case was the Espace Calpe Mexicana publishing house. The commission ruled that its publishing was in the interest of Mexican industrialization, and therefore approval was granted. A precedent was set.[85]

Following the end of the war, it became necessary for the U.S. authorities to find new devices to maintain the same degree of close contact with industries below the border. No longer did wartime rationing mean that the U.S. embassy's help was required in order to import products from the United States. It was not clear that its economic diplomats in Mexico would still enjoy government help in conducting surveys of resources and production. In no area did access to Mexican resources matter as much as in the mining field. The Big Seven mining companies, as they were called, were accustomed to the wartime resource surveys to help them find materials to be exploited. As the war came to an end, Horace Braun of the State Department and Carl Fries, Jr., of the U.S. Geological Survey presented a plan that would continue to allow "the type of mining investigation and development of properties such as were practiced during the war." Technical advising and the training of Mexican geology students would be the basis of an ongoing program of exploration. This was to be "acceptable to the mining interests, including the 'big seven' now operating in the field."[86]

At times there were threats to the newly emerging policy of allowing reentry of foreign capital into Mexico. In 1946, in response to the evasion of the 51 percent rule, a project was proposed to limit the rights of foreigners to incorporate, in order to get around that rule, and then own property. However, little came of the proposal. Clearly, it would have made the 51 percent rule effective, and that was not on the government's agenda. The

legal fiction of a foreign corporation adding "de México" to its name provided the way out.[87]

In short, a number of factors came together and led to a resolution of the battle over foreign investment. Mexicans, in large numbers, thought that a rapid push for industrialization was imperative. Arguments from classical economics over laissez-faire models were irrelevant since almost all participants agreed that the state had a central role in raising capital. New techniques emerged by which foreign investors could enter the country in partnership agreements with powerful Mexicans. Only the world's largest firms, which enjoyed special leverage, could go it alone; and, even in the case of such giants as Ford Motor Company, there was an ongoing battle over their exclusion of Mexican partners. New techniques were designed by U.S. professionals in Mexico to enable investors to get around such provisions of economic nationalism as the 51 percent law, the registration of professionals, and ownership controls.

Foreign firms reentered Mexico with a vengeance, and scholars have traced their return in considerable detail.[88] However, they did not encounter the same rules as in the past. It became more important for foreign investors to have influential Mexican partners to provide them with political cover. With foreign investors, and their influential partners operating in conjunction, the state would serve increasingly as a guarantor of profits and overseas borrowing.

# Notes

1. Merwin L. Bohan to secretary of state, March 5, 1947, USNA/RG 59, 812.50/3-547.
2. *Diario Oficial*, May 14, 1947.
3. Juan de Dios Bojórquez to Miguel Alemán, February 23, 1951, and editors of *Bancos* to Alemán, AGN, PR/MAV, 950/23652.
4. Ashton, *The Industrial Revolution,* 84–85, placed the low interest rates in a key position in leading to the industrialization of the United Kingdom. Japanese interest rates have stayed at the 1.5 to 3 percent level for decades. Similarly, A.C.&Co. bought their vast tracts of land in the Imperial Valley of California, financing the deal at 2.75 percent in the 1950s.
5. Venancio Escalante to Alemán, April 29, 1948, AGN, RP/MAV, 423/99.
6. Isidro Fabela, March 25, 1941, "El Problema de la Energía Eléctrica," ibid.
7. Governor Jorge Cerdán to the president, March 6, 1940, AGN, RP/MAC, 545.11.
8. *Diario Oficial*, June 23, 1947.
9. Manuel Avila Camacho to the Confederación de Cámeras Industriales de los Estados Unidos Mexicanos, October 31, 1944, AGN, RP/MAC, 545.22/262.
10. Lagos, *Inconvenientes del impuesto sobre exportaciónes* .
11. Avila Camacho to Jesús Cruz y Célis, September 26, 1944, AGN, RP/MAC, 545.22/262.

12. "XVIIth Annual Convention of Mexican Bankers' Association," May 16, 1951, USNA/RG 59, 812.14/5-351; May 16, 1951, USNA/RG 59, 812.14/5-1651.

13. Latapi's speech may be found in *El Mercado de Valores*, May 9, 1952. For a U.S. view of the conference see "Convention of Mexican Bankers' Association," May 20, 1952, USNA/RG 59, 812.14/5-2052.

14. *El Popular*, May 5, 6, and 27, 1953.

15. Cámara Nacional de Industrias de Transformación, *Actividades durante el año de 1945*, 11.

16. Antonio Ruiz Galindo to the president, February 10, 1945, AGN, RP/MAC, 545.22/262.

17. José R. Colín to the president, April 22, 1946, AGN, RP/MAC, 523/5.

18. Colín to the president, March 11, 1946, ibid.

19. José de la Mora to Alemán, November 20, 1949, AGN, RP/MAV, 432/461.

20. "The National Chamber of Industry," August 27, 1953, USNA/RG 59, 812.19/8-2753.

21. Cámara Nacional de Industrias de Transformación, *Pacto Obrero-Industrial*, 19–20.

22. Ibid., 19.

23. Antonio Ruiz Galindo to Avila Camacho, February 23, 1945, AGN, RP/MAC, 545.22/262.

24. See Colín to Avila Camacho, AGN, RP/MAC, 523/5, for requests for audiences that were rejected.

25. George Messersmith to Will L. Clayton, March 1, 1946, Truman Library, files of undersecretary of state for economic affairs, 1946–47, Box 4.

26. J. M. O. Monasterio to Clayton, October 12, 1946, Truman Library, Clayton Papers, M folder 1. Monasterio was soon to become the president of the American Bankers' Association.

27. CIA report, December 1951, Truman Library, PSF, 259.

28. Guy W. Ray to Charles Ross, March 1, 1946, Truman Library, Official File 146.

29. Messersmith to Cordell Hull, August 4, 1944, GSM Papers.

30. Bohan to secretary of state, August 18, 1948, USNA/RG 59, 812.50/8-1848.

31. Report to Morris L. Cooke, February 19, 1942, AGN, PR/MAC, 433/310.

32. Lamar Flemming to Clayton, July 19, 1941, Truman Library, Clayton Papers.

33. Walter Thurston to secretary of state, January 8, 1947, USNA/RG 59, 812.51/1-847.

34. Wallace, *The Diary of Henry A. Wallace*, 461.

35. Messersmith to Clayton, July 20, 1945, USNA/RG 59, 812.796/7-2045. For the terms of the agreement see USNA/RG 59, 812.796/8-945.

36. *Business Week*, May 3, 1947.

37. Lew B. Clark to secretary of state, May 29, 1947, USNA/RG 59, 812.50/2947.

38. Messersmith to Clayton, January 25, 1946, Truman Library, files of undersecretary of state for economic affairs, 1946–47, Box 4.

39. Thurston to secretary of state, December 30, 1946, USNA/RG 59, 812.51/12-3046.

40. Clark to secretary of state, March 12, 1948, USNA/RG 59, 812.50/3-1248.

41. Clark to secretary of state, May 4, 1947, USNA/RG 59, 812.50/5-947.

42. Ibid.

43. William K. Ailshie to secretary of state, August 30, 1945, USNA/RG 59, 812.504/8-3045.

44. *Diario Oficial*, December 31, 1946.

45. *New York Herald Tribune*, January 4, 1947.

46. Bohan to secretary of state, January 17, 1947, USNA/RG 59, 812.50/1-1747.

47. Bohan to secretary of state, March 13, 1947, USNA/RG 59, 812.50/3-1347.

48. Clark to secretary of state, May 2, 1947, USNA/RG 59, 812.50/5-247.

49. Ruiz Galindo to Alemán, August 5, 1949, AGN, RP/MAV, 705.2/107.

50. Clark to secretary of state, April 24, 1947, USNA/RG 59, 812.50/4-2447.

51. Bohan to secretary of state, July 16, 1947, USNA/RG 59, 812.50/7-1647.

52. *Diario Oficial*, August 16, 1947.

53. *Journal of Commerce*, August 14, 1947.

54. Clark to secretary of state, February 27, 1948, USNA/RG 59, 812.50/2-2748.

55. Bohan to secretary of state, November 6, 1947, USNA/RG 59, 812.50/11-647.

56. *Excélsior*, November 1, 1947.

57. Ibid.

58. *Diario Oficial*, November 13, 1947.

59. Bohen to Otis E. Mulliken, September 11, 1948, Truman Library, Clayton Papers, Box 78.

60. Ramón Beteta to Alemán, February 5, 1948, AGN, RP/MAV, 433/216.

61. Gale F. Johnston to Alemán, October 22, 1947, ibid.

62. Bohan to secretary of state, December 30, 1947, USNA/RG 59, 812.50/12-3047.

63. George Whitney to D. B. Cannafax, December 8, 1944, Truman Library, Clayton Papers, Box 32.

64. Anderson, Clayton, and Company S.A. also operated in Mexico as Compañía Industrial Jabonera del Pacífico and the Banco Mexicano Refaccionario S.A. of Torreón.

65. Flemming to Avila Camacho, April 15, 1942, Truman Library, Clayton Papers, Box 21.

66. Flemming to Clayton, April 18, 1942, and October 3, 1941, Truman Library, Clayton Papers, Box 21.

67. Flemming to Clayton, April 18, 1942, ibid.

68. Flemming to Clayton, November 29, 1943, Truman Library, Clayton Papers, Box 32.

69. Ibid.

70. H. R. Pape to López Padilla, February 1, 1944, AGN, RP/MAC, 523.6/7.

71. Rincón Gallardo to the president, May 17, 1945, AGN, RP/MAC, 545.22/262.

72. Harry Hopkins to secretary of state, November 10, 1949, USNA/RG 59, 812.50/11-1049.

73. "Controversy between Cristales Mexicanos S.A. and Corning Glass Works," April 25, 1952, USNA/RG 59, 812.053/4-2552.

74. *Diario Oficial*, May 25 and October 1, 1945.

75. Ibid., January 25, and January 30, 1947.

76. Bohan to Julius Klein, July 21, 1947, Truman Library, Merwin L. Bohan Papers, Box 4.

77. Bohan cited the May 1947 issue of the *Journal of the Bar Association of Kansas*, ibid.

78. Jess Dalton became a pillar of the U.S. community in Mexico, serving on the board of the ABC Hospital, the Universidad de las Américas, and many other institutions. He eventually controlled a number of the soft drink-bottling firms that he had helped establish in Mexico. In 1980 he fled the country, apparently in trouble with the tax authorities, who seized all of his assets.

79. *Diario Oficial*, June 7, 1944.

80. Bohan to secretary of state, April 2, 1947, USNA/RG 59, 812.50/4-247.

81. Ibid.

82. *Excélsior*, March 24, 1947.

83. *New York Herald Tribune*, March 25, 1947.

84. Bohan to secretary of state, April 2, 1947, USNA/RG 59, 812.50/4-247.

85. Clark to secretary of state, June 24, 1948, USNA/RG 59, 812.50/6-2448.

86. Bohan to secretary of state, April 2, 1947, USNA/RG 59, 812.50/4-247.

87. Francisco Castillo Nájera to Avila Camacho, January 9, 1946, AGN, RP/MAC, 201.1/5.

88. Ceceña, *México en la orbita imperial*, 125–238; Baird and McCaughan, *Beyond the Border*, and the appendix by Marc Herold, 190–203.

# 8 The Political Nature of Industrialization

The importance of political decision making in the Mexican industrialization process cannot be overestimated. The favors that the government could grant to approved projects in that area were so lucrative that the private sector was caught up in the political machinations of the day. It was common for the Mexican president to rule on important industrial matters, and a favorable decision could mean a gift of free land, tax relief, customs holidays, cheap utilities, grants of resources, guaranteed purchase contracts, and a host of other subsidies. The rewards for successful proposals were so direct and obvious that intense competition existed for political favors. Since accountability for state subsidies was minimal, powerful vested interests vied for control of resources.

## Mingling of Elites

With Mexico and the United States separated by one of the most dramatic borders in the world, it is easy to underestimate the degree to which the elites of these two countries interact. From time to time the historical record gives us striking glimpses of their intimate contact, despite their profoundly different cultures, languages, problems, histories, and perspectives. In the period under study, contacts were being cultivated at the top that molded the policies of both governments. Key figures in the private sector could call upon each other for information, help, and favors, which were frequently returned. These personal and business contacts led to the formation of state policy as the elites interacted in ways that changed the course of the Mexican Revolution. A surprisingly small number of people who were especially interested in the politics of industrialization set the rules for the nation's development.

There was a network of insiders—not all of whom held public office—who interacted in ways that were not open to view. It is striking to see how finely attuned members of the elite were to each other. Normally, a mere word passing between these men carried more clout than a mass political movement. A figure such as Ambassador George Messersmith is extremely valuable in helping us understand this process, since he was able to move in

both the public political world and the private business sphere, frequently facilitating contact between the two.

The proliferation of official committees between the two countries brought people in the public and private sectors closer together around the goal of increasing production for the war effort. Donald Nelson, head of the War Production Board, immediately contacted such figures in the private sector, arguing that if one did not gain the enthusiastic cooperation of the business elite, then production for the war effort would languish. The dollar-a-year men worked for the common goal, but they also kept the interests of their firms and industries in mind, and Mexico was new territory for expansion.

A long-time U.S. businessman in Mexico, Floyd D. Ransom, had headed the Rubber Reserve Company, an offshoot of the Commerce Department's Reconstruction Finance Corporation, during the early part of World War II. When Messersmith went to Mexico in 1942 he selected Ransom as his number two man since he knew the business community from previous experience. Messersmith made an enemy of Dean Acheson over the appointment, but in his view that did not matter since, without Ransom's intimate knowledge of U.S. and Mexican business circles, the integration of Mexico into the war effort would have been much longer in coming. After the war Ransom returned to Mexico and became the president of Proveedor de Oficinas S.A., representing Monroe Calculators, Royal Office Machinery, Ditto Reproducers, Soundscriber Recorders, and Diebold Safes. In Mexico, the business elite also provided staff for positions on the economic side of the war effort. Jesús Rivero Quijano, a Spanish citizen who owned Almacenes Textiles S.A. and Atoyoc Textiles S.A., was made a member of the Consejo de Coordinación y Fomento de la Producción, under General Rodríguez. Will Clayton immediately congratulated him.[1]

The new president, Miguel Alemán, was certainly one of the politicians most deeply involved in creating links between the U.S. and Mexican elites. From his early days in Hollywood, throughout his presidency, and even after he left office, he pursued that goal. He moved from the presidential office to head the Tourism Department for the remainder of his active life, which enabled him to offer the pleasures of Acapulco to powerful contacts. A constant stream of corporate leaders passed through Alemán's Acapulco, cementing deals while enjoying the good life.

Many of the public figures who headed up the economic effort during the war also established the terms for entry of foreign capital into Mexico when hostilities ended, and many public figures were beholden to a powerful capitalist such as Will Clayton. George Messersmith wrote to Clayton asking for investment advice: "I have so much money in government bonds that I would like to buy a bit of stock."[2] Luis G. Legorreta, when visiting Washington, called on Clayton for counsel on matters of business, politics,

and finance.[3] Even political figures whom we normally do not think of in terms of business networks were involved. Allen Dulles was on a retainer from Clayton in 1941; and, before moving to intelligence work, he had represented the Clayton interests in Latin America in a number of cases.[4]

Clearly, we are dealing with powerful networks in which political and economic decisions intermingled with private interests. When the Mexican ambassador to Washington went to an economic conference in Rome in 1947, his visit provided an opportunity for the United States to do him a favor. Major General Harry Vaughan, military aide to President Harry Truman, wrote to James C. Dunn, the U.S. ambassador to Italy. Indicating that "Dr. [Espinosa de los] Monteros is one of our good friends for whom we would like to do any favor within reason," he instructed the ambassador "without publicity . . . to loan the good doctor a car for his holiday in Italy."[5]

When the Avila Camacho administration came to power, Ambassador Messersmith acted to try to build personal links with friendly members of the new government, and in the process woo them away from the radical nationalists of the Cárdenas era. In 1943, when Señora Padilla and Señora Torres Bodet wanted to visit the United States, Messersmith wrote to Will Clayton, "It is a very fine occasion for us to pay some attention to the wife of Padilla and of the under-secretary, both of them being our great and good friends and most helpful to us in so many ways."[6] All the stops were pulled out. Oliver Stevens, head of the U.S. railroad mission, offered his private car on the Missouri-Pacific Railroad for the journey, something that doubtless impressed Señora Padilla since her father, Señor Couttolenc, had owned land and several small branch railways that were expropriated by the Mexican government. Messersmith reassured Clayton, then the assistant secretary of commerce, that the Missouri-Pacific understood that "no charges would be incurred."[7]

The impact of this hospitality upon these women can only be imagined; however, to be feted by an assistant secretary of commerce, who was also the personal owner of the world's largest cotton brokerage, must have been impressive. It is revealing to notice that, before their visit, the two women were so unfamiliar with the United States that Señora Padilla asked Ambassador Messersmith if there were any shops in Houston, Texas. New links were being forged.

When Luis Montes de Oca stepped down as head of the Banco de México, he informed Will Clayton of the fact at once. Joe Sharp, head of Clayton's interests in Mexico, penned a note on the letter to the effect that Montes de Oca's sympathies were on their side, and Clayton did entertain him. Similarly, when Luis G. Legorreta visited Washington in 1941, Nelson Rockefeller acted as his host. Indeed, a few academics even had access to these networks. Raul Prebisch, for example, sent Clayton a case of champagne for Christmas in 1940.[8]

### Political Favors

Favors were not necessarily based upon corruption or even the fruits of network building. It was when dominant theories of development interacted with vested interests that a truly formidable combination emerged. Being able to explain the decision of the moment in terms of development strategy elicited support from people other than the recipients of favors. But where favors coincided with development arguments, then that combination was powerful. These networks of favoritism paid high dividends.

Altos Hornos was a centerpiece of the Cárdenas industrialization project. In 1948 it still suffered from poor initial planning. In the wake of the oil expropriation, the cabinet had invited U.S. capital to participate in the venture even though previously the plan had been to go it alone. A decade later its viability was still in question as President Alemán sent Minister of the National Economy Antonio Ruiz Galindo to Monclova to evaluate the continuing difficulties. The mill still could not produce the steel pipe that PEMEX desperately needed; seamless pipe had to be acquired from Monterrey or the United States. The pace of production was slow and the enterprise still suffered acutely from a bizarre location in Coahuila, far from the natural resources required for steel making. The poor transportation network in the region was a major impediment. Even though Monclova had grown from four thousand inhabitants when the project started to twenty thousand in 1948 (with a monthly payroll of one million pesos), the community still lacked adequate basic amenities such as water, sewage, pavements, electric lighting, and health services.

Ruiz Galindo acknowledged all of the problems that made the cost of steel excessive, but he concluded that the government had no alternative but to continue to fund the project because the factory "now is an economic reality." The predominance of politics over economics was striking.[9] Steel making was viewed as a central industry upon which industrial progress depended, and no matter how inefficient the venture, there was no turning back—especially since the governing party was so closely identified with it. The case of Altos Hornos demonstrates how a clear business failure, when subsidized by the state, could endure for decades. In that case, the project was justified because steel was one of the fundamental industries that the country lacked.

The Mexican "doctrine of industrial saturation" provided another rich field where influence counted. Reacting against the kind of human misery so apparent after 1929, the Mexican authorities decided that if an industry expanded to the point where its further development would be detrimental to the interests of labor, capital, or the public—and they kept the definitions broad and vague—then they would declare it, by means of an executive order, to be in a state of saturation. No further development would be allowed in order to maintain a balance between fair wages, fair profits, and

fair prices. Ironically, they based this anticompetitive doctrine upon the authority of the antimonopoly provisions (Articles 20 and 28) of the 1917 constitution. Mexican governments seized rather broad powers of economic intervention and regulation and further expanded them in subsequent legislation.[10]

The implementation of the "doctrine of industrial saturation" shows how things that started in one way changed profoundly over time. The rayon industry was the first one declared to be saturated, in 1937.[11] It was a curious story. The rayon industry had developed out of the tiny silk industry in the 1930s, as a result of the invention of that new material, which was lower in cost and very attractive in use. The products—dress goods and hosiery—were so profitable that the field attracted a large number of entrants of all sizes, from cottage industries to major participants. It turned out that the largest and smallest firms did well, the former due to cheap access to supply and the latter due to the payment of miserable wages. As some plants failed within a context of fierce competition, the workers took over the operations, forming cooperatives in a pattern common to Cardenismo.

In order to aid the cooperatives and what it called the respectable industrialists, the Cárdenas government established a semiofficial raw material importing and distributing agency called Importadora y Distribuidora de Artisela. By controlling the importation of rayon yarn, initially from Italy, the agency announced its intention to use this power to penalize producers who ignored the terms of the labor contract law, aimed at protecting workers. At that time there was a community of interests between the cooperatives, large producers, and the government to work against the small sweatshop producers.

The Ministry of the National Economy was empowered to register and regulate the country's producers to ensure that the labor code was respected in all workplaces.[12] After Mexico joined the war effort, the initial attempt to control the sweatshops was inadvertently cancelled as wartime cooperation took precedence over social reform. Therefore, large-scale Mexican industry was generally pleased that the war effort had implied the end of pressure against the sweatshops as well as relief from foreign competition. As rayon imports dried up from Italy, the U.S. embassy allocated wartime supplies to Mexico. As the war ended, and supplies again became available, pressure grew on the Avila Camacho administration to deregulate imports. Producers, caught between ceiling prices and wartime excess-profit taxes in the United States, found it tempting to unload their output to the south (Mexican industrialists called it dumping). By 1946 calls to deregulate had changed to pressure on the government for protection, through an import quota system. So the decision to place rayon on the saturation list related to an attempt to defend the infant industry from the large U.S. producers.[13]

The match industry was the second one declared to be saturated.[14] Although there were sixteen factories, it was in reality a duopoly; one firm

was owned by a German family named Krueger, and the other by Mexicans. The government granted this industry special protection as a result of excess productive capacity.[15] The flour milling industry was also saturated.[16] At the height of the wartime food crisis, ND&R's regulatory role was a windfall to the industry. As one diplomatic dispatch of the day put it, "the major portion of the mills located in and around Mexico City, as well as certain individual mills located in other parts of the Republic, is controlled by a powerful and and wealthy group of Mexicans of Spanish origin. Trade sources believe that these mills are individually owned and that the group of owners work together merely as a syndicate for the sake of advantage to be obtained from co-operation."[17]

So the saturation law was implemented in the face of a food crisis, and rapid increases in the price of bread, in order to protect the oligopoly position of the Cámara Central de la Industria Harinera Mexicana, which still had excess milling capacity! Socialism may have been the most radical doctrine of the day; however, competition was not to be allowed either.

Another odd use of the saturation powers was in the rubber industry. The wartime shortages of tires did not prevent the application of the saturation principles.[18] Initially justified as an emergency war measure, the decree was a form of rationing. U.S. diplomats believed that there was no ulterior motive and that the industry would be deregulated after the emergency ended.[19]

The cigarette industry was another matter.[20] Confronting a French near-monopoly in the 1920s, a dozen small firms had entered the market using obsolete equipment. Then, in the early 1930s, a major U.S. tobacco company overwhelmed the market. An agreement was reached in which the French and the American firms, operating under different names in Mexico City and Monterrey, divided up the market. The United States then raced ahead, followed by the French firm and, finally, by a small Spanish company; the dozen-odd Mexican firms withered as they produced an inferior product at higher prices. A trade agreement of 1936 failed to protect the Mexican producers. So in 1944 a coordinating commission was established, as the industry was declared to be saturated. The commission, made up of industry representatives and the Ministry of the National Economy, divided the producers into three groups: the largest U.S., the intermediate French and Spanish, and the small Mexican. Certain regions and product niches were thus guaranteed to the Mexican producers. Buyers were required to take a certain percentage of the local products along with the output of the large firms. In short, the arrangement guaranteed the large producers an oligopoly position in return for allowing the small domestic producers a niche in which to survive. Foreign producers were reported to be happy with the arrangement in that it was a virtual form of insurance against adverse government action.[21]

The use of the "doctrine of industrial saturation" varied considerably from industry to industry, depending upon the perceptions of the government and the influence of the industrialists involved. It is clear that a highly politicized form of industrialization was emerging. Initial impulses to protect national industry and to implement the labor law could easily be diverted to the interests of powerfully connected industrialists, either Mexican or foreign. Even though the number of formal cases was limited, broader patterns of government participation in policy applied to other industries, even in areas where the doctrine was not formally invoked.

At times, motives overlapped. The president of the Compañía Panamericana Comercial S.A. wrote to Miguel Alemán in his position as minister of the interior in 1942. As he suggested to the minister, a group of the president's friends, for whom he spoke, wanted to organize an industrial bank that would concentrate on funding higher levels of technical production in the country. They had targeted the formation of a factory to make laminate iron and steel products, and they were particularly interested in the process of electroplating. In this they were profoundly opposed by ASARCO, since that mining giant wanted to continue to export only semirefined copper. It turned out that by doing the final smelting in plants in the United States, the company had, in effect, found an indirect and very lucrative way to export gold and silver from Mexico, since precious metals in an unrefined state were taxed only as unrefined copper. This was a case where personal friendships, and a seemingly good idea, clashed with the interests of one of the largest foreign firms in Mexico.[22]

During the war years, the fate of an industry rested upon the ability of an industrialist to gain inclusion on the government's priority list. Fernando Flores Muñoz, the head of Productora de Aceites Vegetales S.A., wrote to the president complaining that his attempt to produce fertilizers, which by today's standards was quite organic, was all for naught since he could not finish the fertilizer without potassium salts. Marte Gómez had not been helpful, so he petitioned the president to have these items included on the purchasing list from the United States.[23] Flores Muñoz was out of luck; he received word that his potassium salts were not to be included.[24] This kind of episode illustrates not only the political vulnerability of industries without adequate political cover, but also why the small firms that were producing environmentally less damaging organic fertilizers lost out to the giant petrochemical firms. Of course, in the 1940s there was no concern for environmental issues where a project of industrialization was involved.

Favors were reciprocated. At the beginning of World War II, A.C.&Co. was well positioned to take advantage of the demand for processed edible oils. The problem was the Mexican labor law, which in the view of company officials prevented a third shift in A.C.&Co.'s factories. Joe Sharp wrote to the firm's general manager, Lamar Flemming, stating that

"[Eduardo] Suárez volunteered to present their [A.C.&Co.'s] point of view and the national interest in exports to the Minister of Labor and the labor leaders themselves."[25] Similarly, the A.C.&Co. interests lobbied hard for the expansion of the Matamoros-Victoria highway since it would "enlarge the territory tributary to our Matamoros oil mill."[26] As Export-Import Bank loans funded the project and the importance of the highway was clear, there was a community of interests.

The postwar Export-Import Bank loan for the Monclova steel mill was presented to the bank by the American Rolling Mills Company, which had obtained an equity share in the project. As the bank's president explained, "We are convinced of the possibilities of sound development of the resources of Latin America and are convinced also of the desirability of encouraging private capital in that direction."[27]

Key figures were alert to changing conditions. When Eduardo Villaseñor succeeded Montes de Oca as head of the Banco de México, Joe Sharp immediately extended an invitation to him to go to New York and meet with Will Clayton.[28] Such relationships were important. In 1950–51, A.C.&Co. entered into a rapid period of expansion. It borrowed 25 million dollars (at 2.5 percent for twenty-five years) from Equitable Life Assurance Company (a Rockefeller corporation), and developed the Imperial Valley in California and a number of properties and oil mills in Mexico. The company did not need the money; their profits were 11.9 million dollars on their domestic operations and 13.5 million dollars on their foreign operations in 1950. However, the access to state funds for infrastructure supporting their business was central in that period of expansion. Their Mexican cotton production increased by one hundred thousand bales (it was an expansion in a field as yet untouched by the development of synthetics), and, as such, it rested squarely on the network of new irrigation projects in northwest Mexico and in Tamaulipas. The new oil-milling plants at Monterrey and Empalme directly serviced this production, much of it on A.C.&Co. lands, which were irrigated by loans from the Export-Import Bank and serviced through NAFISA.

This was a classic case of the privatization of gain (the land, the cotton production, the processing, and the marketing by A.C.&Co.) and the socialization of costs (the Mexican taxpayer ultimately underwrote the borrowing and assumed the risk of devaluation through NAFISA). The Empalme plant was built by Brown and Root Construction Company (which habitually financed Lyndon Johnson's political career). However, there was a problem; A.C.&Co. had many enemies in Mexico. It was clearly the kind of firm that opponents of imperialism disliked. Apparently the company ran into some unhelpful government functionaries as it tried to gain the title to the oil mill at Empalme. As a manager of the Houston office boasted to Clayton, the acquisition of the title was a hassle, which was only resolved by aid from powerful Mexican friends and "six months of effort."[29]

Political favors for agreements of which the government approved could be quite substantial, and they covered a large number of fields. Instrumentos Científicos de México S.A. of La Barca, Jalisco, in association with the Neptune Meter Company of New York City, had a plan to manufacture water and electricity meters in Mexico under the catchy name of Planta Armadora, Fábrica de Medidores y Equipos de Saneamiento S.A. Amadeo Solórzano, the president and general manager, confided to President Alemán that the negotiations were at a touchy point in September 1948. Solórzano had already written to the U.S. firm promising federal tax exemptions for a minimum of five years, protection from competition offered by Mexican tariffs, and low labor costs.[30] However, that was not enough. Solórzano asked the president to instruct the Department of Water Resources, the Department of the Federal District, and other dependencies to suspend the annual purchase of 250,000 meters from abroad. In addition, General Luis Alamillo Flores gave the firm land, a building, and equipment next door to the factory of Motores y Maquinaria Anáhuac S.A. on the Calzado Puebla.[31]

There is an eternal tension between planners' views of the economy and business leaders' views of their own situation. There are always dangers in looking at economics exclusively from a theoretical viewpoint. Aggregate statistics, efficiency, productivity, and theories can give one perspective; however, as an executive put it, "the Export-Import Bank loans don't do these [Mexican] firms any good that they can see. These loans look good in the Latin American newspapers, but the average importer is more likely to be impressed if he can see benefit to himself."[32]

Subtle and indirect techniques of influence were more useful. The link between the U.S. automobile industry, the U.S. government, and their Mexican counterparts provides a case in point. American automobile manufacturers were competing for a share of future Mexican markets at a time when their preeminence was stunning. There were 52.7 million automobiles in the world in March 1948, of which 37.6 million were in the United States. Mexico had only 238,000 cars. Nine U.S. manufacturers of cars and trucks (Ford, General Motors, Chrysler, Nash, Hudson, Packard, Mack, International Harvester, and Studebaker) were trying to gain a foothold in the Mexican market.[33]

The Asociación Mexicana de Caminos formed as an industry pressure group to push for more road construction funds. Its president was Rómulo O'Farrill, who also ran the Automotriz O'Farrill (Packard and Mack Trucks) and was president and general manager of *Novedades*. The association enjoyed close relations with Minister of Communications and Public Works Agustín García López. Other political figures within the PRI, such as Abelardo Rodríguez (Studebaker Panamericano S.A.), also had a stake in this industry. The association was eager to press for plans for road construction and the development of the industry, and it formed a technical wing, bringing civil engineers together in the Afiliados Contratistas de la AMC.

The U.S. embassy came to the party by organizing a 10-million-dollar loan for the purchase of road-building machinery, since the attempt to use manual labor was already seen as an impediment to the completion of a road network. The Export-Import Bank was mobilized to finance the machinery, with Nacional Financiera guaranteeing the loans. In addition, a Point Four grant organized a series of technical missions, scholarships, and links between U.S. and Mexican civil engineers to ensure that the technical aspects of the two countries' road-building projects would be compatible. The U.S. secretary of commerce, Charles Sawyer, visited Mexico and finalized these negotiations.[34]

At times an industry developed in ways that seemed set to destroy the multiplier effect. The case of the dairy industry is a good example. After World War II, and the campaigns against hoof-and-mouth disease, Mexico experienced a shortage of dairy products. The government was particularly sensitive to shortages in the Federal District. The new Alemán administration established a consultative council under Francisco Doria Paz to study the situation; it, in turn, brought in U.S. dairy experts to study the problem. In the view of industry experts, it was unlikely that Mexico would be able to produce the milk needed due to the poor quality of the stock, the difficulties of providing food for the cattle, and the "horrific hygienic conditions" of the industry. Thus, the decision makers proposed to form a new corporation, Lechería Nacional S.A., that would enter into an agreement with the Kraft Corporation to bring powdered milk from Wisconsin to be reconstituted in a new factory on the Calzada Atzcapotzalco in Mexico City.

In a parallel deal, Nestlé's Milk Products set up a powdered milk factory to produce milk under the label "Borden" in Ciudad Obregón, Sonora, in November 1942.[35] The same pattern of importing the final product and, therefore, cutting out the earlier stages of production and the spin-off effects of peripheral activities was also evident. Taking advantage of the long list of tax breaks that by this time had been instituted, the new corporation listed its shareholders as Joaquín M. Bourde, William A. O'Connell, Francisco Doria Paz, David Cázares Nicolín, and Lamberto Urrieta. (Frequently in Mexico some false names were registered on charters of incorporation in order to hide the real ownership of new corporations.) The plan was to purchase powdered milk, f.o.b.Wisconsin at 4.87 pesos per kilo. Transportation added another 33 centavos to the cost. Converting milk (8.3 liters to a kilo of powdered milk) and selling it from between 65 centavos wholesale and 73 centavos delivered, the operation planned to keep the factory—which employed 161 workers, 48 employees, and 3 technicians—running around the clock.[36]

Based upon a study made by U.S. industry sources, Francisco Doria Paz of the Lechería Nacional S.A. made ample use of some dozen state favors, as the firm set out to supply milk to the Federal District. Through the sale of some sixty thousand liters per day, at an average of 70 centavos

per liter, the firm generated a monthly sales figure of 1,620,000 pesos (4.85 pesos=1 dollar). The total monthly payroll for workers, employees, and technicians, including delivery of milk, was only 88,978 pesos. There obviously were running costs apart from wages; however, most of the spin-offs from the industry went back to dairy producers in Wisconsin. Two thirds of the price of milk in Mexico remained in the United States; in addition, patent and administration fees were paid to the Kraft Corporation.

There is no doubt that a profitable industry had been started, one that helped fill the country's need for milk. However, this is a clear case where the multiplier effect was exported. Unlike other milk-producing regions in Europe, New Zealand, or even the United States, a profitable dairy industry would not generate a prosperous rural sector and a series of associated industries. Neither would the kind of rural industry based upon dairy products grow to provide employment opportunities in rural Mexico. Only the 212 employees and the owners would benefit.

In the case of Motores y Maquinaria Anáhuac S.A., an internal faction of the ruling party became central to the development of an industry. Motor manufacturing emerged as a project of the Cardenista wing of the party. Immediately after the nationalization of the petroleum industry it became apparent that management would have to upgrade PEMEX's machine shop capabilities, a project to which the director, Efraín Buenrostro, applied himself. Buenrostro, a Cardenista, made contact with a Spanish refugee and engineer, Francisco Cárdenas Ponga, who had been associated with Hispano-Suiza factories in Europe. Cárdenas Ponga convinced Buenrostro of the need to upgrade the machine shop to a manufacturing plant for gasoline engines. Apparently the Cardenista faction took on the project as a special interest and the former president's backing ensured continued support.

When the Alemán administration came to power, PEMEX's investment in the plant was supplemented by a major infusion of funds from Nacional Financiera. Reorganized in 1947, it was named Motores y Maquinaria Anáhuac S.A. and the management was turned over to industrial chemist and economic nationalist José Domingo Lavín. In 1949, Lavín was replaced by General Alamillo Flores, so the management of the firm remained clearly Cardenista. By providing motors, engines, pumps, and equipment to PEMEX, the army, the navy, the railroads, and other industries, the project was an example of the economic nationalists' vision. U.S. engineers saw the plant as putting out "thoroughly satisfactory products from a technical point of view" but at higher prices than U.S. production. Fiat eventually added technical capacity through joint participation.[37] As a product of the Cardenista wing of the party, it seemed to bear fruit. The control of Motores y Maquinaria Anáhuac S.A. was up for grabs in 1950. Alamillo Flores, as general manager, was proud of the accomplishments of the firm: "Allow me to inform you that, for the first time in history, with Mexican raw materials, Mexican labor, and Mexican technology, we have made major repairs

to Durngo transport turbines."[38] The firm had passed through a number of crises and the moment was tense. Even the workers had heard that a group, headed by the banker Montes de Oca, was trying to privatize the firm, which had been started with public funds.

Since 1947 the firm had been administered by economic nationalists (José Domingo Lavín, José María Arguelles, and Miguel Vargas Solórzano), who believed that it was imperative for Mexico to be independent in machine works and basic engineering. It had been set up to manufacture four thousand Panther tractors per year as well as agricultural implements, buses, truck carriages, diesel engines, and carriages for the railroad. The factory had been organized with a capital of 11 million pesos, with Nacional Financiera holding 579 shares and PEMEX another 528 shares. It used U.S. technology, for which it paid a royalty.[39]

By 1948 the president's close business associate, Carlos Bush, had proposed a reorganization that made Alamillo Flores the director general and Bush the manager of Motores y Maquinaria Anáhuac S.A. The project had run at a loss, and there had been recent controversy over the alienation of ejido land for the project.[40] However, a far more basic issue of the control of the firm concerned General Alamillo Flores in 1950. In his view, the Montes de Oca group, with strong foreign participation, represented an abandonment of the nationalist goals of the project. Alamillo Flores believed that Ramón Beteta was unsympathetic to that cause and that the growing involvement of foreign capital threatened the nation's control of the project. Clearly, the fate of the factory was decided at the highest level of government, and the Alemán administration's decision meant that the large state investment should become privatized, much to the consternation of the general manager. It was a familiar pattern. The nation put up the capital in the name of economic emancipation, with Nacional Financiera, and in this instance PEMEX, maintaining control for a while. Eventually, a private group of Mexican and foreign industrialists came to own the firm.

The president intervened at the financial level as well as at the immediate production level. In 1947, Gregorio Garza Elizondo applied for a 4-million-peso loan for the Productora de Papel S.A. from Nacional Financiera. The factory was going to produce newsprint and kraft paper to ease the importation requirements. There was no possibility that such a project would proceed without official backing. The decision to support it went to the presidential level. Here again, the state was moving to decide which projects would proceed, this time by means of control over loans.[41]

## Ripe for the Picking: The Mexican Chemical Industry

The chemical industry in Mexico was the scene of high political machinations in the 1940s. The I. G. Farben interests had controlled some

95 percent of the basic chemical industry before World War II. These companies were some of the most prominent and profitable firms on the Allies' blacklist after the United States entered the war. Initially, there was little protest as the Avila Camacho administration turned the chemical corporations over to the Alien Property Custodian. However, the firms soon suffered from neglect, and their capital base was rapidly dissipated.

The U.S. journalist, Drew Pearson, blew the lid off the story in the spring of 1943. In a bold investigative article, he charged that former German drug and chemical companies were about to be handed over to American Cyanamid Company, a firm "which itself had monopoly agreements with the Nazi cartels before Pearl Harbor." Pearson went on to add tantalizing details: "Suárez was looking for a plan to operate the dozen or so German Drug and Chemical companies orphaned, when Joe Rovensky suggested that American Cyanamid take them over."[42]

In addition to raising the issue of a U.S. corporation developing a monopoly in Mexico in possible contravention to U.S. legislation and objecting to a firm that had "patent hook-ups" with the Nazis, Pearson also raised the issue of a conflict of interest. Joseph C. Rovensky was an assistant to Nelson Rockefeller in his post as coordinator of the Office of Inter-American Affairs. However, before the war Rovensky had been a vice president of Chase National Bank, controlled by the Rockefeller family. In fact, he was on loan to the government from that bank. Since Chase National was also the banker to American Cyanamid, Pearson raised the possibility of a major scandal.

Certainly the Mexican embassy in Washington took notice of Pearson's charges and, in his report to Foreign Minister Ezequiel Padilla, staff member Rafael de la Colina commented that the Pearson column had created "certain complications."[43] Interestingly enough, it was not only the Mexican embassy that paid attention to Pearson's article, but also embassy officials quickly met with F. H. Russell, head of the State Department's Division of World Trade Information. Russell pointed out that other U.S. chemical companies were complaining that the American Cyanamid move would cut them out of the Mexican market for the foreseeable future, and they too spotted the ambiguities in Rovensky's role. Russell, therefore, opposed the plan to turn the Mexican chemical and pharmaceutical industry over to American Cyanamid.[44] By this time, Foreign Minister Padilla was requesting background information from the economic ministries. Finally, Ambassador Francisco Castillo Nájera reported the entire story to his boss, who apparently had been unaware of the situation.

According to the Mexican ambassador in Washington, the origin of the proposed takeover of the Mexican chemical industry was to be found in a casual conversation between Colonel Pope, president of American Cyanamid, and a lawyer of the Rockefeller interests, who informed the executive that the I. G. Farben interests in Mexico had been placed in the hands of the

Alien Property Custodian. Pope then raised the matter with Nelson Rockefeller; the latter put him in contact with Joe Rovensky, who encouraged the plan. At that point the Mexican entrepreneur, Valentín Garfías, stepped into the picture by urging the consolidation of all of the Farben firms into a single Mexican corporation. His plan was that this firm would then sign a management contract with American Cyanamid. Garfías's close relationship with Avila Camacho made it appear that the government approved of this plan. As the Mexican ambassador confided, "The contract includes all of the known devices for assuring the unlimited control by the management corporation, and the maintenance of practices in the making of chemical products, drugs, and medicines in Mexico along the lines heretofore worked out by the German chemical trust, I. G. Farben."

In Washington high administration officials were startled. The Anti-Trust Division of the Department of Justice began to examine the monopolistic aspects of the plan, and Alien Property Custodian Leo Crowley strongly opposed the proposal. Crowley's prewar background in the chemical industry and his previous employment with a rival of American Cyanamid undoubtedly strengthened his opposition to the plan. Suárez quickly retreated, indicating that his approval was dependent upon the final U.S. position that emerged. In Castillo Nájera's account, "apparently the American Embassy in Mexico City, through Dean Acheson of the State Department, misrepresented the position taken by Suárez, stating that the latter had, in fact, given his approval to the contract, subject to the confirmation by Washington. Both Messersmith and Acheson pressed urgently for a favorable answer from the Department of State."[45]

Vice President Henry Wallace also opposed it, although Nelson Rockefeller, with equal vigor, supported the plan. The Mexican ambassador added that I. G. Farben's annual prewar profit level, approaching 70 percent, placed the products of the industry "beyond the reach of workers, whose wages were totally inadequate to buy quinine and other drugs which are absolutely essential." Recent price increases of 300 to 400 percent on some products had convinced Castillo Nájera that the proposed monopoly served Mexico poorly. It was with considerable satisfaction that he reported the final resolution of the matter: "Fortunately a few government officials in Washington, whose sense of public responsibility has not been dulled by the prospect of establishing American big business in Mexico on a monopoly basis, at the expense of Axis interests as well as of the Mexican people, managed to bring the deal to a halt."[46]

Franklin D. Roosevelt, Leo Crowley, and Attorney General Francis Biddle asserted themselves in a dramatic way. After FDR instructed the State Department to kill the deal, a memorandum was drafted distorting the president's instructions. According to one account, the distortion was so blatant that FDR called in a young Texan named Creemore Faith, of the Board of Economic Warfare, who had been following the case most closely

within the administration. After hearing the details of the machinations from the young man, FDR said, "Any time you want to come up and see me again, just call up and tell 'Pa' Watson [General Watson was in charge of Roosevelt's calendar of appointments] that another Cyanamid is being pulled off." FDR then "bawled out" the offending State Department functionaries and wrote to President Avila Camacho explaining that the United States would not be a party to the creation of such a monopoly.[47] Thus, in the interests of Mexican consumers, the top New Deal politicians blocked a deal between U.S. and Mexican elites.

At times there were cases in which the interaction of U.S. and Mexican elites created classic examples of dependency. The Mexican electronics industry was one such case. Industrias Electrónicas Mexicanas (IEM) was a domestic company in 1941–42. The initial capital came from NAFISA and, therefore, represented a commitment of repayment from the entire Mexican community, through its fiscal system. At first Westinghouse went into a joint production venture with IEM, in which they exchanged patents and expertise for free blocks of stock. For a while it seemed to be a clash of national capital, with Luis Legorreta representing IEM shares and Antonio Carrillo Flores organizing a dramatic increase in Westinghouse's participation to 25 percent of the IEM shares. However, in the end the bargain-basement takeover by Westinghouse accommodated Legorreta's interests, and the chief executive officer, Mr. White, was the only casualty of the takeover, apart from the Mexican public who effectively underwrote West-ing-house's capital.[48]

The governments of the period noted, from the perspective of the consumer, that the procurement of continuous and efficient products and services at the lowest price was the goal. From the producer's perspective, the objective was the highest possible profit. From the point of view of government officials, the provision of goods and services within the context of public service was the main criterion. Having said that, they saw that the essence of government was to regulate the relationship between private firms and the public. From these general principles, legislation emerged to ensure that the state would "guarantee the investor a 'reasonable profit' on the investment" after the firm had paid its costs and taxes, had provided for recapitalization requirements, and had contributed to other services and special funds, as required by the state. Thus emerged the ultimate cost-plus contracts, with the state underwriting private profits. It was a government commitment that investors would be guaranteed a profit and that the consumer would have "a public service that would not end." The Finance Ministry then set out to implement many of these general principles, at the level of accounting rulings. Specifically, the problem of evaluating padded figures on the amount of capital invested, excessively generous schedules of depreciation, and the like were addressed, quantified, and collated into an interpretation that would guarantee a required rate of expansion and a

"reasonable profit" for the seven principal private power companies in the republic.[49]

The country's industry was well organized. The Law of the Chambers of Commerce and Industry of 1941 required that any firm, with a capital of more than 500 pesos, was required to join its organization. By 1947 there were some 255 Chambers of Commerce and another 35 Chambers of Industry operating in Mexico. In addition there were 37 cooperatives and additional professional organizations of the kind that are found everywhere in the West. Services offered by these organizations included credit reports, the accumulation of statistics and market information, trade adjustments, and arbitration. They also were the agencies through which the government, at least at times, negotiated with an industry. The CONCAMIN was the most aggressive and powerful, given its influence over large industry.[50]

It was a very broad corporativist commitment, indeed, and it is within this context that the revealing quotation from Agustín Legorreta, director of BANAMEX, should be understood: "The State and private enterprise are fundamentally the same thing."[51] There are many examples of the kinds of favors that were commonly extended. As early as 1941 there was a project to create a Fondo de Fomento a la Industria y de Garantía de Valores Mobiliarios. Directed by the Banco de México, the fund was organized to guarantee markets, prices, and, indirectly, the profits in selected industries. An early test case related to a price guarantee for the Empresa "Acra" S.A. and the cacao industry, which had been in decline since 1939.[52]

At the end of 1949 the government had to decide what to do about the claim for indemnization that Generals Federico Montes and Juan Barragán had made for the Ingenio de San Miguel. According to the claim, the mill had represented an investment of 2.9 million pesos by the government and an investment of 650,000 pesos by Montes and Barragán. General Acosta also retained a share in the refinery, without investing, due to his friendship with Avila Camacho. In the intervening years, the value of the mill had appreciated to 4.2 million pesos. Both Generals Montes and Barragán were claiming an effective 10 percent share of the current value and another 10 percent for the widow of General Acosta. The government and Azúcar S.A. had suffered losses, since they held mortgages on the plant. The recommendation to the president was that each be paid 500,000 pesos for their share and that a building under mortgage be returned to them in compensation for their share in the sugar mill.[53]

It is abundantly clear from the record that the former president and governor of Sonora, Abelardo Rodríguez, was the power behind the fishing industry in the northwest. Therefore, when Juan G. Brittingham, a partner in La Reductora de Pescado S.A., approached Marte Gómez in November 1942 to convince the F.C. Sud Pacifico de México to provide fifteen tons of ice and the refrigerated cars to bring the catch from Guaymas, Agiabampo,

Topolobampo, and other West Coast ports to the United States, he was almost certainly speaking for Abelardo Rodríguez. The railroad agreed.[54]

Wartime pricing was politically sensitive. Carlos Prieto, head of Compañía Fundidora de Fierro y Acero de Monterrey S.A., approached the president many times over prices. On December 2, 1944, the government authorized Ferrocarriles Nacionales a 20 percent increase in tariffs, except for metals and minerals that were strategic for the war effort, as judged by the Ministry of Finance (*Hacienda*). On February 26, 1945, the same price increase was extended to coke; however, Ferrocarriles Nacionales did not extend the price exemptions for the war effort to the products of the Fundidora on the grounds that neither strategic nor military production was involved. Prieto based his argument for exception on the fact that the Fundidora sold its products to: the railroads, 38.5 percent; public works, 18.5 percent; the mining industry, 15 percent; other industry, 17 percent; and the remainder, 11 percent. In January 1946 the new tariff on coke was implemented and the transportation tariffs were increased by 100 percent.[55]

The Confederación de Cámaras Nacionals de Comercio petitioned the government to require Ferrocarriles Nacionales to implement a standard tariff on the transport of petroleum. Merchants in Guadalajara, Culiacán, and the northwest in general thought that they were paying too much for transport, and they centered their efforts on oils since they were viewed as a necessity, even in wartime. Enrique Estrada responded by denying the concession that the Guadalajara merchants wanted. Noting that Mexican costs of rail transport were an average of 31.76 pesos per ton and that the Guadalajara merchants wanted the cost reduced to 17.13 pesos (they longed for the 11.98 cost that Mexico City enjoyed in shipping oil from Tampico), Estrada pointed out that comparable costs in the United States were 48.1 pesos.[56] Several points are clear: first, political decisions determined transportation pricing; second, Mexico was probably subsidizing all transportation costs through its federal budget; third, Mexico City received the largest subsidy of all; fourth, unions were frustrated at not being able to charge higher tariffs; and fifth, Eduardo Suárez's policy of holding railroad tariffs low was also keeping wages low.

The Atenquique paper and industrial cellulose project was given a high wartime allocation for equipment. A series of grants, from 1939 to 1941, allowed the exploitation of the forests of the Volcán Nevado and the Volcán de Colima. The paper industry was authorized to take three hundred thousand cubic meters of timber, of which one half was to go to the United States. The costs were primarily those of putting in access roads and purchasing earth-moving equipment. (Reforestation was a minuscule .056 percent of the projected budget.) The U.S. Department of Agriculture and the Mexican Ministry of the National Economy agreed that the project was of high importance, so the Unión Forestal and the Fábrica de Papel Atenquique took their place as a top war priority. Additional subsidies were extended

by the Ferrocarriles Nacionales, in the form of reduced tariffs.[57] They also received special exemptions from the requirement in the general forestry code to provide railway sleepers (*durmientes*, or ties), a move that had been precipitated by the railroad's suspension of service to the project to make them comply with the legal provision on sleepers. Petitioning to the president to overrule the railways, Enríque Anisz was successful.[58] The project was financed by Fomento Industrial y Mercantil S.A. and the Banco Refaccionario de Jalisco S.A. for a total of 1,900,000 pesos, of which 200,000 was taken by Sáenz's Financiera Industrial Azucarera S.A. For the fiscal year ending June 30, 1943, it returned 23.16 percent profit on the capital, of which five sixths were distributed to shareholders.[59]

Since 1936 the Mexican government had been pressing for the merger of the country's two telephone systems. On December 23, 1947, the articles of merger were finally signed. (The Mexican press announced it on December 24.) General Abelardo Rodríguez, governor of Sonora, was elected president of the board of directors of Teléfonos de México S.A. Stockholders at the time of the merger with the Ericsson system were Axel Wenner Gren, Bruno Pagliai, Adalberto Saldaña, José de la Mora, Luis Montes de Oca, and Marcos Wallemberg. Wenner Gren reportedly held 51 percent of the stock in Teléfonos de México, and the group paid 190 million pesos for the Ericsson system.[60]

Private banking had atrophied in Mexico. *Agiotistas*, or private moneylenders, had predominated—at times even in the sphere of public finance—before the revolution. Even after the founding of the Banco de México and the development of a large number of banks, private moneylending played a major role in the financial arena, especially in rural areas. By the time of the great industrial push, Sanford Mosk characterized the financial system of Mexico under three headings: commercial banks, *financieras*, and savings banks. In his view neither commercial banks nor private *financieras* were willing to invest, to a significant degree, in industrial projects. It was safer and more profitable to make short-term loans. After being granted a free hand in 1941, the private *financieras* that had proliferated copied the commercial banks in entering the medium- to short-term lending business. Even savings banks, which were unknown in Mexico before 1930, as they had increased their assets from 63 million pesos in 1942 to 286 million pesos in 1946, had largely followed this pattern. Some 98 percent of the savings banks deposits in 1946 were loaned for less than a year, with the majority of funds loaned for less than six months, for the simple reason that in Mexico short-term lending was more profitable. Thus, the entire private capital market was unwilling to act as the agent to mobilize funds for the industrialization push to which the government and major segments of the community were committed.

It was into this vacuum that Nacional Financiera stepped. The government controlled 51 percent of the stock in NAFISA, so it was able to con-

centrate on longer-term investments for industry. The Ministry of Finance was deeply involved with the industrialization push. The Dirección de Aforos y de Estudios Financieros was constantly evaluating specific plans within a broader context of the national effort. Translating the broad goals of the Plan de Movilación Agrícola into specific import proposals from the United States, the Finance Ministry provided a powerful link. Quickly focusing upon the problems of rail transportation and the wartime interruptions to shipping, they set up a broad classification of investment priorities. These projections set priorities for state investment in a wide range of industries for years to come.[61]

State favors were being distributed. At times the documentary record allows one to go only so far; however, the aggregate budget figures offer some help. The 1948 federal budget was the largest one up to that point in Mexico's history.[62] Beteta explained that the increase mainly reflected the inclusion of all government expenditures of the day into the budget. One study showed that the largest single area of increase was in the category of "additional expenditures," which a U.S. embassy economic officer understood to be "largely subsidy payments or rebates on taxes paid by import and export groups and tax-exempt new industries." Whereas spending on education increased by 25 percent in nominal terms, or on defense by 20 percent, subsidies increased by fully 163 percent.[63] Simultaneous heavy reliance upon indirect taxes made the system doubly regressive.

## Tax Breaks

The president granted special rights to the DDF to decide which industries ought to be established in the Federal District. For projects thus favored, a series of concessions applied. The *impuestos de traslación*, established by the Ley de Hacienda, would not apply. Only 10 percent of the public registry fees were applicable. The land tax (*impuesto predial*) would only be charged on the basis of unimproved rural land and would not be upgraded to reflect construction or improvements. There would be a ten-year exemption from taxes affecting mercantile and industrial activities, and invested capital would not be taxed.[64]

In other cases the degree of favor seemed to vary. In the case of the development of the tourist industry in Baja California, Impulsora La Paz S.A. and Fomento Peninsular La Paz S.A. received an 80 percent tax reduction for a period of twenty years from Governor and General Agustín Olachea Avilés. By contrast, the individual income-tax schedule of the period went from 3.3 percent for incomes below twenty-four hundred pesos to the high of 20 percent for incomes in excess of five hundred thousand pesos.

One of the unique Mexican devices used to finance industrialization projects emerged out of the battle against inflation during the period of

wartime austerity. Banks were required to lodge 50 percent of their sight deposits with the Banco de México. The government's idea was to tap these funds to finance industrialization. Bankers were never very happy about the provision, since it eroded their prerogative of deciding which projects to finance. The government had sweetened the deal for them, however, by making the interest paid to the banks for those sight deposits tax free. According to William B. Richardson, manager of the Mexico City branch of the National City Bank of New York, the Banco de Comercio in 1949 "obtained the bulk of its profits from these bonds rather than from its ordinary operations." By 1949 this tax gift amounted to one million pesos for the Banco de Comercio.[65] Needless to say, when the minister of finance proposed to eliminate this welfare for the banks, it provoked a storm of protest. Interestingly, the Banco Nacional de México split away from the Bankers' Association and supported the proposal, so close was the link between BANAMEX and the government.

Perhaps even more important than direct subventions, tax breaks formed the contours of the playing field. Industrial development was supported because the community, in large measure, thought that it was high on the national agenda. So the terms of the development became central. Those who knew how to start, or copy, an industry enjoyed great leverage. However, with the involvement of the economically active state in Mexico, the question of costs and benefits, guarantees, and repayment became central to the politics of industrialization. The subtle interplay of interests can be seen clearly in the case of the largest foreign enterprise operating in Mexico during these years.

## Mexican Light and Power Company (MEXLIGHT)

Increased electricity generation was central to every conceivable project of the era. Foreign-owned power companies constantly complained that they had few profits and that they were blocked in raising quotas to cover costs, much less to raise new capital for further development of power-generating capacity. However, we have also seen that company accountants figured their costs in a way that siphoned off high payments to parent firms well before the final profit-and-loss calculations were made. In 1947, George Messersmith returned to Mexico as the head of MEXLIGHT. His superb connections in both the United States and Mexico made it natural for him to press for a major loan of 23.5 million dollars from the Export-Import Bank and the International Bank for Reconstruction and Development (the World Bank) in 1948–49.

When Messersmith raised the idea of the loan with Minister of Finance Ramón Beteta, he was assured that there was no problem with the plan. However, Rogerio de la Selva, the president's private secretary, sent quite different instructions to Antonio Ruiz Galindo, who was then representing

Mexico at the Havana Conference in 1948. In a confidential memorandum, the issue of guarantees became central. According to the Messersmith proposal, the power company would receive the funds; however, Nacional Financiera would guarantee repayment of the debt and carry the risk of added costs that might result from devaluation. Given the fact that the company had been unable to pay its obligations in the past, that made the risk real.

Since this was the largest loan proposal for Mexico in the postwar period, and since the United States was eager to go to the conference at Bogotá with evidence that it was helping to organize credit for Latin American development, Mexican officials thought they held trump. De la Selva argued that it would be unfortunate for such a development loan to go to a firm owned by foreign investors. This plan would have represented far more than equal treatment of foreign investors; it would have been a favor to Messersmith's company at the expense of the CFE.[66]

The confluence of politicians of national and international importance with major capitalists was even more strikingly illustrated after the war. MEXLIGHT was the Mexican subsidiary of SOFINA, a Belgium-based holding company that represented some of the most established capital of Europe. U.S. capital was also represented as a major shareholder on the board through a company named Amitas. Reggie Leeper, an important director on the board, was tied up with De Beers and Oppenheimer interests in South Africa, as was director Nathaniel Samuels of Brussels. Another director, Dannie Heineman, was a financial adviser to the king of Belgium and chairman of the board of SOFINA. British capital—some hinted at the participation of the royal family—was also represented in the company. George Messersmith called Dannie Heineman his "best friend," and it was Heineman who arranged for Messersmith to be appointed chief executive officer of MEXLIGHT after President Truman became disgusted with his bickering with Spruille Braden over policy toward Argentina's Juan Perón and sacked both diplomats.[67] Dannie's son, Jimmy, was Messersmith's assistant in running MEXLIGHT until he became bored with the business. Jimmy then decided that he wanted to join the CIA, so Messersmith made contact for him with Allen Dulles.

The Mexican Light and Power Company had not paid any dividends to its stockholders for many years. The company argued that it was, therefore, impossible to attract new capital for future power development. (MEXLIGHT spokesmen ignored the fact that the company had been repatriating substantial sums under guises other than dividends.) The World Bank was constantly consulted in matters of appointments and acted as an advocate for the company in dealing with the Mexican government. As the elder Heineman explained it to Messersmith, "He [Eugene Black] seems very happy to know that the company seems satisfied with Carrillo Flores' suggestion [on new power rates] and the 8 percent net return. He asks me if I know what Beteta's future plans are."[68]

Messersmith's connections in the United States were still invaluable in pressing the company's case. In turn, MEXLIGHT officials kept a close watch on various Mexican politicians. They viewed Ramón Beteta and Carrillo Flores as being of great value to the firm but thought that Alemán was too "inactive."[69] Messersmith was clear in his belief that Carrillo Flores was his best ally against the "left elements" in the government. Since he viewed him as the "#2 man in the government," his service was invaluable.

Favors were extended at all levels. When John Snyder left the job as secretary of the treasury, Eugene Black intervened with Heineman to look after Snyder: "The matter was insistently raised by Gene [Black] who stated that the [World] Bank would be happy and grateful to see John [Snyder] become associated with the Company. I understand that Gene and John are quite close friends and quite apart from Gene's desire to be helpful to John personally, he feels that his association with MEXLIGHT can only be constructive."[70]

These officials were well rewarded for their efforts, even in years when profit figures were low. Messersmith enjoyed a mansion at Genova No. 44 in the Federal District and a grand house in Cuernavaca. As he was heading toward retirement, he complained about moving from the mansion in the Zona Rosa to a house at Sierra Paracaima No. 1285 in Lomas de Barrilocco. He called it a "chicken coop" even though the dining room sat fourteen people "easily." Company executives found innovative ways to bring selected Mexican officials into their circle of privilege.[71]

MEXLIGHT decided to try to create a junior board for cooperative politicians. The idea was that they would be brought into a Mexican Advisory Committee, and the unstated implication was that such a position might lead to the eventual invitation to membership on the board of directors of MEXLIGHT, and the concomitant contact with SOFINA might be forthcoming for a few men. In fact, Luis Legorreta, Eduardo Suárez, and Guillermo Barrosa were named to the MEXLIGHT board in 1955. (That freed up places for industrialist Carlos Prieto, Carlos Mendieta of BANCOMER, and banker Juan Monasterio.)[72]

The first meeting of the MEXLIGHT board with the Mexican Advisory Committee took place in October 1954 and was timed to coincide with the inauguration of the new plant at Patla and the new substation at El Salto. A lavish meal at the Del Prado Hotel in Mexico City was served to over 250 guests. Hernández Delgado, director of NAFISA, was positively gushy in his praise of MEXLIGHT in "carrying forward such sound and constructive policies . . . not only for itself, but for the country in which it worked." Ramírez Ullola, head of the CFE, publicly stated that the company needed a "good return" on its capital and denied that the CFE was selling power to MEXLIGHT at too low a price, a charge that was widely reiterated at that time. That Ramírez Ullola took this position in spite of the fact that com-

pany officials thought that he really believed in public ownership of utilities shows something of the mood of the day. Even the head of the company's union praised the Patla plant as a triumph of private enterprise. As Messersmith reported to Dannie Heineman, "You and I know that it is a far cry from what we used to get from a labor leader, and especially [one] in our company."[73]

By the end of the period a number of precedents had been set, and the balance of forces increasingly favored business over labor. In 1953, George Messersmith happily wrote to the board members assuring them that they need no longer worry over the possibility that Mexico might pass laws "guaranteeing [or limiting] dividends of certain public service companies." Messersmith's political tactics had served his employers well.[74]

It is important to realize that we are witnessing complex interaction of vested interests. The Mexican authorities under Ruiz Cortines were less automatically procompany than they had been under Alemán. Under the Eisenhower administration, the State Department lost considerable influence on Latin American policy to the Treasury, and that implied that business interests would be limited by fewer alternative considerations than had formerly been the case. As George Messersmith explained it to young Jimmy, "The 'new set up' at the Export-Import Bank is that the State Department is off the board" and that "[Treasury Secretary George] Humphrey, Buryess and Overby will be running the Ex-Im Bank together with Bill Martin."[75]

The attempt to bring Mexican policy into line with U.S. thinking was aided by the availability of the loanable funds from the Export-Import Bank that were so extremely useful to MEXLIGHT. As Messersmith admitted, "I need not tell you that had it not been for the discreet aid of the World Bank and the United States Government, and a combination of circumstances, we would not be getting this [tariff] relief at this time. We really are going ahead."[76]

Messersmith did worry that his successor and chairman of the board, Draper, had been indiscreet. President Ruiz Cortines had invited Draper and Messersmith to return to Mexico City with him after inspecting a power plant. During the drive Draper indicated that MEXLIGHT wanted to acquire Monterrey Power and American and Foreign Power, profitless companies. In conjunction with Draper's ex-ante statement that MEXLIGHT would be paying 10 percent dividends again this year, Messersmith feared that this slip might convince the authorities that power generation was profitable and thus expose the company to renewed pressure for nationalization. Company officials thought that Ruiz Cortines was not entirely immune to such thoughts, as had been his predecessor.[77] Messersmith pondered his tactics. "I sometimes wonder whether it was worse to have a bad leader like Rivera Rojos or a weak one like Preciado."[78] In the case of the electricity-generating industry, the threat of nationalization had been thwarted, largely

by linking key Mexican officials with the MEXLIGHT board. From time to time, the threat of nationalization still returned; its meaning, however, was far from obvious.

## Lemon Socialism

The threat of nationalization could imply one of several things. Apart from the obvious threat to private property, it might provide a powerful weapon for unions to force a more favorable settlement rather than opening up a debate over public ownership. Alternatively, there were times when there was a push for nationalization of industries because the firm in question was in economic trouble. There is a record of a harmonious meeting between two directors of Electric Bond and Share (David Matson, Mr. MacKenzie), Edward Miller (assistant secretary of state), Antonio Martínez Baez (minister of the national economy), Manuel Sánchez Cuen (undersecretary of the national economy), and Antonio Carrillo Flores (NAFISA), in which these directors discussed the necessity of nationalizing the electricity installations of the smaller power-generating firm, Electric Bond and Share. The reasons why these people supported what on the surface appeared to be a radical program was that the industry was unprofitable, the political context made it impossible to raise rates, and new capital was needed. Therefore, for the right price, the owners were more than happy to get their capital out of the electrical industry.[79] Although the possibility of a broad-based program of nationalization had retreated, there still might be cases of the nationalization of unprofitable operations or the threat thereof for the purposes of industrial bargaining. This had the useful effect of blurring the political debate as to the economic policies of the postrevolutionary governments.

Hidden behind patriotic calls for, and enthusiasm over, industrialization were complex political deals that determined the contours of the Mexican industrial landscape. The highly skewed nature of income distribution, the lack of concern over the environmental impact of industrialization, the concentration of industrialization in the Federal District, and the return of the giant U.S. corporations to Mexico were characteristic of this politicized program of development. It is important to realize that the most important political and business figures created this world; we are not dealing with abstract and remote laws of economics.

## Notes

1. Jesús Rivero Quijano to Will Clayton, November 7, 1942, Truman Library, Clayton Papers, Boxes 24, 46.
2. George Messersmith to Clayton, December 6, 1945, Truman Library, Clayton Papers, Box 46.

3. Luis G. Legorreta to Clayton, October 5, 1940, Truman Library, Clayton Papers, Box 22.

4. Clayton to Rupert Allmond, head of A.C.&Co. in Lima, July 11, 1941, Truman Library, Clayton Papers, Box 18.

5. Harry Vaughan to James C. Dunn, August 7, 1947, Truman Library, Clayton Papers, Box 146.

6. Messersmith to Clayton, April 2, 1943, Truman Library, Clayton Papers, Box 32.

7. Messersmith to Clayton, April 7, 1943, Truman Library, Clayton Papers, File M, folder 1.

8. Luis Montes de Oca to Clayton, December 31, 1940, Truman Library, Clayton Papers, Box 23.

9. Antonio Ruiz Galindo to Miguel Alemán, March 8, 1948, AGN, RP/MAV, 432/135.

10. *Diario Oficial,* August 31, 1934.

11. Ibid., June 21, 1937.

12. Ibid., July 5, 1938.

13. File of assistant secretary of state for economic affairs, "The Mexican Doctrine of Industry Saturation," January 31, 1946, Truman Library, Box 4, File M, folder 1.

14. *Diario Oficial*, April 14, 1941.

15. File of assistant secretary of state for economic affairs, "The Mexican Doctrine of Industry Saturation," January 31, 1946.

16. *Diario Oficial,* May 17, 1943.

17. File of assistant secretary of state for economic affairs, "The Mexican Doctrine of Industry Saturation," January 31, 1946.

18. *Diario Oficial,* July 7, 1943.

19. File of assistant secretary of state for economic affairs, "The Mexican Doctrine of Industry Saturation," January 31, 1946.

20. *Diario Oficial*, April 25, 1944.

21. File of assistant secretary of state for economic affairs, "The Mexican Doctrine of Industry Saturation," January 31, 1946.

22. A. Kleyff to Alemán, January 3, 1942, AGN, PR/MAC, 111/309-4.

23. Fernando Flores Muñoz to Avila Camacho, June 8, 1943, AGN, RP/MAC, 705.2/468.

24. J. Jesús González Gallo to Flores Muñoz, June 20, 1942, ibid.

25. Lamar Flemming to Clayton, August 1, 1941, Truman Library, Clayton Papers, Box 21.

26. Ibid.

27. William McC. Martin to Clayton, June 10, 1948, Truman Library, Clayton Papers, Box 74.

28. Eduardo Villaseñor to Clayton, November 8, 1940, Truman Library, Clayton Papers, Box 24.

29. Jack M. Johnson to Clayton, October 5, 1951; "Report to Stockholders" for fiscal year ending July 31, 1951, Truman Library, Clayton Papers, Box 96.

30. Ortega Cantero to Neptune Meter Company, September 11, 1948, AGN, RP/MAV, 705.2/102.

31. Amadeo [Solórzano] to Rogerio [de la Selva], February 10, 1949, ibid. Alemán issued a directive to that effect, January 28, 1949, AGN, RP/MAV, 705.2/107.

32. Frazier Potts to Clayton, January 30, 1941, Truman Library, Clayton Papers, Box 23.

33. *El Autómovil Americano*, March 1938.

34. Rómulo O'Farrill to Alemán, September 9, 1949, AGN, RP/MAV, 606.3/235.

35. Juan G. Brittingham to Marte Gómez, November 16, 1942, AGN, RP/MAC, 523/64.

36. Hurtado Alvarado to the Department of Industry of the Ministry of the National Economy, January 28, 1947, AGN, RP/MAV, 523.1/14.

37. "Rumored Purchase of Interest Mexican Anáhuac Motor Plant by Fiat," August 28, 1950, USNA/RG 59, 812.053/8-2850.

38. Luis Alamillo Flores to Roberto Amoros, February 14, 1950, AGN, RP/MAV, 705.2/165.

39. Carlos Bush to Alemán, March 15, 1949, ibid.

40. *Diario Oficial,* May 14, 1949.

41. Rodríguez y Rodríguez to Nacional Financiera, October 20, 1947, AGN, RP/MAV, 523.1/84.

42. Drew Pearson, "Mexico Is Now Scene of First Major Test of Postwar Monopoly," *Washington Post,* April 25, 1943.

43. Rafael de la Colina to Ministry of Foreign Relations, April 26, 1943, SRE, III-918-5.

44. Memorandum of conversation, Sánchez Gavito and Russell, July 1, 1943; further memorandum of June 9, 1943, ibid.

45. Ibid.

46. "Monopolio American Cyanamid," Francisco Castillo Nájera to Ezequiel Padilla, August 17, 1943, ibid.

47. Drew Pearson, "The Washington Merry-Go-Round," *Washington Post,* July 9, 1943. In Mexico, *Hoy* and *El Mundo* accused Francisco Javier Gaxiola of being behind the deal. *Hoy* and *El Mundo*, July 14, 1943.

48. Messersmith to J. Heineman, August 21, 1951, GSM Papers.

49. "Memorandum acerca de la Industria Eléctrica en México" from the Ministry of Finance, June 15, 1943, AGN, RP/MAC, 550/44-2.

50. Merwin L. Bohan to secretary of state, August 6, 1947, USNA/RG 59, 812.50/8-647.

51. Cockcroft, *Class Formation, Capital Accumulation, and the State*, 145.

52. Francisco Javier Gaxiola to Avila Camacho, October 21, 1941, AGN, RP/MAC, 545.22/262.

53. Federico Montes and Juan Barragán to Avila Camacho, December 16, 1949, AGN, RP/MAV, 704.595.

54. Juan G. Brittingham to Gómez, November 16, 1942, AGN, RP/MAC, 523/64.

55. Carlos Prieto to Avila Camacho, January 9, 1946, AGN, RP/MAC, 513.7/10.

56. Felix Díaz to Enrique Estrada, January 26, 1942; Estrada to González Gallo, June 4, 1942, AGN, RP/MAC, 513.7/10.

57. *Diario Oficial,* September 15, 1943.

58. Directors and major shareholders of the project included Enrique Anisz, Aarón Sáenz, Antonio Espinosa de los Monteros, and above all Celanese Mexicana S.A., a subsidiary of the U.S. parent. It manufactured wood products through Chiapas y Triplay S.A., a subsidiary of United States Plywood.

59. Enrique Anisz to Avila Camacho, January 24, 1944; González Gallo to Anisz, August 16, 1943, AGN, RP/MAC, 545.22/182.

60. Bohan to secretary of state, December 30, 1947, USNA/RG 59, 812.50/12-3047.

61. Extractive industry, 50 million pesos; manufacturing, 220.1 million pesos; public services, 5.2 million pesos; agriculture, 109.8 million pesos; transportation, 125.4 million pesos; miscellaneous, 38.7 million pesos, for a total of 549.2 million pesos; this represented only one year's detailed budget. "Coordinación y Fomento de la Producción," AGN, RP/MAC, 550/44-2.

62. *Diario Oficial,* December 31, 1947.

63. Bohan to secretary of state, December 30, 1947, USNA/RG 59, 812.50/12-3047.

64. Presidential decree, September 3, 1945, AGN, RP/MAC, 545.22/178.

65. McVittin to Foreign Office, February 10, 1949, PRO/FO, 371/74086.

66. Rogerio de la Selva to Ruiz Galindo, June 10, 1948; Ernesto P. Uruchurtu to Congress, November 21, 1949, AGN, RP/MAV, 565.4/903.

67. Messersmith to D. Heineman, March 25, 1949, GSM Papers.

68. D. Heineman to Messersmith, February 13, 1953, ibid.

69. Messersmith to Ruth Mason Hughes, September 18, 1952, ibid.

70. J. Heineman to Messersmith, February 13, 1953, ibid.

71. Ibid.

72. Messersmith to René Brosens, chairman of the board of SOFINA, August 18, 1955, GSM Papers.

73. Messersmith to D. Heineman, October 26, 1954, ibid.

74. Messersmith to John Snyder, January 6, 1953, Truman Library, Papers of John W. Snyder, Box 243.

75. Messersmith to J. Heineman, September 14, 1954, GSM Papers.

76. Ibid.

77. Messersmith to D. Heineman, October 26, 1954, GSM Papers.

78. Messersmith to J. Heineman, February 17, 1954, ibid.

79. "Situation Surrounding Electric Bond and Share Companies in Mexico," March 19, 1952, USNA/RG 59, 812.053/3-1952.

# 9 Mexico and the Postwar Settlement

The end of World War II was a rare historical moment in which a single dominant power—to an unprecedented degree—set the rules of international political and economic contacts for the foreseeable future. As the only Great Power to emerge unscathed from the Second World War, the United States occupied a position of relative strength greater than any single power at the Congress of Vienna after the Napoleonic Wars, or at the Treaty of Versailles after World War I. At those general peace settlements, the decision-making authority was shared among the victorious allies. By contrast, after World War II, the United States was able to set the rules virtually by itself; from our perspective in the 1990s it is difficult to imagine conditions under which a single power could ever again exercise such dominance.

As the Great Power rivalry between the United States and the USSR shifted attention to the perimeter of the Soviet Union, Mexico, formerly valued as a frontline state against fascist expansion and an economic ally during the war, soon became marginalized. The Cold War hit inter-American relations like a tidal wave, sweeping away many other issues. The United States increasingly identified itself in terms of a worldwide ideological battle against communism, and so that project was forced upon the region, however ill the fit. Since the Communist Party of Mexico was so minuscule—after the purge of 1940 it was declining in the quantity and quality of its membership—Cold War rhetoric provided a thin veneer to cover more pressing issues.[1] At the daily level, U.S. officials continued their fight against policies of economic nationalism with great vigor. But at the strategic level, Mexico's bargaining position with the United States was reduced acutely.

Support for U.S. policy and its global strategy continued unabated after the war, although Mexican officials never generated the intense enthusiasm for the Cold War demanded by the United States. In the event of war between the United States and the Soviet Union, President Harry Truman was informed: "The Department of State has been assured informally by the Mexican government that the United States could count on its support in the event of a show down with the Soviet Union."[2] In a retrospective mood, Mexican diplomats assured Washington of their country's commitment to continue to furnish raw materials, as it had during World War II.

On the U.S. side the military priorities shifted significantly, and a new set of goals emerged. Mexico's military importance diminished in the new bipolar world. Washington officials began to look at the Mexican military as an institution to influence rather than as a possible ally in the event of war, as had been the case from 1939 to 1942. As President Truman's military aide, Major General Harry Vaughan, put it, "The primary objective has now become the standardization of the armament and training of the armed forces of our two countries."[3] Perpetual innovations in equipment, as well as the economic power of the United States, made it inevitable that the Mexican military would be influenced by its neighbor.

U.S. diplomats exercised a great deal of influence over the selection of major figures in the Mexican government. Ambassador Messersmith told the secretary of state, upon the appointment of a new Mexican ambassador to Washington: "I wish to assure you that there is no doubt that Espinosa [de los Monteros] has the most categoric instructions from the president of Mexico to collaborate with us for the consolidation of the American-Mexican relationship on sound lines."[4]

As Mexico's strategic importance diminished, the United States again placed Open Door policies toward Latin America at the heart of its relations with that country. It is important, however, not to see the United States as a homogeneous unit pressing against a solid door, which is being held back gamefully by all Mexicans.[5] There were always protectionist sentiments, especially within the legislative branch; and, as we have seen, even President Truman insisted upon an "escape clause" to make certain that free-trade principles did not unduly damage U.S. interests. When the Mexican international account deteriorated dramatically after World War II, U.S. influence and leverage increased notably.

As the Truman years gave away to the Eisenhower era, the importance of Latin America diminished, at least in terms of the attention that the administration paid to the region. As Merwin L. Bohan explained to Nelson Rockefeller, "The operating, mainly sub-cabinet level of the administration, although not always consciously aware of it, has set the objective of making Latin America safe for private initiative, which is in no way surprising given the dominance of banking and business thinking within its ranks."[6] In practice this meant that close monetary supervision of the region was managed so that the dollar value of foreign investments would not be diminished, that only "grudging provision of minimum public credit" would be granted, that there would be an "almost exclusive emphasis" on the role of private capital, and that the United States would press for ever better conditions for private investment.

The diminished role of Latin America in world affairs made it difficult for New Deal diplomats to sustain their personal belief that Mexico and the United States shared a community of interests in which each country benefited from contact with the other. There was something of a crisis of confi-

dence as Washington turned away from her allies in Latin America and post-war inflation quickly eroded the region's savings. That generation of U.S. diplomats actually believed that they were fighting for democracy in the hemisphere, and therefore the need to accommodate dictators in the name of the Cold War was repugnant.

Merwin Bohan, one of the top U.S. diplomats in Mexico, knew the country well; his father had been a division manager of Waters Pierce Oil Company, and after he retired he lived out his life in Puebla. His papers in the Truman Library show the same disillusionment with U.S. foreign policy toward Latin America, of the sort that influenced Laurence Duggan to take his life during the McCarthy era. By the Nixon years Bohan had become so disillusioned that he wrote: "If a person, such as myself, who during the first fifty years of his life believed in the essential honesty and and morality of the presidency and of our conduct of foreign policy, can become so disillusioned as to question every statement of our highest officials, is it any wonder that cynicism has eroded our authority at home and abroad?"[7]

The United States was primarily concerned with setting the rules of international relations to favor its own interests. New Deal diplomats, such as George Messersmith, prided themselves on noninterference in Mexican politics; however, invariably what they meant was nonintervention in the electoral process. In this respect, U.S. diplomats were scrupulous. Yet if one defines politics more broadly than elections, thereby encompassing the use of state power and the way in which the broad parameters of public life are set, then it is clear that key figures in both the public and private sectors played a crucial role in Mexican politics.

This can be seen in even small matters. The United States had always exercised power arrogantly when dealing with Mexican issues on its own soil. Such was the case of the 6 million dollars that 160,000 Mexican railroad workers paid into the U.S. Railroad Retirement Fund during the war. As we know, those temporary workers were not going to be around to collect that money upon their retirement, so Mexican diplomats pressed for its return. The case went back and forth for years. It took the direct intervention of President Truman to return the money to Mexico, with 3.5 percent interest.[8] It was natural that U.S. officials would have a say over internal matters.

At times, matters of high policy were decided with breathtaking speed. The Truman Library holds the appointments diary of Robert L. Gardner, vice president of the International Bank for Reconstruction and Development (the World Bank) in 1947, a remarkable document. Several times each hour presidents, prime ministers, finance ministers, and other economic officials passed through his office, and Gardner instructed them on the appropriate economic policies for their countries. Typical of the tone of the top officials, Gardner noted with great satisfaction that, during negotiations with PEMEX executives, the Mexicans told him that they had "learned" a

lot from his instructions.[9] The issue that most clearly demonstrates the U.S. preeminence arose when the victorious allies turned their attention to the postwar monetary system.

## Mexico at Bretton Woods

Mexico went to the Bretton Woods Conference, in the summer of 1944, in an unusual position of favor. From the U.S. perspective on the eve of the Cold War, the Avila Camacho administration had changed enough policies to relegate the Mexican Revolution to the past. The country had fulfilled its role as a purveyor of raw materials for the war effort. Moreover, two influential ambassadors in a row had convinced President Roosevelt that the country was an important ally, and for an administration that had made the Good Neighbor policy a major innovation, Mexico was of obvious importance.

The forty-four nations that gathered in the White Mountains of New Hampshire faced great issues. The impending victory over the Axis forces raised concerns associated with the postwar political settlement. The need to reorganize the world's economic system in order to avoid the repetition of the recent depression was foremost on the delegates' minds. The victors thought that protectionism, the resultant decrease in world trade, and the collapse of an international monetary system had brought on the Great Depression of the 1930s; therefore, they knew they had to do something about the world's monetary system.

Money was the problem. It was widely recognized that the breakdown of the world's monetary system had partially been responsible for turning the collapse of the overheated New York Stock Exchange into an international depression. Practical politicians and economists were forced to ponder the nature of money at a level usually ignored. To people who work in a stable environment, money is taken for granted as a repository of value and a medium of exchange. However, the century before Bretton Woods had seen an unending series of monetary upheavals. Banking collapses, competing monetary standards, and depressions were induced, at least partially, by restricting money supplies; these recurring problems highlighted the necessity of designing a more adequate world monetary system.

Since all states issue money, and since it is so tempting for governments to solve immediate problems by simply printing money, a degree of discipline was indispensable. Unfortunately, much of the traditional discipline had its origin in an increasingly anachronistic illusion. The myth was that the value of money was based, for reasons of historical custom, on gold. Indeed, there was an ancient tradition of people preferring to hold metal coins rather than paper money, since it was less likely that governments could so easily debase metal coins. The belief that money was, or at least should be, based on gold reserves was sacred to central monetary au-

thorities. However, the Second Industrial Revolution had doomed the gold standard. There simply was not enough gold on which to base the world's business transactions, and the quantum theory of money clearly showed how by simply reducing the amount of money in circulation too far, a depression could be precipitated. Increasingly in the modern era, the strongest world currencies and silver competed to join in the privileged role as an international standard of value.

During depressions, orthodox economists and bankers reverted to beliefs in balanced budgets. This implied stringent money supplies and deflationary policies which, in turn, exacerbated the Great Depression. Britain, the classic example of the phenomenon, returned to the gold standard in 1925. This was, in John Maynard Keynes's view, a lesson illustrating that economic orthodoxy had intensified the Great Depression. As Charles Kindleberger refined the argument, the United States and Britain followed this deflationary policy by refusing to maintain relatively open markets, by refusing to provide countercyclical lending in rough conjunction with the decline caused by the stock market crash, and by its discounting policies.[10] These policies had the effect of converting a financial collapse in New York into a severe depression around the world. Orthodox reaction—cutting public expenditures—only made the situation worse, and even the pump priming of the New Deal was negated by greater contractions of public expenditures at the state and local levels. The brutal fact was that the depression in the United States took another downturn in 1937, and it was only the unprecedented deficit financing of World War II that truly brought the country out of its decline. The delegates at Bretton Woods had decided that restrictions to trade had caused the depression. They were, above all, committed to freeing trade within a context of fixed exchange rates. U.S. strength in a world of war-torn powers and crumbling empires made its tradition of the Open Door policy enforceable at the global level.

Harry Dexter White emerged as the central figure in the U.S. team that went to Bretton Woods. The ideas man behind Treasury Secretary Henry Morgenthau, White took on no one less than Keynes in proposing the fundamental aspects of the postwar monetary system, and White largely prevailed. The decision makers at Bretton Woods were primarily motivated by a desire to open the world's economic system to free flows of trade, capital, and investment. No longer would trading blocs (of the Axis powers, France, the Dutch, the United Kingdom, or the USSR) be allowed to exclude U.S. interests from markets and access to resources.

The International Monetary Fund (IMF) was to be the powerful new agency to facilitate trade and finance—a sort of super central bank to the central banks of each country. The carrot that the IMF extended was the prospect that it would help to stabilize each country's currency as well as facilitate the daily clearing of international accounts between all countries. It also promised to alleviate the dollar shortage that was already appearing

in Europe, due to the singular strength of the U.S. economy in a war-torn world.

It was less obvious at the time that the IMF would also wield such a heavy stick. The Fund required each country to purchase its own currency from other countries if reserves accumulated beyond prescribed limits. But how could a country buy back its own currency, and with what? This was a vexing problem. Everyday assumptions about money quickly became unclear if one questioned the ultimate value of money. But, of course, the delegates at Bretton Woods were not thinking only in terms of theoretical economics.

Franklin D. Roosevelt came to power in 1933 at the height of the banking collapse, and he quickly achieved his greatest economic coup. He brilliantly combined closing the banks with pegging the price of gold to the dollar (in quite an arbitrary way), and, simultaneously, he prohibited U.S. citizens from owning gold. Using stirring rhetoric, he effectively maintained the gold fiction, all the while really basing the currency on faith and trust in what the dollar will buy, which is all that money is in the last analysis. The point of prohibiting ownership of gold was not to allow the speculators to test the thirty-five-dollar price of gold. FDR's call to faith against "fear itself," and the federal insurance of small bank deposits, was the great economic achievement of the New Deal. By contrast, the profound economic confusion that was encapsulated in the NRA—essentially an attempt to outlaw low prices—was minor compared with the initial achievement in saving the banks and the nation's monetary system. However, the New Deal saved the banks more effectively than it solved the depression. In a sense, the Roosevelt administration created an arrangement for the world's money system at Bretton Woods that paralleled its domestic monetary settlement. All countries were required to peg and defend their currencies at a fixed price. But fixed to what?

At this point Mexico's role at Bretton Woods became significant.[11] On the eve of the great conference Mexico had launched a diplomatic effort aimed at convincing as many countries as possible that silver, as well as gold, should be the basis of the world's new money system. As Mexican diplomats pursued their case from China to the Middle East and throughout Latin America, they created a silver bloc comprising the majority of countries attending the conference.[12]

Knowledgeable smiles frequently greeted Mexico's effort, as it was the world's leading silver producer and delegates could easily view its actions as self-serving. Still, Mexican diplomats were well coached in arguing that, by basing the world's money system on silver as well as gold (they pushed a very optimistic 10-to-1 ratio), this accommodated silver-saving nations as well as silver producers and provided a degree of relief for countries that did not have gold. As a statement on the silver issue argued, "It is easy to misunderstand our position. Mexico produces 40 percent of all the silver,

therefore, one could think, Mexico is interested above all in furthering the interests of her mining industry. However, we do not come before this high Assembly of Nations as the largest producer of silver. Certainly nobody could believe that the gold producing nations are represented here to further their own interests."[13]

The Mexican delegate had touched on two critical issues. The countries that produce monetary specie enjoyed an enormous advantage, one that flowed from the accident of nature's mineral endowments. The question of the IMF's impingement on national sovereignty also emerged in Antonio Espinosa de los Monteros's statement of July 14: "Mexico is strongly opposed to the original formula [White's plan] according to which a uniform change in the gold parities of all currencies can be effected by the decision of three major powers alone."[14]

In the Mexican view, a role for silver accommodated the interests of more countries than the extremely limited number of gold producers. Their proposal also recognized that a large number of nations had historically accumulated silver coinage, and they argued that the bimetal system would help those nations. The Mexicans even pointed out that they had accepted payment for their raw materials during World War II in specie even though "no nation has ever committed itself to buy that gold from Mexico at the same price she paid for it." Mexican diplomats did not address themselves to the fundamental problem of a bimetal standard, the difficulty of pegging money, as a unit of account, to two prices that change constantly in relation to each other.

The U.S. position on silver was not immediately clear; however, other tenets were emerging rapidly. Preliminary discussions had taken place between the United States and technical experts from thirty countries. Eventually, there emerged a consensus behind the U.S. view: the IMF should be established to implement exchange stability, to provide multilateral payment facilities, and to monitor the currencies of all member nations. It should also combat discriminatory currency practices or multiple currency arrangements.[15] On these fundamental questions, we may conclude that Mexico was informed rather than consulted, since the Ministry of Foreign Relations was given only two days' notice that the "Joint Statement of Experts of the United States and Associated Nations on the Establishment of an International Monetary Fund" was to be released.[16]

In the face of minimal preliminary consultation, it is something of a surprise to learn that Mexico was given a place of honor at Bretton Woods. Possibly, this reflected the country's role as a producer of raw materials for the war effort, but it is more likely it was an attempt to commit the world's major silver producer to the monetary settlement. The conference was divided into three commissions. Commission I, headed by Treasury Secretary Morgenthau, with Harry Dexter White at his right hand, was charged with setting up the International Monetary Fund. Commission II, led by Lord

Keynes, was to create the International Bank for Reconstruction and Development, later known as the World Bank. Commission III, charged with coordinating all other forms of economic cooperation, was headed by the Mexican finance minister and leader of the country's delegation, Eduardo Suárez, who was feted in order to win over the silver bloc.

In this position, Suárez was neatly placed to press for bimetalism, or at least so it seemed. There still was an important, if not dominant, silver lobby in the U.S. Congress, and Mexican diplomats met with representatives of that group before the conference, in Atlantic City, on their way to New Hampshire. FDR was willing to give silver a voice. Mexico and the silver lobby could count on the support of virtually all of Latin America, China, India, and assorted other countries; they represented the majority of nations at the conference.

The third commission was, in the end, the least effective one. Mexico was not even able to win it over to its silver cause, for as New Zealand delegate Edward C. Fussell summed up in the commission's final report, the issue of silver was too hard; it was "impossible to give sufficient attention to this problem at this time in order to make definitive recommendations."[17] Mexico was only able to gain a statement that the matter deserved further study, a certain death for bimetalism. In fact, Commission III was more effective in bringing attention to the issue of looted Nazi treasure. Norway also tried, unsuccessfully, to convince it to have the Swiss-based Bank of International Settlement dismantled as a punishment for its intimate collaboration with the Axis finance ministers.

The reason that Mexico and so many other countries failed in their attempt to return to bimetalism was simply that the United States opposed the idea. In spite of the presence of delegates from forty-four nations in the New Hampshire resort, and apart from the rhetoric about Allied cooperation, the conference was hardly an exercise in economic democracy. The IMF was set up with the proviso that when countries representing 65 percent of the Fund's capital signed the articles of association, the Fund would become reality. Of the total of 8.8 billion dollars in subscriptions, the United States subscribed 2.75 billion and the United Kingdom another 1.3 billion. Once any three countries of these four—China, Canada, India, or France— joined, the Fund was deemed to be in operation. The rest of the world faced a fait accompli. The promise of multilateral currency clearing was a powerful drawing card, and the threat of exclusion from the new system seemed awesome to all countries outside of the Soviet bloc. The United States finally decided that the world's currency would be based upon a fixed ratio between the dollar and gold. All other countries were required to defend their currencies in a fixed relationship to that standard.

Only a few countries offered any alternative to the U.S. plan. Australia tried holding out for a commitment to an "employment obligation" that would take precedence over concern for financial stability. In their final submis-

sion to Commission III, the Australian delegates, led by Leslie G. Melville of the state-owned Commonwealth Bank, argued: "The experience of the interwar period shows that the volume of international trade depends far more on domestic policies of employment than upon any international arrangements. When employment and prosperity have been high, trade has flourished notwithstanding tariffs and subsidies and unstabilized currencies."[18] The Australian challenge on employment policies ultimately fell on deaf ears.

The Mexican representatives also challenged the Bretton Woods monetary settlement by posing an alternative to the gold/dollar standard for the world's monetary system. Their argument that the emerging system would disadvantage the poor countries was prophetic: "It is not fair that the economically weaker peoples should carry the weight of their silver stocks, as well as the heavy losses caused by the wide fluctuation of their international value, and carry besides their proportionate share of the gold stocks."[19]

Mexico fought for a better deal for poor countries, arguing that silver would help one half of the nations in the world. A country in trouble with its international trade account would then have an additional way to make good its obligations and not be completely dependent on gold or U.S. dollars to achieve its trade balance. However, by the end of the conference, it was clear that, as an editorial in the financial press in London put it, "American silver groups and other bi-metalists are wasting their time."[20] After protesting the U.S. decision, the Mexican delegates quickly took no for an answer.

It was not, however, only from the underdeveloped countries that such protests emerged. John Maynard Keynes also objected to the return to the gold/dollar standard. He proposed an alternative system of organizing the world's trade and currency. Keynes's idea was that the new international currency should not be controlled by any single country but should be issued by the new international monetary authority; he called the supercurrency the "bancor," with an equivalency of gold. At the heart of his proposal was the idea that the new Fund should have a mechanism by which countries with a favorable balance of "bancors" should help countries with deficits.

Keynes and White had issued the preliminary drafts of their respective plans simultaneously in April 1943. Jacob Viner's classic critique of the two proposals stressed that while Keynes's plan was more effectively written, White's proposal for the international monetary system had better mechanisms. White's approach was to discipline countries to stabilize their currencies via the gold mechanism, whereas Keynes wanted to compensate imbalances.[21] Keynes was vulnerable to the charge that he was playing Santa Claus by compensating countries for trading deficits. Moreover, given the dollar shortage in Europe, he was suspected of raising British national interests to a level of high principles, not unlike the Mexican convergence of

principles and vested interests in the bimetal issue. Between the time that Keynes and White floated their respective plans in 1943 and the meeting in Bretton Woods, a French plan, a Canadian plan, and an updated U.S. plan were all proposed; however, the United States had the economic votes, and there was never any doubt that its proposal would prevail.

In his closing comments to the conference, Lord Keynes admitted that the men of Bretton Woods stood too close to the edifice they were building to see clearly the contours of the new system. Four decades later the view has improved. The IMF has become, not all at once, but over the years, the ultimate economic policeman, a sort of international bailiff spreading economic misery wherever its letters of intent are sent. The gold/dollar standard—among other factors—meant that many of the poor countries would fall even further behind.

The gold/dollar standard also enabled the United States to abuse the international monetary system by printing mountains of dollars. From the 1960s on, the United States financed the war in Vietnam, the War on Poverty, domestic budget deficits, and massive trading deficits without either raising taxes to cover expenditures or receiving an IMF letter of intent. As Charles de Gaulle aptly put it, the United States enjoyed the "exorbitant privilege" (until 1971) of printing dollars and forcing the central banks of the world to accept cheapened dollars because of the IMF's requirement to defend the fixed exchange rate. Even President Richard Nixon's 1971 decision to drop the gold fiction only created, in Robert Triffin's apt phrase, the "p ᴛr dollar standard."

When the debt crisis of the 1980s created a crisis of distribution on a global scale, the question of the ultimate meaning of money again arose. The U.S. Federal Reserve Bank is said to have a plan to take over bad debts, should a major debtor default, and simply carry the bad paper as assets on its balance sheet. This would simply be relabelling bad money as good money, an ultimate extension of the Bretton Woods mechanism.

With the economic shocks of recent decades, it is fascinating to reflect upon the alternative proposed by the silver bloc (that is, the majority of countries at Bretton Woods). The gold/dollar standard gave the United States and the gold producers the great privilege of making the world's money. Many problems of poor distribution flowed from that privilege. Had the gold/dollar system (and the paper dollar system after 1971) been superseded by a gold/silver/dollar system, then more countries could have shared the privilege.[22]

That was not to be. IMF member nations faced an array of requirements. No special restrictions on the flow of currency were to be allowed. No differential exchange rates—to allow hard currency to be channeled to productive activities rather than opulent consumption—were to be tolerated. No barter deals were to form between poor countries, and no economic secrets were to be kept from the Fund. The charter stated that the

IMF should have the right to any information "that it should deem necessary." Reserves of gold and currencies and all trade and invisible flows were to be the Fund's business. National income accounts were to be kept according to the new U.S. system, and that was the immediate issue that forced the USSR out of the IMF, in spite of that country's initial enthusiasm, even to the point of increasing its subscription from 900 million to 1.2 billion dollars during the first Bretton Woods sessions. There was, however, a requirement that the information given to the Fund was not to be so detailed as to refer to specific individuals or companies. In short, capital was to have secrets, nation-states were not.[23]

Control of the IMF also was narrowly based. Voting was allotted on the basis of capital contributions to the Fund rather than to countries per se. The Fund was never to be taxed, nor was it subject to legal regulations, juridical procedures, or other regulations by member nations. Its archives were to be kept secret and inviolable, and it could not be held liable for its actions under any country's laws. The Fund's directors would both interpret and implement the IMF's charter, and they were accountable to only the largest contributors. The headquarters was to be in the country that had the largest participation in the IMF.[24] All of these factors, and many others, have created a set of rules that is profoundly skewed against poorer countries. To take one example, in 1988, 4.6 billion more dollars flowcd out of Latin America than entered the region, according to the IMF's own report. The rules of the game matter.

Following Mexico's fascinating role at Bretton Woods, and the experience of being party to such fundamental determinations (Dean Acheson modestly entitled his memoirs relating to these events *Present at the Creation*), matters returned to a more terrestrial level. To the world it appeared that the United States had turned away from an interest in Latin America; however, it was an inattentiveness based upon supremacy. As the head of an informal empire, the United States became very effective at setting the broad rules of international contact in which its principles and its interests were very much in harmony.

The extent to which U.S. rules permeated Mexico's society and were internalized by its rulers is an amazing feature of the postwar era. In some ways Mexico is an even better place to study the operations of the informal empire than Cuba, Nicaragua, or Chile—corners of the empire where the natives rebelled. For in the case of Mexico one finds a state where a clear differentiation exists between rules that are central to the effective running of the international system and areas where its citizens are allowed a higher degree of national autonomy. As such, the Mexican case provides a striking example of the degree and kinds of erosion of sovereignty that have taken place within the informal U.S. empire.

One fundamental rule was that international capital could enter Mexico with only minor degrees of interference. Vestiges of economic nationalism

had ensured that if foreign capital entered and allowed participation by some well-connected Mexicans in either the public or private sector, then those investments would be secure. Apart from that, it was very dangerous to go it alone.

Although the rules of the game had been set by the United States, Mexico had a wild card with which to apply pressure: the threat of nationalization. That threat was credible because of the history of the revolution. Business and government might be reassured; however, the Mexican government could use the threat, or the fact, of nationalization to raise the country's bargaining leverage. Labor, too, could increase its leverage with management by placing the issue of nationalization on its not-so-hidden agenda.

On June 16, 1948, the government gave notice to the Mexican Telegraph Company, a subsidiary of Western Union Telegraph Company, and to All America Cables that, in accordance with Article 37 of the contract, it was going to invoke the terms of its 1926 contract and allow this one to expire. The companies could, therefore, dispose of the 3.5 million dollars (book value) in assets and presumably sell the nation's telegraph system for whatever salvage value the cables might bring. The threat quickly facilitated a more favorable settlement.[25]

An interesting corollary followed. The Left's deeply held belief in the need for the nationalization of the means of production created for the government, on the one hand, a powerful weapon to keep international business in line (and the occasional nationalization of a utility, a resource, or a national monopoly increased the government's bargaining power); on the other hand, it provided a means to feed left and/or nationalistic sentiment with just enough tidbits to keep left and labor forces generally within the coalition of the revolutionary family.

There were two major exceptions to this rule. In the case of major international corporations such as Ford, American Cyanamid, and Du Pont, there was the possibility that a multinational giant might go it alone in Mexico; usually that was because it offered some product for which there was no adequate substitute. The other exception to the rule of Mexican participation occurred when the level of technical skill did not exist domestically or when the capital requirement was too great. In the petroleum industry, for example, the Avila Camacho government decided that the exhaustion of petroleum fields, except Poza Rica, was creating a problem that could not be met by PEMEX either in terms of capital requirements or technical skills. Therefore, the president invited private U.S. firms to reenter the field of petroleum exploration on a shared participation basis with PEMEX. However, unlike the period before 1938, the foreign firms would have to incorporate under Mexican law and accept Mexican corporate participation.[26] Miguel Alemán toyed with the idea of returning PEMEX to the private sector, but even he paused before crossing that line.

Another fundamental rule was that the United States would participate in all Latin American organizations. U.S. diplomats worked hard to prevent the formation of a regional bloc (as proposed by Vicente Lombardo Toledano) rather than the Pan-American movement that included the United States. (Ambassador Messersmith used the operative phrases "being against us" and "being for us.") As he reported to the president after an important meeting with Joe Grew, Jimmy Dunn, Will Clayton, and Nelson Rockefeller in January 1945, "There are very definite attacks being made constantly, some of them in an insidious and dastardly form, against the policy of collaboration with the United States." The ambassador alerted his colleagues over the role of former President Cárdenas: "To be absolutely frank, General Cárdenas, who is still a very important and powerful influence in the Mexican picture, while it cannot be said that he is openly against us, he is certainly extremely nationalistic to the point that he still views us with distrust. . . . Cárdenas, for example, is among those who have been helping along the idea that the Latin American countries should work together very closely, and he has been pressing forward the idea of Latin American collaboration in contradistinction with the idea of American collaboration. . . . He is profoundly and blindly extremely nationalistic."[27] The United States needed to find new techniques to replace the leverage that the system of wartime allocations had provided.

## Aid: Worth Many a Foreign Legion

In these battles over policies, aid in its various forms was of great value. Thomas S. Lamont, formerly head of the Bankers' Committee, had made the famous quip about his Mexican colleagues that "you can lead them anywhere, but you can't drive them an inch." It was as though the U.S. leaders had found in the aid mechanism an application of Lamont's dictum.

At the end of the 1951 meeting of the Mexican Bankers' Association, Secretary of the Treasury John W. Snyder addressed the convention on President Truman's Point Four program. The idea of aid for Latin America was "very well received, despite the fact that a substantial proportion of the audience could not understand English"![28] Snyder's warm reception, language notwithstanding, reflected the Mexicans' belief that the United States was going to help with their push for industrialization. So it was a matter of considerable bitterness for Latin American leaders after World War II to see the Marshall Plan for Europe take precedence over their hope for a major aid program to industrialize their region. It made the existing loan programs through the Export-Import Bank and the promise of the World Bank increasingly significant.

The stabilization agreement on currency was another of the main pressure points at which U.S. aid was contingent upon change in economic policy.

In 1948, on the eve of the first postwar devaluation, the United States was able to insist upon a number of policy changes before allowing the stabilization agreement to kick into effect. The U.S. Treasury was extremely powerful in matters of economic diplomacy, although it kept a very low profile. When the Treasury speaks, it often sets the rules. Secretary Snyder insisted on the following: first, prompt ratification by Mexico of the bracero agreements, which were stalled over some technical issues (and acceptance of the railroad workers' pension fund settlement by Mexico on U.S. terms); second, reduction of Mexican export restrictions on certain items (hides, chicle, cotton, and timber); and third, the strengthening of import controls and their extension to nonessential articles (the United States preferred this alternative to a general increase in protectionism). Since Mexican excess reserves had plummeted to merely 319,000 dollars, Secretary Snyder made these elements a prerequisite before allowing the stabilization agreement to start. Only then did the first 5 million dollars go to Mexico; and each time that country tapped the funds, Ambassador Espinosa de los Monteros was required to reiterate these agreements in an aide-mémoire.[29]

By June additional items were required from Mexico for the continuing implementation of the agreement. The Banco de México was to follow a contractionist monetary policy, to restrict imports, and to refuse loans to Mexican borrowers who could find financing in the private market. In the face of low domestic interest rates and backlogs of export orders, U.S. representatives followed this course, all the while working to open Mexico to their firms. Measures to keep the cotton crop at home were not to be allowed; and although the hand of Will Clayton is not directly visible in the surviving documents, the policy was not too far away from the interests of his firm. The possibility of imposing excise taxes on automobiles in Mexico was opposed, so as not to disadvantage U.S. imports. Mr. Overby of the IMF was also drawn into the supervision of Mexican international economic policies.[30]

Once his administration agreed to the reentry of U.S. capital into Mexico, President Alemán used Donald Nelson, whom he had hired to organize a study of the country's industrialization program, to negotiate with the United States. As we learned in Chapter 6, Nelson urged the Mexicans to think not only of the official sources of capital such as the Export-Import Bank or the World Bank but also of private sources, a point that Under Secretary of State Will Clayton and Spruille Braden had also been pushing to the Mexicans. Guy Ray, of the embassy in Mexico City, stressed this in conjunction with what he viewed as the inadequate performance of the transport sector and PEMEX. The latter only produced 45 million barrels per day when, he argued, it should be able to produce 200 million.

At U.S. urging, Mexican officials agreed that the average Mexican's standard of living could only be increased after production generated enough exports to cover the cost of imports, and not by restricting those imports.

As we know, Nelson was able to tell them that if they agreed to move in this direction, as they did, he "was going from the [State] Department to the White House" to discuss the matter with the president.[31] Thus, the broad pattern of postwar development was set; Mexicans were not to be allowed to consume whatever they could produce until imports were purchased. The battle of the economic nationalists to limit imports and thereby create an autonomous industry was lost. When Mexico tried to limit its exports in such industries as cotton so as to guarantee a supply of textiles for the home market, U.S. diplomats worked actively against that tradition, and by 1948 success was claimed in that effort.[32]

It is curious that, given the enormity of these decisions, so much attention at the time was paid to the renewal of the Reciprocal Trade Agreement between the United States and Mexico, rather than to policies affecting development strategy and the standard of living.[33] The failure to come to a meeting of the minds on the Reciprocal Trade Agreement in 1947 was widely viewed as the key international economic issue of the day between the two countries. In retrospect, the decisions to hold down the standard of living in order to finance the industrial imports required for import-substitution industrialization and export-oriented production can now be seen as far more important than the battle over reciprocal trade.

Within Mexico such remote decisions were quickly felt by most people. Increases in productivity would not be converted into higher wages. In 1947–48 the unions were in a state of crisis as internal political disputes reflected consternation over the PRI's antilabor policies. Vicente Lombardo Toledano finally abandoned his line that since the CTM had nominated the presidents of the 1940s, they had to accept anything they did. Returning to the strategy of the 1930s, he began to organize an umbrella labor organization, the Unión General de Obreros y Campesinos de México (UGOCM), which copied the CGOCM of a decade before. It was one thing to give up wage increases in the flush of the patriotic war effort; however, as the war ended, organized labor became outraged that wartime austerity measures were to be a permanent fixture.[34]

Despite organizational similarities, the story of the UGOCM did not resemble the CGOCM. By 1947–48 labor did not enjoy the backing of the president as it had a decade earlier. So when the Sindicato de Trabajadores Petroleros de la República Mexicana (STPRM), in their Fourth Extraordinary Convention in December 1947, vowed to withdraw from the CTM and the PRI, it was understood as a political declaration of war against the government. Independent unions eventually lost in spite of the support that the STPRM received from the miners, railroad workers, and other union members.

In each case, a dominant PRI faction clashed with an independent group, which wanted to support the petroleum workers' union. The Comité Ferrocarrilero de Depuración Sindical purged the union of independent and/

or radical unionists. At the height of the battle, they told President Alemán that "our friendship for the regime is sincere, but not unconditional."

From the point of view of the development program, the unionists' nonwage demands were extremely revealing, as they protested against public subsidies to foreign business. Their leaders wanted to increase freight rates, which had been frozen since the Cárdenas years. The PRI unionists blamed "bankers and businessmen" for protecting foreign interests, in effect subsidizing the shipping to the United States. In a report from a U.S. economic diplomat, they commented that:

> The same syndicate bought display space to charge that "bankers and businessmen" were defending the "foreign mining companies" and were responsible for the fact that the freight rates on minerals had not been increased, thereby causing losses to the Railways of more than 25 million pesos in 1946 alone. Parenthetically, it is interesting to note that the admittedly low mineral freight rates do not stem from any objection to increases on the part of "bankers and businessmen" but are the result of a deliberate policy on the part of the wily ex-minister of finance. Lic. Suárez was willing to divide the lion's share of the increased mineral prices between mine labor and taxes, but felt that if he permitted increased freight rates, these would not help the railways as they would be immediately siphoned off through wage demands from railway labor.[35]

The enormously complex labor battles of the 1940s were contained by the government by means of a combination of bribery, force, and manipulation. It was a dirty war, fraught with a generous application of state terrorism. Clearly, the government of President Alemán used all means at its disposal to make certain that workers' demands would not get in the way of the emerging model of development.[36]

Another fundamental aspect of this model was that the countryside was to subsidize the cities. Each year the countryside would grow or raise its products; the trucks would come by, take the products, and little would be gained by the villagers. No profits remained for subsistence agriculture. One mechanism after another guaranteed that surplus was extracted from the countryside. Cheap food subsidized the urban population, and wages were held pitifully low. (Some argue that the very concept of wages has little meaning in rural Mexico.) A generation of rural dwellers got the message and migrated to the urban slums—some of which grew in size to have the population of major cities. Others looked for work in the United States. Agency after agency was established to deal with the rural problems. In the end the numerous state agencies provided employment for the middle class rather than a solution for rural Mexico. In village after village, government programs failed to get through to the local level; however, the policies that meant low prices for the peasants touched every field. Farmers had to

produce corn without price increases since they could only sell to the state monopoly. At the same time, land and resources were shifted into agribusiness.

As inflation skyrocketed in the face of food shortages in 1943, Nacional Distribuidora y Reguladora S.A. responded with legal coercion against price increases for the subsistence sector. Nazario S. Ortíz Garza, general manager of ND&R, for example, wrote to the state governors under the president's war powers authority ordering them not to allow price increases for corn. He demanded that at least 40 percent of all corn crops be sold to ND&R, that traditional corn farmers increase their acreage in that grain by at least 25 percent, and that no farmer be allowed to sow less than 10 percent of his fields in corn.[37] By contrast, even at the height of the food crisis, the Mexican government placed the highest priority on the importation of grain for beer manufacture by Malta S.A. of Monterrey, rather than food provisioning.[38] Similar decrees and orders proliferated during the war. They established a pattern of state regulation of staple production that became an enduring part of the Mexican development program.

The sugar industry provides an example of the way policies impoverished the country without producing an adequate supply. In one report to the president, Ortíz Garza noted that sugar subsidies for 1944 had been 34.4 million pesos.[39] However, it is not so clear where the money went. Admitting that there were great "losses," Ortíz Garza's reports dealt in global terms, disguising the money trail. A group of small farmers and *ejiditarios* who produced sugarcane at Acatlán de Juárez and Villa Corona, Jalisco, told quite a different tale. They complained to the president that they had to sell their sugar for 43 centavos per kilo, which left them only 10 centavos per kilo for their effort. Industry profits were shifted to the sugar mill, and the small producers were on the verge of collapse. Interestingly enough, they provided a much more detailed account of the costs of sugar production than ND&R reported in its budget. They were dealing with a monopoly at the local level, since they had to take whatever price the sugar mill offered. They certainly did not receive any of the ND&R subsidies.[40] Producers were particularly bitter about the subsidies to the employers' organization, the Unión Nacional de Productores de Azúcar, and the legal compulsion to force them to plant only sugarcane, even though there was little profit in that industry. The situation was doubly frustrating since there were considerable shortages of sugar and they could not even sell their products for the market price. Government analysts blamed the situation on the 1935 *convención obrero-patronal* covering the country's six hundred sugar refineries, which purported to be proworker; however, the producers blamed the refinery's monopoly position. The solution to the problem, in their view, was to extend long-term, low-interest loans to the industry, to raise the price of sugar, to increase subsidies to producers rather than to the mills, to cut taxes on the industry, and to hold down wages in the face of inflation.[41]

The problem was politically sensitive because, in addition to shortages and low prices to the consumers, the Unión Nacional de Productores de Azúcar had made a major sale of twenty-six thousand tons of subsidized sugarcane to the Pepsi-Cola Corporation, for export, starting in 1943. Since the United States had a contract to buy the entire Cuban sugar crop during the war, Mexico had to ask Washington to make a special case and allow it to buy enough Cuban sugar to make up for the shortfall.[42]

Rather than addressing the structure of particular industries, the Alemán administration set out on an ambitious project of building infrastructure for the nation's development on the assumption that such an approach would solve these bottlenecks. Roads, communication systems, and dams were foremost on the list of projects for which the Alemán government borrowed from the Export-Import Bank and the World Bank. President Alemán was tapping the deeply felt need for development throughout the community. Public borrowing was justified in the name of agricultural development. The circuit of borrowing to finance Mexican development pledged the repayment of the funds in dollars. Nacional Financiera farmed out the funds for public works and, in some cases, to private firms. The projects were justified in the name of "Mexico's" development. But what was "Mexico," and which Mexicans benefited?

An important project shows the way in which the state borrowing for rural development worked. As the Palmito Dam was completed in the region of the Laguna, in 1950, a presidential order directed that the water of the Río Nazas, now freed by the dam, should be used for the production of wheat and grains that would feed the population.[43] The order actually came from the manager of Irrigation District No. 17, and it reflected the need that had been obvious during the wartime food shortages.

Joe Sharp, head of the Anderson, Clayton, and Company interests in Mexico, and W. T. Burns of the company's Monterrey office alerted the home office in Houston to this order. They immediately saw a threat to A.C.&Co. if the precious water was allowed to be used for traditional production rather than for their agribusiness interests. Sharp and Burns arranged for Will Clayton to call upon Ramón Beteta and have the directive reversed. "We are informed the restriction measures have been rescinded and the farmers will plant cotton using water from the dam preferably for cotton. . . . It is my guess that the Laguna reversal of policy may serve as a precedent and that other areas will have no trouble."[44]

This exchange is absolutely central to understanding how infrastructure development failed to help the vast majority of rural Mexicans. Even though the irrigation project was justified upon developmental grounds for the entire nation, and even though the population ultimately underwrote the cost of the borrowing through the public finance system, the new production was to be channeled into the A.C.&Co. network. This was not an example of market forces at work.

The regulation of grain prices meant that producers of corn would not be allowed to benefit from high demand for their crops. Peasant producers faced low regulated prices and restricted credit opportunities. Now, Ramón Beteta and Miguel Alemán even directed that the newly provided water would not go to the small farmers and *ejiditarios*. In response to Clayton's pressure, they made sure that A.C.&Co.'s cotton, rather than food for the the domestic market, received the water. Food subsidies have frequently been seen as evidence of the subsistence sector's inefficiency. However, in this important case we see that political pressure from A.C.&Co. decided that the resources of the Laguna would only be routed for agribusiness.[45] Since fully half of the company's profits came from its international operations, this was important indeed. And as Joe Sharp noted, a pattern had been established.

Rural producers were locked into submarket prices, and as subsidies poured into the agribusiness sector, the enemies of the *ejido colectivo* blamed the small farmers and peasants. Urban decision makers determined not to place capital in the hands of the poor farmers. Rather, they created a series of scandal-ridden banks, which were directed by the top private bankers in the country, men who were enemies of the very ejido system that their banks ostensibly had been formed to finance. By reacting to symptoms rather than causes, they also created a massive bureaucracy in the name of doing something about what they called the agrarian problem.

A close examination of the government's agrarian effort, however, reveals a different reality. There is a detailed budget—not merely a summary statement—for the Departamento Agrario as of October 31, 1946. The most striking aspect of this detailed budget is that almost all of the department's expenditures were administrative. Replicating a general tendency of the development program to remove rewards from those who directly produce, the Departamento Agrario spent most of its money on salaries, trips for officials, offices, and a vast array of other expenditures. As one looks for investment that was going directly to support rural production, the closest was a category called *ayuda al campesino* (help to the peasant). Its meaning was not spelled out; but whatever that money was used for, it only represented 18,000 pesos out of 2.8 million pesos, or .006 percent of the total monthly budget. More money was spent on sports programs, machine parts, or gasoline than on agricultural extension work, much less the direct financing of poor peasants.[46] It is very difficult to avoid the conclusion that the agricultural bureaucracy was, in effect, an employment-generating scheme for the urban middle class.

There were even more direct attacks on the small farmer and *ejiditario*. The governments of the 1940s required that half of the demand deposits in Mexican banks be channeled into productive investments in development projects rather than into sterile bidding up of existing real assets. Once in office, the Alemán administration moved in a powerful way to modify that

requirement in order to deprive small farmers and *ejitarios* of capital. In 1950 it decided to add an apparently technical series of changes to the reserve bank requirements. Cash deposits outside the Federal District, as a percentage of demand liabilities, were reduced from 30 percent to 20 percent; total reserves required to be in productive investments were increased from 50 to 60 percent. However, investment in agriculture was removed from the list of productive investments, thus prohibiting banks from financing small and ejidal agriculture, even if they so desired. The decapitalization of the rural sector was state policy effected under the guise of technical adjustments.[47]

At the same time that massive subsidies flowed from the public to the private sector, there was no comparable sympathy for collective efforts that were unrelated to a corporativist structure of the state. This was clear in the case of the cooperative movement in Mexico in the 1940s. President Cárdenas had organized the enabling legislation that allowed cooperatives to eliminate the intermediary, thus providing for basic items at cheaper prices. Consumer, producer, and credit cooperatives were proposed in the 1930s and, a decade later, many were in operation. During the Avila Camacho years, two conflicts focused on the cooperative sector. There was a jurisdictional dispute between the Ministry of the National Economy and the Ministry of Labor, and there also was a battle over the ideology and scope of the cooperative movement.

The battle for the co-ops was between the minister of the national economy, Francisco Javier Gaxiola, and the minister of labor, Ignacio García Téllez. Each man wanted the right of supervision and control of the cooperative movement and each claimed that right by citing different sections of the law. Normally, this kind of jurisdictional dispute was uninteresting, except perhaps to the functionaries involved. However, in this case the administrative conflict masked a deeper division.

The ideological issues were promoted by Gaxiola, who was a protégé of Abelardo Rodríguez and so was quite unsympathetic to the procooperative principles enunciated in the law. He decided to challenge the ministry's control over all cooperatives. His position was that the Ministry of Labor should have control "only over the consumer cooperatives trading in articles of subsistence." By limiting the cooperative movement to subsistence products he was in fact striking a severe blow at cooperatives in general; there was no doubt that talk about exploitation, double exploitation, intermediaries, and monopolists would be unwelcome in the Ministry of the National Economy.[48]

The Ministry of Labor cited a number of extra-economic considerations in arguing its case. These included the protection of the principle of equality of all co-op members, the defense of the poor against speculation and exploitation, the battle against intermediaries and/or monopolists, and the defense of human capital. These concepts had been written into the law

during the Cárdenas administration, and García Téllez was one of the remaining ministers clearly associated with Cardenismo. The cooperative movement wanted to combat the "double exploitation" that workers faced at the level of production, consumption, and finance, so they saw Gaxiola's position as a threat. As the 1940s passed, these principles were less welcome in the cabinet.[49]

The government favored Gaxiola's position; although it allowed consumer cooperatives to produce more than articles of subsistence, all co-ops were placed under the administrative control of the Ministry of the National Economy. It was a severe blow to the movement. Successful cooperatives became rare. A few, like the Cruz Azul cement plant, succeeded in spite of the government; however, most found the environment ever less favorable.[50]

The Fábrica de Fibras Duras Atlas in San Luis Potosí (which produced bags and other products from hard fibers) provides a case in point. In 1938, President Cárdenas had expropriated the factory, thus converting it into a cooperative. It was a case of "lemon socialism," since the factory was running at a loss. In order to let the cooperative begin operations, the Banco Nacional Obrero de Fomento Industrial loaned the enterprise 188,000 pesos. Unfortunately, the terms of the cooperative's charter were not propitious. The former employees were owed considerable back wages and the former owner, Gerónimo Elizondo, also took legal action to recover his losses. These battles continued into the 1940s. In 1943 the cooperative opted for a negotiated settlement with the former owner, as indicated by the Ministry of the National Economy. Continued borrowing to pay past obligations doomed the attempt to shift to new technologies. Increasing profits became losses after 1944, resulting in a 5-million-peso debt to the Banco del Ahorro Nacional S.A. and to the Banco Nacional de Fomento Cooperativo S.A. by 1949. The co-op management blamed inadequate electricity supply and the original burden of debt for their situation. The managers asked the government for a subsidy, but government auditors were not sympathetic. In their view the cooperative had been producing at a loss, a shortcoming they attributed to the directors. Of course, the auditors factored in the cost of servicing the borrowing. Although this reasoning was fair enough from an accounting perspective, it essentially reflected the political decision to make the new cooperative responsible for past debts. It is clear that it received no government favors remotely paralleling the grants being extended to private enterprise.[51]

Another example is the case of the cooperative at Atencingo in Puebla. For decades the *ejidatarios* had been in conflict with mill owner William Jenkins, his manager Manuel Espinosa Yglesias, and their political protectors Maximino Avila Camacho and Governor Bautista. The cooperative was locked into a set of rules that constrained its potential. As late as March 1949 a combined intersecretarial commission investigated the situation at

the mill and ruled that "the cooperative agrees not to pursue any project that has not been approved by the Company and the Cooperative."[52]

The cooperative had to accept the company's charges for the use of its equipment, cost of transportation, material used in milling such as lubricating oils, and repairs on its rapidly deteriorating machinery, without a possibility of looking elsewhere, since it was bound into production on the company's terms. There was conflict each year after the sugar harvest as the company presented its accounts and the cooperative felt exploited. In the 1947–48 harvest, for example, the company managed to figure that the long list of complex charges (9,729,086 pesos) exceeded the value of the crop (7,950,097 pesos). Under its charter, the cooperative was even denied the possibility of seeking alternative productive activities for its land. The *ejidatarios* became ever more disillusioned, and observers confused cause and effect by blaming the cooperative techniques of production for poor showings of the ejido. Time and again they petitioned the president to be allowed to present the co-op's case—at "any day and hour"—and each time they received no answer. Dissident workers frequently charged cooperative leaders and administrators with being on Jenkins's payroll, and with accepting bribes from the firm so as not to challenge the company's accounts. Jenkins's political leverage even allowed the company to deny access to the government's mixed commission that was investigating the cooperative's charges of malfeasance. Clearly, the rules were stacked against the *ejidatarios*.[53]

The banking industry's relationship to land reform illustrates how a reform could be invalidated in practice. The scarcity of credit for ejidos is well known. An inadvertent result of trying to protect the *ejidatarios* made it impossible for them to mortgage their land. Agricultural production without credit is obviously impossible, especially in the move away from village subsistence agriculture. The Alemán administration clearly decided that private agriculture was the modern way. Such groups as the Popular Committee for Private Agricultural Credit emerged. At its convention on May 20–22, 1948, it called for government guarantees, including the same maximum rediscount facilities from the Banco de México that were available for private farmers; crop insurance; credit at subsidized interest rates (they suggested 6 percent rather than the 10 to 12 percent prevalent in the private credit markets); and treatment of presidential statements as equal in law to guarantees of private titles. It also called for the prompt response by the military in case of disputes with ejidatarios or land invaders (*paracaidistas*). Nazario Ortíz Garza, now the minister of agriculture, reassured the farmers that total security of land titles was in order.

The most fundamental spirit of the age was the tendency to privatize gain and socialize loss. By 1948 the state had guaranteed 37.4 million dollars from the World Bank and the Export-Import Bank for the Mexican Light and Power Company and for the American and Foreign Power Company.[54]

Similar loans were also extended to private companies throughout the country, even to the Fundidora in Monterrey. By contrast, the poor were on their own. The private banking sector was unwilling to lend to small agrarian operations and to small artisan producers, for reasons of class as much as economics. Private moneylenders still charged exorbitant rates of interest in the countryside. The banks fought a long battle with the state and the industrialists over investing in industry; they were more comfortable with loans for real estate and commerce, as was their historical practice.

Whereas the entire banking sector was quite pleased to have Nacional Financiera underwrite investment borrowing and take the risk of exchange rate deterioration (since the government borrowed from international organizations in dollars and loaned those funds to the private sector in pesos), some bankers were unwilling to share the investment decision-making role with the state. The Avila Camacho government won a considerable battle with the banks during the war by requiring that they place a substantial part of their funds in government investments, mainly Nacional Financiera. Certainly one of the techniques in Mexico by which rapid growth in industry was realized was that reserve requirement. Yet throughout the period, while many of the country's traditional private bankers resented the state's intrusion into investment decision making and constantly called for an end to the reserve requirements, it is interesting to note that some powerful private bankers, such as Luis and Agustín Legorreta, who were close to the government, found new opportunities. The fact that the state was bearing the risk for the private sector made the new deal attractive.[55]

There was profound resistance to the payment of taxes in the private sector. An under secretary of the treasury estimated that 50 to 60 percent of the registered private firms in Mexico paid no taxes at all. A campaign in 1948 to implement an excess-profits tax floundered. That proposal was so modest that even when bank profits hit 20 percent, the tax had not yet gone into effect. The campaign revealed that a bank that earned 5.5 million pesos in profits paid only 4,200 pesos in taxes. The PRI ran a campaign against tax evasion under the banner "The National Economy Is Not the Patrimony of a Few Potentates"; but apparently it was a public relations exercise, since the campaign had limited effect and the government reduced taxes a few months later.[56]

At both the national and international levels, advantages flow to the strong. Ironically, just as political leaders disadvantaged the poor in Mexico, they came face to face with raw economic power in their dealings with New York's financial community.

## Pan American Trust Company

Mexican officials did occasionally try to redress the balance of power with their neighbor to the north. They were quite aware of the degree

to which the normal functioning of the economic system worked to their disadvantage. An episode that perhaps best characterizes this unequal relationship is seen in the attempt by Mexico to purchase the Pan American Trust Company of New York City. The story makes it abundantly clear where real power resided and who set the rules of the game.

Just as the *ejidatarios* at Atencingo had to pay any accounts from William Jenkins, Mexico, too, could only gain access to world markets via the U.S. financial institutions. Deprived of markets in much of the world due to the early gains of the Axis forces (and the British retaliation over the expropriation of petroleum), New York became Mexico's only financial window on the world. For this, it paid exorbitant discount rates, financial fees, and charges.

After the Nazi conquest of the European mainland, Mexico had to depend upon the goodwill of the United States to protect its shares and assets in conquered countries; this raised complicated legal issues of vesting, double vesting, and subrogating claims on property between two or more countries. In addition, broader precedents of attacking private property—even in enemy territory—were raised, and these were issues of extreme sensitivity. The United States, in one opportunistic moment, even interpreted Mexico's request for assistance in pursuit of its European claims as conceding "Mexico's desire to subrogate itself to the bondholders' rights to the trust fund." That is to say, its claims over assets in Europe would be set against the old foreign bondholders' claims against Mexico. The issue, in the U.S. and British view, became one of offsetting Mexico's right to its European assets against bondholders' indirect claims on undistributed funds over bonds held in Axis countries. Clearly, the United States was placing top priority on the protection of property rights; as one economic diplomat put it, "The protection of the interests of bondholders in occupied territory would still constitute a basis for United States intervention."[57]

These claims and counterclaims formed the background to the Pan American Trust issue. Mexico decided to ask the United States to defend its assets in occupied Europe since the lattter could get at them more easily than Mexico could. The United States said no.[58] It was a complex legal problem, one in which even the state courts of New York could rule in favor of bondholders if the United States accepted subrogation. These issues were also complicated by claims of governments in exile in the conquered territories. The Departments of Treasury, Justice, and the Alien Property Custodian were unsympathetic to Mexico's request.[59]

On December 15, 1943, Mexico vested all nonregistered bonds in NAFISA as trustee. That included the right of ownership of the title and the right to collect interest, since unregistered securities were presumed to be in enemy hands. It was easier to pass such a law than to enforce it, so Mexico again turned to the United States, asking it to pursue its bonds and securities that were held in Europe. Subrogating its rights to the United States,

Mexico was, in fact, taking the route opened up by the Inter-American Conference on Systems of Economic and Financial Control, which had met in Washington from June 30 to July 10, 1942. In those discussions the issue of legal fees was significant, and that issue continued to underpin Latin American complaints about U.S. preeminence through November 1943.

At the same time Mexico paid exorbitant legal and banking fees. Eduardo Suárez pointed out that in one recent transaction alone, his country was charged 700,000 dollars for access to its own funds. He was told that the matter was being discussed by Under Secretary Dean Acheson and the ubiquitous Adolf Berle.[60] In response, at a conference in Washington on June 29, 1944, between Suárez and officials of the State Department, Mexicans were told that the old Committee of Bankers in New York might have a claim on the pursuit of Mexican assets in Europe. In effect, to question high banking fees might reopen the old issues of the debt that had been resolved in 1941. Suárez obviously opposed the return of former members of the old Committee of Bondholders, now recrudescent as the Committee of Bankers in New York. By August 7, U.S. officials discussed whether the funds should be merged with other funds administered by the Alien Property Custodian and then turned over to Mexico. This proposal would require an act of Congress, or, as Mexico preferred, the property rights might be pursued through the U.S. courts. After continuing the protest about the excessive legal and financial fees that Mexico was being forced to pay, Acheson promised to discuss the matter with the attorney general.[61]

In 1943, Eduardo Villaseñor had gone directly to London to try to buy some of the outstanding bonds of the external debt at the best price he could negotiate, and to try to find bargains in the bonds of the outstanding railroad debt. A new compact was proposed between his country and the United States to solve the problem; however, that pact did not eventuate and, as a result, Mexico tried to salvage the loss by another means, inadvertently creating the Pan American Trust issue.

Mexico's most successful wartime financial measure was to issue a decree providing registration points abroad for individuals and corporate entities holding its bonds. If outstanding bonds were not duly registered, they were then considered to be enemy owned. In this masterstroke the country thus eliminated an estimated 55 percent of its external debt and proceeded to pay registered bondholders 20 cents on the dollar. Mexico entered into another agreement to this effect with the International Committee of Bondholders, headed by Thomas Lamont. On October 12, 1943, the Mexican ambassador requested that the secretary of state in Washington recognize this as a sovereign act and provide recognition and enforcement in U.S. courts.

In January 1944, Antonio Carrillo, representing Suárez, requested the Alien Property Custodian to refrain from vesting that percentage of distributable funds corresponding to the unregistered bonds (presumed to be in

enemy hands) with the International Committee of Bondholders. He also suggested that the two governments enter into an agreement so recognizing the situation and transfer unregistered funds to the Mexican Alien Property Custodian and NAFISA.

In an aide-mémoire, the State Department on February 21 "regretfully concluded" that it could not accede to Mexico's proposal, stating: "The Department of State has been assured by the Alien Property Custodian he will not vest any part of the above-mentioned fund without prior consultation with the Department, and the Department will consult with the Mexican Government in advance of any vesting." Negotiations were suspended until October 12, when Mexico requested that the U.S. government take steps to prevent the dissipation of the fund by the International Committee of Bankers.

On October 25, 1944, Mexico reversed its position in a meeting with the Departments of State, Justice, Treasury, and the Alien Property Custodian. It then asked that the U.S. Alien Property Custodian vest bonds held by the enemy in the International Committee of Bankers with the understanding that these should be turned over to Mexico. The U.S. position at the meeting was that, if they were so vested, they would be for the use of the United States, unless Congress provided otherwise. At this point the negotiations broke off, awaiting a new position from Suárez.[62] The possibility that Mexico would now have to convince the U.S. Congress was exasperating.

Frustrated by the combination of technical difficulties and dependency, Mexico opted for another way to protect its international financial interests. For slightly more than one million dollars the Banco de México, on October 11, 1944, purchased 32,500 of the 40,000 outstanding shares in the Pan American Trust Company of New York—a small bank and trust company managed by John B. Glenn. Mexico's purpose in acquiring this institution, which was registered with the Federal Reserve System, was to centralize the various international transactions that had formerly been rendered by such New York banks as Chase Manhattan and National City Bank. Pan American Trust would be able to process a wide variety of these transactions: administration of the debt obligations, coordination of international borrowing, collection of anticipated import duties, covering the costs of Mexico's foreign consular services, and generally facilitating international transactions. The bank's legal section would also be extremely useful in the case of the foreign bonds.

The attempt to save considerable sums in financial and banking commissions, as well as associated legal costs, was clearly behind the move. Plans were made to increase the capital of the bank to 2.5 million dollars at once. It seemed clear that the potential growth of such a bank doing the Republic of Mexico's business was great, especially when we realize that one single commission—on the annual payment of interest to the foreign

bondholders—was over 800,000 dollars. The Pan American Trust Company belonged to the private Banco Nacional de México, and the director, Luis Legorreta, had decided that the returns were too small to justify holding the company. The bank had been known as the Harbor State Bank of New York before BANAMEX bought it in the 1930s.[63]

According to directors of the Federal Reserve System, Mexico's ploy was ingenious. To that date no other government had thought of such a plan. It immediately set off a flurry of activity in New York and Washington. On December 6, 1944, officials of the Federal Reserve System, the State Department, and the Treasury met to consider this innovation. Speaking for the Federal Reserve System, Bray Hammond and Walter Gardner stated that Mexico's action raised matters of high policy. They denied that it was acceptable for a central bank of a foreign country to conduct its operations directly in another country through branches or affiliates. Noting that the practice contravened no U.S. legislation, but arguing that it was a "generally recognized principle of central banking," the Federal Reserve Bank strongly disapproved of the possibility that Mexico could compete with private banks in international markets. The bankers noted that while the scope of Mexico's activity was not too great, if the central banks of major countries such as Britain adopted these practices, it "might constitute a serious interference with the execution by the authorities of the monetary policies of that country and cause or occasion international friction and misunderstandings." The Federal Reserve directors noted that there were few modern precedents for the practice, with the exception of the operation of the Federal Reserve Bank in Cuba which, even they conceded, "might seem to be an exception." They lamely argued that the U.S. operations in Cuba were different, since Cuba had no central bank at the time and since the Treasury ran Cuba's monetary system.[64]

Unaware of the degree to which this imaginative solution was about to earn the wrath of the Federal Reserve System, Villaseñor granted a press interview. He was enthusiastic about having conceived and executed such an efficient and clever move.[65] William F. Busser, second secretary of the U.S. embassy, visited Villaseñor on December 6. Busser reported that he was surprised that the Federal Reserve Bank was interested in Mexico's purchase of "a little banking institution in New York," and he suggested that ownership could be transferred to the Banco Nacional de Comercio Exterior if the United States was worried about a central bank owning a bank in New York. The U.S. embassy took the tack of eliciting background information from Villaseñor and querying whether banking officials would want diplomatic immunity. Villaseñor reiterated what he had expressed to bankers at a dinner in New York City. He was not planning to break off existing commercial relations with U.S. private banks (the diplomat seemed to assume that there would be something inherently wrong with that course of action). Busser asked Villaseñor what Mexico's attitude would be if the

Federal Reserve System were to open a branch in Mexico. The situations were not analogous, said Villaseñor. As he put it, "Mexico's acquiring an institution in New York might be said to be in the nature of a poor man sending someone to a rich man's table to observe happenings, whereas the rich man's sending an observer to a poor man's table might be looked upon with some suspicion and alarm."[66]

The position of the Federal Reserve Board was made difficult in that there was no precedent for the Mexican action and no U.S. statute was broken. It expressed concern about having to deal with the Mexican embassy in order to implement its policies and raised the example of the Federal Reserve System asking Mexico to dismiss a functionary found wanting, as was common practice within the domestic banking system. Ultimately, Marriner S. Eccles, chairman of the board of governors of the Federal Reserve Board, characterized the situation as "a little fast work on the part of the Banco de México."[67]

The Federal Reserve Board assigned the matter of Mexico's purchase of the Pan American Trust Company to Mr. Szymczak, of the board of governors of the Federal Reserve System. By December 8, Chairman Eccles wrote to Secretary of State Cordell Hull that "we feel that if anything is to be done, it is important that it be done promptly before the transaction is carried further and becomes harder to undo."[68]

At another meeting between the Federal Reserve System and the State Department on December 18, U.S. officials agreed that the Mexican move "would be a violation of the generally recognized principle of central banking that one country would not conduct its operations in the market of another by means of branches of affiliated corporations."[69] They also agreed that none of the other four government-owned banks in Mexico (the Banco Nacional de Comercio Exterior S.A., the Banco Nacional de Crédito Agrícola S.A., the Banco Nacional Hipotecario Urbano y de Obras Públicas, and the Banco Nacional de Crédito Ejidal S.A.) would be allowed to purchase the Pan American Trust Company. The following day the same group met with Messersmith, who agreed with the officials of the State Department and the Federal Reserve System. Messersmith confided to the meeting that Director Villaseñor "was not a good friend of the United States and that anything that he was mixed up in should be watched very carefully." He further surmised that Villaseñor's motivation had been to save fees in Mexico's international transactions and to offer the same services to other Latin American countries. At that point they brought Harry Dexter White, Morganthau's assistant at the Treasury Department, into their calculations, and that same day, Edward R. Stettinius and Governor Eccles confirmed their subordinates' decisions.[70]

Mexico had broken the rules. It had tried to avoid being a price-taker in the international financial arena. Neither the natural justice of a poor country trying to defend its interests, nor the legality of the move, nor the inge-

nuity of the maneuver would be allowed. Power resided in the North. Mere cleverness was not going to affect the basic rules of the system.

## Epilogue: A Reconfirmation of the Fundamentals

In a curious way, the early experience of the Ruiz Cortines administration (1952–1958) reconfirmed the new political economy of Mexico. Adolfo Ruiz Cortines was a long-time collaborator of Miguel Alemán. A friend and business partner in Veracruz, long before either rose to national prominence, Ruiz Cortines seemed to be a safe choice for the departing president. However, a bit like appointing a Supreme Court Justice in the United States, the new president, upon arriving at the pinnacle of formal political power, found himself in a position that was totally different from the condition that brought him to power. A high degree of autonomy replaced the subservience that allowed the candidate to emerge from the shadow of his mentor. Miguel Alemán, like Cárdenas and Calles before him, found that once his successor was installed, gratitude was without currency.

Ruiz Cortines was not a healthy man. Although he had been party to a few of President Alemán's business deals, on the whole he had been far more scrupulous about the treatment of public funds than had his two predecessors. Indeed, the main charge leveled against him was that he had done very well as minister of the interior under Avila Camacho, but that had resulted from a milking of vulnerable citizens of the Axis powers rather than a misuse of public funds. After the open split between President Alemán and his nephew Fernando Casas Alemán, the coast was clear.[71] Ruiz Cortines had easily handled General Miguel Henríquez Guzmán's challenge at the time of the 1952 election, undoubtedly because, as a major contractor to the government public-works program and the largest shareholder in the Altos Hornos steel mill, Henríquez Guzmán was dependent on government favors.[72] And even the old charges that Ruiz Cortines had aided the Yankee invaders in Veracruz in 1914, at age twenty, were no longer credible.

The new president surprised his former associate by starting his term with a campaign against his predecessor's corruption. This was the first of what was to become the obligatory anticorruption drive at the beginning of every new Mexican administration. The public awareness of the corruption of the Alemán administration and the pressure generated as a new elite prospered in the midst of rising prices and frozen wages were so great that the new president decided to use the campaign to divert opposition.

Ruiz Cortines also displayed some sensitivity to the growing problem of income inequity. Although he did not change the patterns, he did voice his disapproval, at least enough to anger his former colleagues. Years later, Ramón Beteta still expressed annoyance as he reflected upon the change in attitude toward the masses of the population. In an interview with James

Wilkie, Beteta acknowledged that Ruiz Cortines saw the Alemán prosperity as being based on the pattern that "que los ricos se hicieran más ricos, y los pobres más pobre." However much that charge angered the Alemanistas, Ruiz Cortines did not go very far in rectifying the system.[73]

After a few minor culprits were put on public display, business returned to normal. The main economic adjustment that Ruiz Cortines then made was to hold down the prices of the staples consumed by the poor. Those state subsidies helped employers pay low wages, and it was possible to gain a certain amount of political credit by this means. However, by keeping prices in the campo low, especially in the peasant/village/ejido sector, he was creating a situation that forced the rural poor into the urban slums. In essence, by limiting the corruption drive to small fish, and by making minor adjustments to the profoundly unequal distribution of income, Ruiz Cortines, in fact, reconfirmed the existing system. Not until the 1980s and 1990s, when neo-liberalism came to Mexico with a vengeance, would there be as fundamental a set of changes to the rules of the game as those that had occurred in the 1940s. The administrations of the 1940–1952 period, in conjunction with their U.S. partners in and outside of government, had changed the rules definitively.

# Notes

1. Aware that the PCM was in decline, U.S. diplomats shifted away from the hunt for communists toward an identification of what they called the "communist line" in Mexico. See also Carr, "Crisis in Mexican Communism," and his *Marxism and Communism in Twentieth Century Mexico.*

2. James Webb to Harry Truman, April 9, 1951, Truman Library, PSF, Box 183.

3. Annual report to the president, July 1, 1945, to June 30, 1946, ibid.

4. George Messersmith to Secretary of State James F. Byrnes, October 22, 1945, Truman Library, Clayton Papers.

5. Hess, "After the Tumult," 483–501.

6. Merwin L. Bohan to Nelson Rockefeller, February 24, 1955, Truman Library, Papers of Merwin L. Bohan, Box 2, Correspondence File 11.

7. Bohan to Harold Randell, May 30, 1974, ibid.

8. William G. MacLean to Truman, July 19, 1946, Truman Library, Official File 146.

9. Diary entry for April 10, 1947, Truman Library, Robert L. Gardner Papers.

10. Charles Kindleberger, *The World in Depression,* 291–94; and Keynes, *Essays in Persuasion,* 244–70.

11. The Mexican delegation was headed by Eduardo Suárez, minister of finance, and included Antonio Espinosa de los Monteros, manager of Nacional Financiera; Rodrigo Gómez, manager of the Banco de México; Daniel Cosío Villegas, head of the Department of Economic Studies of the Banco de México; and Victor Urquidi, then an economist with the Banco de México.

12. "Acuerdo presidencial," June 28, 1944, SRE, III-1177-1 (1).

13. Statement of July 5, 1944, SRE, III-1180-1 (7). For the detailed Mexican arguments in favor of silver see SRE, III-1177-1 (1), Padilla to Suárez, June 13, 1944, as well as SRE, III-1178-1 and 2.

14. Ibid.

15. U.S. embassy to Secretaría de Relaciones Exteriores, April 13, 1944, SRE, III-1177-1 (1).

16. Ibid., April 20, 1944.

17. Final report for Commission III, July 21, 1944, SRE, III-1180-1 (7).

18. See Australia's final submission to Commission III, July 10, 1944, ibid.

19. "Mexico's Proposal on Silver," ibid., document 189.

22. *Financial News*, London, October 9, 1944.

21. Viner, "Two Plans for International Monetary Stabilization."

22. Kindleberger, *A Financial History of Western Europe*, 55–57.

23. "Convenio para la Creación de un Fondo Monetario Internacional," July 1–22, 1944, SRE, III-1177-1 (1).

24. The final articles of agreement were published in Young, *Conference at Bretton Woods*. FDR spoke to Congress in support of the plan on February 20, 1945.

25. Bohan to secretary of state, July 1, 1948, USNA/RG 59, 812.50/7-148.

26. Francisco Javier Gaxiola to Avila Camacho, May 7 and July 5, 1943, AGN, RP/MAC, 550/44-2.

27. Messersmith to Franklin D. Roosevelt, January 8, 1945, USNA/RG 59, 812.002/1-845; Messersmith to Edward R. Stettinius, January 8, 1945, ibid.

28. "XVII Annual Convention of the Mexican Bankers' Association," May 16, 1951, USNA/RG 59, 812.14/5-351.

29. Southard to John W. Snyder, February 20, 1948, Truman Library, J. W. Snyder Papers, Box 21.

30. Southard to Snyder, June 18, 1948, ibid.

31. Memorandum of conversation: Donald Nelson, Fernando Buch de Parada, Guy Ray, and MacLean, April 29, 1947, USNA/RG 59, 812.50/4-2947.

32. Lew B. Clark to secretary of state, February 3, 1948, USNA/RG 59, 812.50/2-348.

33. The Reciprocal Trade Agreement was initially signed in Washington on December 23, 1942, and finally ratified by both countries on January 30, 1943.

34. Bortz, *El Salario en México*.

35. Bohan to secretary of state, January 22, 1947, USNA/RG 59, 812.50/1-2247.

36. Espinoza Toledo, "La Consolidación del Sindicalismo," 301–12.

37. Nazario S. Ortíz Garza to the state governors, September 2, 1943, AGN, RP/MAC, 545.2/83; and González Gallo to Alemán, July 7, 1944, ibid.

38. Ortíz Garza to Avila Camacho, November 23, 1943, ibid.

39. Ortíz Garza to Avila Camacho, March 1, 1945, AGN, RP/MAC, 521.8/188.

40. Florentino Coral to Avila Camacho, September 27, 1943, and the Frente Unico de Ejiditarios y Pequeños Agricultores de Caña de Azúcar y Similares, from Córdoba, Veracruz, October 7, 1945, AGN, RP/MAC, 521-6/7.

41. "Estudio sobre la actual situación de la Industria Azucarera de la República Mexicana," June 1945, AGN, RP/MAC, 545.22/304.

42. Aarón Sáenz to Avila Camacho, December 31, 1943, AGN, RP/MAC, 564.2/244.

43. *Excélsior*, October 27, 1950.

44. Joe Sharp to W. T. Burns, October 27, 1950; Clayton to Sharp, October 30, 1950; Burns to Clayton, November 2, 1950, Truman Library, Clayton Papers. The effort was fruitful: Sharp to Clayton, November 8, 1950, ibid.

280 War, Diplomacy, and Development

45. Ronfeldt, *Atencingo*, 25–32.

46. Budget, October 31, 1946, AGN, RP/MAC, 545.2/37.

47. "Mexican Reserve Requirements," May 16, 1950, USNA/RG 59, 812.14/5-1650.

48. Luna Arroyo to the president, October 13, 1941, AGN, RP/MAC, 545.2/12.

49. Ignacio García Téllez to the president, January 28, and August 12, 1942, ibid.

50. Agreement between the Ministry of Labor and the Ministry of the National Economy, April 6, 1942, ibid.

51. Pedro Belaunzarane to Alemán, December 20, 1949, and the cooperatives' memorandum, June 19, 1949, AGN, RP/MAV, 432/99.

52. Report of the commission to the president, November 24, 1949, AGN, RP/MAV, 423-2/3.

53. Petition of the cooperative to the president, July 14, 1948, ibid.

54. "Electric Power in Mexico," August 9, 1948, USNA/RG 59, 812.50/9-248.

55. "The XII National Banking Conference," March 21–23, 1946, AGN, RP/MAC, 433/477.

56. *El Universal,* January 14, 1949; *Diario Oficial,* July 4, 1949.

57. Bernard Metzler to Frederick Livesey and Berle, October 20, 1943, USNA/RG 59, 812.51/2734.

58. Reeves to Livesey, October 27, 1943, USNA/RG 59, 812.51/2734. See also files 812.51/2734 and 812.51/2735 for additional documents relating to these claims.

59. *Diario Oficial,* October 24, 1942.

60. Memorandum of conversation in the State Department, June 28, 1944, USNA/RG 59, 812.51/6-2944.

61. Memorandum of conversation between Suárez and others and E. G. Collado, USNA/RG 59, 812.51/8-744.

62. Attorney general to secretary of state, December 9, 1944, USNA/RG 59, 812.51/12-944.

63. Busser to secretary of state, "Acquisition by Banco de Mexico S.A. of Controlling Interest in Pan American Trust Company," October 17, 1944, USNA/RG 59, 812.516/10-1744. See also *El Universal* and *Excélsior*, October 13, 1944.

64. Memorandum of conversation between officials of the Federal Reserve Bank and the State Department, December 6, 1944, USNA/RG 59, 812.516/10-1744.

65. *Excélsior*, November 1–4, 1944.

66. Memorandum of conversation between Villaseñor and Busser, December 6, 1944, USNA/RG 59, 812.516/12-644.

67. Marriner S. Eccles to Collado, December 6, 1944, ibid.

68. Eccles to Hull, December 8, 1944, USNA/RG 59, 812.516/12-844.

69. Memorandum of conversation between officials of the Federal Reserve Board, the Federal Reserve Bank, and the State Department, December 18, 1944, USNA/RG 59, 812.516/12-1844.

70. Memorandum of conversation between officials of the State Department, the Federal Reserve System, and Messersmith, December 19, 1944, USNA/RG 59, 812.516/12-1944; and Stettinius to Eccles, December 18, 1944, USNA/RG 59, 812.516/12-844.

71. "Mexican Elections in 1946 and 1952—Comparisons and Contrasts—Observations as to Progress Achieved," February 12, 1952, USNA/RG 59, 712.00/2-1252.

72. "Relation of Altos Hornos de México to Mexican Presidential Campaign," September 17, 1951, USNA/RG 59, 812.331/9-1751.

73. Wilkie and Wilkie, *México visto en el Siglo XX*, 48.

# Conclusion: The Great Evasion

Certain images can sum up great and complex events. The legions of people who flocked to the January 1950 opening of Anderson, Clayton, and Company's state-of-the-art processing factory in Monterrey revealed an enthusiasm for industrial development that already separates the 1950s from the present. Although this popular enthusiasm was widely shared, there was no comparable consensus on the way to attain the goal of industrialization. Broadly, there were two fundamentally divergent approaches: economic nationalism and international integration. One of the most basic aspects of dismantling the Cardenista project of the 1930s was the change from the former to the latter. The leaders of the 1940s shifted the political project in a far more conservative direction. The ability of Presidents Manuel Avila Camacho and Miguel Alemán to change the program of the Mexican Revolution did not depend on the will of these men alone.

After the nationalization of petroleum, Mexico sent out urgent signals to the United States that its economic radicalism would go no further and that the petroleum companies would be compensated for their losses. Its leaders, starting with President Cárdenas, then committed Mexico unreservedly to the Allied side, and the wartime economic cooperation saw U.S. policymakers develop an unprecedented degree of influence over that country. Mexico's wartime strategy was to exchange support for the war effort for help in achieving industrialization.

Although the historic project of industrial modernization brought the masses along, even in the face of an acute reduction in their standard of living, images of cynicism surround the actions of the decision makers. The record of corruption and the self-serving use of state power was so great as to offer one explanation of the failure of the Mexican development program. Even the activities of those who spoke in the name of the people were questionable. Vicente Lombardo Toledano, the leader of the CTM, was followed by FBI agents into surreptitious meetings in New Jersey at which the distribution of pirated petroleum was being decided. The G-men believed that they were shadowing a dangerous radical.

The opulent resort of Acapulco provides another image. State terrorism was used to separate the villagers from their land so that tourism could be the leading edge of development, thus providing jobs, business opportunity, and progress. Yet the small island with the abandoned estate in front of

Caleta Beach is another reminder of the era. Worthy of a novel by Joseph Conrad or Graham Greene, the mansion that Avila Camacho built on the land he took from the national patrimony now sits gathering mold while victims of alienated village lands and their heirs continue to search for jobs serving jet-setters in the posh resort. If there was ever a case to demonstrate the failure of the trickle-down theory of economic development, it certainly is Acapulco. A short trip inland from the glitter of the beach hotels reveals some of Mexico's most appalling poverty.

It is useful to reflect upon what U.S. policymakers most disliked, as they monitored events in Mexico. Before the war the New Deal diplomats worked hard not to allow the petroleum companies to dominate foreign policy. U.S. strategists were convinced that they should work for a solution to the conflicts over debt, oil, land, and economic nationalism as war approached. That strategy served the United States well after Pearl Harbor. During the war Allied diplomats monitored Axis activities, real and imagined, in Mexico. When the Germans attacked the USSR, Mexico's Left enthusiastically joined the war effort, thus creating a period of national unity. The United States singled out Miguel Alemán as the least helpful minister in its anti-Axis efforts and this, plus the ambassador's obvious fondness for Ezequiel Padilla, prevented Alemán from being identified with Washington's interests until after he took office. Thus, Lombardo Toledano rushed back from the founding of the United Nations in San Francisco and used the last of his political influence to block Padilla in favor of Alemán, to save the revolution.[1]

Economic cooperation cemented the political accommodation between the two countries and made way for a massive entry of foreign capital into Mexico after the war. U.S. participation in Mexican public affairs, as a result of wartime regulations, made this era different from all others. During the 1940s diplomats were participants and decision makers, not mere observers. The Mexican goal of industrialization merged with the desire to join in the Grand Alliance in the battle against fascism; that created enough political unity to allow the leaders to reverse the course of the Mexican Revolution.

After the Allied victory U.S. diplomats quickly shifted their priorities, much to Mexico's consternation. A highly valued ally soon became a neighbor of minor importance, in Washington's view. That was revealed even in the choice of embassy personnel. After sending two top diplomats, Josephus Daniels and George Messersmith, as ambassadors to Mexico City, the United States then sent a quiet professional, Walter Thurston, followed by a political embarrassment, William O'Dwyer.[2]

It took a while for these diplomats to realize just how conservative the Mexican Revolution was becoming. Anticommunism swept like a tidal wave across the United States; even the Truman administration found that it was unable to control the base forces it had unleashed. In Mexico, there were

few communists, if one defines a communist as someone who belongs to a communist party. U.S. diplomats were constantly disappointed by the lack of enthusiasm that Mexican politicians exhibited in battling communism, yet they inadvertently revealed the real importance of the Communist Party of Mexico by shifting their reports from party activities to what they called "the communist line," that is to say, radical ideas of which they disapproved.[2] Although, by 1949, Mexican authorities did run an anticommunist campaign, they did so with only tepid enthusiasm, and their primary targets soon became leaders of independent unions.

U.S. diplomats on the scene had a more immediate target than agents from Moscow. Economic nationalism was the real enemy. However, the majority of Mexican politicians and journalists, especially those on the left, were convinced that the United States wanted to subvert the Mexican electoral process. Many also believed that their real purpose was to prevent the country from industrializing so as to maintain a monopoly over modern techniques. On both of these scores they were in error. The United States was fundamentally interested in shaping the rules of the game, and therefore diplomats could say, with a significant degree of veracity, that they were not interfering in the electoral process. The 1946 election is a good example. Ambassador Messersmith favored Ezequiel Padilla over Miguel Alemán. He wrote to Secretary of State Acheson: "It has been a very difficult matter for this Embassy and for our Government to be kept out of this electoral struggle but it is absolutely essential. There is no question that we have a very definite interest in the outcome of this election, but we are powerless in this matter."[3]

New Deal diplomats, in contrast to their predecessors, maintained their integrity by refraining from meddling in electoral politics. Yet if one looks beyond the electoral arena, those same diplomats were highly skilled at imposing their will on the Mexican decision makers. They did so by changing the rules of the game to their own advantage. This was the political prize. U.S. officials and capitalists did not want to keep Mexico from industrializing. What they wanted was a large slice of the action. In this respect the personal and political interests of power brokers, on both sides of the border, coincided during the 1940s. With the establishment of the fundamental elements governing the relationship between the two countries, it really did not matter who would enforce and even interpret those rules.

Before the war, a three-corner contest pitted enemies on both the right and the left against U.S. interests; that situation gave Latin America room to maneuver. At the best of times, our diplomats even supported democratic forces against dictators. After FDR's death a simple bipolar Cold War formulation overwhelmed inter-American relations. Latin Americans (and some New Deal diplomats) were bitter that former allies such as Mexico had much less leverage in their relationship with the United States. Their exclusion from the Marshall Plan left bitter memories. It was not for decades, until

their demands for loans were met, that the world system caught the region in a "debt trap," to use Cheryl Payer's phrase. The borrowing of the 1970s, together with the dictatorships of that period, brought untold misery to the region.

An episode that took place during the Ruiz Cortines campaign shows how pervasive U.S. influence in Mexico had become. The great artist, Diego Rivera, had painted a mural entitled *Nightmare of War and Dreams of Peace* to represent his country at an exhibition in Paris. The Alemán administration decided not to send the painting as it had planned, objecting that it expressed sympathy with the North Korean charge that the United States had used bacteriological warfare in the Korean War. In it, Rivera portrayed Chairman Mao and Marshal Stalin sympathetically, whereas he characterized the United States, Britain, and France as warmongers. The artist complained that his freedom of expression had been compromised by President Alemán, and he suggested that the United States was behind the suppression, an accusation denied at the time. However, one document of the period carries a revealing footnote: "The [Mexican] government's decision was based upon representations made by Ambassador O'Dwyer but, of course, this was not disclosed by the Foreign Office so as not to make it appear that Mexico had yielded to foreign influence."[4] Before the incident, the National Institute of Fine Arts had agreed to allow the controversial mural to be shown at the Palacio de las Bellas Artes in Mexico City. Upon reflection, however, Directors Fernando Gamboa and Carlos Chávez returned the mural to the artist.

Still, there were also moments of cooperation to solve mutual problems. The outbreak of hoof-and-mouth disease in November 1946 provides an example. As we know, the tragedy of destroying the herds belonging to poor rural families was almost of Biblical proportions. Some 1,300,000 cattle plus sheep and goats were killed. President Truman allocated 9 million dollars to compensate those affected, and the 40 million pesos actually reached some victims and was of considerable help. The director of the project, Oscar Flores, worked closely with his U.S. counterpart, M. S. Shahan.[5] When U.S. technology solved immediate problems, it provided diplomats with a weapon to counter voices on the left, which charged the United States with economic imperialism. Technical expertise also gave the internationalists an advantage over the economic nationalists in the business community, as the Point Four program demonstrated.

Since the rise of the socialist left, the issue of imperialism has been contentious. Ambassador Walter Thurston bought into the debate at the Sixty-fourth General Congress of the American Institute of Electrical Engineers, held in Mexico City in June 1948. Directly confronting charges of economic imperialism, Thurston argued that the Declaration of Independence and the Constitution of the United States guaranteed the dignity and freedom of all men. He was, he said, distressed that his country was so fre-

quently charged with imperialist policies by those who believed they had "ulterior designs in our foreign aid program and that we are alleged to begrudge and oppose the industrial development of other lands."

Taking it for granted that no one any longer accused the United States of wanting "political or military imperialism" (that is, direct military expansion), he turned to the charge of economic imperialism. If, he argued, economic imperialism meant the export of surplus capital, then he was happy to acknowledge that "what a blessing the investment abroad of accumulated capital has been to the world!" Even the United States developed in that way. Thurston cleverly charged spokesmen for the Mexican left with wanting it both ways. In this view, the export of surplus capital was economic imperialism; however, he argued that they also "upbraid us for refusing to develop other lands." In any case, the United States traded primarily with developed nations (a decade later this argument came to be known among economic historians as the Fieldhouse thesis). What the United States wanted was a prosperous neighbor who benefited from foreign investment in airplanes, railways, light and power, and industries.[6]

Harry Turkel, of the embassy staff, produced a more detailed critique of the Mexican Left's charges of economic imperialism. Acknowledging that "in Mexico, it is true that many phases of economic life are controlled by nationals or corporations of the United States. [He mentioned American Smelting, Phelps-Dodge, Eagle Picher, Gold Fields, Cananea, National Lead, Electric Bond and Share, Pan American Airways, and American Airlines.] . . . This is not imperialism. It is simply the free enterprise system abroad." Stripped of the rhetoric, Turkel's argument was that only if profits of foreign firms were excessive by the standards of similar national firms (later known as the Landes thesis), or if they were using harsher labor methods, could the charge of imperialism stick. Considering the reluctance of wealthy Mexicans to invest in industry rather than pursue rentier activities, he continued, foreign firms were in fact contributing to the country's much-wanted industrial development. "In short, without these American companies there would be a great many more Indians silent upon their peaks in Mexico."[7] This is an important record of U.S. diplomats privately working out their own response to the charges of economic imperialism. It also anticipates many of the positions so intensely elaborated in academic circles during the Cold War.

The surviving historical record of this period indicates that the Thurston-Turkel position was an interesting mixture of certainties and untruths. Direct military conquest was a thing of the past. The two men were correct in spotting a deep contradiction in Mexicans who simultaneously equated economic imperialism with the export of surplus capital while charging the United States with trying to block Mexico's industrial development. In this, they revealed a weakness in the Hobson-Lenin theory of imperialism. It is also true that many, but certainly not all, rich Mexicans were happier to

stay with rentier activities. This assertion, however, was hypocritical, since its economic diplomats had led the charge against the economic nationalists for years. There were also serious misrepresentations and misunderstandings in the Thurston-Turkel view. U.S. aid was used for ulterior purposes, as was demonstrated by the Pan American Trust Company case, the political leverage of Point Four, and the use of the Export-Import Bank, the World Bank, and IMF loans. These proved to be a more powerful force than landing the Marines.

We now see that the idea that U.S. firms operating in underdeveloped regions would bring living standards up to their levels was, at best, a profound misunderstanding. It was easier to reconstruct the war-ravaged economies of Japan and Europe, which had formerly been industrialized, than to bring Mexico along. At times the record of unfulfilled human needs is poignant. The battle against *carestía* in Mexico continued after the end of the war. Attempting to fight high prices on essential items, and reacting to the deeply held popular belief that intermediaries were responsible for high prices, the government opened markets to link producers with consumers directly, on August 14, 1948. A graphic account, featured on the front page of *Excélsior*, stated that a 40 percent reduction in the price of staple foodstuffs had been achieved. The reporter covering the opening was moved: "We saw our women crying with emotion as they purchased with one peso, foodstuffs which forty-eight hours earlier were unobtainable at [these] low prices."[8]

By the end of the period, the old underconsumptionist nightmare had returned. By defining progress in terms of national income accounting, by using state subsidies, by basing capital accumulation on the plethora of state favors to industrial producers, by starving the campo of investment funds, by having the countryside subsidize the city, by holding agricultural prices low, and by restraining wages in an era of inflation, industry produced more than it could sell. According to the report of CONCAMIN, more than 13 percent of the industrial production for 1953 was accumulating in warehouses, and the percentage was increasing.[9]

Clearly, Fordism—mass consumption as the motor force behind domestic sales from the end of World War II to the crisis of 1973—would not be allowed in Mexico. Tiny modern sectors would continue to consume, but in the long run the government, through the debt and fiscal mechanism, would have to provide markets as well as subsidies for its hothouse industries. The decision to base the development program upon a starving of the rural and artisan economy (and culture) was the fundamental error of the Mexican development program, upon which all other tragedies were based. And the regressive income distribution of that policy continues to crush the country to this day.

Mexico was trapped in a pattern in which the state intervened in all areas of economic activity; this reflected a belief in industrial development

as the way to overcome the backward business sector. Well-meaning planners longed to intervene in the development process, and a vast bureaucracy emerged as problem after problem generated new government agencies. A pattern emerged: initially a critical problem was identified; an agency was established and funded; new programs then clashed with the vested interests benefiting from the status quo; the new agency was neutralized; and baroque administrative complexity replaced a clear sense of mission. Unfortunately, those agencies proliferated even after their purpose became obscure.

The hypertrophy of the government sector also reflected a second cruel reality: even the expansion of industry did not create many jobs in the private sector, since industry was increasingly based upon production techniques that had been designed abroad to maximize capital input and minimize ongoing labor costs. The state grew, in effect, as an employment-generating project for the urban middle class. Today, a complete description of the bureaucracy requires many volumes, but the list of grassroots successes in combating the symptoms of underdevelopment would be short indeed.

Many functionaries had a not-so-hidden agenda of nationalizing an increasing number of firms. That program helped the bargaining position of decision makers in both the public and private sectors. Unfortunately, the pathetic record of performance on the part of many of those public enterprises has led to a recrudescence of neo-liberal ideology and a call for privatization in the name of company efficiency. My own view is that a return to the mythology of laissez-faire is no solution to the problems of underdevelopment. It will only worsen the plight of the majority. The evidence for this is already clear. Only the United States still enjoys the singular ability of off-loading its problems (such as the burgeoning debt) onto poor countries through the Bretton Woods mechanism.

My analysis reaffirms the fact that decisions made at the level of international relations do shape the world in which we live. There is no better example than the postwar industrialization plan for Mexico City. By legitimizing state favors to the industrialists it linked them to the international elites. Political leverage, subsidies, favors, and support for industry combined with a model of rural development to starve the peasantry. As we know, the countryside subsidized the industrial project, and this highly political industrialization required manufacturing firms to locate in Mexico City. Technology did not solve the "inconvenient gases and smoke that will bother the inhabitants," as planners anticipated. This model of development crammed rural people into the great city; the UN estimates suggest that Mexico City will have over thirty-one million inhabitants by the year 2000. The strategy of industrialization shifted away from import substitution, based upon Mexican consumption, in favor of an export model. Within the accountant's logic, therefore, there could be no limit to the reduction of wages. The full formula for disaster was in place.

Today, the present regime is experimenting with monetarist policies that leave people defenseless against the rapacity of the most privileged members of the Mexican business elite and the representatives of international capital. It is imperative to move away from the slogans of the past and focus upon the ways that the fundamental rules of the economic game shape the society in which we live.

The proper role of the state is to set those rules, not to mortgage the people through the public finance system to ill-conceived government-run industrial projects. State intervention should exist to deal directly and immediately with those human needs not being met by market forces. New approaches to problems of underdevelopment must be found at the local level. Massive bureaucratic expenditures have gone into the agricultural projects of the Mexican Revolution, with pathetic results in the field. It is difficult to avoid the conclusion that the government might have accomplished more by dividing funds by the number of ejidos and mailing checks directly to poor producers. That way, rural people might have been able to purchase Mexican products and help the country minimize the debt; the rural economy might have prospered, thus allowing more of the population in the countryside to stay there. Surely the evidence is now conclusive that an export-based strategy of development creates unmitigated disaster.

The use of the state to socialize loss and privatize gain must be resisted. Development must be redefined in ways that reject the implications of the U.S. system of national income accounting. In addition to finding new solutions for the old problems of a reprehensible class system, poverty, and injustice, an adequate definition of development must now take into consideration the rapidly multiplying problems of global contamination. Gone are the days when Mexicans can view concern for pollution as a luxury of rich countries. Clearly, Mexico City, as much as any place in the world, bears tragic testimony to Manfred Max-Neef's observation: "Contrary to what is stated in textbooks, the last link of the economic process is not consumption but the generation of waste."[10]

Above all, it is imperative to resist the notion that economic progress can exclude the majority of the population. The tendency of Mexico's decision makers and its foreign allies to do just that might be called the great evasion, for which that country is now paying the most severe price.[11]

Perhaps the most telling moment in shaping the development program came at that important meeting in Washington at the end of July 1947. Officials from both countries were negotiating the terms of reentry of foreign capital into Mexico. As they agreed that living standards would be held down in the face of inflation so that high profits could finance foreign borrowing for projects of industrialization, a young Mexican delegate objected. This would mean, he said, that even the success of industrialization would fail to alleviate the poverty of most Mexicans.

There was a prolonged silence.

## Notes

1. George Messersmith to Dean Acheson, January 12, 1946, USNA/RG 59, 812.00/1-1246.

2. Folsom, "Mexican Elections in 1946 and 1952," February 12, 1952, USNA/RG 59, 812.00/2-1252.

3. Messersmith to Acheson, January 12, 1946, USNA/RG 59, 812.00/1-1246.

4. "Major political developments in Mexico in March, 1952," April 7, 1952, USNA/RG 59, 712.00/4-752.

5. Merwin L. Bohan to secretary of state, July 2, 1947, USNA/RG 59, 812.50/7-247.

6. Bohan to secretary of state, July 1, 1948, USNA/RG 59, 812.50/7-148.

7. Ibid.

8. *Excélsior*, the Sunday after August 14, 1948.

9. *El Universal,* April 13, 1953.

10. Max-Neef, *Experiences in "Barefoot Economics,"* 48–50.

11. For an analysis of the links between the 1940s and later development see Niblo, "Development without the People," 50–64.

# Bibliography

## *Archives and Manuscript Collections*

Archivo General de la Nación, Mexico City
    Ramo de Presidentes
        Lázaro Cárdenas, 1934–1940
        Manuel Avila Camacho, 1940–1946
        Miguel Alemán Valdez, 1946–1952
        Adolfo Ruiz Cortines, 1952–1958
Biblioteca Miguel Lerdo de Tejada, Mexico City
Biblioteca de la Secretaría de Relaciones Exteriores, Mexico City
Columbia University, New York City
    Oral History Project
Hemeroteca Nacional de México, Mexico City
Library of Congress, Washington, DC
    Josephus Daniels Papers
National Archives, Washington, DC
    Bureau of Foreign and Domestic Commerce, Record Group 151
    General Records of the Department of State, Record Group 59
    General Records of the Department of the Treasury, Record Group 56
    Records of the Office of Inter-American Affairs, Record Group 229
Public Record Office, London, England
    Records of the Foreign Office (FO 371)
Franklin D. Roosevelt Library, Hyde Park, New York
    Adolf A. Berle Papers
    Henry Morgenthau, Jr., Papers
    Franklin D. Roosevelt Papers
        President's Personal File
        President's Secretary's File
        Press Conferences
Harry S. Truman Library, Independence, Missouri
    Merwin L. Bohan Papers
    Will L. Clayton Papers
    Robert L. Gardner Papers
    Roman L. Horne Papers
    Edward G. Miller, Jr., Papers
    John W. Snyder Papers

Harry S. Truman Papers
  President's Personal File
  President's Secretary's File
  Press Conferences
University of Delaware, Newark
  George S. Messersmith Papers

## Primary Sources

Acheson, Dean. *Present at the Creation: My Years in the State Department.* New York: W. W. Norton, 1969.

Alamillo Flores, Luis. *Memorias: Luchadores ignorados al lado de los grandes jefes de la Revolución Mexicana.* Mexico: Editorial Extemporaneos, 1976.

Almazán, Juan Andreu. *Memorias de General Juan Andreu Almazán: Informes y documentos sobre la campaña política de 1940.* Mexico: Editorial Quintana-Impresor, 1941.

Bassols, Narciso. *Obras.* Mexico: Fondo de Cultura Económica, 1964.

Campa, Valentín. *50 años de oposición en México.* Mexico: UNAM, 1979.

Cárdenas, Lázaro. *Ideario político.* Mexico: Editorial Era, 1972.

Carrillo, Alejandro. *La revolución industrial en México.* Mexico: Universidad Obrera, 1945.

Catton, Bruce. *The War Lords of Washington.* New York: Harcourt, Brace, and Company, 1948.

Duggan, Laurence. *The Americas: The Search for Hemispheric Security.* New York: Henry Holt and Company, 1949.

Galbraith, John Kenneth. *A Life in Our Times: Memoirs.* Boston: Houghton Mifflin, 1981.

Gaxiola, Francisco Javier. *Memorias.* Mexico: Editorial Porrúa, 1975.

Hull, Cordell. *The Memoirs of Cordell Hull.* 2 vols. New York: Macmillan Company, 1948.

Jones, Jesse H., with Edward Angly. *Fifty Billion Dollars: My Thirteen Years with the RFC (1932–1945).* New York: Macmillan Company, 1951.

Laborde, Hernán. "Cárdenas, reformador agrario." *Problemas Agrícolas e Industriales de México* 4 (January–March 1952): 57–86.

Portes Gil, Emilio. *Autobiografía de la Revolución Mexicana.* Mexico: Instituto Mexicano de Cultura, 1964.

Suárez, Eduardo. *Comentarios y recuerdos (1926–1946).* Mexico: Editorial Porrúa, 1977.

Vandenberg, Arthur H., Jr. *The Private Papers of Senator Vandenberg.* Boston: Houghton Mifflin, 1952.

Villaseñor, Eduardo. *Memorias-Testimonio.* Mexico: Fondo de Cultura Económica, 1974.

Villaseñor, Victor Manuel. *Memorias de un hombre de la izquierda.* 2 vols. Mexico: Editorial Grijalbo, 1976.

Wallace, Henry A. *The Price of Vision: The Diary of Henry A. Wallace, 1942–1946,* edited by John Morton Blum. Boston: Houghton Mifflin Company, 1973.

# Other Documents

Armour Research Foundation. *Proceedings of the Mexican-American Conference on Industrial Research, September 30–October 6, 1945.* Chicago: Armour Research Foundation, 1945.

Cámara Nacional de Industrias de Transformación. *Actividades durante el año de 1945.* México D.F.: Cámara Nacional de Industrias de Transformación, 1945.

Colín, José R. *Materias primas y capital extranjero.* México D.F.: Cámara Nacional de Industrias de Transformación, 1945.

———. *Requisitos fundamentales para la industrialización de México.* México D.F.: Cámara Nacional de Industrias de Transformación, 1945.

Lagos, Licos. *Inconvenientes del impuesto sobre exportaciónes.* México D.F.: Confederación de Cámaras Industriales, n.d.

Lavín, José Domingo. *La industria química nacional.* México D.F.: Cámara Nacional de Industrias de Transformación, 1945.

———. *Materias primas y capital extranjero.* México D.F.: Cámara Nacional de Industrias de Transformación, 1943.

———. *De la necesidad de formar la industria química mexicana.* México D.F.: Cámara Nacional de Industrias de Transformación, 1943.

———. *Plan inmediato de industrialización en México.* México D.F.: Cámara Nacional de Industrias de Transformación, 1945.

National Foreign Trade Council. *Proceedings of the National Foreign Trade Council.* New York: National Foreign Trade Council, various dates.

*Primer Congreso Nacional de Economía de Guerra.* México D.F.: N.p., 1942.

Quijano, José Manuel, ed. *La banca: Pasado y presente.* México D.F.: CIDE, 1983.

Senate Committee on Banking and Currency. *Study of the Export-Import Bank and World Bank.* 83d Cong., 2d sess. Washington, DC: Government Printing Office, 1954.

Sindicato Nacional de Telefonistas and other unions. *La justicia social en México.* México D.F.: N.p., 1945.

Special Committee on Post-War Economic Policy and Planning. *Economic Problems of the Transition Period.* 78th Cong., 2d sess., and 79th Cong., 1st sess. Washington, DC: Government Printing Office, 1945.

United Nations. *Human Development Report, 1992.* New York: Oxford University Press, 1992.

———. *Second World Food Survey.* New York: United Nations, 1952.

U.S. Board of Economic Warfare. *Confidential Report on the Mexican Economy.* Washington, DC: Government Printing Office, 1942.

# Books

Acuña, Rodolfo. *Occupied America: A History of Chicanos.* New York: Harper and Row, 1988.

Alcázar, Marco Antonio. *Las agrupaciones patronales en México.* México D.F.: El Colegio de México, 1970.

Alonso, Antonio. *El movimiento ferrocarrilero en México, 1958–1959*. México D.F.: Editorial Era, 1972.

Ambrose, Stephen E. *Eisenhower, the President*. London: George Allen and Unwin, 1984.

Ankerson, Dudley. *Agrarian Warlord: Saturnino Cedillo and the Mexican Revolution in San Luis Potosí*. De Kalb: Northern Illinois Press, 1984.

Apter, David E. *Rethinking Development: Modernization, Dependency, and Postmodern Politics*. Beverly Hills: Sage Publications, 1987.

Arrow, Kenneth J. "Economic Development." In *The Collected Papers of Kenneth J. Arrow* 6:183–207. Cambridge: Belkamp Press of Harvard University, 1985.

Ashby, Joe. *Organized Labor and the Mexican Revolution under Lázaro Cárdenas*. Chapel Hill: University of North Carolina Press, 1967.

Ashton, T. S. *The Industrial Revolution*. London: Black, 1937.

Aubey, Robert T. *Nacional Financiera and Mexican Industry*. Los Angeles: Latin American Center, UCLA, 1966.

Baird, Peter, and Ed McCaughan. *Beyond the Border: Mexico and the U.S. Today*. New York: NACLA, 1979.

Bartra, Roger, et al. *La izquierda en los cuarenta*. México D.F.: Centro de Estudios del Movimiento Obrero y Socialista, 1985.

Basurto, Jorge. *Cárdenas y el poder sindical*. México D.F.: Ediciones Era, 1983.

Bazant, Jan. *Historia de la deuda exterior de México (1823–1946)*. México D.F.: El Colegio de México, 1968.

Bennett, Robert L. *The Financial Sector and Economic Development: The Mexican Case*. Baltimore: Johns Hopkins University Press, 1965.

Blasier, Cole. *The Hovering Giant: U.S. Responses to Revolutionary Change in Latin America, 1910–1985*. Pittsburgh: University of Pittsburgh Press, 1985.

Bleaney, Michael. *Underconsumptionist Theories: A History and Critical Analysis*. London: Lawrence Wishart, 1976.

Bortz, Jeffrey. *El salario en México*. México D.F.: Ediciones "El Caballito," 1988.

Braeman, John, ed. *The New Deal*. 2 vols. Columbus: Ohio State University Press, 1975.

Buhite, Russell D. *Patrick J. Hurley and American Foreign Policy*. Ithaca: Cornell University Press, 1973.

Cárdenas, Enrique. *La industrialización mexicana durante la Gran Depresión*. México D.F.: El Colegio de México, 1987.

Caro, Robert A. *The Years of Lyndon Johnson: The Path to Power*. New York: Alfred A. Knopf, 1982.

Carr, Barry. *Marxism and Communism in Twentieth Century Mexico*. Lincoln: University of Nebraska Press, 1992.

Carr, Barry, and Anzaldúa Montoya, eds. *The Mexican Left: The Popular Movements and the Politics of Austerity*. La Jolla: Center for U.S.-Mexican Studies, 1986.

Ceceña, José Luis. *México en la orbita imperial*. México D.F.: Ediciones "El Caballito," 1970.

Clark, Colin. *National Income and Outlay*. London: Macmillan and Company, 1937.

Cline, Howard F. *The United States and Mexico.* Cambridge: Harvard University Press, 1967.

Coatsworth, John H. *Growth against Development: The Economic Impact of the Railroads in Porfirian Mexico.* De Kalb: Northern Illinois University Press, 1981.

Cockcroft, James D. *Mexico: Class Formation, Capital Accumulation, and the State.* New York: Monthly Review Press, 1983.

Cole, Wayne S. *Roosevelt and the Isolationists, 1932–45.* Lincoln: University of Nebraska Press, 1983.

Conn, Stetson, and Byron Fairchild. *The Framework of Hemispheric Defense: The United States Army in World War II.* Washington, DC: Government Printing Office, 1960.

Contreras, Ariel José. *México 1940: Industrialización y crisis política: Estado y sociedad civil en las elecciones presidenciales.* México D.F.: Siglo Veintiuno Editores, 1977.

Córdova, Arnaldo. *La formación del poder político en México.* México D.F.: Ediciones Era, 1972.

———. *La ideología de la Revolución Mexicana: Formación del nuevo régimen.* México D.F.: Ediciones Era, 1973.

———. *La política de masas del cardenismo.* México D.F.: Ediciones Era, 1974.

Divine, Robert A. *Foreign Policy and U.S. Presidential Elections, 1940–1948.* New York: New Viewpoints, 1974.

———. *Second Chance: The Triumph of Internationalism during World War II.* New York: Atheneum, 1967.

Domínguez, Jorge I. *Mexico's Political Economy: Challenges at Home and Abroad.* Beverly Hills: Sage Publications, 1982.

Durand Ponte, Victor M. *Las derrotas obreras, 1946–52.* México D.F.: UNAM, 1984.

Everest, Seymour. *Morgenthau, the New Deal, and Silver.* New York: Da Capo Press, 1973.

Fajnzylber, Fernando, and Trinidad Martínez Tarragó. *Las empresas transnacionales: Expansión a nivel mundial y proyección en la industria mexicana.* México D.F.: Fondo de Cultura Económica, 1976.

Falcón, Romana. *Revolución y caciquismo: San Luis Potosí, 1910–1938.* México D.F.: El Colegio de México, 1984.

Foss, Murray F., ed. *The U.S. National Income Accounts: Selected Topics.* Chicago: University of Chicago Press, 1983.

García Treviño, Rodrigo. *Precios, salarios y mordidas.* México D.F.: Editorial América, 1953.

Gardner, Richard N. *Sterling-Dollar Diplomacy.* Oxford: Oxford University Press, 1956.

Garrido, Luis Javier. *El partido de la revolución institucionalizada: La formación del nuevo estado en México (1928–1945).* México D.F.: Siglo Veintiuno Editores, 1982.

Germán Parral, Manuel. *La industrialización en México.* México D.F.: Imprenta Universitaria, 1954.

Gimbel, John. *The Origins of the Marshall Plan*. Stanford: Stanford University Press, 1976.

Good, Loretta Louise. *United States Joint Ventures and National Manufacturing Firms in Monterrey, Mexico: Comparative Styles of Management*. Ithaca: Cornell University Press, 1972.

Green, David. *The Containment of Latin America: A History of the Myths and Realities of the Good Neighbor Policy*. Chicago: Quadrangle Books, 1971.

Green, Rosario. *El enduedamiento público externo en México*. México D.F.: El Colegio de México, 1976.

Haber, Stephen H. *Industry and Underdevelopment: The Industrialization of Mexico, 1890–1940*. Stanford: Stanford University Press, 1989.

Halberstam, David. *The Best and the Brightest*. New York: Random House, 1972.

Hamilton, Nora. *The Limits of State Autonomy: Post-Revolutionary Mexico*. Princeton: Princeton University Press, 1982.

Harris, Seymour. *Problems in Price Controls: Stabilization Studies, 1942–46*. Washington, DC: Government Printing Office, 1947.

Hefley, James C. *Aarón Sáenz: Mexico's Revolutionary Capitalist*. Waco, TX: World Books, 1970.

Hewitt de Alcántara, Cynthia. *La modernización de la agricultura mexicana, 1940–1970*. México D.F.: Siglo XXI, 1978.

Kaufman, Burton I. *Trade and Aid: Eisenhower's Foreign Economic Policy*. Baltimore: Johns Hopkins University Press, 1982.

Keynes, John Maynard. *Essays in Persuasion*. London: Macmillan and Company, 1931.

Kindleberger, Charles P. *A Financial History of Western Europe*. London: George Allen and Unwin, 1984.

———. *The World in Depression, 1929–1939*. Berkeley: University of California Press, 1973.

Knight, Alan. *U.S.-Mexican Relations, 1910–1940*. La Jolla: Center for U.S.-Mexican Studies, 1987.

Kolko, Gabriel. *The Politics of War: The World and United States Foreign Policy*. New York: Vintage Books, 1968.

Kuznets, Simon. *National Income and Its Composition, 1919–1938*. New York: National Bureau of Economic Research, 1941.

León, Samuel, and Ignacio Marván. *La clase obrera en la historia de México*, vol. 10, *En el cardenismo (1934–1940)*. México D.F.: Siglo Veintiuno Editores, 1985.

Loyola, Rafael, ed. *Entre la guerra y la estabilidad política: El México de los 40*. México D.F.: Grijalbo, 1986.

Max-Neef, Manfred A. *From the Outside Looking In: Experiences in "Barefoot Economics."* Uppsala: Dag Hammarskjöld Foundation, 1982.

McCartney, Laton. *Friends in High Places: The Bechtel Story—The Most Secret Corporation and How It Engineered the World*. New York: Simon and Schuster, 1988.

Medin, Tzvi. *Ideología y praxis política de Lázaro Cárdenas*. México D.F.: Siglo XXI, 1972.

Medina, Luis. *Historia de la Revolución Mexicana, periodo 1940–1952: Civilismo y modernización del avilacamachismo.* México D.F.: El Colegio de México, 1979.

Medina, Luis, and Blanca Torres. *Historia de la Revolución Mexicana, periodo 1940–1952: Del cardenismo al avilacamachismo.* México D.F.: El Colegio de México, 1978.

Meyer, Jean. *Le sinarquisme: Un fascisme mexicain? 1937–1947.* Paris: Hachette, 1977.

Meyer, Lorenzo. *México y los Estados Unidos en el conflicto petrolero (1917–1942).* México D.F.: El Colegio de México, 1972.

Michaels, Albert A. *The Mexican Election of 1940.* Buffalo, NY: Council of International Studies, 1971.

Millon, Robert A. *A Mexican Marxist: Vicente Lombardo Toledano.* Chapel Hill: University of North Carolina Press, 1966.

Morgenstern, Oskar. *On the Accuracy of Economic Observations.* Princeton: Princeton University Press, 1965.

Morris, David M. *Measuring the Condition of the World's Poor: The Physical Quality of Life Index.* New York: Pergamon Press, 1979.

Mosk, Sanford A. *Industrial Revolution in Mexico.* Berkeley: University of California Press, 1954.

Nash, Hugh, ed. *Progress as if Survival Mattered.* San Francisco: Friends of the Earth, 1977.

Navarette, Ifigenia M. de. *La distribución del ingreso y el desarrollo económico de México.* México D.F.: Instituto de Investigaciónes Económicas, UNAM, 1960.

Negrete, María Eugenia. *Crecimiento y distribución de la población de la Ciudad de México.* México D.F.: El Colegio de México, 1968.

Nuncio, Abraham. *El Grupo Monterrey.* México D.F.: Editorial Nueva Imagen, 1982.

Offner, Arnold. *The Origins of the Second World War: American Foreign Policy and World Politics, 1917–1941.* New York: Praeger Publishers, 1975.

Powell, Thomas G. *Mexico and the Spanish Civil War.* Albuquerque: University of New Mexico Press, 1981.

Pruessen, Ronald W. *John Foster Dulles: The Road to Power.* New York: Free Press, 1982.

Quijano, José Manuel, ed. *La banca: Pasado y presente.* México D.F.: CIDE, 1983.

Rabe, Stephen G. *Eisenhower and Latin America: The Foreign Policy of Anticommunism.* Chapel Hill: University of North Carolina Press, 1988.

Raby, David L. *Educación y revolución social en México.* México D.F.: Sepsetentas, 1974.

Radosh, Ronald. *Labor and American Foreign Policy.* New York: Vintage Books, 1969.

Reynolds, Clark W. *The Mexican Economy: Twentieth-Century Structure and Growth.* New Haven: Yale University Press, 1970.

Rodríguez, Antonio. *El rescate de petróleo: Epopeya de un pueblo.* México D.F.: Ediciones "El Caballito," 1975.

Rodríguez, Jaime O., ed. *The Revolutionary Process in Mexico: Essays on Political and Social Change, 1880–1940.* Los Angeles: UCLA Latin American Center Publications, 1990.

Ronfeldt, David. *Atencingo: The Politics of Agrarian Struggle in a Mexican Ejido.* Stanford: Stanford University Press, 1973.

Rout, L. B., and J. F. Bratzel. *The Shadow War: German Espionage and United States Counterespionage in Latin America during World War II.* Frederick, MD: University Publications of America, 1986.

Sampson, Anthony. *The Seven Sisters: The Great Oil Companies and the World They Shaped.* New York: Viking Press, 1975.

Samuel, J. Walker. *Henry A. Wallace and American Foreign Policy.* Westport, CT: Greenwood Press, 1976.

Sanderson, Stephen. *Agrarian Populism and the Mexican State.* Berkeley: University of California Press, 1981.

Saragoza, Alexander M. *The Monterrey Elite and the Mexican State, 1880–1940.* Austin: University of Texas Press, 1988.

Schumacher, Ernst F. *Small Is Beautiful: A Study of Economics as if People Mattered.* London: Blond and Briggs, 1973.

Sepúlveda, Bernardo, Olga Pellicer de Brody, and Lorenzo Meyer. *Las empresas transnacionales en México.* México D.F.: El Colegio de México, 1974.

Shafer, Robert J. *Mexican Business Organizations: History and Analysis.* Syracuse: Syracuse University Press, 1973.

Shoup, Laurence, and William Minter. *Imperial Brain Trust: The Council on Foreign Relations and U.S. Foreign Policy.* New York: Monthly Review Press, 1977.

Smith, Gaddis. *American Diplomacy during the Second World War, 1941–45.* New York: John Wiley, 1965.

Solís, Leopoldo. *La realidad económica mexicana: Retrovisión y perspectivas.* México D.F.: Siglo Veintiuno Editores, 1970.

Stiller, Jesse H. *George S. Messersmith: Diplomat of Democracy.* Chapel Hill: University of North Carolina Press, 1987.

Taracena, Alfonso. *La vida en México bajo Avila Camacho.* 2 vols. México D.F.: Editorial Jus, 1977.

Torres Ramirez, Blanca. *Historia de la Revolución Mexicana, periodo 1940–1952: Hacia la utopía industrial.* México D.F.: El Colegio de México, 1984.

———. *Historia de la Revolución Mexicana, periodo 1940–1952: México en la Segunda Guerra Mundial.* México D.F.: El Colegio de México, 1977.

Vatter, Harold G. *The U.S. Economy in World War II.* New York: Columbia University Press, 1985.

Vernon, Raymond. *The Dilemma of Mexico's Development: The Roles of the Private and Public Sectors.* Cambridge: Harvard University Press, 1965.

———. *Public Policy and Private Enterprise in Mexico.* Cambridge: Harvard University Press, 1964.

Weil, Martin. *A Pretty Good Club: The Founding Fathers of the U.S. Foreign Service.* New York: Norton, 1978.

Wilkie, James W. *The Mexican Revolution: Federal Expenditure and Social Change since 1910.* Berkeley: University of California Press, 1970.

———, and Edna Monzón de Wilkie. *México visto en el siglo XX: Entrevistas de historia oral.* México D.F.: Instituto de Investigaciones Económicas, 1969.

Wilkins, Mira. *The Maturing of Multinational Enterprise: American Business Abroad from 1914 to 1970.* Cambridge: Harvard University Press, 1974.

Wills, Garry. *Reagan's America: Innocents at Home.* London: Heinemann, 1988.
Wright, Harry K. *Foreign Enterprise in Mexico: Laws and Politics.* Chapel Hill: University of North Carolina Press, 1971.
Yergin, Daniel. *Shattered Peace: The Origins of the Cold War and the National Security State.* Boston: Houghton Mifflin, 1977.
Zorilla, Luis G. *Historia de las relaciones entre México y los Estados Unidos de América.* 2 vols. México D.F.: Editorial Porrúa, 1963.

## Articles and Chapters

Beals, Carleton. "Army Action Lessens Cedillo Peril." *Philadelphia Record,* May 22, 1938.
Bernstein, Michael A. "Numerable Knowledge and Its Discontents." *Reviews in American History* 18, no. 2 (June 1990): 151–64.
Bortz, Jeffery. "Wages and Economic Crisis in Mexico." In *The Mexican Left: The Popular Movements and the Politics of Austerity,* edited by Barry Carr and Anzaldúa Montoya, 1986.
Carr, Barry. "Crisis in Mexican Communism: The Extraordinary Congress of the Mexican Communist Party." *Science and Society* 50, no. 4 (Winter 1986): 391–414; and 51, no. 1 (Spring 1987): 43–67.
Carson, Carol S. "The History of the United States National Income and Product Accounts: The Development of an Analytical Tool." *Review of Income and Wealth,* ser. 21, no. 2 (1975): 153–81.
Espinoza Toledo, Ricardo. "La consolidación del sindicalismo institucional en México." *CEMOS Memorias* 2 (May–June 1988): 301–12.
Fitzgerald, E. V. K. "The State and Capital Accumulation in Mexico." *Journal of Latin American Studies* 19, no. 2 (November 1978): 263–82.
Haines, Gerald K. "Under the Eagle's Wing: The Franklin Roosevelt Administration Forges an American Hemisphere." *Diplomatic History* 1, no. 4 (Fall 1977): 373–88.
Hess, Gary R. "After the Tumult: The Wisconsin School's Tribute to William Appleman Williams." *Diplomatic History* 12, no. 4 (Fall 1988): 483–500.
Lira, Maximo. "La larga marcha de Prebisch hacía la critica del capitalismo periférico y su teoría de transformación de la sociedad." *El Trimestre Económico* 53, no. 3 (July–September 1986): 451–76.
Merla, Pedro. "El Convenio Suárez-Lamont." *La República,* December 26, 1942.
Meyer, Lorenzo. "La resistencia al capital privado extranjero: El caso del petróleo, 1938–1950." In *Las empresas transnacionales en México,* edited by Bernardo Sepúlveda et al., 1974.
Michaels, Albert L. "The Crisis of Cardenismo." *Journal of Latin American Studies* 2 (May 1970): 51–79.
Niblo, Stephen R. "British Propaganda in Mexico during the Second World War: The Development of Cultural Imperialism." *Latin American Perspectives* 10, no. 4 (Fall 1983): 114–26.
———. "Decoding Mexican Politics: The Resignation of Francisco Javier Gaxiola." *Anales: The Australasian Journal of Iberian and Latin American Studies* 2, no. 1 (1993): 23–39.

―――. "Mexico: Development without the People." *Journal of the West* 27, no. 4 (October 1988): 50–63.

―――. *The Impact of War: Mexico and World War II*. Bundoora: La Trobe University Institute of Latin American Studies, Occasional Paper #10, 1988.

―――. "The Recrudescence of Silver: Mexico at Bretton Woods." *Anales: The Australasian Journal of Iberian and Latin American Studies* 2, no. 2 (1993): 99–114.

North, Lisa, and David Raby. "The Dynamics of Revolution and Counter-revolution under Cárdenas." *LARU Studies* 2, no. 1 (Latin American Research Unit).

Olmedo, Luna. "Algunos aspectos de la balanza de pagos." *El Trimestre Económico* 9, no. 3 (July–September 1942): 14–52.

Peláez, Gerardo. "Un año decisivo." *Boletín de CEMOS/8* 1, no. 8 (January–February 1985): 177–78.

Ruggles, Richard. "The United States Income Accounts, 1947–1977: Their Conceptual Basis and Evolution." In *The U.S. National Income Accounts: Selected Topics*, edited by Murray F. Foss, 1983.

Seers, Dudley. "The Meaning of Development." *International Development Review* 9, no. 4 (December 1969): 2–6.

Tice, Helen Stone. "Comments on Richard Ruggles." In *The U.S. National Income Accounts: Selected Topics*, edited by Murray F. Foss, 1983.

Viner, Jacob. "Two Plans for International Monetary Stabilization." *Yale Review* 33 (Autumn 1943): 77–107.

# Newspapers

*El Automóvil Americano* (Mexico City), 1938.
*Diario Oficial* (Mexico City), 1934–1949.
*Evening Star* (Washington, DC), 1938.
*Excélsior* (Mexico City), 1938–1950.
*Financial News* (London), 1944.
*Jornadas Industriales* (Mexico City), 1954.
*Journal of Commerce* (New York City), 1947–1954.
*El Mercado de Valores* (Mexico City), 1952.
*El Nacional* (Mexico City), 1941–1945.
*New York Herald Tribune* (New York City), 1938–1947.
*New York Post* (New York City), 1941.
*New York Times* (New York City), 1938–1941.
*El Norte* (Monterrey), 1944–1950.
*Novedades* (Mexico City), 1939–1943.
*Philadelphia Record* (Philadelphia), 1938.
*El Popular* (Mexico City), 1942–1944.
*El Porvenir* (Monterrey), 1944.
*La Prensa* (Mexico City), 1940–1943.
*La República* (Mexico City), 1942.
*El Universal* (Mexico City), 1940–1953.
*Valley Morning Star* (Brownsville, TX), 1938.

*La Voz de México* (Mexico City), 1940.
*Voz Patronal* (Mexico City), 1946.
*Washington Daily News* (Washington, DC), 1938.
*Washington Post* (Washington, DC), 1938–1983.
*Washington Times* (Washington, DC), 1938.
*Washington Times-Herald* (Washington, DC), 1940–1941.

## Dissertations

Adler, Ruth. "Experiments in Worker Participation in the Administration of Industry in Mexico during the Presidency of Lázaro Cárdenas." Ph.D. diss., La Trobe University, 1991.

Brown, Lyle C. "General Lázaro Cárdenas and Mexican Presidential Politics, 1933–1940: A Study in the Acquisition and Manipulation of Political Power." Ph.D. diss., University of Texas, 1964.

Clash, Thomas Wood. "United States-Mexican Relations, 1940–1946: A Study of U.S. Interests and Politics." Ph.D. diss., State University of New York at Buffalo, 1972.

Niblo, Stephen R. "The Political Economy of the Early Porfiriato." Ph.D. diss., Northern Illinois University, 1972.

Schuller, Friedrich Engelbert. "Cardenismo Revisited: The International Dimensions of the Post-Reform Cárdenas Era, 1937–1940." Ph.D. diss., University of Chicago, 1990.

# Index

Abbott Laboratories, 177
Acción Cívica, 169
Acción Nacional, 170
Acero Estructural S.A., 5
Acheson, Dean, 90, 222, 234, 259, 273, 285
Acosta, General, 236
Adams, Sr. (bureaucrat), 212
AFL-CIO, 11
Agrarian reforms: controversy over, 172–73
Agriculture: in Mexico during WWII, 93–95, 127–39
Aguilar Alvarez, Guillermo, 177
Aguirre, Steve, 38
Ailshie, William K., 10
Airline industry: growth of, in Mexico, 202–3
Alamillo Flores, Luis, 229, 231–32; on Mexican technology, 231–32
Alarcón, Pablo O., 68
Alemán, Fernando Casas, 277
Alemán, Miguel, 6, 8, 13, 78, 82, 114, 116, 118, 146, 165, 171, 185, 187, 194, 199, 204, 210, 215, 222, 224, 227, 229–31, 242, 260, 264, 266, 277–78, 283–84; attempts to influence newspapers, 149; enlists Nelson in obtaining U.S. aid, 262; industrialization and, 5, 180–84; Messersmith and, 102, 285; on income distribution, 17, 159; price indexing and, 147; privatization and, 22; relations with business, 184–85; water diversion controversy and, 266–67
Alianza de Uniones y Sindicatos de Artes Gráficas, 12
Alien Property Custodian, 233–34, 273–74
Allen, Henry E., 118
Almazán, Carlos, 68

Almazán, Juan Andreu, 47, 66, 68, 105, 166, 169
Altos Hornos de México S.A.: steel mill, 3, 43, 107, 110, 113, 213, 224
Alvarez, Miguel Gleason, 175
Alvaro Obregón Dam, 182
Amador, Armando C., 108, 205
American Airlines, 287
American Cyanamid Company, 110, 260; controversy involving, 233–35
American Smelting and Refining Company (ASARCO), 39–40, 92, 141, 150, 183, 227; silver production, 43–44
American Zinc, Lead, and Smelting Company, 52, 270
Amitas Limited, 111
Anaconda Copper Corporation, 184
Anáhuac Construction Company, 169
Anderson, Arthur M., 56
Anderson, Clayton, and Company, 110–11, 198, 211, 213; financial standing of, 202; opens factory in Monterrey, 28–29, 283; water diversion controversy and, 266
Anisz, Enríque, 117, 238
Ankerson, Dudley, 46
Anti-Comintern Pact (1936), 63–64
Anuario Estadístico, 148
A. P. Green Fire Bricks Company, 177
Aragón, Agustín, 81
Araiza, Evaristo, 7, 10, 107–8, 114, 172
Arguelles, José María, 232
ARMCO International Corporation, 110, 111, 113
Armour Foundation, 185; Mexican industrialization and, 175–77
Armstrong, Hamilton Fish, 64
Arnold, Henry "Hap": on Mexican troops, 97

Arthur Anderson and Company, 185
Asando Bussan Kabushiki Kaisha, 72
Así (magazine), 99
Atlantic Charter: Cabrera and, 180
Atoyac Textile Mill, 109
Australia: delegation at Bretton
    Woods Conference, 256–57
Avila Camacho, Manuel, 6, 8, 13, 22,
    47, 68–69, 78–79, 95–96, 100,
    103, 106–8, 116, 132–33, 151–
    54, 169, 173, 177, 182, 185, 187,
    199, 225, 233, 235, 252, 260,
    268, 271, 283–84; agriculture in
    WWII and, 128; cabinet of, 171;
    conservatism of, 167; granted
    emergency powers, 80; inaugura-
    tion of, 65; industrialization and,
    180; laissez-faire tactics and,
    195; Lombardo Toledano on, 83;
    meets with FDR, 173–74;
    Messersmith and, 90, 223;
    military organization and, 97;
    Monterrey Group and, 169–70;
    oil nationalization and, 165–66;
    on Anderson, Clayton, and
    Company, 211–12; on deportation
    of Axis nationals, 102; on U.S.
    recruiting Mexicans into military,
    98; probusiness attitude of, 170–
    71; public works expenditures
    and, 205; reaction to Axis attacks
    on Mexican shipping, 78;
    relations with Allies, 80–83;
    response to attack on Pearl
    Harbor, 77–80; seeks U.S.
    industrial help, 111; support for
    WWII and, 84–85; touts industri-
    alization, 15; Treasury circulars
    and, 204
Avila Camacho, Maximino, 9, 82, 99,
    155, 172, 194, 269
Axis: agents of, in Mexico, 66–67,
    101–4; alliance with Mexico, 46;
    seized assets of, 103; Vanderbilt
    alleges Mexican ties with, 80–81
Azcárraga, Emilio, 168
Azienda Generale Italiana Petroli
    S.A., 73

Bach, Federico, 24, 108
Bakers' Union: strike of, 49–50
Ball, George, 22

Balleres, Raúl, 151
Banco de México, 8, 24, 80, 151, 185,
    262, 270; cost-of-living figures
    and, 146; foreign exchange and,
    208; gold reserves and, 55, 183–
    84; Pan American Trust and,
    274–75; run on silver and, 44;
    sells bonds, 192
Banco de Pequeño Comercio: interest
    rates, 192
Banco del Ahorro Nacional S.A., 269
Banco Nacional de Comercio Exterior
    S.A., 276
Banco Nacional de Crédito Agricola
    S.A., 131, 276
Banco Nacional de Crédito Ejidal
    S.A., 131, 276
Banco Nacional de Fomento
    Cooperativo S.A., 269
Banco Nacional de México
    (BANAMEX), 24, 69–70, 112–
    13, 236, 240, 275
Banco Nacional Hipotecario Urbano y
    de Obras Públicas, 276
Banco Nacional Obrero de Fomento
    Industrial, 269
Bank of America, 184
Bankers' Association of Mexico, 6
Bankers' Club (Mexico), 151
Banking: fees paid by Mexico, 273;
    Mexican debt issue and, 55;
    regulations of Mexican govern-
    ment, 157–58; wartime condi-
    tions for, 238–39
Bar Association (Mexico), 6
Barkley, Alben, 48
Barragán, Juan, 68, 236
Barragán, Manuel, 168
Bateman, Alan M., 92
Bateman, C. H., 98; on price controls,
    157
Batista, Fulgencio, 38
Bautista, Sr. (governor of Puebla),
    269
Baz, Gustavo, 6
Beals, Carleton, 51
Bechtel, Steve, 110
Bechtel Corporation, 110
Berle, Adolf, 46, 52, 273; ridicules
    Hoover's views, 67
Beteta, Ramón, 8, 40, 101, 116, 182,
    204, 240–42; Alamillo Flores on,

232; changing political views of, 186; free trade and, 210; investment views of, 195–96; on limiting imports of luxury items, 207; on Mexican budget increases, 239; on Ruiz Cortines, 278; seeks to attract foreign capital, 208; supports U.S.-Mexico trade agreement, 209; water diversion controversy and, 266–67

Bethlehem Steel Export Corporation, 213

Biddle, Francis: chemical company controversy and, 234–35; on Mexican economic development, 108

Black, Eugene: MEXLIGHT and, 241–42

Blacklisting: in Mexico during WWII, 101–4

Blocher, Mr. (American consul general), 47

Blumenthal, A. C., 151

Bobadilla, Luis, 167

Bobay, Robert, 213

Bodet, Torres, 78, 182, 223

Bohan, Merwin L., 7, 184, 206, 209, 214–15, 250; economic role of, 23–24; on U.S. Latin American policy, 63

Bonus Army, 51

Borah, William, 64

Bortz, Jeffrey: wage analysis of, 147

Boulder Dam, 184

Bourde, Joaquín M., 230

Bourgerie, Elmer H.: Mexican price indexing and, 146–47

Bowers, Claude: relationship with Daniels, 38

Braceros (agricultural laborers), 100–101

Braden, Spruille, 8, 104, 181, 241, 262; on pro-Nazi U.S. firms, 74

Braniff Airlines, 203

Braun, Horace H., 184, 216

Bretton Woods Conference (1944), 25, 26, 141, 289; Mexico and, 252–61

Brieschke, Eugen, 73; visits Mexico, 74

Briggs, William Patrick, 39

British American Tobacco Company, 73

British Security Coordination, 74

Brittingham, Juan G.: fishing industry and, 236–37

Brogan, S. T.: advocates annexation of Mexico, 46

Brown and Root Construction Company, 228

Brunt, William L., 67

Buch de Parada, Francisco: U.S. business and, 180–81

Buenrostro, Efraín, 155, 231

Burns, W. T., 266

Bursley, Herbert, 39, 47

Buryess, Mr. (banker), 243

Bush, Carlos, 232

*Business Week*, 203

Busser, William F., 275

Bustamante, Eduardo, 8

Butler, N. K.: on Mexican oil sale to Axis, 74

Cabrera, Luis, 11, 81–82, 103, 179; Atlantic Charter and, 180

Calder, Curtis E., 52

Calles, Plutarco Elías, 5, 79, 82, 97, 168, 277; relations with U.S., 35

Cámara Central de la Industria Harinera Mexicana, 226

Cámara Nacional de Comercio, 196

Cámara Nacional de Industria, 196

Cámara Nacional de Industrias de Transformación (CNIT), 6, 8, 178, 196, 206, 210

Camp, George, 185

Campa, Valentín, 13

Cananea Corporation, 287

Capital: Mexican resources and development of, 172–73; postwar shortage of, 191–94

Carbonífera Unidad de Palau S.A., 113

Cárdenas, Lazaro, 70, 78–79, 96–97, 100, 153, 158–59, 165, 167, 185, 224, 261, 264, 269, 277, 283; accuses oil companies of assisting Cedillo, 50; anti-Axis measures of, 102; cooperatives and, 268; cotton expropriation and, 211–12; economic development under, 41–43;

Cárdenas, Lazaro (*cont.*)
    industrialization and, 4; land
    policies of, 6; moderates policies,
    49–50; New Deal and, 47–48; oil
    nationalization and, 40–41, 52–
    57; on compensation after
    nationalization of oil industry,
    37; on military cooperation with
    U.S., 75–77; recalled to military
    service, 77; reforms of, 16;
    relations with U.S., 35–37, 55–
    57; U.S. sugar interests and, 39–
    40
Cárdenas Ponga, Francisco, 231
Cárdenas R., Rafael, 193
Carrillo, Alejandro, 82, 91, 186; on
    Mexican industrialization, 10
Carrillo Flores, Antonio, 8, 13, 196,
    235, 241–42, 244, 273
Cartón Titan S.A., 113
Cashew-nut oil: for industrial use, 94
Castellón, Marqués de, 78
Castillo Nájera, Francisco, 49, 53, 96,
    233–34; on Cárdenas and military
    relationship to U.S., 75
Cázares Nicolín, David, 230
Cedillo, Saturnino, 38; rebellion of,
    against Cárdenas, 45, 50
CEIMSA (labor organization):
    commodity trading and, 212
Celanese Corporation of America,
    111–12, 114, 176
Celanese Mexicana, 114
Centros Patronales, 196
Cerdán, Jorge, 194
Cervecería Cuauhtémoc, 170
Cervecería La Laguna S.A., 109
CGOCM: labor organization, 263
CGT: labor organization, 12, 79
Chapultepec Conference (1945), 200,
    205–6
Chase Manhattan Bank, 274
Chase National Bank: American
    Cyanamid and, 233–34; on
    business conditions in Mexico,
    186
Chavarría, Manuel, 24
Chávez, Carlos, 82, 286
Chávez, Dennis, 51
Chemical Bank and Trust Company
    (New York), 184
Chemical industry: in Mexico, 232–39

Churchill, Winston: ridiculed, in
    Mexico, 83
Ciudad Industrial S.A., 177–78
Clark, Colin, 26
Clark, Lew B., 184
Clay, Lucius D., 22
Clayton, Will L., 106, 110, 181, 209,
    222–23, 261–62; free trade and,
    210; investments of, 28–29, 202;
    Messersmith seeks advice of,
    134–35; water diversion contro-
    versy and, 266
Clayton Plan, 209
CNC: peasant organization, 166
COCM: labor organization, 12
Colín, José R., 7–8, 10, 15; attacks
    Truman's tariff position, 206; on
    Mexican capitalism, 197–98
Collado, Emilio G., 82, 202
Collado, Pete: U.S.-Mexican debt
    issue and, 55
Comisión Federal de Electricidad
    (CFE), 110
Comisión Federal de Fomento:
    creation of, 180
Comisión Nacional de Planeación
    para la Paz, 15
Comisión Nacional para el Estudio de
    los Problemas de México en la
    Posguerra, 179
Communist Party: in Mexico, 7, 249,
    284–85. *See also* PCM
Compañía Carbonífera de Sabinas
    S.A., 114
Compañía de Luz y Fuerza, 193
Compañía Financiera Industrial y de
    Comercio Exterior, 116
Compañía Fundidora de Fierro y
    Acero de Monterrey S.A., 14–15,
    91, 107, 113–14, 172, 237
Compañía Internacional de Comercio
    S.A., 69
Compañía Internacional de Drogas
    S.A., 69
Compañía Mexicana de Aviación,
    203
Compañía Mexicana de Petróleos El
    Aguila S.A., 70
Compañía Mexicana de Petróleos "La
    Laguna" S.A., 68
Compañía Panamericana Comercial
    S.A., 227

Compañía Petrólera La Nacional S.A., 110
Compañía Petrólera Veracruzana S.A., 68
Compañía Productora e Importadora de Papel S.A., 113
CONCAMIN, 196, 236, 288; urges protectionism, 209
CONCANACO: urges protectionism, 209
Confederación de Cámaras Industriales (CCI), 9, 13, 180; urges protectionism, 209
Confederación de Cámaras Industriales de la Ciudad de México, 195
Confederación de Cámaras Industriales de los Estados Unidos Mexicanos, 195, 237
Confederación de Cámaras Nacionales de Comercio, 181
Confederación de Trabajadores de América Latina, 13
Confederación Nacional Cinematográfica, 9
Confederación Patronal de la República Mexicana (COPARMEX): formation of, 168
Connally, Tom, 52
Consejo de Coordinación y Fomento de la Producción, 107, 222
Consejo Supremo de la Defensa Nacional: organized, 78
Constructora Rosoff S.A., 118
Consumers: industrialization and, 13–15
Continental Grain Company, 138
Cooke, Morris L.: Sinclair's settlement with Mexico and, 54
Cooperatives: Cárdenas and, 268; problems regarding, 269–70
Copper: Mexican wartime production of, 92
Cordóva, Arnaldo: on Cárdenas's reforms, 16
Corn: wartime shortage of, 130–31
Corning Glass Works, 213
Cortéz, José Lino, 173
Cosío Villegas, Daniel, 25
Coughlin, Charles E., 105
Council on Foreign Relations, 64, 180, 201

Covarrubias, Miguel, 82
CPN: labor organization, 12, 79
Crampton, W. D.: on Mexican oil markets, 71
Crawford, David L.: Mexican agriculture and, 129
Creel, George, 104, 174
Cristales Mexicanos S.A., 213
CROM: labor organization, 12, 79
Crowley, José: on status of Mexico to industrialized world, 186; reacts to government policies, 196
Crowley, Leo, 234
Cruise, Gerald, 175
Cruz y Célis, Jesús, 7, 15
Cruz y Célis, José, 9
CTM (labor organization), 9–12, 13, 78–80, 82, 166–67, 197, 209, 263, 283; oil nationalization and, 36; urges response to Axis attacks, 78
Cuban Revolution (1959), 63
Currie, Laughlin, 95
Curtis Wright Aircraft Company: Mexican negotiations with, 48

Dalton, Hugh, 203
Dalton, Jess, 215
Daniels, Josephus, 35, 39, 52, 70, 74, 89, 129, 284; contradicts Vanderbilt, 81; fears Mexican oil sales to Japan, 73; oil nationalization and, 40–41, 47; on Cárdenas's policies, 45; on French holdings in Mexican firms, 69–70; on Mexican election of 1940, 167; on possibility of revolution in Mexico, 45; relationship with Bowers, 38
Davidson, I. D., 83
Davies, Ralph, 110
Davis, William Rhodes, 52, 80; death of, 74; Mexican oil industry and, 71–74
De Boal, Pierre L., 38–39
De Iturbe, Luis, 103
De Iturbide, Aníbal, 195
De la Colina, Rafael, 233
De la Huerta, Adolfo, 97
De la Huerta-Lamont Agreement (1922), 55

De la Madrid, Miguel, 56
De la Mora, José, 198, 238
De la Mora, Pepe, 212
De la Peña, Gonzalo, 14
De la Peña, Joaquín, 210; on
    Mexican industrialization, 4; on
    protectionism, 206–7
De la Selva, Rogerio: MEXLIGHT
    and, 240–41
De Witt, John, 96
Debt issue: between U.S. and Mexico,
    55–57
Defense Supplies Corporation, 113
Degolyer mission (1942), 110
Deitcher Brothers, 69
Del Río, Dolores, 82
Delgado, Hernández: MEXLIGHT
    and, 242
Delgado, Ramón Jimenez, 97
Deloitte, Plender, Haskins, and Sells,
    185
Dentistry: in postwar Mexico, 13
Deutsch-Amerikanische Petroleum, 72
*Diario de la Guerra* (newspaper),
    102
Díaz, Pablo, 213
Díaz, Porfirio, 14, 45, 47, 54
Dirección de Aforos y de Estudios
    Financieros, 239
Dirección General de Profesiones, 214
Distribuidora de Petróleos Mexicanos,
    36
Distribuidora Mexicana S.A., 207
Doheny, Edward, 36
Doria Paz, Francisco, 230
Douglas Aircraft Company: Mexican
    negotiations with, 48
Dr. Pepper Company: investment in
    Mexico, 214–15
Draper, Mr. (MEXLIGHT), 243
Drumm, James: Mexican industrial-
    ization and, 175–76
Du Pont Company, 260
Duce, James T., 110
Duggan, Laurence, 116–17; Mexican
    agriculture and, 134; ridicules
    Hoover's views, 67; suicide of,
    251; U.S.-Mexican debt issue
    and, 55
Dulles, Allen, 223, 241
Dunn, James C., 223, 261

E. Jolly Poe and Associates, 183
Eagle Picher Corporation, 287
Eastern States Petroleum Company,
    72–73
Ebasco Services, 185
Eccles, Marriner S., 276
Echeverría, Luis, 56
Economic imperialism: charges of, by
    Mexican Left, 287
Economic nationalism: Mexico and,
    196–99; opposition to, in
    Mexico, 199–202
Eisenhower, Dwight D., 63, 250–51
*Ejiditarios*: problems of, 265–70
El Boleo Copper Company, 70
*El Economista*, 6
El Márquez Dam, 182
*El Mundo*, 83
*El Nacional*, 216
El Palmito Dam, 93–94
*El Popular*, 10, 107, 149
*El Universal*, 150
Election of 1940 (Mexico): Monterrey
    Group and, 167–72
Electric Bond and Share Company,
    287
Electrical Workers' Union: prowar
    stance of, 82
Elizonodo, Gerónimo, 269
Embick, Stanley Dunbar, 96
Emerson, Earl, 213
Escobár, Gonzalo, 168
Espinosa de los Monteros, Antonio,
    111, 116, 154, 213, 223, 250; at
    Bretton Woods Conference, 255;
    U.S.-Mexican debt issue and, 55
Espinosa Yglesias, Manuel, 269
Estrada, Enrique, 95
*Examen de la Situación Económica de
    México*, 24
*Excélsior*, 66, 81, 100, 107, 288; as
    organ of PCM, 168–69
Export-Import Bank (EXIMBANK),
    64–65, 96, 106, 128–29, 182,
    202, 216, 228, 230, 262, 266, 270
Export Managers' Club (New York):
    203

Fabela, Isidro, 193; argues against
    military cooperation with U.S.,
    76–77

Fábrica de Casados, 198
Fábrica de Fibras Duras Atlas, 269; effects of power outages on, 193
Fábrica de Máquinas S.A., 113
Fábrica de Medidores y Equipos de Saneamiento S.A., 229
Fábricas de Hilados y Tejidos San José de Mayorazgo, 198
Fageol, Frank A., 104, 174
Faith, Creemore: chemical company controversy and, 234–35
*Faja de Oro* (ship): sunk, 78
Falcón, Romana, 46
Farish, W. S., 53
Federal District (Mexico): industrialization of, 177–78
Federal Reserve System: role in Pan American Trust issue, 274–76
Feis, Herbert, 56
Ferrocarriles Nacionales de México, 237–38
Fibro-Tambor S.A., 113
Fifty-one Percent Law (1944): aspects of, 215–17
Fish, Hamilton: on FDR's role in Mexico, 50
Fishing industry: in Mexico, 236–37
Flack, Edward, 175
Flemming, Lamar, 227; on communism in Mexico, 212–13; on honoring Mexican trading rights, 211–12
Flores, Oscar, 286
Flores Esponda, Luis, 68
Flores Muñoz, Fernando: fertilizer and, 227
Flynn, Ed, 171
Foglio Miramontes, Fernando, 212
Fomento Peninsular La Paz S.A.: tax breaks for, 239
Ford, Bacon, and Davis: consulting firm, 175
Ford Motor Company, 217, 260; reacts to oil nationalization, 41
Foreign investment: controversy over, in Mexico, 191–217
Foucher, Rodolfo Brito: as pro-Axis speaker, 102
Franco, Francisco, 102
Free trade: U.S. and, 200
Frente Nacional Proletario, 149

Frente Patronal: economic nationalism and, 200
Fries, Carl, Jr., 216
FSTSE: labor organization, 82
Fuentes, Carlos, 150
Fulton Iron Works, 44
Fussell, Edward C.: at Bretton Woods Conference, 256

Galbraith, John Kenneth: on GNP as economic indicator, 21
Gamboa, Fernando, 286
García, Macario, 100
García López, Agustín, 229
García Naranjo, Nemesio, 99
García Telléz, Ignacio: cooperatives and, 268–69
Garde, Earle E., 110
Gardner, Robert L., 251–52
Gardner, Walter, 275
Garfías, Valentín R., 107; chemical company controversy and, 234
Garrido, Luis Javier: on moderation of PRM, 170
Garza, Isaac, 167
Garza, Luis, 168
Garza, Virgilio, Jr., 169
Garza Domínguez, Humberto, 213
Garza Elizondo, Gregorio, 232
Gaulle, Charles de: on U.S. economic policy, 258
*Gavillas* (Mexican gangs), 150
Gaxiola, Francisco Javier, 90, 180; cooperatives and, 268–69; price controls and, 155–56; resignation of, 156
Gay, Edwin, 17
General American Transportation Company, 177
General Electric Corporation: oil nationalization and, 41
General Motors Corporation, 73
German Oil Import Board, 73
Germán Perra, Manuel, 207
Germany: economic relations with Mexico broken, 101; effect of aggression on Mexican economy, 48; influence of, in Mexico, 64–66; rise of, as factor in U.S.-Mexican relations, 45–46. *See also* Axis

Getty, J. Paul, 71; interests in Mexico, 105

Gibbs, J. Bernard: on U.S. food exports to Mexico, 136

Gillette Company: opens factory in Mexico, 213

Glenn, John B., 274

Goering, Hermann, 172

Gold: depletion of Mexican reserves, 48

Gold Fields Corporation, 287

Gold standard: debated at Bretton Woods Conference, 257

Goldschmidt, Emile, 213

Gómez, Marte, 93, 131–32, 212, 227; corn shortage and, 133

González Cadena, Miguel S., 96

González Gallo, J. Jesús, 155

González Palavicini, Agustín, 68

Good Neighbor policy, 45, 57

Goodrich and Dalton, 215

Goodyear Company: Oxo rubber factory, 5

Grain: distribution of, in Mexico, 137–38, 266

Gran Canal del Desagüe, 115

Grand Coulee Dam, 184

Gray International Corporation, 109

Green Revolution, 129

Grew, Joe, 261

Gross national product (GNP): analysis of Mexican, 15–21; wartime, in Mexico, 139; wartime, in U.S., 26

Grovas, Jesús, 9

Guggenheim family: Mexican mining and, 39, 92

Gurza, Tomás: industrialization and, 177–78

Gutiérrez, Juan: resignation of, 49

Haber, Stephen: on difficulty of Mexican industrialization, 5

Hamilton, Alexander, 197, 206

Hammond, Bray, 275

Hansen, Alvin: economic influence of, 8

Harbor State Bank (New York), 275

Hastings, John A., 104, 174

Havana Conference (1947), 209–10

Hay, Eduardo, 50, 166; on compensation after oil nationalization, 40

Hearst, William Randolph, 39; price paid by, for Mexican land, 49

Heineman, Dannie, 241, 243

Heineman, Jimmy, 241, 243

Helm, A. K.: on Mexican oil sales to Axis, 74

Hemmingway, W. L., 153

Henderson, James E.: on Mexican industrialization, 9

Henequen: Mexican production of, during WWII, 94–95

Henríquez Guzmán, Miguel, 277

Hernández, Manuel A., 6

Herramientas de México S.A., 5

Hertslet, J. G. A., 73; visits Mexico, 74

Heyser, Jorge, 7

Hierro Fundido de México, 113

Hierro Maleable de México, 113

Hillman, Sidney, 10, 181

Hitler, Adolf, 89; Anti-Comintern Pact and, 63–64; Davis and, 73

Hojalata y Lámina S.A., 113

Holland, Maurice: Mexican industrialization and, 176

Hoof-and-mouth disease: epidemic of, in Mexico, 286

Hoover, J. Edgar, 104; and Axis agents in Mexico, 66–67; on Cárdenas, 46; on Japan-Mexico oil agreement, 69

Hopkins, Harry: on Mexican steel production, 91

Horton, Herman H.: on attitude of Mexican government toward industry, 47

Houston, George, 174; Mexican industrialization and, 175–76

Houston and Jolles, 104, 174–75

*Hoy* (magazine), 6; attacks Gaxiola and price regulation, 156; on U.S. conscription of Mexicans, 99

Hoyo, Mario Javier, 108

Huerta, Victoriano, 45

Hull, Cordell, 53, 63, 82, 84, 95, 104, 106, 110, 116, 133, 153, 167, 201; Lombardo Toledano on, 12; on Daniels, 35; on oil nationalization, 47, 70; rethinks position on oil nationalization, 75

Humphrey, George, 243; U.S. Latin
American policy and, 63
Hurley, Patrick J., 51

I. G. Farben, 232–33
Ickes, Harold, 52, 110, 117
Illinois Institute of Technology:
Mexican industrialization and,
175–77
Importadora y Distribuidora de
Artisela, 225
Impulsora La Paz S.A.: tax breaks for,
239
Industria Eléctrica de México S.A., 5
Industrial Rayon Corporation, 184
Industrialization: consumers and, 13–
15; in Mexico after WWII, 3–29;
in Mexico in 1940s, 15–16; forty-
year plan for, 43; plans for
postwar Mexico, 165–87;
relationship to labor, 9–13;
relationship to politics, 221–44
Industrias Electrónicas Mexicanas
(IEM), 235
Inflation: in postwar Mexico, 265; in
wartime Mexico, 154–59
Instituto de Estudios Económicos y
Sociales, 6
Instrumentos Científicos de México
S.A., 229
Inter-American Development Com-
mission, 180
Inter-American Statistical Institute,
23
Interest rates: postwar, 192
International Agrarian Claims
Commission, 39
International Bank for Reconstruc-
tion and Development, 181–82,
256
International Committee of Bankers:
Mexican debt issue and, 55
International Committee of Bond-
holders: Mexican dealings with,
273–74
International Electric Corporation:
reacts to oil nationalization, 41
International Harvester Corporation
(IH): pro-Nazi disposition of, 74
International Monetary Fund (IMF),
23, 205, 258–59, 262; creation
of, 253–54

Japan: interests of, in Mexico, 68;
Mexico breaks relations with, 77
Jara, Heriberto, 78, 149
Jenkins, William: cooperatives and,
269–70
Johnson, Alfred Wilkinson, 96
Johnson, Lyndon B., 52, 228
Johnston, Eric A., 106, 174–75
Joint Mexican-American Commission
for Economic Cooperation, 107
Joint Mexican-United States Defense
Commission, 116; created, 77, 96
Jones, Gus T.: counterintelligence of,
103
Jones, Jesse, 47, 64, 175
Jones and Laughlin Corporation, 213
Jovellanos, Gaspar Melchor, 196

Keynes, John Maynard, 253, 255–56;
gold standard and, 257–58;
influence of, on Mexican
thinking, 7–8
Kirk, Betty: on resurgence of Mexican
gangs, 150
Klein, Julius, 214
Klein and Saks, 214
Kluckhohn, Frank L.: attacks Mexican
government, 50
Kniffin, L. M.: Mexican water supply
and, 42–43
Kokasai Seiyaku Kabushiki Kaisha,
69
Krüger, Hilda, 102, 105
Kuznets, Simon, 26; economic theory
of, 17–19
Kyle, Martin: Lombardo Toledano on,
12

La Consolidada steel mill, 5
*La Nación*, 10, 99
La Nacional S.A., 5
*La Prensa*, 107
*La Voz de México*, 166
Labor: relationship to industrializa-
tion, 9–13; shortages in Mexico
during WWII, 100–101
Laborde, Hernán, 13
Lacaud, Julio, 213
Laminadora de Acero S.A., 5
Lamont, Thomas S., 55–56, 273; on
Mexican colleagues, 261
*Lamont v. Travelers Insurance*, 55

Lard: Mexican consumption of, 136
Latapi, Luis, 196
Lavín, José Domingo, 6, 10, 13, 210,
    231, 232; Messersmith on, 199–
    200
Lead: Mexican wartime production of,
    92
Lechería Nacional S.A., 230
Leeper, Reggie, 241
Legorreta, Agustín, 9, 167, 236, 271
Legorreta, Luis G., 53, 167, 172, 235,
    271, 275; asks Clayton for
    advice, 222–23; foreign invest-
    ment and, 194; MEXLIGHT and,
    242; on oil nationalization, 47–48
Leishman, Morton S., 213
Lend-Lease program, 96–97
Lewis, John L.: Davis and, 72;
    Lombardo Toledano and, 11;
    reacts to Pearson's column, 73
Linder, Gregory, 68–69, 177
Little, Arthur D., 185
Lobatón, Aurelino, 13
Lockett, Thomas H., 103, 108; meets
    with Villaseñor, 152
Lombardo Toledano, Vicente, 7, 46,
    50, 69, 72, 81–82, 167, 197, 199,
    261, 263, 284; as Marxist, 12;
    attempts link with U.S. labor, 11;
    defends Cárdenas, 83; election of
    1940 and, 166; FBI and, 283; on
    U.S.-Mexican relations, 11
Loyo, Gilberto, 23–24
Luna Olmedo, Agustín, 24
Lynch, Arthur, 177

Macedo, Pablo, 213
MacKenzie, Mr. (Electric Bond and
    Share), 244
MacVeagh, John H., 38–39
MacVeagh, Mrs. John H. (Bobbie),
    38–39
Maffry, August: examines Mexico's
    national debt, 25
Maier, Gerard: relationship with
    Cárdenas, 46
Mallory, Walter H., 64
Malloy, John, 213
Maloney, Paul H., 95
Marquette Cement Company, 176–77
Marshall, George C.: on Mexican
    military forces, 97–98

Marshall Plan, 23, 261, 285
Martin, Bill, 243
Martínez Baez, Antonio, 244
Marxism: as influence on Mexican
    labor, 10; Lombardo Toledano
    and, 12; Marxist Roundtable
    (1947), 13
Matson, David, 244
Max-Neef, Manfred: on economic
    process, 290; on the poor, 20
Maya Construction Company, 115
Mayberry, Joe W., 67–68
McAdoo, William Gibbs, 174
McCabe, Thomas B., 106
McCone, John A., 110; transisthmian
    oil pipeline and, 68–69
Meana, Juan A., 110
Melville, Leslie G.: at Bretton Woods
    Conference, 257
Mendieta, Carlos: MEXLIGHT and,
    242
Mendoza Machine Gun Company, 113
Mercantile Trust Company (Saint
    Louis), 184
Merla, Pedro: opposes U.S.-Mexican
    debt settlement, 57
Messersmith, George S., 64, 78–79,
    95, 97, 99, 110, 116, 118, 134,
    151–52, 202, 221, 234, 250–51,
    284; airlines' role in Mexico and,
    203; as head of MEXLIGHT,
    240–44; becomes ambassador to
    Mexico, 89; Clayton and, 134–
    35, 222; economic nationalism
    and, 201; election of 1946 and,
    285; Mexican agriculture and,
    130, 132–33; on Alemán and
    business, 181; on Cárdenas, 46,
    261; on deportation of Axis
    nationals, 102; on Lavín, 199–
    200; on Mexican forces in
    WWII, 97–98; on transfer of U.S.
    firms to Mexico, 109; on U.S.
    trade with Mexico, 108; Pan
    American Trust issue and, 276;
    pessimism regarding Mexican
    economy, 148; relationship with
    Avila Camacho, 204, 223;
    revaluation of peso and, 153–54;
    role as ambassador during WWII,
    89–91; Villaseñor's policies and,
    152–53

Mexican-American Commission for
Economic Cooperation, 107, 112,
174, 179
Mexican Export Oil Company, 72
Mexican Light and Power Company
(MEXLIGHT), 70, 115, 270;
policies regarding, 240–44;
restricts power, 193
Mexican Telegraph Company, 260
Mexico: agriculture in, during
WWII, 93–95; analysis of
wartime production in, 139–46;
banking fees paid by, 273;
breaks relations with Germany,
101; breaks relations with Japan,
77; Bretton Woods Conference
and, 252–61; capital resources
and development in, 172–73,
193–94; chemical industry in,
232–39; enacts new tariff policy
(1947), 209–10; entry into
WWII, 63–85; foreign investments in, 191–217; GNP of, 15–
21, 139; impact of WWII on,
123–59; military forces during
WWII, 96–98; military relations
with U.S., 74–77; national debt,
25; national income, estimated,
24; nationalization of oil
industry, 35–37; payroll of
government employees, 44–45;
postwar industrial strategies,
165–87; postwar role, 249–78;
predictions for economic future
of, 289–90; price controls during
WWII, 154–59; railroads in,
during WWII, 95; U.S. involvement in economy of, 105–9;
Vanderbilt alleges ties with Axis,
80–81; wartime cooperation with
U.S., 89–119
Mexico City: pollution in, 21–22
MEXTELCO, 202
Military conscription: draft of
Mexican residents in U.S., 98–
99
Military forces: Mexican, during
WWII, 96–98; relations with U.S.
and, 74–77
Milk processing: in Mexico, 230–31
Miller, Edward, 244
Milmo, Patricio, 167

Minerals: Mexican production during
WWII, 91–93, 143; seizure of
mines, 40
Mirador Tunnel, 119
Miranda, Francisco P.: nutrition and,
137
Missouri Pacific Railroad, 95, 223
Mitchell, Wesley, 17
Mitsui and Company, 72
Monasterio, Juan: MEXLIGHT and,
242
Monetary issues: at Bretton Woods
Conference, 252–61
Monsanto Chemical Corporation, 184
Monterrey: industrialization boom in,
15–16
Monterrey Group, 113–14, 175;
election of 1940 and, 167–72
Monterrey steel works. *See* Compañía
Fundidora de Fierro y Acero de
Monterrey S.A.
Montes, Federico, 236
Montes de Oca, Luis, 166–67, 212,
228, 238; foreign investment and,
194; Messersmith on, 200;
resigns from Banco de México,
223
Montes de Oca-Lamont Agreement
(1930), 55
Moreno, Mario, 151
Morgenstern, Oskar: on Kuznets's
methodology, 18
Morgenthau, Henry, 52, 174, 255,
276
Morín, Gómez, 11
Morones, Luis: on wartime trade
problems, 149
Morrison, Knudsen, and Company,
184
Morrow, Dwight, 35
Morrow-Calles Agreement (1928), 35
Mosk, Sanford, 238; on Mexican
industrialization, 7
Motores y Maquinaria Anáhuac S.A.,
231
Múgica, Francisco, 46
Muguerza, José, 167
Murchison, Clint W., 71
Murillo, Rafael, 68
Murphy, Frank, 90
Mustard, Lewis, 89
Mustard, Marion, 89

Nacional Distribuidora y Reguladora
    S.A. (ND&R), 137–38, 154–55,
    265; famine relief and, 135
Nacional Financiera (NAFISA),
    113, 157, 183, 228, 235, 238–39,
    271, 272; offers bonds for sale,
    157
National Association of Manufactur-
    ers (NAM), 201–2
National City Bank (New York), 274
National Lead Corporation, 287
National Planning Association, 201–2
Nation's Business, 184
Nelson, Donald, 111, 118, 222, 262–
    63; War Production Board and,
    181
Neptune Meter Company, 229
Neruda, Pablo, 82
Ness, Norman, 202
Nestlé's Milk Products Company:
    establishes factory in Mexico,
    230
Nevarez, Raúl, 155
New Deal: Cárdenas and, 47–48
New York Herald Tribune, 50; on
    Alemán and industrial develop-
    ment, 205–6
New York Times, 50; claims Axis-
    Mexican relationship, 51
Newspapers (U.S.): assert Mexican-
    Axis relationship, 51; on U.S.-
    Mexican relations, 50–51
Newsweek: on U.S.-Mexican relations,
    51
Nicolaus, Georg, 103
Nixon, Richard: gold standard and,
    258
Norris and Elliot Company, 185
Novedades, 107, 206

Obregón, Alvaro: assassination of,
    168
O'Brian, Jack, 174
O'Connell, William A., 230
O'Connor, John R., 104
O'Dwyer, William, 284, 286
O'Farrill, Rómulo, 116, 229
Office of Inter-American Affairs, 66,
    130, 175, 233
O'Hara, John, 104
Oil industry: nationalization of, in
    Mexico, 35–57; Seven Sisters

and, 50–51, 70–71; transisthmian
    pipeline, 68–69. See also
    Petróleos Mexicanos
Olachea Avilés, Agustín, 239
Olivo, Angel, 82
Olney, Fred, 67–68
O'Neill, William, 104
Orive Alba, Adolfo, 184
Ortíz, José F., 173
Ortíz Garza, Nazario S., 155, 270;
    corn price increases and, 265
Ortíz Rubio, Pascual, 97, 168
Osorio, Adolfo León: Pro-Neutrality
    Patriotic Committee and, 67
Overby, Mr. (banker), 243, 262

Padilla, Arturo, 168
Padilla, Ezequiel, 6, 11, 82, 99, 110,
    116, 154, 166, 215, 223, 233,
    284; financial policies and, 152–
    53; Messersmith and, 285; urges
    war against Axis, 78
Pagliai, Bruno, 151, 238
Palavicini, Felix: on agrarian reform,
    173
Palazuelos, Leopoldo H., 43
Palm oil: for industrial use, 94
Palmito Dam, 266
Pan American Airways, 203, 287
Pan American Conference: (1936), 63;
    (1938), 64; (1940), 64
Pan American Trust Company:
    Mexico's attempts to purchase,
    271–77
Pan American Union, 23
Panama Canal: possibility of Axis
    attack on, 96
Pani-Lamont Agreement (1925), 55
Pape, Harold, 213
Paper industry: in Mexico, 111, 113–
    14, 237–38
Partido Revolucionario Mexicano
    (PRM): organization of, 37
Payer, Cheryl, 286
PCM (Mexican Communist Party), 7,
    78, 82, 168–69
Pearl Harbor: Mexican response to
    attack on, 77–80
Pearson, Drew: breaks German
    chemical story, 233; on Davis and
    Hitler, 73
Pearson, Weetman, 36

Peat Marwick, Mitchell, and Company, 185
Pepsi-Cola Corporation: in Mexico, 94, 117, 266
Petróleos Mexicanos (PEMEX), 155, 183, 224, 231–32, 260, 262
Petroleum Workers' Union (STPRM): oil nationalization and, 36, 263
Phelps-Dodge Corporation, 287
Pierson, Warren Lee, 96; Mexican economy and, 106
Pineapples: Mexican cultivation of, 115–16
Point Four program, 95, 115, 185–87, 261
Political favoritism: as factor in Mexican-American relations, 224–32
Politics: industrialization and, 221–44
Poodevan, Videl, 91
Pope, Colonel (American Cyanamid), 233
Portes Gil, Emilio, 68, 97, 166, 168
*Potrero del Llano* (ship): sunk, 78
Pous Cházaro, Rafael, 68
Prebisch, Raúl, 29, 186, 223; on postwar inflation, 158
Preciado, Sr. (political leader), 243
PRI: political party, 263–64, 271
Price, Waterhouse, and Company, 185
Price controls, 196; in wartime Mexico, 154–59, 236
Prieto, Carlos, 114; MEXLIGHT and, 242; pricing and, 237
Privatization: Alemán advocates, 22
Pro-Neutrality Patriotic Committee, 67
Productores de Artisela S.A., 112
Productos Químicos de San Cristóbal, 112
Protectionism: Mexican advocates of, 197, 205–10; Mexican business-men and, 6–7; U.S. views on, 200

Quintanilla, Luis, 103
Quintanilla, Teresa, 103

Racism: against Mexicans in U.S., 100–101
Railroad Retirement Board, 101
Railroad Workers' Union (STFRM), 38

Railroads: in Mexico during WWII, 95, 149, 237–38; postwar, 263–64
Ransom, Floyd D., 90, 222
Ray, Guy, 181, 262; Mexican media and, 79
Rayburn, Sam, 186
Raymond Concrete Pipe Company, 68, 184
*Reader's Digest*: supports WWII, 84
Reciprocal Trade Agreement (1947), 263
Reconstruction Finance Corporation, 64–65
Republic Steel Corporation, 213
Reyes, Bernardo, 14, 168
Reynolds, Clark: on Mexican economy, 126
Reynolds, Robert R., 69
Reynolds Internacional de México S.A., 5
Reynolds Metal Company, 111
Ricardo, David, 196
Richardson, Sid, 71
Richardson, William B., 240; on Japanese interests in Mexico, 68; on 1940 Mexican election, 46–47
Richberg, Donald R., 51
Rivera, Diego, 286
Rivera R., José, 9
Rivera Rojos, Sr. (political leader), 243
Rivero, Valentín, 167
Rivero Quijano, Jesús, 222
Road construction: in Mexico, 229–30, 266
Robles, Gonzalo, 108
Rocha, Joel, 168–69
Rockefeller, Nelson, 66, 108, 132, 175–76, 180, 223, 233–34, 250, 261; Mexican agriculture and, 130
Rockefeller Foundation, 128
Rodríguez, Abelardo, 5–6, 9, 79, 82, 97, 156, 194, 213, 222, 229, 236, 238, 268; as revolutionary industrialist, 107; named director of national production, 78
Rodríguez, Nicolas, 78
Rohen y Galvez, G. A., 108
Rolland, Modesto C., 42, 68; industrial development and, 43

Roosa, Robert, 18
Roosevelt, Franklin D., 38, 41, 52–53, 55, 65, 72–73, 89–90, 106, 111–12, 128, 252, 285; financial policies of, 254; involvement in chemical controversy, 234–35; Lombardo Toledano on, 12; meets with Avila Camacho, 173–74; oil nationalization and, 47–49; on economic nationalism, 201; on invasion at Tampico, 96; on Mexican industrial plans, 171–72; on Pan American system, 64; on Villaseñor's policies, 15; opposes U.S. soldiers of fortune in Mexico, 5; protectionism and, 200; ridiculed, in Mexico, 83; settlement of U.S.-Mexican debt issue and, 56–57
Roosevelt, Theodore, 104
Rosenbleuth, Fernando J., 108
Rosoff, Samuel R., 118–19, 151
Rovensky, Joe, 233–34
Royal Dutch-Shell Corporation, 70
Rüge, Karl: Axis agent in Mexico, 103
Ruggles, Richard, 17
Ruiz Cortines, Adolfo, 12, 243; characteristics of, 277–78, 286
Ruiz Galindo, Antonio, 7, 15, 23, 199, 207, 240; cost of steel and, 224; injured, 16; protectionism and, 197
Russell, F. H., 233

Sada, Francisco, 167
Sada, Roberto G., 168
Sáenz, Aarón, 5, 9–10, 108, 168, 238; business interests, 114
Sáenz, Josué, 8, 12, 24, 108
Salas y López, Pablo, 168
Saldaña, Adalberto, 238
San Juan de Amandi textile factory, 198
San Rafael paper mill, 111
Sanalona Dam, 184
Sánchez, Graciano, 84, 167
Sánchez Cuen, Manuel, 244
Sánchez de Tagle, Miguel: estimates Mexico's national income, 24
Sánchez Hernández, Tomás, 96

Sánchez Pontón, Luis: dismissal of, from cabinet, 171
Sánchez Tapia, Rafael, 47
Santos, Gonzalo N., 166
Saragoza, Alexander: on PRM and Acción Nacional, 170
Savage, John A., 119, 182
Sawyer, Charles, 230
Schuller, Friedrich: on Axis agents in Mexico, 67
Sears, Roebuck Company, 184; opens store in Mexico City, 191
Seers, Dudley: economic theory of, 22
Selective Service Act (U.S.), 98
Seybold, G. I., 110
Shahan, M. S., 286
Sharp, Joe, 212, 223, 227–28; water diversion controversy and, 266–67
Shaw, George P.: on Mexican war effort, 83–84
Sheppard, Morris, 52
Siderurgia Veracruzana, 105
Signoret, Antonio, 213
Silva Herzog, J.: report on oil industry, 36
Silver: U.S. purchase of, from Mexico, 43–44, 141
Silver lobby (U.S. Congress), 141, 256
Sinclair Oil Company: oil nationalization and, 54–55
Sindicato de Trabajadores Petroleros de la República Mexicana (STPRM), 36, 263
SITTFDS: labor organization, 12
Sleepy Lagoon racism case (1942), 100
Smith, Adam, 196
Smith, Ben, 151, 171
Smoot-Hawley Tariff, 200
Snodgrass, C. Stribling, 110
Snyder, John W., 216, 242, 261–62; visits Mexico, 182
Social security system: in Mexico, 9
SOFINA: Belgian holding company, 70, 241–42
Solís, Leopoldo, 126
Solórzano, Amadeo, 229
Solórzano, Miguel Vargas, 232
Sosa Texcoco S.A., 110
Southwest Research Institute, 185

Spencer, White, and Prentis: construction company, 184
*Spencer Kellogg* (ship): oil sales to Axis and, 74
Standard Oil Company, 72; on oil nationalization, 51
Statistics: Mexican economy and, 124–27; Mexican wartime production, 139–46
Stephenson, William, 74
Stettinius, Edward R., 276
Stevens, Oliver, 95
Stimson, Henry: on Japanese in Mexico, 79
Suárez, Eduardo, 8, 51–52, 69, 72–74, 90, 92, 103, 111, 151, 154, 172, 212, 228, 273–74; agrarian reform and, 173; as economic official, 78; at Bretton Woods Conference, 256; chemical company controversy and, 233–34; labor and, 36; on transfer of U.S. firms to Mexico, 108–9
Suárez, Manuel, 9
Suárez-Bateman Agreement (1942), 92, 128–29, 141
Suárez-Lamont Agreement (1942), 56
Sugar: Mexican consumption of, 136; postwar prices of, 265–66; U.S. interests and, 39–40, 44
Sullivan, Mr. (entrepreneur), 117
Szymczak, Mr. (Federal Reserve System), 276

Tampico: as Axis invasion site, 96
Tariffs: Mexican positions on, 205–10, 237
Tax breaks: for industry in Mexico, 239–40
Taylor, Wayne C., 106, 108
Teléfonos de México S.A., 238
Tennessee Valley Authority: as model for Mexican dam projects, 182–83
Textile industry: in Mexico, 109
Thurston, Walter, 204, 284, 286–87; on Mexican Left, 287–88; on Mexican productivity, 8
Tobacco industry, 226–27
Tourism, 114; tax breaks for, 239
Triffin, Robert, 258
Tri-Partite Pact, 9

Trotsky, Leon, 166
Trouyet, Carlos, 213; on Armour Foundation, 206
Truman, Harry S., 183, 203, 223, 241, 249–50, 284–86; advocates tariff reductions, 206; Point Four program and, 261
Tsuru, Kisso, 68–69
Turkel, Harry, 287; on Mexican Left, 287–88
Turner Construction Company, 184

Ugarte, Salvador, 112, 172, 180; on bonds, 157
Ullman Grain Company, 138
Ullola, Ramírez: MEXLIGHT and, 242–43
*Ultimas Noticias* (newspaper), 66, 102
Unión General de Obreros y Campesinos de México (UGOCM), 263
Unión Mexicana de Dentistas Libres, 13
Unión Nacional de Productores de Azúcar, 113, 265–66
United States: aid to Mexico, 261–71; at Bretton Woods Conference, 252–61; encourages Mexican industrialization, 16–17; GNP of, 26; halts purchase of Mexican silver, 43–44; hegemony in Mexican economy, 105–9; military relations with Mexico, 74–77; possible intervention after oil nationalization, 45–47; protectionism and, 200; relations with Cárdenas administration, 35–37, 55–57; wartime cooperation with Mexico, 89–119
United Sugar Company, 39
Upson, Maxwell M., 68
Urquidi, Victor, 25
Urraza, Angel, 10
Urrieta, Lamberto, 230
U.S.-Mexican Commission for Wartime Cooperation, 95
U.S.-Mexican Committee on Economic Cooperation, 116
U.S.-Mexican Mixed Commission: on Mexican industrialization, 147

U.S.-Mexican Trade Agreement
    (1947), 210
U.S. Railway Mission, 95

Vagtborg, Mr. (Armour Foundation),
    175
Valadés, José C., 99
Valsequillo Dam, 118–19
Vanderbilt, Cornelius: on Axis
    influence in Mexico, 80–81
Vargas Llosa, Mario, 20
Vasconcelos, José, 81
Vásquez Gómez, Elena, 76
Vaughan, Harry, 250; on Espinosa de
    los Monteros, 223
Véjar Vásquez, Octavio, 10, 82, 171–
    72, 179; postwar planning and, 4
Velázquez, Fidel, 13, 82; CTM and,
    80; postwar electricity reduction
    and, 149
Vera Estañol, Jorge, 212
Villa Michel, Primo, 107–8, 174
Villalobos, Antonio, 36
Villaseñor, Eduardo, 103–4, 107, 154,
    173, 228; attempts to buy bonds,
    273; on Armour Foundation, 177;
    on Axis agents in Mexico, 101–2;
    on Mexican industrialization,
    151–52; on Mexican investment,
    27; Pan American Trust issue
    and, 275
Villaseñor, Jesús M., 68
Villaseñor, Victor Manuel, 179, 275
Viner, Jacob, 257
Von Collenberg, Rüdt, 70
Von Schleebrugge, Friedrich Karl:
    Axis agent in Mexico, 103

W. R. Davis and Company: dealings
    with Mexico, 70–74
Wallace, Henry A., 65–66, 202, 234;
    attends Avila Camacho's inaugu-
    ration, 65, 128
Wallemberg, Marcos, 238
War Production Board (U.S.), 109,
    181
Ward, Bernardo, 196
*Washington Daily News*, 50; claims
    Mexican-Axis relationship, 51

*Washington Evening Star*, 50
*Washington Times*, 50
Watson, Mr. (FDR secretary), 235
Watson-Flagg Engineering Company,
    177
Welles, Orson, 82
Welles, Sumner, 38–39, 53, 64, 75,
    96, 118; Mexican wartime
    industrialization and, 110–11
Wenner Glen, Axel, 105, 171–72, 238
Western Hemisphere Trade Corpora-
    tion, 214
Western Union Telegraph Company,
    260
Westinghouse Corporation, 176, 235;
    oil nationalization and, 41
Wheat: Mexican production of, 266;
    U.S. embargo of, 137–38
White, Harry Dexter, 106, 174, 255,
    276; at Bretton Woods Confer-
    ence, 253, 257–58
Whitney, Alfred, 24
Whitney, George, 57
Whitney, Richard, 57
Wickard, Claude, 93, 133–34, 148
Wickard, Louise, 134
Wilcox, Clair: on U.S. economic
    diplomacy, 203–4
Wilkie, James, 277–78; on Mexican
    "poverty index," 126
Wilson, Charles E., 201
Woodward and King: trading firm,
    212
Worker-Employer Pact (1945), 13
World Bank, 23, 256, 262, 266, 270
World War II: effect of, on Caribbean
    trade, 148–49; events leading to
    Mexico's entry into, 63–85;
    impact of, on Mexico, 123–59;
    opposed by many Mexicans, 83–
    85

Zacatecas sugar mill, 44
Zevada, Manuel J.: and Sinclair's
    settlement, 54–55
Zimmerman Telegram, 65
Zinc: Mexican wartime production of,
    92
Zoot-Suit Riots (1943), 100

# Latin American Silhouettes
## Studies in History and Culture

*William H. Beezley and*
*Judith Ewell*
Editors

**Volumes Published**

William H. Beezley and Judith Ewell, eds., *The Human Tradition in Latin America: The Twentieth Century* (1987). Cloth ISBN 0-8420-2283-X Paper ISBN 0-8420-2284-8

Judith Ewell and William H. Beezley, eds., *The Human Tradition in Latin America: The Nineteenth Century* (1989). Cloth ISBN 0-8420-2331-3 Paper ISBN 0-8420-2332-1

David G. LaFrance, *The Mexican Revolution in Puebla, 1908–1913: The Maderista Movement and the Failure of Liberal Reform* (1989). ISBN 0-8420-2293-7

Mark A. Burkholder, *Politics of a Colonial Career: José Baquíjano and the Audiencia of Lima*, 2d ed. (1990). Cloth ISBN 0-8420-2353-4 Paper ISBN 0-8420-2352-6

Kenneth M. Coleman and George C. Herring, eds. (with Foreword by Daniel Oduber), *Understanding the Central American Crisis: Sources of Conflict, U.S. Policy, and Options for Peace* (1991). Cloth ISBN 0-8420-2382-8   Paper ISBN 0-8420-2383-6

Carlos B. Gil, ed., *Hope and Frustration: Interviews with Leaders of Mexico's Political Opposition* (1992). Cloth ISBN 0-8420-2395-X Paper ISBN 0-8420-2396-8

Charles Bergquist, Ricardo Peñaranda, and Gonzalo Sánchez, eds., *Violence in Colombia: The Contemporary Crisis in Historical Perspective* (1992). Cloth ISBN 0-8420-2369-0   Paper ISBN 0-8420-2376-3

Heidi Zogbaum, *B. Traven: A Vision of Mexico* (1992). ISBN 0-8420-2392-5

Jaime E. Rodríguez O., ed., *Patterns of Contention in Mexican History* (1992). ISBN 0-8420-2399-2

Louis A. Pérez, Jr., ed., *Slaves, Sugar, and Colonial Society: Travel Accounts of Cuba, 1801–1899* (1992). Cloth ISBN 0-8420-2354-2 Paper ISBN 0-8420-2415-8

Peter Blanchard, *Slavery and Abolition in Early Republican Peru* (1992). Cloth ISBN 0-8420-2400-X Paper ISBN 0-8420-2429-8

Paul J. Vanderwood, *Disorder and Progress: Bandits, Police, and Mexican Development*. Revised and Enlarged Edition (1992). Cloth ISBN 0-8420-2438-7 Paper ISBN 0-8420-2439-5

Sandra McGee Deutsch and Ronald H. Dolkart, eds., *The Argentine Right: Its History and Intellectual Origins, 1910 to the Present* (1993). Cloth ISBN 0-8420-2418-2 Paper ISBN 0-8420-2419-0

Jaime E. Rodríguez O., ed., *The Evolution of the Mexican Political System* (1993). ISBN 0-8420-2448-4

Steve Ellner, *Organized Labor in Venezuela, 1958–1991: Behavior and Concerns in a Democratic Setting* (1993). ISBN 0-8420-2443-3

Paul J. Dosal, *Doing Business with the Dictators: A Political History of United Fruit in Guatemala, 1899–1944* (1993). ISBN 0-8420-2475-1

Marquis James, *Merchant Adventurer: The Story of W. R. Grace* (1993). ISBN 0-8420-2444-1

John Charles Chasteen and Joseph S. Tulchin, eds., *Problems in Modern Latin American History: A Reader* (1994). Cloth ISBN 0-8420-2327-5 Paper ISBN 0-8420-2328-3

Marguerite Guzmán Bouvard, *Revolutionizing Motherhood: The Mothers of the Plaza de Mayo* (1994). Cloth ISBN 0-8420-2486-7 Paper ISBN 0-8420-2487-5

William H. Beezley, Cheryl English Martin, and William E. French, eds., *Rituals of Rule, Rituals of Resistance: Public Celebrations and Popular Culture in Mexico* (1994). Cloth ISBN 0-8420-2416-6 Paper ISBN 0-8420-2417-4

Niblo, Stephen R., *War, Diplomacy, and Development: The United States and Mexico, 1938–1954* (1995). ISBN 0-8420-2550-2

Summ, G. Harvey, ed., *Brazilian Mosaic: Portraits of a Diverse People and Culture* (1995). Cloth ISBN 0-8420-2491-3 Paper ISBN 0-8420-2492-1

ISBN 0-8420-2550-2

## DATE DUE

| | | | |
|---|---|---|---|
| | | | |
| | | | |
| | | | |
| | | | |
| | | | |
| | | | |
| | | | |
| | | | |
| | | | |
| | | | |
| | | | |
| | | | |
| | | | |
| | | | |
| | | | |
| | | | |